THE FUNCTION OF HUMOUR IN ROMAN
VERSE SATIRE

The Function of Humour in Roman Verse Satire

Laughing and Lying

MARIA PLAZA

OXFORD

UNIVERSITY PRESS

This book has been printed digitally and produced in a standard specification in order to ensure its continuing availability

OXFORD
UNIVERSITY PRESS

Great Clarendon Street, Oxford OX2 6DP
Oxford University Press is a department of the University of Oxford.
It furthers the University's objective of excellence in research, scholarship,
and education by publishing worldwide in
Oxford New York
Auckland   Cape Town Dar es Salaam   Hong Kong   Karachi
Kuala Lumpur Madrid Melbourne Mexico City   Nairobi
New Delhi Shanghai   Taipei Toronto
With offices in
Argentina Austria Brazil Chile Czech Republic France Greece
Guatemala Hungary Italy Japan South Korea Poland Portugal
Singapore Switzerland Thailand Turkey Ukraine Vietnam

Oxford is a registered trade mark of Oxford University Press
in the UK and in certain other countries
Published in the United States
by Oxford University Press Inc., New York

© Maria Plaza 2006

ISBN 978-0-19-928111-4

Matri Optimae

Preface

The writing of this book was made possible by a grant from the Swedish Research Council, which I held between 2001 and the spring of 2004.

During this time I have spent one term (Michaelmas 2001) at Corpus Christi College, Oxford; and I have presented my project at the seminars of Stockholm University, Göteborg University, and the University of Oslo—to all these environments I express my gratitude for their kind reception and many helpful suggestions.

Throughout my work on the satires I have received different kinds of help from many quarters, and I would like to thank the following people: Monika Asztalos, Ewen Bowie, Bracht Branham, Sandy Hardie, Stephen Harrison, Nicholas Horsfall, Paolo Leva, Elena Merli, Ruurd Nauta, Magnus Wistrand, and Maaike Zimmermann. Special thanks are due to Susanna Morton Braund and Inga Gerkan.

Finally, I am very grateful to the Oxford University Press, especially to Hilary O'Shea and the two anonymous readers of the Press.

All the above have helped make this a better book; the remaining imperfections are entirely my own responsibility.

M.P.

Contents

A Note on Editions and Translations

The primary Latin texts are quoted from the following editions:

Lucilius: F. Marx, (ed.), *C. Lucilii Carminum Reliquiae*
                      (Leipzig, 1904).
Horace: D. R. Shackleton Bailey, (ed.), *Q. Horatius
                      Flaccus: Opera, Editio quarta* (Leipzig, 2001).
Persius and Juvenal: W. V. Clausen, (ed.), *A. Persi Flacci et D. Iuni
                      Iuvenalis Saturae* (2nd, rev. edn., Oxford,
                      1992).

Unless otherwise indicated, the translations of the Latin and Greek quotations are my own, though they are indebted to extant English translations I have consulted, especially Niall Rudd's renderings: *Horace: Satires and Epistles, Persius: Satires. A Verse Translation with an Introduction and Notes by Niall Rudd* (London, 1973; repr. with revisions, 1997) and *Juvenal: The Satires. A New Translation by Niall Rudd* (Oxford, 1992). It needs to be stressed that my aim has only been to make literal translations, not literary ones.

Introduction

THE FUNCTION OF HUMOUR IN ROMAN SATIRE

The present study is about the function of humour in the verse satires of Horace, Juvenal, and Persius, with a glance at the fragments of Lucilius. Humour is generally acknowledged as a major element of Roman verse satire, yet it has not been seriously examined by most scholars. When the satirists themselves make explicit statements about their art, as in their so called programme satires,[1] they describe humour as (1) a means of expressing their main message (moral criticism and teaching), and (2) as a pleasing element, making the moral message more palatable. Trusting the speaker in these satires—the satiric persona—many critics have taken these statements at face value and, as a consequence, seen humour as a separable, 'entertaining' ingredient, which the reader would have to see through in order to grasp the serious kernel of the satire.

Yet this is not the whole truth about humour in satire. Humour, in satire as elsewhere, carries with it its own ambivalence. On the understanding adopted here, humour always entails a breach of rules—linguistic, behavioural, aesthetic etc.—and an acknowledgement of the breach. It follows that humour always has at least two possible meanings: on the one hand the joy of breaking the rule, with the suggestion that the rule is oppressive, unacceptable; and on the other hand, the insistence on the rule, with the implication that the breach is ridiculous and unacceptable. At its softest, humour may make a pronouncement less categorical, and give the speaker the excuse of 'just joking'. At its strongest, it may completely revert the

---

[1] Hor. S. 1.4, 1.10, 2.1; P. 1; J. 1, cf. also J. 10.

meaning of an utterance, as happens in harsh irony and sarcasm. Humour may lead the eye away from a weak point in the argument, or blacken an antagonist with entirely fictional associations not easily washed off.[2]

All of this and much more happens in Roman satire. It may perhaps be said to be peripheral. Yet, to paraphrase a memorable claim in a study of inversion: what is statistically peripheral is often symbolically central.[3] It is, I believe, no coincidence that readers have found it painfully difficult to agree on the exact overall moral message in Horace's or Juvenal's satires. In these authors the periphery of potentially subversive humour interferes with the central message so much as to blur the contours of this centre and render its shape difficult to grasp.

My main thesis is thus that the Roman satirists do not deliver what they expressly promise to deliver, i.e. well-deserved ridicule of vice and vicious people, but rather give us a much more sprawling and ambiguous product, where humour is in fact more widespread than the criticism it is supposed to sweeten. This is not an accident, but an incongruity built into the very foundation of the genre: while the Roman satirist needs humour for the aesthetic merit of his satire, the ideological message inevitably suffers from the ambivalence that humour brings with it. While acknowledging the importance of social pressures, I argue that there is also an aesthetic ground for the curious, hybrid nature of Roman satire, and that the double mission of criticism combined with humour drives the satirists to build their art on paradox from the very beginning.

The paradox of teaching and joking creates a residue of meaning and opens up for cheating in different ways. One kind of satirical cheating is to pretend to attack one thing (e.g. the ruler) while

---

[2] This was well known to the rhetoricians in antiquity, and so Cicero teaches these and other ways to use humour for the orator's aims in his treatise on the laughable, in *De Or.* 2.235–90.

[3] Barbara Babcock says in an introductory discussion of the cultural phenomenon of inversion: 'What is socially peripheral is often symbolically central' (B. A. Babcock, *The Reversible World: Symbolic Inversion in Art and Society* (Ithaca, NY: Cornell University Press, 1978), 32). If we think of 'subversive humour' where she speaks of 'inversion and other forms of cultural negation', the rest of her sentence is relevant to our present context as well: 'and if we ignore or minimize inversion and other forms of cultural negation we often fail to understand the dynamics of symbolic processes generally.'

actually attacking another (e.g. a competing poet). The members of the highly intellectual Russian Decabrist movement of 1825 found Juvenal inspirational reading for their anti-autocratic, revolutionary ideas,[4] whereas it has recently been argued that Juvenal is flattering the new emperor (Hadrian) by disparaging the old (Domitian).[5] How can such disparate readings of the same text be at all possible? My answer is that humour makes it possible to make several statements at once. If for instance, Juvenal derides a certain emperor who is safely dead and gone, but does so by dressing him up as a bloodthirsty monster of The Emperor, then he has made a cowardly attack on a dead and disrespected man, but at the same time, the attack *sounded* noble and bold. And since language is the material of literature,[6] he has, in some sense, also made the bold attack; it is there in the language to be read.[7] The exaggeration, the grotesque humour of the image, has multiplied the statement's potential mean-

[4] V. S. Durov, 'La fortuna di Giovenale in Russia', *A&R* 25 (1980), 52–3.

[5] E. S. Ramage, 'Juvenal and the Establishment. Denigration of Predecessor in the "Satires" ', *ANRW* II.33.1 (1989), 640–707; S. H. Braund, 'Paradigms of Power: Roman Emperors in Roman Satire', in K. Cameron (ed.), *Humour and history* (Oxford: Intellect, 1993); A. Hardie, 'Juvenal, Domitian, and the Accession of Hadrian (*Satire* 4)', *BICS* 42 (1997–8), 117–44.

[6] See Lotman, *Analysis of the Poetic Text*, ed. and trans. D. Barton Johnson (Ann Arbor, Mich.: Ardis, 1976), esp. the chapter entitled 'Language as the Matériel of Literature'.

[7] I have found it instructive to compare Janice Radway's *Reading the Romance: Women, Patriarchy, and Popular Literature* (Chapel Hill: University of North Carolina Press, 1984), a feminist analysis of romantic consumer's literature. Radway begins her study by setting up, side by side, the contrasting utterances of on the one hand women who enjoy reading the romances under discussion, and on the other hand, feminist critics of the same romances: the former group tends to say that they find themselves morally improved (kinder, more understanding etc.) after the reading, while the latter group says that readers of these books will be brainwashed by patriarchal propaganda and induced to participate in their own humiliation. After a thorough and illuminating analysis Radway basically subscribes to the verdict of her feminist colleagues, though after having suggested an explanation to why the women who read these romances see them so differently. Another feminist critic, Lisbeth Larsson, has taken the issue further, arguing that there is even more to the readers' positive response than Radway acknowledges—that they do in fact see a utopian possibility in their reading, which they invest with real emotional energy in favour of the utopia (L. Larsson, *En annan historia: om kvinnors läsning och svensk veckopress.* ('*Another Story: on Women's Reading and the Swedish Weekly Press.*') (Stockholm: Symposion, 1989)). This real energy is not, Larsson argues, ultimately reducible to connivance in their own humiliation, but potentially goes in another direction, and could be channelled into revolutionary energy.

ings and made it ambivalent, in a way that a serious statement would not have been.

Another kind of cheating is to undercut the speaker by irony, or other humorous devices, so as to avoid taking responsibility for what he is saying—that way the satirist can both say 'the speaker's statement' and un-say it. This may be used when the utterance is prejudiced and banal, but the poet still wants it said, or—*in bonam partem*—to present several points of view and criticize even those with which he basically agrees.

Still another way of cheating is to speak of something different altogether, which is not directly relevant to either the target (object) of the satire nor to the speaking subject. This kind of humour occurs when the satirist as if inadvertently reveals that he is not really all that interested in straightforward moral teaching. He lets slip that he is more interested in describing the human condition—comically, and in purely human terms. In this, he comes near to hijacking the ambition of epic (to speak of man's place in the universe), just as satire has hijacked the metre of epic, the hexameter.[8] Here the fact that Roman satire was to epic what comedy was to tragedy, i.e. a kind of comic double,[9] is at its clearest. From this point of view it becomes tempting to toy with the idea that Roman satire, with its personal perspective, its interest in moral questions, and its centrifugal humour, served as a link in the chain from antiquity's broadest genre, epic, to the broadest modern genre, the novel.

It is further my contention that the authors are far from unconscious of an intrinsic twist in satire's essence, brought about by the element of humour. This is, I argue, expressed in their own statements about their writing; only not in the official, main part of their programmes, but in casually dropped lines, e.g. in what I shall call the

---

The problem of this gap between benevolent and critical readers is, *mutatis mutandis*, similar to the one I speak of in reading the Roman satire. It can probably not be hidden that I stand closer to Larsson's solution than to Radway's.

[8] S. H. Braund, *Roman Verse Satire*. Greece & Rome: New Surveys in the Classics 23 (Oxford: Oxford University Press, 1992), 3.

[9] For this 'ratio', see e.g. W. S. Anderson, 'The Roman Socrates: Horace and his Satiresa', in J. P. Sullivan (ed.), *Critical Essays on Roman Literature: Satire* (London: Routledge & Kegan Paul, 1963), 12.

'programmatic jokes', the jokes that round off Horace's, Persius', and Juvenal's programme satires. These meta-literary statements will receive particular attention.

It may be seen that I have been selective in my analysis, concentrating on cheating humour and not looking in much detail at the (apparently) straight joking in line with the moral message of the satire in which it is found. I have done this for three reasons. First, straight joking can fight for itself, having been defended and explained by the poets themselves and generations of critics; second, to show that straight joking is not as dominant as one might be tempted to think; and third, because by looking at the cheating joking we shall also learn something about the straight kind.

My method is literary, and all my analyses take their beginning in close readings of a humorous passage (or several humorous passages). The method has a Formalist slant to it in that I take the original texts themselves as my primary, and main, material. In consequence, I see everything in the text as *textual realities* of the same dignity—thus metaphors, flights of fancy, and even downright lies in the texts are considered just as substantial as, for instance, historical facts recounted by the satirists. When necessary, I will move between different planes (such as the plane of narrated events and the metaphorical plane), since I deem them to be united by their common textuality.

After this introduction, my study is arranged in three chapters around the orientation of the satirists' humour: (1) humour directed at an object (a person, a quality, an era); (2) humour directed at the persona, including self-irony; (3) non-aligned humour, where the target is not obvious, as when the satirist puts on a side show which has no direct bearing on the main subject matter. Since I am more interested in the similarities than the differences between the satirists' use of humour, the main stress will be put on the overarching themes, though the authors will be treated consecutively within each theme.

The approach by the orientation of humour, instead of by different kinds of humour, has been dictated by the question I pose: I am asking *how* satiric humour works, not *what* it is. Humour is here regarded as a process rather than as a stable ingredient, and so I begin with the question of its direction.

SURVEY OF HUMOUR THEORIES

The present study is not concerned to make statements about humour as such, nor to give an exhaustive description of humour in Roman satire—my aim is to investigate how humour is used in this genre. The study is not dependent on any one humour theory, and observations will be eclectically evoked from different theories along the way of the analyses. Nevertheless, my basic view of humour is in accord with the so called Incongruity theory, especially with the model developed by Susan Purdie in her book of 1993. Thus, I will only give a very brief survey of the wide field of humour studies, placing more emphasis on Purdie's model, treated last.[10] Since this is a literary study, laughter as a physical act, and humour as a psychological trait ('he has a sense of humour') fall outside my focus, but will enter in the theories recounted below, as laughter and humour have often been studied together, and even—unfortunately—treated synonymously.

---

[10] For more comprehensive surveys, see P. Keith-Spiegel, 'Early Conceptions of Humor: Varieties and Issues', in J. H. Goldstein and P. E. McGhee (eds.), *The Psychology of Humor* (New York and London: Academic Press, 1972); A. J. Chapman and H. C. Foot, *Humour and Laughter: Theory, Research, and Application* (London: Wiley, 1976); M. L. Apte, *Humor and Laughter: An Anthropological Approach* (Ithaca, NY: Cornell University Press, 1985) (from the point of view of anthropology); J. Morreall (ed.), *The Philosophy of Laughter and Humor* (Albany, NY: State University of New York Press, 1987) (philosophy); F. Ceccarelli, *Sorriso e riso. Saggio di antropologia biosociale* (Turin: Einaudi, 1988); P. Santarcangeli, *Homo ridens: estetica, filologia, psicologia, storia del comico* (Firenze: Olschki, 1989); S. Attardo, *Linguistic Theories of Humor* (Berlin: Mouton de Gruyter, 1994) (linguistics). For humour in antiquity in particular, see M. Grant, *The Ancient Rhetorical Theories of the Laughable*. University of Wisconsin Studies in Language and Literature 21 (Madison: University of Wisconsin, 1924); W. Preisendanz and R. Warning (eds.), *Das Komische*. Poetik und Hermeneutik 7. (Munich: Fink, 1976); W. Schindler 'Komik-Theorien—komische Theorien? Eine Skizze über die Deutung des Lachens von der Antike bis Heute', *AU* 29 (1986), 4–19; S., Halliwell, 'The Uses of Laughter in Greek Culture', *CQ* 41 (1991), 279–96; and M.-L. Declos (ed.), *Le rire des Grecs: Anthropologie du rire en Grèce ancienne* (Grenoble: Editions Jérôme Millon, 2000)—the last two are on Greece, but are also instructive for the student of Latin literature and Roman culture. I have also drawn on my own exposition of humour theories in the introduction to my study on Petronius (M. Plaza, *Laughter and Derision in Petronius' Satyrica: A Literary Study* (Stockholm: Almqvist & Wiksell, 2000), 3–10).

Today the field of humour studies is a fertile one and there are currently more than a hundred humour theories used in different disciplines, such as biology, psychology, cognitive science, anthropology, linguistics, and literary criticism. There are, however, substantial overlaps between the various theories, and they can well be grouped, as e.g. in the common and useful tripartite grouping into Superiority theory, Relief theory, and Incongruity theory.

All humour theories which have come down to us from antiquity belong to the Superiority category, characterized by the belief that we laugh at what is ugly and/or bad. The first proponent of such an explanation is Plato, who in *Philebus* 48–50 claims that the laughable is a kind of vice, more specifically a lack of self-knowledge, and amusement a kind of malice, as we take pleasure in others' faults. Interestingly, he hints at the ambivalent nature of humour in concluding that the pleasure from laughing is mixed with the pain of malice. He also suggests that the amusing is a neighbour of the hateful, in saying that weak self-ignorance is funny while strong self-ignorance is hateworthy—a thought which will echo down the history of the thinking about humour. Plato's suspicion of laughter is also evident in another passage, *Republic* 388e, where he stresses that the guardians of the ideal state should avoid laughter because of its tendency to provoke violent reactions and that literature should be censored so as not to show respectable characters laughing.

The next version of the Superiority theory is sketched by Aristotle in his *Poetics* 5.1449^a, where he defines the laughable as that which is ugly without being painful. In the *Nicomachean Ethics* 4.8 Aristotle discusses how far humour should be carried by a well-bred and educated man, and dismisses excessive humour as a feature of vulgar buffoons. The latter passage, often termed Aristotle's description of 'the liberal jest', was early seen to have been a major impulse for Horace's theory of satiric humour as expressed primarily in his *S.* 1.4 and 1.10.[11]

On Roman ground, Aristotle's consideration of the decorum of humour was taken up and developed in some detail by Cicero (*De Or.* 2.235–90, *Orat.* 26. 87–9), who was later followed by Quintilian (*Inst.* 6.3). In his extensive discussion of the laughable in

---

[11] More on this in the survey of critical literature below.

De Oratore, Cicero shows himself as an adherent of the Superiority theory in saying that the ridiculous is a kind of the ugly which is not worthy of either great hate or great compassion, censored in no ugly way:

haec enim ridentur vel sola vel maxime, quae notant et signant turpitudinem aliquam non turpiter. (*de Or.* 2.236)[12]

people laugh mostly, or only, at that which censures and points out something offensive in an inoffensive manner.

Cicero's is also the first extant discussion to introduce the difference between verbal and thematic jokes. In general, however, his treatment is a practical guide to the effective use of humour by the orator rather than a theoretical contribution, and he even explicitly refuses to deal with the question of what laughter is (*De Or.* 2.235). Like Aristotle, Cicero discusses what kind of humour becomes a gentleman (both in *De Oratore* and in *De Officiis* 1.104), but he allows that the illiberal kind, unbefitting for the orator, may nevertheless be very funny.

In the modern era, important advocates of the Superiority theory have been Thomas Hobbes, who offered a very drastic formulation,[13] and Henri Bergson (1900), who offered a mild version, arguing that ultimately laughter has a positive purpose, as it is used to remove mechanical encrustations from life and so promote free and well-adapted behaviour.[14] The latter also paid close attention to incongruity, and his model may in fact be regarded as a mixture of Superiority- and Incongruity theory.

Within the frame of the Superiority theory, Umberto Eco has added an interesting twist to the definition of humour in his article

[12] For a full discussion of Cicero's views on humour, see A. Corbeill, *Controlling Laughter: Political Humor in the Late Roman Republic* (Princeton: Princeton University Press, 1996), ch. 1.
[13] T. Hobbes, *Leviathan* (London, 1651), ch. 6: '*Sudden glory*, is the passion which maketh those *Grimaces* called LAUGHTER; and is caused either by some sudden act of their own that pleaseth them; or by the apprehension of some deformed thing in another, by comparison whereof they suddenly applaud themselves. And it is incident most to them, that are conscious of the fewest abilities in themselves; who are forced to keep themselves in their own favour, by observing the imperfections of other men.' This definition will be further discussed in Ch.1 below.
[14] H. Bergson, *Le rire. Essai sur la signification du comique* (1900; 17th edn. Paris: Alcan, 1919).

'Il comico e la regola', 1981.[15] To the customary claim that we laugh at what is a breach of rules, ultimately in order to expel it from society, Eco adds that the rule broken in such cases needs to be left unuttered, merely implied—if the rule is spelled out the breach becomes tragic rather than comic. This has a certain bearing on Roman satire, since the rules of right behaviour are often explicitly spelled out in the 'preaching' passages, especially in the earlier satirists (Lucilius, Horace). This does indeed have a cooling effect on the derision of those who break these rules. To avoid it various strategies are employed, such as not joking at exactly the same vice that has been seriously chided—we shall encounter this in our analyses below.

Today the Superiority theory is much used in anthropology and, in its Bergsonian version, in some literary studies.[16] For the reason that Graeco-Roman antiquity offers this view of laughter and humour in its theoretical discussions, the Superiority theory is also popular among classicists. As will be seen in the survey of secondary literature below, this is not least the case among those who study Roman satire.

The Relief theory, popular in the field of psychology, stresses the physiological and psychological aspects of laughter and humour. First presented by Herbert Spencer (*The Physiology of Laughter*, 1860) and receiving its most famous formulation in Sigmund Freud's *Der Witz und seine Beziehung zum Unbewussten*, 1905 (a work perhaps indirectly influenced by Spencer's ideas),[17] the Relief theory regards the perception of something ludicrous as leading to a saving of psychic energy, and laughter as the release of that energy. Apart from being the choice of psychologists, the Relief theory is also used by Freudians in literary criticism. No thoroughly Freudian readings of humour in Roman verse satire are known to me. However, Amy Richlin's 'Priapic model', mainly a Superiority theory, certainly has traits of Relief theory, such as the claim that the Roman humorists

---

[15] Republished in Eco, *Sette anni di desiderio*, 1983: 253–60.
[16] Within classics, a rightly celebrated example is E. Segal, *Roman Laughter: The Comedy of Plautus* (Cambridge Mass.: Harvard University Press, 1968), a Bergsonian discussion on the humour in Plautus.
[17] G. B. Milner, 'Homo Ridens: Towards a Semiotic Theory of Humour and Laughter', *Semiotica* 5 (1972), 7.

use humour as a pretext for the expression of violent sexual and aggressive impulses.[18]

Different versions of the Incongruity theory share the core idea that humour is born out of a mismatch—an incongruity—between two or more components of an object, event, idea, social expectation etc. This group, too, may be traced back to Aristotle, to a passage in the *Rhetoric* (3.2), where it is said that a speaker can raise a laugh by flouting certain expectations which he has built up in his audience. The principle of incongruity can also be said to be approached in Cicero's description of the most common type of joke: 'sed scitis esse notissimum ridiculi genus, cum aliud expectamus, aliud dicitur.' ('but you know that the best known kind of joke is when a saying goes against our expectations' *De Or.* 2.255). Fuller versions of the Incongruity theory, however, were not developed until the eighteenth and nineteenth centuries, notably by Kant and Schopenhauer.[19] A later influential exponent of an incongruity-based view has been Arthur Koestler with his 'bisociation theory'.[20] He maintains that humour is experienced when two essentially different elements are yoked together in the same situation and bring about a rapid oscillation of thought from one associative realm to another. Our feelings cannot move as quickly, and the resulting emotional tension is resolved in laughter.

The Incongruity theory is most widespread in humour studies today, as its basic tenets have the advantages of viewing humour as value neutral, and of being easily adaptable to different cultural or literary contents, since 'incongruity' is so vague a concept. On the other hand, while these tenets seem to present a necessary condition of humour (it is difficult to find examples of the laughable that do not contain some kind of incongruity), they have to be further qualified in order to become a sufficient condition (it is easy to imagine other reactions than humour to incongruity), and no agreement has been reached on such further qualifications. It should also be pointed out

---

[18] A. Richlin, *The Garden of Priapus: Sexuality and Aggression in Roman Humor* (1983; 2nd, rev. edn., Oxford: Oxford University Press, 1992), 57–70; see also the survey of critical literature below.

[19] I. Kant, *Kritik der Urtheilskraft* (1790; 4th edn. Leipzig: P. Reclam, 1878), Part I, Div.1.54; A. Schopenhauer, *Die Welt als Wille und Vorstellung* (1819; 3rd edn. Leipzig, 1859), Book I and Supplement to Book I, ch. 8.

[20] A. Koestler, *The Act of Creation* (London: Hutchinson & Co, 1964).

that the Incongruity theory is compatible with both Superiority- and Relief theory, and that different blends of these are not uncommon.[21]

As has already been mentioned, a variant of the Incongruity theory which I have found particularly persuasive is that presented by Susan Purdie in her study *Comedy: The Mastery of Discourse*, 1993. Bringing in Jacques Lacan's concept 'Symbolic order',[22] which in a strongly simplified explanation may be described as the sphere a human being first enters when s/he acquires a language (complete with the basic rules of social behaviour) and in which s/he lives from then on, Purdie argues that what is funny is always a trespassing of the rules of the Symbolic order. At the linguistic level, for instance, one rule of communication requires that a word mean only one thing at a time. A pun will transgress this rule by making us think of two meanings at the same time. It is crucial, Purdie further points out, that in humour the break is conscious, and marked as such by the joker. According to this model, humour requires a minimum of two actors: joker and audience. (A third actor, the butt, is optional.) As the joker makes a marked break of the Symbolic order, the audience understands both moves, and acknowledges them. Both actors sense that they know the rules so well as to be able to play with them—they master the discourse. They congratulate themselves and each other on this mastery; this *feels* good. Since the arrangement of the Symbolic order varies with time, culture, social group etc., this becomes a

---

[21] I do not treat Mikhail Bakhtin here, since his theory is one of *laughter* (understood in a very special sense), not *humour*, as he expressly says (M. M. Bakhtin, *Rabelais and his World*. Russian original 1965, trans. H. Iswolsky (Cambridge, Mass.: MIT Press, 1968), 11). This is often not understood, and misreadings spring from the treatment of 'humour' and 'laughter' as synonyms. A recent study of humour in the Middle Ages oddly makes the opposite misreading, taking Bakhtin to mean that what he terms 'the culture of folk laughter' somehow *excludes* humour (O. Ferm, *Abboten, bonden och hölasset: skratt och humor under medeltiden*. [*The Abbot, the Peasant, and the Hay-cart: Laughter and Humour in the Middle Ages*] (Stockholm: Atlantis, 2002), 14). Bakhtin's ideas on laughter's regenerative force and on the grotesque body will be used in my analyses below, and will be summarized when this is needed.

[22] S. Purdie, *Comedy: The Mastery of Discourse* (Hemel Hempstead: Harvester Wheatsheaf, 1993). Purdie spends much of her first chapter ('Joking as Discourse', 3–70) unravelling the obscure psychoanalytic/ linguistic model of Lacan; she then corrects his concepts at several points. (She draws especially on J. Lacan, *Écrits* (Paris: Seuil, 1966) and id., 'Les quatres concepts fondamentaux de la psychanalyse', in *Le Séminaire de Jacques Lacan*, xi (Paris: Seuil, 1973).) It seems to me, however, that her model of the comic may stand very well on its own.

broad and flexible view of humour. Depending on where one puts the emphasis, on the breach of the rule or the recognition of the breach and thus the reinstatement of the rule, the funny event will allow its players to rejoice in the freedom from the pressures of rules, or in the contentment with the normal order after a welcome relaxation; potentially every joke or funny event entails both.[23] To this explanation Purdie adds that a joke may be strengthened by sexual, aggressive, or otherwise taboo-breaking content, thus opening up for admixture of Superiority and Relief elements.

Purdie's model has two considerable advantages over other views of humour. First, it approaches the form, not the content of humour. It thus explains how the same joke structure can be filled with different sense (as for instance, in 'wandering' ethnic jokes); and how it is that we may be tricked into laughing at a joke whose subject matter we find offensive, or even enjoy a joke with whose content we disagree (as long as we do not disagree too strongly)—this latter phenomenon has some bearing on modern readers of Roman satire. Secondly, this explains why humour basically always feels good for the joker and the audience that understands him/ her and is willing to play the game, no matter how offensive or 'black' its content may be. This captivating force of humour is also of importance for Roman satire.

As my working definition, then, I understand humour as arising from an incongruity which may, but need not, be strengthened by aggression or other taboo-breaking. The basic mechanism of its working is understood along the lines of Purdie's model: the joker is the satirist (often, though not necessarily, through the mouthpiece of his persona), the audience is the reader, the butt (optional) I call object, s/he or it is often also the object of the satire as a whole. The discourse game is played with every reading, as sketched above.

No mechanical criteria for how to identify humour have been set up.[24] Instead I have tried to take as my examples such passages as are

---

[23] It must be noted that while Purdie acknowledges the existence of both poles, her interpretation stresses the conservative, rule-asserting pole much more. This may be connected to the fact that her examples are taken from English Renaissance comedy.

[24] Within the confines of this note I may confide that *vestigia terrent*: when elaborate mechanical criteria for humour are set up, the results of the analysis are often meagre or downright false, whereas more interpretative approaches may lead to impressive explorations.

fairly obviously meant to be funny; where I have deviated from this, I have been careful to explain why the passage in question should be considered funny.[25] Nor do I use technical terms for different kinds of humour; 'joke', 'hilarity' and so on, will be employed according to ordinary English usage.

One special case is *irony*, which will be understood as a subspecies of humour,[26] and defined as: saying something other than what one means (often the opposite), but with the intention that both the incongruous, 'perverse', surface meaning and the true meaning underneath be understood by the audience. The oscillation between the two meanings will be perceived as humorous.[27]

SURVEY OF CRITICAL LITERATURE ON HUMOUR IN ROMAN SATIRE

In order not to digress too far from my own question I will strictly limit this survey to the works that exclusively or primarily deal with humour in one or more Roman satirist(s).[28]

The intersection between two vast fields, humour studies and studies of Roman satire, is relatively small. Studies of Roman satire before the second half of the nineteenth century hardly regarded humour in itself as a topic worthy of discussion. As has already been mentioned above, it was—and is often still—seen as an embellishment on a moralistic kernel. Even as studies devoted to the topic

---

[25] It is only after much deliberation that I have decided to forego fixed criteria for the identification of humour, but I take courage from two facts: that literary criticism is a hermeneutic, not an exact discipline, and that my judgement may count as reasonable, since I am, after all, also one of Roman satire's readers.

[26] I am thus not concerned with such non-humorous kinds as e.g. 'Romantic irony'.

[27] My definition of irony is inspired by the discussions in Douglas C. Muecke, *The Compass of Irony* (London: Methuen, 1969); W. Booth, *A Rhetoric of Irony* (Chicago and London: University of Chicago Press, 1974); and V. Sack, *Ironie bei Horaz*. Diss. (Würzburg, 1965).

[28] Although most commentaries and studies of Roman satire mention humour at some point, these scattered observations usually do not amount to a view of humour. Important observations will be recorded in connection with the passages analysed below.

began to appear, they were regarded as trifling, sometimes by their authors as well. Most critics have focused on one satirist, and only a very few have discussed the humour of all the Roman satirists (plus a couple of scholars who have included satire in an overview of humour in Latin literature). For a survey such as this, the arrangement which most readily suggests itself is thus one that treats the secondary literature for every satirist in turn. However, since it is my aim in this study to look at similarities between the satirists rather than their obvious differences, I will arrange the secondary works in this survey thematically.

Three groups will be discerned: (1) inventories, i.e. works which catalogue humorous passages, sometimes with a certain amount of commentary; (2) those works which categorize different kinds of humour, often using formal categories; (3) those which analyse humour beyond mere categorization. The third group will then be further subdivided according to the main thesis of their analysis.[29]

Inventories

The first to appear in the group of inventories is Theodor Oesterlen, who generously enumerates all the passages deemed humorous in Horace, not only in the *Sermones*, but in all Horace's writings.[30] Oesterlen adds his own descriptions to the effect of the humour, and sets up certain haphazard categories such as 'cynical humour', or satires 'filled with a humorous spirit', without however giving any criteria for these regulations.[31] While it is easy to criticize him for his enthusiastic monotony and his almost complete lack of theoretical framework,[32] he is to be commended for undertaking this laborious

---

[29] The last two groups are close (categorization being a rudimentary form of analysis), and will be seen to overlap somewhat.

[30] T. Oesterlen, *Komik und Humor bei Horaz. Ein Beitrag zur römischen Litteraturgeschichte* (3 vols., Stuttgart: Verlag der J. B. Metzlerschen Buchhandlung, 1885–7). Vol. i, 1885, treats the *Sermones*.

[31] 'Cynical humour' is his label for S. 1.2; 2.7; *Epodes* 8 and 12; 'satires filled with a humorous spirit' for S. 1.9; 2.8; 1.6; 2.6; 2.3.

[32] Cf. the merciless evaluation of him by Sack: '[die] Arbeit Oesterlens, der das Wesen der horazischen Ironie mit ebensowenig Geschick wie Erfolg durch eine bloße Paraphrase des Inhalts zu erklären sucht' (Sack, *Ironie*, 6).

ground work, as well as for being a sensitive reader, whose acute notes often make up for the missing stringency in terms and argumentation.

Although there is no full analysis of the humour aspect, much attention to humour is still paid by Niall Rudd in his classical study on Horace's satires (1966). Here is a wealth of fine observations and good judgement.[33]

Inventories on the same scale have not been made for the other verse satirists. In a more modest format, a couple of scholars have battled with the accusations of 'humourlessness' against Persius, highlighting his funny passages.[34]

Lists of humorous passages have repeatedly been drawn up for Juvenal.[35]

Finally, Mary Grant (1924) and Wilhelm Süss (1969) touch upon Roman satire within the frame of broader discussions of humour in antiquity.

Categorizations

Most attempts at categorizing satirical humour have been attracted by Horace, both because he is often regarded as the funniest and most ironic among the Roman satirists, and because he has teasingly laid down the foundation for such humour categories himself. The

[33] The same may also be said for his broadened study of 1986, *Themes in Roman Satire* (London: Duckworth, 1986), though the percentage of comments on humour is perhaps less there.

[34] R. G. M. Nisbet, 'Persius', in J. P. Sullivan (ed.), *Critical Essays on Roman Literature: Satire* (London: Routledge & Kegan Paul, 1963); M. Squillante Saccone, 'Techniche dell'ironia e del comico nella satira di Persio', *BollStLat* 10 (1980), 3–25, going through the humour in Persius' *Satires* 1 and 3.

[35] By J. Jessen, 'Witz und Humor bei Juvenal', *Philologus* 47 (1889), 321–7 (with emendations to increase the funniness!); F. S. Dunn, 'Juvenal as a Humorist', *CW* 4 (1911), 50–4; J. R. C. Martyn, 'Juvenal's Wit', *GB* 8 (1979), 219–38; and A. T. Bendoriute, 'Humoras Juvenalio satyrose', ('Das Humor in den Satiren von Juvenalis'), *Literatura* (Vilnius) 25/3 (1983), 39–47. Humour in several of Juvenal's satires has been stressed by Alex Hardie in articles primarily devoted to other questions ('Juvenal and the Condition of Letters: the Seventh Satire', *Papers of the Leeds International Latin Seminar*, 6 (1990), 145–209; and id., 'Domitian'), though the view he expresses is not simply an enumeration, but gravitates towards the position of William S. Anderson and others, which will be discussed below.

category of irony in his writings has been separately treated by several critics, most thoroughly by Volker Sack (1965), who subdivides the phenomenon into: (*a*) irony that helps express the satiric message, (*b*) self-irony, and (*c*) irony as a means of artistic expression. Sack has made an often acute linear reading of ironic passages in Horace's satirical writings.[36]

As for Horace's own meta-literary comments on the comic in the *Sermones*, these were seen to have been inspired by Aristotle's thoughts about 'the liberal jest' as early as 1900 by George L. Hendrickson in his article 'Horace, *Serm.* 1.4: A Protest and a Programme'. This is one of several impressive readings of Roman satire by this scholar. After Hendrickson's signal a number of treatments of Horace's humour as 'Aristotelian'[37] have appeared, some mostly intuitive, some truly stringent and illuminating.[38]

For Persius a kind of humour categorization has been made by John Bramble, who has illuminated many passages of sexual humour in his brilliant, difficult study *Persius and the Programmatic Satire*, 1974. These passages he tends to take as 'ironic'. His reading of Persius' humour has recently been challenged by the claim that far from being sophisticated irony, Persius' laughter is a deliberately impolite guffaw.[39] The reading of this satirist's laughter as impolite

---

[36] Sack treats the first book each of the *Sermones* and the *Epistles*. Apart from Sack, cf. the treatments by Zoja Pavlovskis ('Aristotle, Horace, and the Ironic Man', *CP* 63 (1968), 22–41) and Ernst Zinn ('Ironie und Pathos bei Horaz', in A. Schaefer (ed.), *Ironie und Dichtung. Sechs Essays* (Munich: Beck, 1970)).

[37] 'Aristotelian' here roughly meaning 'gentlemanly', 'non-vulgar'.

[38] Examples of intuitive categorizations are A. K. Michels, '*Παρρησία* and the satire of Horace', *CP* 39 (1944), 173–7; L. Radermacher, *Weinen und Lachen. Studien über antikes Lebensgefühl* (Vienna: R. M. Rohrer, 1947); H. A. Musurillo, *Symbol and Myth in Ancient Poetry* (New York: Fordham University Press, 1961); E. de Saint-Denis, 'L'Humour dans les Satires d'Horace', *RPh* 38 (1964), 24–35; L. Giangrande, *The Use of Spoudaiogeloion in Greek and Roman Literature* (The Hague: Mouton, 1972).

An example of a stringent reading of Aristotelian humour in Horace is Alison Parker's dissertation on comic theory in the *Sermones* (A. R. Parker, 'Comic Theory in the Satires of Horace', Ph.D. thesis (University of North Carolina at Chapel Hill, 1986)), where she argues that the satirist not only expressly espouses an Aristotelian ideal of the comic, but also adheres to it in practice, drawing near to the comic style of New Comedy. In fact, Parker's study could be regarded as an analysis, as I do for Freudenburg's study of the same question (K. Freudenburg, *The Walking Muse: Horace on the Theory of Satire* (Princeton: Princeton University Press, 1993)). I have placed Parker here because her book poses the problem much more narrowly than Freudenburg.

[39] J. C. Relihan, 'Pardoning Persius' laughter', *Mnemosyne* 44 (1991), 433–4.

is a well-needed warning against making the notoriously obscure Persius into too much of an intellectual.

Juvenal received the analogue of Sack's study for Horace with Alba Claudia Romano's *Irony in Juvenal*, 1979, a conscientious treatment of ironic passages with subdivisions into various kinds of irony, and with percentage charts over their distribution. Romano's book contains many valuable observations which have been of great help for the present study among others. However, it suffers from the gap between its inescapably hermeneutic assignment of a passage to a certain category and its mathematically rigid conclusions. As has been noted, some necessarily subjective judgements sway the results of the tables and make the conclusions less exciting than they might have been.[40] Nevertheless, Romano's work is an important step in the exploration of Juvenalian humour.

Minor categorizing discussions of this satirist's humour have been offered in articles by various scholars.[41]

Another particular category of satirical humour is caricature, which has been briefly treated for all the Roman satirists by J.-P. Cèbe (*La caricature et la parodie*, 1966).

---

[40] C. J. Classen, 'Überlegungen zu den Möglichkeiten und Grenzen der Anwendung des Begriffes Ironie (im Anschluß an die dritte Satire Juvenals)' in (eds.), U. J. Stache, W. Maaz, and F. Wagner *Kontinuität und Wandel. Lateinische Poesie von Naevius bis Baudelaire*. Franco Munari zum 65. Geburtstag (Hildesheim: Weidmann, 1986); S. H. Braund, *Beyond Anger: A Study of Juvenal's Third Book of Satires* (Cambridge: Cambridge University Press, 1988), 25 n. 6 (on p. 206).

[41] By de Saint-Denis ('L'Humour de Juvénal', *Inform.Litt.* 4 (1952), 8–14) F. J. Lelièvre ('Parody in Juvenal and T. S. Eliot', *CP* 53 (1958), 22–6); R. Marache ('Rhétorique et humour chez Juvénal', in M. Renard and R. Schilling (eds.), *Hommages à Jean Bayet* (Brussels: Latomus, 1964)); and in parts of H. A. Mason's now classical article of 1963, 'Is Juvenal a Classic?' (in J. P. Sullivan (ed.), *Critical Essays on Roman Literature: Satire* (London: Routledge & Kegan Paul, 1963)). Mason's argument, that there is much lascivious, Martialian humour in Juvenal, has been countered by E. Rodríguez-Almeida ('Martial—Juvenal: entre *castigatio per risum* et *censura morum*', in M. Trédé and P. Hoffmann (eds.), *Le rire des anciens* (Paris: Presses de l'École Normale Supérieure, 1998)). Rodríguez-Almeida maintains that Juvenal's humour is censorious and exactly opposed to that of Martial. Anderson's article '*Lascivia* vs. *ira*: Martial and Juvenal' (*CSCA* 3 (1970), 1–34. Reprinted in *Essays on Roman Satire* (Princeton: Princeton University Press, 1982)), also stresses the difference between the two poets, but does so in favour of Juvenal, not in favour of Martial like Rodríguez-Almeida.

Analyses

Developing meta-literary comments in the satires

Among the works that analyse satirical humour beyond arranging it
in categories certain trends may be discerned on a time-scale. The
oldest, most traditional approach is to follow the indications that
seem to have been given, in the form of metaliterary comments, by
the satirists themselves. These have often been straightforwardly read
as proposing superiority humour in the sense that the satirist means
to deride what is morally wrong.[42] The critic has then analysed all the
humour in accordance with this programme. Within this approach
there are, with some simplification, two attitudes that critics take.
Either they endorse the derision of the objects chosen by the satir-
ist(s), greeting it as morally upright and witty, finding that it is as it
should be, *or* they read against the author, questioning his insistence
that what he mocks is vicious—rather than, say, threatening to his
social status. Those who adopt the latter position, a more modern
one, occasionally even take up the part of the satirist's butt against
him.

Gilbert Highet's well-known book *Juvenal the Satirist*, 1954, may
exemplify the former position. Highet understands Juvenal's mockery as superiority humour. Despite some hypotheses such as assum-
ing that Juvenal had had bad experiences with women, Highet's study
is basically in sympathy with this humour. The headings that Highet
gives to his discussions of the individual satires underline Juvenal's
explicit claims.[43] In effect, the critic *continues* the satirist's mockery.

From the opposite scholarly camp, Amy Richlin's feminist study
on sexuality and aggression in Roman humour, *The Garden of Priapus*, 1983,[44] also sees superiority derision in Juvenal, but instead
of accepting it, opposes it. Richlin achieves this in several ways:
by questioning Juvenal's motivation in attacking these groups, by

---

[42] See my discussion below, section 'Programmatic statements on humour in
Roman satire'.

[43] G. Highet, *Juvenal the Satirist: A Study* (Oxford: Oxford University Press, 1954).
For instance, J. 2, on homosexuals, Highet labels 'The Fairie Queenes'; J. 6, the great
misogynist poem, is claimed by Juvenal to be against marriage, and this is followed—
'Advice to those About to Marry'.

[44] Revised edition 1992; I quote from this latter edition.

throwing into relief the social enmity between attacker and attacked, by probing the proposed scope of the target (does J. 6 treat *bad wives*, as claimed, or women in general?), even by expressly criticizing Juvenal's attitude. The camp represented by Richlin may be in danger of becoming anachronistic, but it offers more of an analysis in not unquestioningly following the directions of the author, and its resistance to the assumptions of superiority humour makes it more clear-eyed.

Still, both camps are limited by their unwillingness to go beyond the humour that the satirists parade before their readers. To the former camp belong several traditional-minded studies of humour in satire.[45] In the opposite camp, Richlin has been followed above all by gender-oriented critics, among whom John Henderson deserves particular mention.[46]

Focusing on the technical quality

A smaller group consists of critics who wish to see Roman satire's humour as artistically sophisticated. A fine example is Ulrich Knoche's article on Horace's humour,[47] but the most influential champion of this view, for all the satirists, is William S. Anderson.

---

[45] e.g. E. A., Schmidt, 'Vom Lachen in der römischen Satire', in S. Jäkel and A. Timonen (eds.), *Laughter down the Centuries*, ii (Turku: Annales Universitatis Turkuensis, 1995); and Vogt-Spira, G. 'Das satirische Lachen der Römer und die Witzkultur der Oberschicht', in S. Jäkel, A. Timonen, and V-M. Rissanen (eds.), *Laughter down the Centuries*, iii (Turku: Annales Universitatis Turkuensis, 1997), who have written on all the satirists; and Rochefort, who in a dissertation on laughter in Juvenal's *Satires* ('Laughter as a Satirical Device in Juvenal', Ph.D. thesis (Tufts University, 1972)) has claimed that explicit laughter in them expresses superiority.

[46] Henderson, '...When Satire Writes "Woman" in S. Braund (ed.), *Satire and Society in Ancient Rome* (Exeter: University of Exeter, 1989) and *Writing down Rome: Satire, Comedy, and Other Offences in Latin Poetry* (Oxford: Oxford University Press, 1999), has written on all the verse satirists; cf. also Gold, 'Humor in Juvenal's Sixth Satire: Is It Funny?' in S. Jäkel and A. Timonen (eds.), *Laughter down the Centuries*, ii (Turku: Annales Universitatis Turkuensis, 1994) and ead., ' "The House I Live In Is Not My Own": Women's Bodies in Juvenal's *Satires*', *Arethusa* 31/3 (1998), 369–86, on Juvenal: P. A. Miller, 'The Bodily Grotesque in Roman Satire: Images of Sterility', *Arethusa* 31 (1998), 257–83; and Walters, 'Making a Spectacle: Deviant Men, Invective, and Pleasure', *Arethusa* 31 (1998), 355–67, on Juvenal.

[47] 'Über Horazens satirische Dichtung: Witz und Weisheit', *Gymnasium* 67 (1960), 56–72. Another fine example in the same year is Ernst Zinn, 'Elemente des Humors in augusteischer Dichtung', *Gymnasium* 67 (1960), 41–56 and 152–5.

In a number of articles, Anderson has fought for the acceptance of satire as literary art, and not least for the acceptance of its humour as *literary* humour.[48] Analyses of this kind have also been sketched by other critics, who usually concentrate on one satirist.[49] This approach has proved rich in insights and excellent readings, but its drawback is that it risks coming to a standstill of aesthetical admiration, where the analysis turns into the recommendation of a connoisseur instead of the scrutinizing splitting of the chemist.

Reading against the grain

A modern kind of analysis focuses on humour that *goes against* the overt moral-ideological message of the satire. This orientation has been best developed on the material of Juvenal, where Anderson was again the pioneer.[50] He argued that far from inviting us to laugh with his aggressive speaker (= persona), Juvenal *the author* is mocking this very *speaker*, and wishing his readers to catch this. The view has been richly expanded in several studies by Susanna M. Braund, and is also followed by Martin Winkler, and to a certain extent by Alex Hardie.[51]

For Persius, the seeds of an against-the-grain reading have been sown with the suggestion that his satire contains Aristophanic humour and occasionally invites the reader to laugh with the persona's enemies.[52]

---

[48] Especially 'Horace, the Unwilling Warrior; *Satire* I,9', 1956; 'Studies in Book 1 of Juvenal', 1957; 'Imagery in the Satires of Horace and Juvenal', 1960; 'Part versus Whole in Persius' Fifth Satire', 1960; 'The Roman Socrates: Horace and his Satires', 1963; 'Roman Satirists and Literary Criticism', 1964; '*Lascivia* vs. *ira*: Martial and Juvenal', 1970; and 'The Form, Purpose, and Position of Horace's *Satire* I,8', 1972. All are conveniently collected in W. S. Anderson, *Essays on Roman Satire* (Princeton: Princeton University Press, 1982).

[49] J. K. Whitehead, 'Towards a Definition of Etruscan Humor', *EtrStud* 3 (1996), 9–32, and K. Reckford, 'Reading the Sick Body: Decomposition and Morality in Persius' Third Satire', *Arethusa*, 31 (1998), 337–54, for Persius; J. Baumert, 'Identifikation und Distanz: Eine Erprobung satirischer Kategorien bei Juvenal', *ANRW* II 33.1(1989), 734–69, for Juvenal.

[50] Especially in his articles 'The Programs of Juvenal's Later Books' and 'Anger in Juvenal and Seneca' (1962, 1964, both reprinted in Anderson, *Essays*).

[51] Braund, *Beyond Anger* and *Roman Satire*; M. M. Winkler, *The Persona in Three Satires of Juvenal* (Hildesheim: Olms, 1983); Hardie, 'The Condition of Letters' and 'Domitian'.

[52] Reckford, 'Reading the Sick Body'. I do not find these suggestions persuasive; see further below, Ch. 3, p. 301–5.

For Horace's humour reading against the current results in a totally different picture than it does for Juvenal's. Where Juvenal parades his fierce anger, Horace parades his mildness and fairness and commensurate laughter—thus a questioning analysis of Horatian humour will argue that there is *more* aggressiveness in it than the author wants to own up to. Such readings have been performed with great subtlety by Kirk Freudenburg and Ellen Oliensis.

Freudenburg began in the area of Horace's own theory of humour in the *Sermones*,[53] and unearthed there, in addition to the Aristotelian view, a layer of much sharper, Cynic and iambographic theories of laughter. He showed these to be intertwined with the milder Aristotelian credo into an 'impossible and absurd combination'[54] made very real in Horace's satires. In his second book, *Satires of Rome*, 2001, Freudenburg has broadened his scope to all three Roman satirists. His main thesis in this analysis is that from Horace onwards, all the satirists of Rome suffered from a 'Lucilius problem' in that they were generically supposed to, but in their historical reality unable to, write a pointed kind of satire with *nominatim* personal jokes. This comes very close to recognizing the basic paradox of satire—the contradiction between serious message and humour—but regards the reasons for it as entirely extra-poetical. Freudenburg assumes that the first Roman satirist Lucilius, in his beneficent social circumstances, was able to write an unproblematic kind of satire, whereas I will argue that this was never possible, since the problem was a poetical one as well, encoded in the very definition of the genre.

Where Oliensis' work on Horace's satire deals with the problem of humour,[55] it offers a similar probing of whether Horace's humour is as mild and commensurate as it promises to be.

Highlighting contradiction

The work that comes closest to my argument in the present study is that of Gustaf Adolf Seeck, primarily in his important article 'Die

---

[53] Freudenburg, *Walking Muse*.   [54] Ibid. 107.

[55] E. Oliensis, 'Canidia, Canicula, and the Decorum of Horace's *Epodes*', *Arethusa* 24 (1991), 107–38; '*Ut Arte Emendaturus Fortunam*: Horace, Nasidienus, and the Art of Satire', in T. Habinek and A. Shiesaro (eds.), *The Roman Cultural Revolution* (Cambridge: Cambridge University Press, 1997); and within the scope of her major Horatian study, *Horace and the Rhetoric of Authority* (Cambridge: Cambridge University Press, 1998).

römische Satire und der Begriff des Satirischen' (1991). Seeck recognizes that there are different kinds of humour in Roman satire: both aggressive and innocent joking. Most importantly, he then highlights the contradiction between their functions. The more aggressive derision ('Spott') has as its function to sharpen the attack made in the non-humorous part of the satire, whereas the innocent humour ('Heiterkeit') has the function of softening the approach of the attack, as part of the process of winning the sympathies of the reader. At least potentially, Seeck says, these functions run in contrary directions. His solution is to plead for a balance between the impulses of 'Spott' and 'Heiterkeit', which when reached neutralizes the impulses. This is perhaps an especially welcome solution in his discussion, since he mostly works with examples from Horace, the great balance-actor. Yet what Seeck's analysis overlooks is that since these are functions, not entities, they cannot be brought to stable balance frozen in time and impact. Functions unravel, they work with every new reading, and undercut each other even when they are equally blended. What I will argue below is that the different humour impulses create not so much a stable balance as a dynamic whirlpool on the site of Roman satire, drawing every new reader into its contradictory currents.

A NOTE ON AUTHOR AND PERSONA

In the present study I use the concept of the satirical *persona* as developed in the studies of Alvin Kernan (*The Canykered Muse*, 1959), Anderson ('Anger in Juvenal and Seneca', 1964), and Freudenburg (*The Walking Muse*, 1993, pp. 3–8).[56] The main persona, speaking in most verse satires, shares the name of the author. Thus in order to uphold the analytical differentiation between persona and author

[56] Cf. also the bibliographical survey of this question in Winkler, *Persona*, 1–22. Recent studies have argued that the advent of New Historicism has rendered obsolete the separation of the literary role of the author from other aspects of his personality (e.g. Oliensis, *Rhetoric of Authority*; C. Keane, 'Satiric Memories: Autobiography and the Construction of Genre', *CJ* 97/3 (2002), 215–31; R. R. Nauta, ' "Lyrisch ik" en *persona* in de bestudering van de Romeinse poëzie', *Lampas*, 35/5 (2002), 363–86; E. Gowers, 'Fragments of Autobiography in Horace *Satires* 1', *CA* 22 (2003), 55–92). Nevertheless, I still find this simplification useful as a tool. I have the greatest respect for the New-Historical approach, and do not find it *wrong*—instead I see the

without cumbersome repetition, I write the name in inverted commas when the persona is meant ('Horace', 'Persius', 'Juvenal') and without them when the author is meant (Horace, Persius, Juvenal). The persona will be regarded as a strong, but not necessarily almighty authority in each satire—although he is the speaker, the author may choose to manipulate the text against the persona, so as to undercut his credibility, by making his speech self-contradictory, excessively emotional, naïve, etc.

Occasionally the primary persona partakes in a dialogue with a dominant interlocutor, as e.g. in Horace's discussions with the Stoics in his second book (*S.* 2.3; 2.7), or in Juvenal's talk with the male prostitute Naevolus in J. 9. In such cases the persona who is the author's namesake is often considerably tuned down, in Horace even turning into part-interlocutor, part-object for the other speaker. In these dialogic satires I will call the other speaker a 'secondary persona'.

The meaning-generating instance above the persona, the author, is here understood as the *implied author*, i.e. the sum of the intentions which can be implied from the text itself, and which do not necessarily coincide with what the flesh-and-blood author actually intended.[57] It follows that by 'intention' I mean the *intentio operis*, as it may be discerned from the complete text.[58]

THE PARADOXES OF SATIRE, AS MAPPED BY ALVIN KERNAN

The fact that satire is a paradoxical genre has been recognized from the beginning of its existence—the first to recognize this were

difference between it and my own Formalist approach as a difference in perspective and method. It is not my contention that the literary persona of an author *cannot* coincide with his biographical person (it may well do so), but simply my choice not to enquire about whether it does or not. By taking this approach I hope to limit my focus and so to perform a more effective analysis.

[57] For the term, see W. Booth, *The Rhetoric of Fiction* (2nd edn. 1961; Chicago: University of Chicago Press, 1983), 71–6 *et passim*.

[58] For a lucid discussion of the notion *intentio operis* (as well as the related claims of *intentio auctoris* and *intentio lectoris*), see U. Eco, '*Intentio lectoris*: The State of the Art', in *The Limits of Interpretation* (Bloomington and Indianapolis: Indiana University Press, 1990).

actually the Roman satirists themselves—but for a long time this fact elicited only the odd shrug of resignation from satire's students. It was not until Kernan's book *The Cankered Muse. Satire of the English Renaissance* (1959) that the paradoxes of satire began to be properly seen as an inherent characteristic of the genus, and more systematically reckoned with in satire scholarship. Kernan's clear-sightedness about satire was made possible by, among other things, his resolute insistence on there being a satiric *persona*, a mask for the speaker in satiric works, whose character was not necessarily identical to that of the author, and whose traits were themselves part of the fiction, and of the generic conventions. By this time the analytic tool of the persona was already being used for other genres of poetry, but lagged behind for satire, possibly because of satire's intensely personal and opinionated appearance—which is meant to be taken as honesty by the reader, and which the scholars had difficulty seeing through. Kernan's work lifted the discussion of satire to a new level of sophistication, and has proved to be of enduring importance for satire studies. The paradoxes mapped by Kernan were paraphrased and put to use for the reading of Roman verse satire by Anderson, most clearly in his article 'Anger in Juvenal and Seneca' (1964). Since these important insights into the trickster nature of satire are essential to the present study, I find it convenient to set them out here, at the beginning, so that the reader may easily consult this section when I refer to 'Kernan's paradoxes', or to Anderson's handling of them.[59]

First of all, Kernan sees a basic paradox in all satire in that the satiric persona (called 'the satirist' by both Kernan and Anderson) expressly insists that he is blunt, honest, and clumsy with words, whereas his practice shows him to be an expert manipulator of rhetoric. This twist of the 'artless artist' should not, Kernan says, be 'solved' by means of stressing one side at the expense of the other, but should be recognized and accepted as a convention of the genre.

From this point Kernan proceeds to establishing a distinction between two sides of the persona, which he designates 'the public personality' and 'the private personality'; the former is what the

---

[59] A. Kernan, *The Cankered Muse. Satire of the English Renaissance* (New Haven: Yale University Press, 1959). My paraphrases in this section draw primarily on the first chapter in Kernan's book, 'A Theory of Satire', esp. 1–7 and 14–30. In this chapter, Kernan speaks of the genre as a whole, and also includes examples from Roman satire.

persona insists on as his true self, the side he likes to show, while the latter is what he is secretly, a character he needs for his job but does not like to stress.

The public personality, which the persona needs in order to be convincing in his fervent indignation, in his horror at the vice he sees around him, and in his unswerving moral judgement, is dominated by the bluntness and honesty mentioned above. These traits are often strengthened by rural origins, suggestive of pastoral innocence and a simple style in writing and living. In line with a country background, the public personality includes a simple, traditional moral code, a view of life in social not philosophical terms, and a tendency to assume heroic postures. Yet in addition to this paraded face, the satiric persona also needs the private personality, characterized by less pleasant features such as aggression, sensationalism, and pride. According to Kernan's scheme, a number of closely related tensions arise from the uneasy coexistence of these two 'personalities' in one persona, as follows:

1. The satiric persona insists on the truth of what he tells, while in reality wildly distorting his material in order to convince his audience of the wickedness of the world.
2. Although he hates vice, he goes out of his way to find it and show it in detail. He is thus 'stained' by the filth which he claims he will clean away, becoming a red-hot sensationalist and something of a 'literary Peeping Tom' in the process.
3. Despite his alleged probity, the sheer violence of his attacks and his anger suggests that he is unreasonable, as well as unkind.
4. His combination of self-righteousness with aggressive criticism of others opens him to accusations of pride. He is an 'egoistic monster' mightily pleased with himself, devoid of any empathy for his victims.

Thus in Kernan there is the overarching paradox of the 'artless artist', followed by four related tensions, which are born of the fusion of the persona's two sides, the public and the private. It must be noted, however, that Kernan never sets up a formal system to delineate the tensions/paradoxes, and that he tends to merge them in his discussion.

What is perhaps most important in his model is that he underlines the necessity of *both* the public *and* the private personality in a functional satiric persona. Although he allows for differences in emphasis—thus the public personality will be foregrounded in milder satire, the private in harsh satire—he insists that both personalities are integral parts of the genre, as well as the ensuing paradoxes:

If...we accept the strange, twisted, contradictory satirist as a fictitious character created in order to achieve the satiric end, the exposure of vice and depravity, then we can direct our attention to the ways in which the authors of great satire manipulate their satirists and exploit them in a thoroughly dramatic fashion.[60]

Taking up Kernan's ideas, Anderson succinctly paraphrased and systematized the paradoxes of satire, in this fashion:

As ('Kernan') demonstrates, the typical satirist experiences or exhibits internal conflicts on at least five levels: (1) he is a plain, blunt, simple artless speaker who yet makes the most skilful use of rhetoric; (2) he proclaims the truth of what he says, while he wilfully distorts facts for emphasis; (3) although he loathes vice, he displays a marked love of sensationalism; (4) despite his moral concerns, the satirist can take sadistic delight in attacking his victims; (5) sober and rational as he may claim to be, he frequently adopts the most shockingly irrational attitudes.[61]

We may note that Anderson brings down the 'artless artist' to the same level as the other points. He also subdivides one of Kernan's tensions into two distinct ones (probity vs. unreasonable unkindness, third in my enumeration above, become Anderson's points 4 and 5), and drops one of them (the last one, about pride). These are no great changes, and the lists correspond closely. Much more significant is Anderson's tendency to still try and solve the paradoxes. So, in his analysis of Juvenal, he uses the persona's twists to dismiss him as an unworthy mouthpiece of the author—this problem will be treated in more detail below.[62]

My thesis in the present study, that there is a tension between the constituents of satire's double mission—criticism and humour—is closely related to Kernan's pattern of tensions/paradoxes. In my

---

[60] Kernan, *Cankered Muse*, 28.
[61] Anderson, *Essays*, 293; Kernan, *Cankered Muse*, esp. 14–30.
[62] Ch. 2, § 'The Question of Trust in Juvenal's Speaker'.

analyses I will make much use of them, occasionally in Anderson's systematized version.

PROGRAMMATIC STATEMENTS ON HUMOUR IN ROMAN SATIRE

All of the Roman satirists whose work has come down to us intact make programmatic statements about the place of humour (laughter)[63] in their satire: Horace in *S.* 1.1 and 1.10, Persius in 1, and Juvenal in 10.[64] Moreover, all of them use jokes in their programmatic satires (Horace 2.1.83–6; Persius 1.119–21; Juvenal 1.170–71), but since these jokes point to a more deviant kind of humour I will postpone the treatment of them until the next section. The more explicit meta-literary statements on humour, however, unanimously suggest exposure, derision, attack.

So Horace's famous tag, 'quamquam ridentem dicere verum | quid vetat?' ('yet what forbids one to tell the truth while laughing?', 1.1.24–5) presents us with a Latin rewording of the Cynic σπουδαιογέλοιον, and brings with it associations of the Cynics' sometimes harsh corrective derision of human vice, particularly the moral flaws of society's grandees.[65] The allusion to the principle of the serio-comic is further

---

[63] 'Risus', 'ridere', and 'ridiculum' are the general terms for humour and humorous writing/ speech in Latin, as may be seen from e.g. Cicero's and Quintilian's discussions of humour (Cic. *De Or.* 2.235–90, *Orat.* 26.87–9; Quint. *Inst.* 6.3). Cf. G. L. Hendrickson, 'Satura Tota Nostra Est', *CP* 22 (1927), 59, for the argument that what we today term 'satire' in an extended meaning would have been expressed with the words 'risus', 'ridere' etc., by the Romans, to whom 'satura' signified a narrow genre and 'had as yet only a fraction of the meaning we attach to it'.

[64] See preliminary 'Note on Editions and Translations'.

[65] A. Kießling and R. Heinze, *Q. Horatius Flaccus. Zweiter Teil: Satiren* (6th edn., Berlin: Weidmannsche Verlagsbuchhandlung, 1957) ad loc.; G. C. Fiske, *Lucilius and Horace: A Study in the Classical Theory of Imitation* (Madison: University of Wisconsin, 1920), 229. Some wariness is in place, however, for the earliest mentions of the Greek term σπουδαιογέλοιον (or σπουδαιογέλοιος) that have come down to us are later than Horace's satires: they are found in Strabo (16.2.29), Diogenes Laertius (9.17), and *Anthologia Palatina* (7.417–18), in all cases in connection with the Cynics. The term κυνικὸς τρόπος is found earlier, when Demetrius Rhetor uses it of Crates' reasoning (*Peri Hermeneias*, §259). The Cynics' use of laughter to repel vice (without the technical term) is also mentioned in the same work, §170.

strengthened in the image of the cake-serving teacher (25–6)[66] and especially in the juxtaposition of *seria* ('serious matters') and *ludo* ('play') in v.27.[67] Generally, the connection of the *Sermones* to Cynic thinking is supported by Horace's own (probable) reference to them as 'Bioneis sermonibus' ('conversations in the style of Bion'), *Ep.* 2.2.60. As regards the immediate context, 'ridentem dicere

The combination of the terms γελοῖα and σπουδαῖα (or synonymous expressions) appears before this, first in Aristophanes' *Frogs* 391–2: καὶ πολλὰ μὲν γέλοιά μ' εἰ — | πεῖν, πολλὰ δὲ σπουδαῖα ('and to say many laughable things, and many serious ones'). The linkage of σπουδάζειν and παίζειν is used of Socrates in *Gorg.* 481b and *Phaedr.* 234d.

Thus we have to agree with R. B. Branham's pessimistic statement that 'the use of the term spoudaiogeloion in antiqity is poorly documented' (*Unruly Eloquence: Lucian and the Comedy of Traditions* (Cambridge, Mass.: Harvard University Press, 1989), 27), and point out that the assumption that the Cynics called themselves σπουδαιογέλοιοι and were thus called by their contemporaries, is a reconstruction, though a fairly certain one. For the term see further Giangrande, *Spoudaiogeloion*, 17–19; for Cynic humour in general, cf. Grant, *Theories of the Laughable*, 53–70; Z. Stewart, 'Laughter in the Greek Philosophers: a Sketch', in S. Jäkel and A. Timonen (eds.), *Laughter down the Centuries*, i (Turku: Annales Universitatis Turkuensis, 1994); Branham, *Unruly Eloquence*, esp. ch. 1, and R. B. Branham and M.-O. Goulet-Cazé (eds.), *The Cynics: The Cynic Movement in Antiquity and its Legacy* (Berkeley and Los Angeles: University of California Press, 1996).

Horace's theory of satire is also influenced by Aristotelian and Epicurean thought, and N. W. DeWitt ('Epicurean Doctrine in Horace', *CP* 34 (1939), 134) correctly pointed out that *ridentem dicere verum* may also allude to the Epicurean idea 'γελᾶν ἅμα δεῖ καὶ φιλοσοφεῖν' ('one must laugh as one philosophises'), *Sent.Vat.* 41 (van der Mühll). However, I consciously focus the Cynic tincture here, since this seems to be more particularly connected to explicit references to laughter/ humour. On Horace's satirical programme in general, see G. L. Hendrickson, 'Horace, Serm. I.4: a Protest and a Programme', *AJP* 21 (1900), 121–42; A. Parker, 'Comic Theory in the Satires', and Freudenburg, *Walking Muse*.

[66] The image is a rephrasal of the comparison of philosophy to medicine, administered by doctors who smear the edge of the cup with honey in order to sweeten the bitter liquid for the patient. Likewise, the teacher of philosophy may serve the lesson in appealing form so as to ease perception. The simile is found in a fragment of Diogenes the Cynic (treated in G. A. Gerhard, *Phoinix von Kolophon* (Leipzig: Teubner, 1909), 41–2) and in Lucretius 1.936–50 and 4.11–25. Cf. Grant, *Theories of the Laughable*, 56; Freudenburg, *Walking Muse*, 80–1.

[67] Radermacher (*Weinen und Lachen*, 135) points out that this is a Latin rephrasing of the term σπουδαιογέλοιον, but is not willing to connect it to the Cynics; rather, he joins it to a mellower, in his view more 'philosophic', variety of the serio-comic, found in Socrates and in Neoplatonist thought. Such a categorization in the case of Horace, however, is not as simple as it might seem at first sight, as Freudenburg has argued with rich examples in his study of Horace's view of satire (*Walking Muse*). Cf. also A. Parker, 'Comic Theory in the Satires'.

verum' is intricately placed between two admonitions not to exaggerate mirth and joking at the cost of serious matters (24–5, 'ne sic ut qui iocularia ridens | percurram' ('so that I may not skip over this as one who tells jokes with a laugh') and 27, 'sed tamen amoto quaeramus seria ludo' ('but, joking aside, let's look into the serious matters'). The first of these admonitions has been read as a reference to Lucilius' excessive joking,[68] but if the general complexity of the passage is taken into account, as well as Horace's evaluation of Lucilius' humour in 1.10, this seems less than satisfactory. Neither in 1.1 nor in 1.10 is the use of *risus* and *ridiculum* criticized as such, and in the latter poem, Lucilius is actually praised for his mordant wit (1.10.3–4). Rather, I would suggest that the interlaced pattern of admonitions to seriousness and laughter in 1.1.24–7 graphically reflects the ideal of the *serio-comic*.

The direct expression of the serio-comic ideal in v.24 is rendered still more complex by being embedded in a question about what obstacles there could possibly be to humorous frankness. Although the question is clearly rhetorical, it is not at all difficult to find answers to it in the case of Horace the historical person: such factors as his low birth, his recent admission to Maecenas' circle, and Augustus' growing power could all hinder the free speech of this unestablished satirist. If, as we read on, we find that Horace is not free-spoken enough, we cannot say that he has not hinted at a warning. With a sly move, Horace manages to both make a bold claim for his poetry and keep his back free.

From the allusion to the Cynics it may be surmised that 'verum' is going to be an unpleasant truth, and this impression is strengthened by the larger context of the statement. Before it, the reader is faced with the criticism of discontent with one's lot, *mempsimoiria*, the introductory theme of the satire, describing the general moral failure which lies behind the more specific vice *avaritia*, the second theme of the satire. The description of *avaritia* begins immediately after our passage (28 ff.). Both themes are developed through alteration of serious preaching and vivid, comic scenes, and both themes belong among the stock targets of Greek diatribe, as does the presumed

---

[68] Anderson, 'Roman Socrates', 22–3.

causal connection between them.[69] The satirist clearly casts himself in the role of the annoying street philosopher.

Somewhat later in the satire it is indicated that not even the reader is exempt from attack, as the speaker suddenly turns on him with the words 'quid rides? mutato nomine de te | fabula narratur' ('what are you laughing at? Change the name, and the story is about you'), 69–70. This device, typical of the Greek diatribe, again underlines the potential dangerousness of the satirist, and at the same time rules out humour in the wrong direction—only the satirist has the right to decide when to laugh and at what.

In 1.4.1–9 we are told that Lucilius, the *primus inventor* of Roman satire, is to be regarded as a descendant of Eupolis, Cratinus, and Aristophanes with their outspoken and humorous branding of immoral people. According to Horace, it is precisely the humour and the sound judgement of Old Comedy that Lucilius followed to good effect ('facetus | emunctae naris' ('witty, with a keen nose'), 6–7).[70] This is developed in 1.10, where Lucilius is applauded for his wit, ('at idem, quod sale multo | urbem defricuit, charta laudatur eadem' ('but I also praise him on the same page, for rubbing down Rome with caustic wit') 3–4, 'comis et urbanus' ('courteous and elegant'), 65) and scorned for his technical flaws (1–3, 5–6, 20–35, 50–1, 56–64, 67–71). After the Lucilius-centred introduction of the satire, there follows another programmatic statement on satire, which both opens and closes with the role of humour and laughter. First Horace insists on its limits, somewhat less than straightforwardly, just as he did in 1.1:

> ergo non satis est risu diducere rictum
> auditoris (et est quaedam hic quoque virtus)	(1.10.7–8)

so it's not enough to make your listener distort his mouth in a grin—though there is some virtue in that as well

---

[69] E. Kraggerud, 'Die Satire I.1 des Horaz. Zu ihrer Einheit und Thematik', *SO* 53 (1978), 133–64, esp. pp. 145–6; P. M., Brown, *Horace: Satires I*, with introd., text, trans., and comm. (Warminster: Aris & Phillips, 1993; repr. with corrections 1995), 89.

[70] See the illuminating discussion by Rudd ('Libertas and Facetus. With Special Reference to Horace *Serm.* I,4 and I,10', *Mnemosyne* 10 (1957), 319–24, 328–36), who however takes the argument that 'facetus' means 'charming' more than 'humorous' too far. Cf. also A. Barbieri, 'Praeco-poeta, sal e urbanitas', *RCCM* 29 (1987), 111–50.

Within the description of ideal satire, the satirist is encouraged often to use a joking style (11), and occasionally to borrow the ways of the urban wit ('urbani', 13), and at the end of the description, humour is allowed a considerably more central role than it seemed to get at first:

> ridiculum acri
> fortius et melius magnas plerumque secat res.   (14–15)

humour is often stronger than fierceness and better cuts through important problems

Finally, Horace rounds off the description by reverting to the ideal of Old Comedy, and tying its wholesome influence on Roman satire firmly to its humour:

> illi scripta quibus comoedia prisca viris est
> *hoc* stabant, *hoc* sunt imitandi   (16–17)

those who wrote the Old Comedy had *this* as their basis, in *this* respect they should be imitated

It seems clear that in these meta-literary statements Horace claims for his satire the bold humour of the Cynics, Old Comedy, and Lucilius, though he puts more stress on 'humour' than on 'bold'.

Like Horace, Persius turns to the examples of Lucilius and Old Comedy when describing his own use of humour, although as a Stoic, he does not allow the Cynics any prominent position. The first reference to laughter in his programme satire in fact turns up the volume to a guffaw, 'cachinno' at 1.12. He tells us that when he looks at the decadence of Roman life and letters he cannot, try as he may, hold back his violent nature and abstain from exploding with laughter. This has been read as an emblem of rough, indecorous humour, excluding more refined devices such as irony,[71] but given the expulsion of boorish jokers at the end of the poem (1.127–34), the outburst is better taken as an insistence on the audacity of Persius' laughter. He boasts that it will out, no matter what obstacles there may be. Much the same boast is repeated in his comparison of his humorous satire to the secret of King Midas' barber (1.119–23). Persius' laugh may be

---

[71] Relihan, 'Persius' Laughter', *contra* J. C. Bramble, *Persius and the Programmatic Satire: A Study in Form and Imagery* (Cambridge: Cambridge University Press, 1974), 70.

buried, but in the end it will ring out to expose and shame the mighty of this world, so the allusion to Midas leads us to believe.[72] Just before this we have heard about the encouraging examples of Lucilius and Horace (114–18), where especially the former was painted as a violent attacker of Rome. Immediately after Persius' boast about his laugh, the three main writers of Old Comedy are enumerated in grand language as authors akin in spirit to Persius' writing. While employing the same convention as his forerunners in satire, Persius sharpens the tone through several devices: the use of the verb *cachinno* instead of the more neutral *rideo* the first time he speaks of laughing,[73] the imagery of *bursting* with laughter, and the warlike portraits of his predecessors: scourging and biting Lucilius (115–16), bold Cratinus (123), angry Eupolis (124), and the threatening figure of a *praegrandis senex* ('grand old man'), Aristophanes (124). The only exception is, significantly, Horace himself, who is presented as a softer kind of mocker (116–18). Thus we see that Persius follows Horace in his humour programme in so far as he recalls the tradition of Old Comedy and the first Roman satirist, but that he is willing to assume an even more violent pose.

As is well known from the tradition which divides satire into two varieties[74]—one smiling (Horatian) and one indignant (Juvenalian)—the programme satire of Juvenal replaces the mention of *risus* with the mention of *indignatio*. Yet humour is present in his work from the first satire onwards, and a discussion of the role of humour does in fact make its appearance later, in the tenth satire (10.28–53). Thus while a programmatic opening on humour seems to be lacking from Juvenal's first satire, Hendrickson has argued (1927)

---

[72] The old idea—proposed in Persius' vita—that v. 1.121 originally read 'auriculas asini Mida rex habet' ('King Midas has ass's ears'), before Cornutus posthumously changed it to the present 'auriculas asini quis non habet?' ('who doesn't have ass's ears?'), is unconvincing in its overdetermination, and currently out of favour. It is nevertheless defended as Persius' original version in Kißel's thorough discussion, with further references (W. Kißel (ed., trans., and comm.), W. *Aules Persius Flaccus: Satiren* (Heidelberg, 1990), ad loc), though not restored by him to the text, since it was not there in the archetype that first met the public with Cornutus' help.

[73] Cf. *TLL* s.vv. 'rideo' and 'cachinno' respectively.

[74] This tradition, which goes back to the Renaissance and I. Casaubon's study *De satyrica Graecorum poesi et Romanorum satira* from 1605, is traced in H. Weber, 'Comic Humour and Tragic Spirit: The Augustan Distinction between Horace and Juvenal', *Classical and Modern Literature*, 1 (1981), 275–89.

that the portrait of Democritus from J. 10 served that same function.[75] The Democritus passage runs as follows:

> iamne igitur laudas quod de sapientibus alter
> ridebat, quotiens a limine moverat unum
> protuleratque pedem, flebat contrarius auctor?
> sed facilis cuiuis rigidi censura cachinni:
> mirandum est unde illi oculis suffecerit umor.
> perpetuo risu pulmonem agitare solebat
> Democritus, quamquam non essent urbibus illis
> praetextae, trabeae, fasces, lectica, tribunal.
> quid si vidisset praetorem curribus altis
> extantem et medii sublimem puluere circi
> in tunica Iovis et pictae Sarrana ferentem
> ex umeris aulaea togae magnaeque coronae
> tantum orbem, quanto ceruix non sufficit ulla?
> quippe tenet sudans haec publicus et, sibi consul
> ne placeat, curru seruus portatur eodem.
> da nunc et volucrem, sceptro quae surgit eburno,
> illinc cornicines, hinc praecedentia longi
> agminis officia et niveos ad frena Quirites,
> defossa in loculos quos sportula fecit amicos.
> tum quoque materiam risus invenit ad omnis
> occursus hominum, cuius prudentia monstrat
> summos posse viros et magna exempla daturos
> vervecum in patria crassoque sub aere nasci.
> ridebat curas nec non et gaudia volgi,
> interdum et lacrimas, cum Fortunae ipse minaci
> mandaret laqueum mediumque ostenderit unguem   (10.28–53)

So why not praise the two philosophers: one of them used to laugh every time he lifted his foot and moved it outside the threshold, while the opposite one used to weep. But the censure of a harsh sneer comes easily to everyone,

---

[75] Hendrickson, 'Satura Tota Nostra', 55. The idea of Democritean laughter on Juvenal's programme has been taken up and developed in D. Eichholz, 'The Art of Juvenal and his Tenth Satire', *G&R* NS 3 (1956), 61–9; Musurillo, *Symbol and Myth*, 165–7, 175; Anderson, *Essays*, 340–61; and Rochefort, 'Laughter as a Satirical Device', 24–8, 48–50, and esp. in his Appendix B, 'Democritus and Heraclitus' 187–97. Rochefort first seems to caution against a too enthusiastic recognition of Democritus as the satirist's ideal, but after a somewhat confused discussion nevertheless agrees that 'rigidi censura cachinni' is the spirit which informs all of satire, including all of Juvenal's work.

the strange thing is that the other one somehow found a sufficient supply of tears. Democritus' sides used to shake with incessant laughter, and this although in their cities there were no togas bordered with purple or scarlet, no rods, no litters, no platform.

What if he would have seen this praetor standing on his lofty carriage, lifted high up amid the dust of the Circus, wearing the tunic of Jove himself and a purple, embroidered curtain of a toga trailing from his shoulders? And with a crown so big that no neck could support it? Why, instead there's a sweating public slave holding it, and he rides in the same carriage as the consul, to stop him from getting above himself. Now don't forget the bird shooting up from his ivory staff; the trumpeters on this side, on that side the long procession of clients walking in front, and the snow-white Roman citizens beside his bridle—the dole he buried in their wallets made them his friends. Still, even in those days Democritus found material for laughter wherever people came together, that man whose wisdom proves that the greatest men, who will set the finest examples, can be born in the fatherland of muttonheads, under a sluggish sky.

He would laugh at the troubles and the joys of the crowd, and sometimes at their tears as well. For himself, he would tell threatening Fortune go hang, and give her the finger.

The strongest reason for taking this as a programme statement is, as Hendrickson rightly observed,[76] that when Juvenal brings on the familiar figure of the laughing Democritus (already used by Cicero, Horace, and Seneca),[77] he makes the Abderitan philosopher look not simply like a satirist, but like a satirist very similar to Juvenal himself. The lines on the targets of Democritus' laughter (10.50–1), 'ridebat curas nec non et gaudia volgi, interdum et lacrimas' ('he would laugh at the troubles and the joys of the crowd, and sometimes at their tears as well') clearly echo the Roman satirist's purpose as stated in the first satire:

> quidquid agunt homines, votum, timor, ira, voluptas,
> gaudia, discursus, nostri farrago libelli est.   (1.85–6)

---

[76] Hendrickson, 'Satura Tota Nostra', 52–5.

[77] Cic. *De Or.* 2.235; Hor. *Ep.* 2.1.194–8; Sen. *De Ira* 2.10.5, *Tr. An.* 15.2–3. The contrast between the laughing Democritus and the crying Heraclitus seems to have been introduced by Seneca's teacher Sotion (Stobaeus, *Flor.* 3.20.53). The history of this contrast is traced in C. Lutz, 'Democritus and Heraclitus', *CJ* 49 (1953–4), 309–14; cf. also the ancient references collected in J. E. B. Mayor, *Thirteen Satires of Juvenal*, vol. ii (3rd edn., London: Macmillan & Co, 1881), 75–6 (to Juvenal 10.28–36).

whatever men do, their prayers, fears, anger, pleasure, joys, their running to and fro—all of this is fodder for my little book

The claim of using as material for satire 'whatever men do', in turn, neatly transcribes a late description of Democritus, οὗτος ἐγέλα πάντα, ὡς γέλωτος ἀξίων πάντων τῶν ἐν ἀνθρώποις ('he laughed at everything, considering all human matters ridiculous').[78] More specifically, *occursus hominum* at 10.48 matches *discursus* at 1.86.

I fully agree with Hendrickson. Indeed his case can be strengthened by several more arguments. First, the verse 'sed facilis cuiuis rigidi censura cachinni' ('but the censure of a harsh sneer comes easily to everyone'), 10.31, reads like a positive counterpart of the negated 'difficile est saturam non scribere' ('it is difficult not to write satire'), 1.30, a connection underlined by the similar metrical pattern of *sed facilis/ difficile est*, and possibly by the near-identical placement of the verses in their satires (vv. 31 and 30 respectively). Furthermore, the scene that makes the observer satirize/ laugh is in both cases the city of Rome,[79] with an emphasis on social indignities, including the absurd elevation of the unworthy and the humiliation of the old Roman nobility (both the view facing the mocker in J. 1 and that in 10 feature raised *lecticae* ('litters') 1.32, 64, 100–2, 109–10, 159, 10.35, and humiliated Roman citizens 1.95–120, 10.45–6). Again, both Democritus and Juvenal particularly despise Fortune (10.52–3 Democritus, 10.365–6 Juvenal). Finally, both are dismissive towards a tearful reaction to the world's folly and decadence: while Juvenal finds it easy to understand the laughter of the one philosopher, he sneers at the crying of the other, Heracleitus, 'mirandum est unde ille

[78] Hendrickson ('Satura Tota Nostra', 52) hails this line from Hippolytus' *Rufutatio Omnium Haeresium* 1.13 (cf. Diels–Kranz 1956, ii. 94, fr. 40 under Democritus) as 'the most clearly defined theory of the function of satire that antiquity affords'. While I cannot agree with this, there is no denying that Juvenal agreed with it in theory—if not in practice. Cf. also the Pseudo-Hippocratic letters (2nd–1st cent. B C), among which nos. 10–17 relate a novella about Democritus' laughter. The texts, with translation and commentary, may be found in Hippocrates, *Pseudoepigraphic Writings*, ed. and trans with an introd. by W. D. Smith. Studies in Ancient Medicine, ii (Leiden: Brill, 1990); rich discussion of the tradition of *Democritus ridens* is found in T. Rütten, *Demokrit—lachender Philosoph & sanguinischer Melancholiker. Eine pseudohippokratische Geschichte* (Leiden: Brill, 1992), esp. 8–53.

[79] Note the thematic development from Hor. *Ep.* 2.1.194–8 to Juv. 10.33–46: in Horace Democritus would have been watching the people gaping foolishly at the games, but there is no twist of social injustice, which is central to Juvenal's scene.

oculis suffecerit umor' ('the strange thing is that the other one somehow found a sufficient supply of tears'), 10.32, just as Democritus himself sometimes laughs at tears, 10.52. As several scholars have emphasized, this is a fitting programme for Juvenalian satire.[80]

If we accept the identification of Juvenal's and the philosopher's outlooks, the next step must be to scrutinize the nature of the humour suggested in satire 10. As in Persius' first satire, we encounter the root *cachinn-*, indicating a less decorous and more markedly derisive humour than *risus* need imply.[81] Moreover, we encounter it in a phrase ('rigidi censura cachinni') which explicitly stresses the element of criticism, presumably of a socio-moral kind, given the associations of 'censura'. Yet the assumption that *rigidus cachinnus* means nothing but criticism, 'a mirthless laugh',[82] seems somewhat hasty when the context is considered. *Rigidus* implies sternness and admonition, and this is perhaps to be expected from the laughter of a philosopher[83]—but it does not imply lack of gaiety in the laugher. The contrast with the crying Heraclitus presupposes the opposite attitude in Democritus for its effect, and the image of the violently laughing philosopher, 'perpetuo risu pulmonem agitare solebat | Democritus' ('Democritus' sides used to shake with incessant laughter'), 33–4, likewise suggests hearty laughter. Against one occurrence of *cachinnus*, there are four instances of the more neutral words of the stem *rid-* in this passage (29, 33, 47, 51), including the sentence which introduces Democritus, 'de sapientibus alter | ridebat' ('one of the two philosophers used to laugh'). From the context, then, I would conclude that the philosopher's laughter is depicted as critical and harsh, but still as real and hearty, far from mirthless.

While the critical *cachinnus* is a trait that Juvenal's programme shares with Persius', Juvenal adds a peculiarly Roman twist to the cackle of the Greek philosopher, and this lies in *censura*, an

---

[80] Hendrickson, 'Satura Tota Nostra', Rochefort, 'Laughter as a Satirical Device', 196–7, Musurillo, *Symbol and Myth*, 166.

[81] Mayor, *Juvenal, with Commentary*, vol. ii, comments ad loc.: 'CACHINNI often implies derision' and compares Cic. *Brut.* 216, 'cachinnos irridentium'.

[82] Eichholz, 'Art of Juvenal', 65; E. Courtney, *A Commentary on the Satires of Juvenal* (London: Athlone Press, 1980), 457.

[83] Although perhaps not this one. *Rigidus* is an adjective repeatedly associated with the Stoics, but the context of J. 10 presents a mixture of different philosophic directions; see Courtney, *Commentary on Juvenal*, 448–54.

authoritative word bursting with connotations of Cato the Censor and the good, stern mores of Old Rome.[84] The practice of Old Comedy is not referred to by Juvenal, and the mention of Lucilius, stripped of his laughter, has been left behind in the first satire. But here, in the tenth satire of Juvenal, we get perhaps the boldest claim that any surviving Roman satirist makes for his humour: it is meant to attack the ways of Rome—where Democritus is mentally imported—with the combined authority of Greek philosophy and the Roman office of the censorship.

This is what the Roman satirists themselves say about their use of humour. However, I will argue that this is not what they do: while insisting on their right to laugh at everything and hinting seductively that this may include utterly important matters and people, they silently put humour to other uses.

PROGRAMMATIC JOKES: THE HIDDEN AGENDA OF AMBIGUITY

In the previous section, I set out the explicit programmatic claims that the Roman satirists make for humour in their satire: these amount to saying that humour will be used to deride vice, and generally to facilitate the teaching of moral lessons. In the analyses below we will see that the promise is not always realized. Yet this gap between what is promised and what is delivered is not unconscious, as is shown by the jokes which round off Horace's, Persius', and Juvenal's programme satires (Hor. 2.1.83–6; Pers. 1.119–21; Juv. 1.170–1). In discussing these jokes, I wish to contend that they have a more significant function than has hitherto been acknowledged. They give a real answer to the pressing question of how to write satire when this is so dangerous, and this answer is: *through joking*. Simultaneously, they warn the reader not to take what is said at face value, but to look for hidden and/or multiple signifieds below

---

[84] In an introductory essay to his translation of Juvenal, Peter Green sketches the common traits of Cato the Elder and Juvenal's persona, concluding with the fine observation that Cato's 'official post as Censor was one to which every satirist unofficially aspired' (*Juvenal, The Sixteen Satires*, trans. with introd. and notes by P. Green (London: Penguin, 1974), 41).

the surface. Further, the fact that all three satirists whose work has come down to us in its entirety end their programmes with a joke implies that this kind of joke became part of the generic tradition. The joke presents the satirist with an escape and suggests multiple meanings instead of one. This means that the satirists' 'cheating' is actually set out in their programmes; that Roman satire is conscious of its paradoxes and its double-play; that other uses of humour than the righteous castigation of vice are not failures but legitimate strategies in a trickster genre.

The existence of a set pattern in the Roman verse satirists' *apologiae*, now widely acknowledged, was established in three articles wholly dedicated to the question: by Lucius Shero in 1922, by E. J. Kenney in 1962, and by John G. Griffith, 1970.[85] The pattern they found and analysed is lucidly summarized by Kenney:

First, a pronouncement, lofty to the point of bombast, of the satirist's high purpose and mission. Second, a warning by a friend or the poet's *alter ego* or the voice of prudence—call it what you will. Third, an appeal by the satirist to the great example of Lucilius. Fourth, a renewed warning. Fifth and last, evasion, retractation, equivocation.[86]

It is this last element of 'evasion, retractation, equivocation', i.e. the concluding joke, that is the object of our interest here. As can be seen from his wording, Kenney does not have a high opinion of these jokes, and this impression is confirmed further on in his discussion, where he calls Juvenal's end-joke a 'flippant evasion', dissimulation 'without urbanity', and a misfiring jest.[87] Shero had ignored the jokes altogether, interpreting the endings merely in terms of self-justification, while Griffith recognized a 'culminating element of surprise', which he saw as a strictly rhetorical device, *not* to be read as 'a note of humour'.[88] Generally these jokes have been regarded in

[85] Cf. also Fiske, *Lucilius and Horace*, 369–78 (on *apologiae* in Lucilius and Horace); C. A. van Rooy, *Studies in Classical Satire and Related Literary Theory* (Leiden: Brill, 1965), 54–5, 146–7; R. A. LaFleur, 'Horace and *Onomasti Komodein*: The Law of Satire', *ANRW* II.31.3 (1981), 1811.

[86] E. J. Kenney, 'The First Satire of Juvenal', *PCPS* 188 (1962), 36.

[87] Ibid. 40.

[88] J. G. Griffith, 'The Ending of Juvenal's First Satire and Lucilius, Book XXX', *Hermes* 98 (1970), 56–72. The first citation is from p. 70; on p. 63 the same phenomenon is called an 'element of παρὰ προσδοκίαν'. The second citation is from a passage where Griffith argues against Kenney, equating humour with 'flippancy' (p. 64).

line with the quotation above, as evasive and flippant, sometimes as disappointing.[89] Although the statements made in these apologetic jokes, especially in Juvenal's case, have occasionally been discussed, the function of these passages *as jokes* has not been seen as meaningful, but rather as an escape from meaning. It is however *a priori* improbable that a poetic programme should have a pointless finale, it is more so when this kind of finale is repeated in poet after poet within the genre, and it is most improbable that *jokes* in the programmes of a genre that defined itself as dependent on *humour* should be meaningless. A closer examination of the jests in question is called for.

Horace

Horace employs the pattern of the satiric apologia in his last and most concentrated programmatic satire, 2.1, in the form of a consultation of the jurist Trebatius. As the satirist answers the various objections raised against his occupation, the poem continuously plays with the two areas of law and literature,[90] and its opening pun on *lex* (v. 2) as both legal law and the law of the genre is matched by its conclusion, punning on *mala carmina* (vv. 82–4), both 'incantations' and 'bad poetry':[91]

> si mala condiderit in quem quis carmina, ius est
> iudiciumque.' 'Esto, siquis mala; sed bona si quis
> iudice condiderit laudatus Caesare? si quis
> opprobriis dignum latraverit integer ipse?'
> 'Solventur risu tabulae, tu missus abibis.'   (vv. 82–6)

---

[89] See e.g. N. Rudd, *The Satires of Horace* (Cambridge: Cambridge University Press, 1966), 129.

[90] See F. Muecke, *Horace: Satires II*, with introd., trans., and comm. (Warminster: Aris & Phillips, 1993), 100, with further references. Illuminating discussions of this satire's intertwining of law and literature are presented in A. D. Leeman, 'Die Konsultierung des Trebatius: Statuslehre in Horaz, Serm. 2,1', in P. Händel and W. Meid (eds.), *Festschrift für Robert Muth.* (Innsbruck: Amœ: Institut für Sprachwissenschaft der Universität Innsbruck, 1983), and F. Muecke, 'Law, Rhetoric, and Genre in Horace, *Satires* 2.1', in S. J. Harrison (ed.), *Homage to Horace: A Bimillenary Celebration* (Oxford: Oxford University Press, 1995).

[91] For the meaning 'incantations'/ 'slander' Griffith confers Horace's own *Ep.* 2.1.152–4: 'quin etiam lex | poenaque lata, malo quae nollet carmine quemquam | describi' [why there is even a punishing law laid down, to stop a man from writing someone down with malicious verses] (Griffith, 'Juvenal's First Satire and Lucilius', 61).

If someone composes foul verses against another man, he will be tried in a court of law.' 'Very well, for *foul* verses, but what if someone composes *fine* verses, and is praised by Caesar? If someone, himself blameless, barks at one who deserves censure?' 'Then the document will be dissolved in laughter, and you will be free to go.'[92]

Historical exactness as regards the law seems to have been sacrificed to the demands of the literary context,[93] but the meaning of the accusation is clear: what is suggested is both casting spells on people (perhaps this is said with an eye to satire's alleged affinity to cursing), and slander, an activity with which satire constantly risked being identified. The answer is equally lucid: 'Horace' writes only *bona carmina*, good poetry, and this pun, while insisting on the satirist's quality as an artist, literally dissolves the legal accusation in laughter.[94] It is essential to recognize that as the court is dismissed and the defendant let off, he is not only freed from all suspicions of breaking the law, but also hailed in his role as a comic writer by the outbreak of laughter, a tribute to his joke. Caesar may have been his judge, 'Horace' may have been fair in his attacks, but not until the laughter of the audience do we see *conclusive* evidence of his innocence, and of his talent. In closing the first book and the previous programmatic satire, 1.10, 'Horace' had hoped that his choice audience would smile at his satires, 'arridere velim' ('I would like them to smile'), 1.10.89. In this confident new beginning of the second book the hope materializes beyond expectation: the reaction is general, and it is violent laughter rather than mere smiling.

While the joke confirms 'Horace''s artistic triumph, it also contains more precise hints as to the nature of his satire. The crucial pun is, of course, a play with words, and the words involved are *mala* and *bona carmina*. This suggests that verbal art, even at a minute level, is central to his work, and that he is a master of twisting words into good poetry (*bona carmina*), but also that he is intent on playing

---

[92] The translation of Horace's wordplay to 'foul/ fine verses' is borrowed from the translation of Rudd, *Horace & Persius*, 1997.

[93] See Cloud, J. D. 'The Client–Patron Relationship: Emblem and Reality in Juvenal's First Book' in A. Wallace-Hadrill (ed.), *Patronage in Ancient Society* (London and New York: Routledge, 1989), 67.

[94] In the discussion about what exactly 'tabulae' refers to I find it easiest to agree with Rudd's opinion that the tablets contain the indictment (Rudd, *Satires of Horace*, 128, 130). There is nothing to suggest that the law itself is invalidated.

with ambiguities and multiple meanings. Furthermore, in the parallel between incantations and poetry the similarity is not only verbal—there is also the common point of swaying the souls of men. Both poetry and magic make use of the mimetic principle.[95] Indeed the witch Canidia haunts the 'angry' poetry of Horace (the *Satires* and the *Epodes*) with her attributes of *mala ars* ('black magic', literally 'bad art') and *mala carmina* as caricatures of the poet's tools of trade.[96] Here the speaker has been accused of changing the lives of men with magic, but is freed when he turns out to be a poet. The suggestion that he has a kind of power over the lives of men lingers on, though he insists that he will use it for artistic purposes only, for *good* purposes—as laughter is his witness.

Even though the pun is the essential part, 'Horace' does not neglect to allude to the Cynic emblem of the dog with the word *latraverit* ('barked'), thus claiming a considerable aggressiveness for his satiric humour, despite his previous protestations that his satire will avoid aggressive derision (1.4.78–103; and in this poem 2.1.39–44). By inserting the image of the dog 'Horace' also lays claim to the paradigm of attacking the powerful from a lowly position.[97] As the satirist has said earlier in this poem, he is a peace-loving but potentially very dangerous person.

This leads us to the final twist of the passage, the question of whether the accusation against 'Horace' has been invalidated, or simply forgotten. The very first lines of this poem refer the accusation that 'Horace' is too aggressive in his satire, and there is hardly anything in the final joke to prove that this is not so, quite the contrary. Good poetry is no evidence in either direction, the flaunting of Augustus' support and the dog image harbour a latent threat. When the laughter resounds, the accused is let off, not properly acquitted.[98] Since Horace is here using humour in court, albeit a

---

[95] In a study on the connection between satire and magic, Elliott comments that if Horace 'was aware of the intimations of forbidden power in the *malum carmen* phrase, he was content to exploit them as a metaphor for poetry' (R. C. Elliott, *The Power of Satire: Magic, Ritual, Art* (Princeton, 1960), 128).

[96] She has made an appearance in 2.1 at v. 48, poisoning her enemies as a parallel to the satirist's art; she will turn up at the end of the last satire (2.8.95), in *Epod.* 5, and again in the last epode, with her art (*artis*) mentioned in its last line (*Epod.* 17.81).

[97] This paradigm will be discussed in more detail below, Ch. 1.

[98] F. Muecke, *Horace: Satires II*, ad loc.

fictional one, it is tempting to compare a statement by Cicero in his discussion of the rhetor's use of humour, in *De Oratore*:

> est plane oratoris movere risum, vel quod ipsa hilaritas benevolentiam conciliat ei, per quem excitata est … maximeque quod tristitiam ac severitatem mitigat et relaxat odiosasque res saepe, quas argumentis dilui non facile est, *ioco risuque dissolvit.* (*De Or.* 2.236, emphasis mine).

> yes, making the audience laugh certainly belongs to the domain of the orator, because merriment arouses goodwill towards him who has stirred it, … but above all because it softens and relaxes gloom and sternness, and because unpleasant points, not easily washed off with argumentation, may often *be dissolved in joking and laughter.*

Horace's 'soluentur risu' is indeed close to 'ioco risuque dissoluit', and it seems at least possible that the beneficent effects of humour described in Cicero are those achieved by the satirist: winning the audience's sympathy, easing excessive seriousness, and getting rid of an unpleasant problem not easily washed off with proof. The concluding joke provides an excellent loophole in the satiric programme, for although Horace does not promise to be less aggressive, he is let off the hook thanks to his command of humour.

Persius

The joke which closes Persius' programme links on to an aposiopesis left behind at the beginning of his first satire. In that exclamation Persius had begun to explain the reason for his laughter, but had not come to the point:

> nam Romae quis non—a, si fas dicere—sed fas
> tum cum ad canitiem et nostrum istud vivere triste
> aspexi ac nucibus facimus quaecumque relictis,
> cum sapimus patruos. tunc tunc—ignoscite (nolo,
> quid faciam?) sed sum petulanti splene—cachinno.   (1.8–12)

For who at Rome hasn't—ah, if it is right to say it—but it is: now that I look at our grey hair and our stern life, and what we do when we have left our marbles behind and turned avuncular. Then—sorry—I don't want to, but what can I do?—it's my unruly spleen—I guffaw.

At the end of the poem, in v. 121, he gives us the rest of the sentence broken off in line 8: 'auriculas asini quis non habet?' ('who doesn't have ass's ears?'). A frame of satirical laughter is thus created around the poetic programme, and the cause for the satirist's laughter is that everybody at Rome has ass's ears (put in the diminutive to stress the contempt of the speaker), i.e. everybody is stupid and garrulous.[99] Furthermore, a defect in ears connotes not only general stupidity, but also specifically the inability to understand good literature, since the ear was the medium for the reception of literature in antiquity.[100] The degeneration of letters, in turn, is the main topic of *Satire* 1 as a whole, on the one hand connected to the exclusivity of Persius' audience, on the other hand readily translated into the moral plane according to the principle that literature mirrors the lives of men, 'talis hominibus fuit oratio qualis vita' ('the speech of men was like their life').[101] In its immediate context, the jest looks as follows:

> me muttire nefas? nec clam? nec cum scrobe? nusquam?
> hic tamen infodiam. vidi, vidi ipse, libelle:
> auriculas asini quis non habet? hoc ego opertum,
> hoc ridere meum, tam nil, nulla tibi vendo
> Iliade.   (119–23)

I'm not allowed to mumble? Not in secret? Not into a hole in the ground? Nowhere? I'll bury it here, though. I've seen it, I've seen it myself, my little book: who doesn't have ass's ears? This secret, this laugh of mine, so nil, I won't sell to you for any *Iliad*.

The allusion is to the story of King Midas, and the joke is of course that although the king's barber hid his secret in a hole, it was soon spread all over Phrygia, because the reeds that grew over the hole whispered the secret in the wind—Persius' little book, it is implied, will function in the same way as the hole. Given the precedent of the Midas story, Persius must know what he is doing. His comic move to evade the interlocutor's warnings is only a charade escape, in actual

---

[99] Cf. Pliny, *NH* 11.114.276: 'auricularum magnitudo loquacitatis et stultitiae nota est' ('big ears are a sign of garrulity and stupidity'); quoted in Bramble, *Persius and the Programmatic Satire*, 27.

[100] As Hendrickson saw, 'The First Satire of Persius', *CP* 23 (1928), 101.

[101] Cf. Seneca, *Ep.* 114.1, but the thought was a widespread one. See further Kenney, 'The First Satire of Juvenal', 36; Bramble, *Persius and the Programmatic Satire*, 23–5.

fact the satirist's alleged secrecy only underlines his ambition to be heard by all people. Thus Persius' programmatic joke merely poses as retraction whilst really insisting on his satire's right to be, and in this it is like Horace's joke.

In other respects, however, it differs from his predecessor's. While Horace's joke was a pun, pointing specifically to verbal humour and the mastery of language, Persius' joke has a political–moral message. Even apart from the fact that a hint at the emperor's (Nero's) ears can hardly be excluded, there is a clear statement: Persius will tell Rome the truth about its hidden self. Beyond this, the image of burying into the ground something that will then emerge again, multiplied, implies the planting of seeds, and looks forward to a passage in the fifth satire, describing the workings of philosophic instruction (5.63–4): cultor enim iuvenum purgatas inseris aures | fruge Cleanthea ('as cultivator you plant the seeds of Cleanthes in the cleansed ears of the young'). There, the seeds to be planted are those of Cleanthes' Stoic philosophy, a parallel which reveals another aspect of the programmatic joke, namely that according to the view propounded by Persius, moral reform must start from within the soul and mind of each individual.

It has been suggested that Persius' gesture to bury his secret is a play on the Epicurean maxim λάθη βιώσας ('live hidden'),[102] but this does not take into account the rest of the Midas story, where the secret is spread out, nor does it seem natural for a devout Stoic to depict an Epicurean tenet in his programme. If, however, the image of burying the truth in the ground is compared to Persius' Stoic advice that moral healing must begin from within, then the match is much more precise. In his moral-philosophical images Persius presents inner qualities as bursting forth and transforming the outside, such as the 'fig-tree' of ambition growing out of the liver (1.24–5), the heart palpitations and rotten breath signalling a man's perdition (3.88–9), or tyrannical masters born deep within a man enslaving him in his life (5.129–31). Persius' own philosophy is parallel to his joke: what is buried inside will break out and affect the outside. Likewise, medicine is to be applied on the inside: inner self-knowledge (4.51–2) as well as cleaning, scorching decocts that

---

[102] Griffith, 'Juvenal's First Satire and Lucilius', 62.

will clear the ears—and the perception they symbolize—so that they can be properly sown with Stoic doctrine (1.126; 5.63; 5.86). The 'truth about Rome' that Persius plants into a hole dug in Roman ground is also a cleansing, scorching medicament that can heal the city, characteristically applied on the inside.[103]

Yet another reading is also possible: just as Persius' *libellus*, and the 'here', *hic*, where he inters his secret, can be seen as lying under the skin of the imperial capital, so this same *locus* can be read as placed under the skin of the speaker. After all, 'Persius' is a man of Rome, and if everyone in Rome has ass's ears, then he has them, too.[104] Persius may be applying his sarcastic knowledge and satiric laughter to himself, turning humour against his own persona. The reference to his laugh as hidden, *opertum*, seems to equate the laugh with the pronouncement about ass's ears, which is likewise hidden, in the ground. The laugh is his, and withheld within him, as is clear both from this passage and from that at the opening of the satire, where he was unable to withhold his laughter (1.11–12). There, his guffaw burst out of him in just the way the ass's-ears secret is bound to do. On this interpretation the satirist's criticism and laughter are directed at his own heart of hearts. This is on the one hand exactly in line with the moral therapy he preaches (and practises in *Sat.* 3[105]), on the other hand problematic as part of a satirical programme. He is beginning with himself, with the Midas in him, from a philosophical belief that this is the right way to cure not only oneself but also the world around one, since what is inside affects the outside. Neronian society can only be cured by starting with 'the Nero inside'.[106] This inward turn is enigmatic when regarded in its role as part of a programmatic statement. It places self-criticism and self-ridicule on

---

[103] Cf. also the following description of his satire as 'aliquid decoctius' ('something more boiled down'), 1.125, properly used of the boiling down of medicine; discussed in E. Gowers, 'Persius and the Decoction of Nero', in J. Elsner and J. Masters (eds.), *Reflections of Nero* (Chapel Hill: University of North Carolina Press, 1994).

[104] Cf. Henderson's comment: 'Specifically, Persius' writing represents, as it declares, a (suitably satiric) "laugh", the "I" laughing ... But it also (suitably) represents "laughs", laughing *at* "me" ' (*Writing down Rome*, 245, original emphasis).

[105] This will be discussed in more detail below, Ch. 2, § 'Persius' splitting self'.

[106] In the happy formulation introduced by Freudenburg, *Satires of Rome: Threatening Poses from Lucilius to Juvenal* (Cambridge: Cambridge University Press, 2001), 134, who discusses this strategy in Persius at pp. 125–83.

the agenda, which do not seem to be included in Persius' satiric programme (= *Sat.* 1) when this is read at the surface level, without particular attention to the programmatic joke. But if this move infers that 'Persius' has ass's ears, and this means that he is stupid, garrulous, and of poor judgement in ethic and aesthetic matters, then this will have considerable consequences for his competence as a moral teacher. The problem can be momentarily escaped if we construe his literary strategy as parallel to his philosophical strategy: during the course of the satires, 'Persius' will first cure himself with laughing criticism, until this medicine bursts forth from him to cure others. Still, the hint that he himself deserves to be laughed at remains, and will at times be realized in the body of his satire, creating an oscillation between authority and non-authority for the persona.

Just as Horace's pun multiplied meaning and suggested ambiguity in his satire, so Persius' programme joke multiplies the meaning of its statement after it has been buried in the earth.

Juvenal

Whereas Persius' programmatic joke only questioned the authority of his persona very slightly, in Juvenal's joke the persona is demolished. Here is the end of his programmatic satire, with the preceding elements of his reference to Lucilius and the interlocutor's last warning:

> 'ense velut stricto quotiens Lucilius ardens
> infremuit, rubet auditor cui frigida mens est
> criminibus, tacita sudant praecordia culpa.
> inde ira et lacrimae. tecum prius ergo voluta
> haec animo ante tubas: galeatum sero duelli
> paenitet.' experiar quid concedatur in illos
> quorum Flaminia tegitur cinis atque Latina.   (1.165–71)

'whenever fiery Lucilius roars, as if with a drawn sword, the listener whose heart is chilled by crimes will flush, and sweat with secret guilt. This is the cause of anger and tears. So think it over in your mind before the trumpet blows—once you have donned the helmet, it is too late to regret going to war.' I'll try what may be allowed against those whose ashes are buried beneath the Via Flaminia and the Latina.

'Juvenal' begins this final section in extremely bold style and imagery: Lucilius the first satirist is introduced to the scene as a blazing warrior with a drawn sword, inflicting terror on his victims, a fierce and fearless enemy of vice. He is an attractive example to follow for our latter-day practician of the same genre, as has already been said close to the beginning of the poem, where 'Juvenal' claimed that he wished to drive down the same field that the great son of Aurunca had steered his horses over (1.19–20). However, here the interlocutor interferes, reminding the satirist that terrified targets of satire are prone to wrath and tears. 'Juvenal' should think twice about the consequences of his actions, the interlocutor warns, for it will be too late to draw back once he has his warrior's helmet on. At this point, rather than defending his just and noble cause, 'Juvenal' makes a full turn and announces that he will try out what can be done against those buried under the Latin and the Flaminian Ways.[107] Instead of a knight ablaze with just indignation he turns out to be a coward after all, as soon as he is faced with a threatening reality. The grand picture of a warrior and the elevated archaism of *duelli* are smashed down against the bleak tomb-rows of familiar streets. Perhaps the scenario is worse still. Since 'Juvenal' has been galloping forth at full speed and in full armour ever since he vowed to follow the chariot of Lucilius, at v.19, and since the image has been intensified towards the end of the poem, the last two lines have the effect of sending him flying head over heels, as if tripped, to attack the dead under the dust of suburban roads. He is a hysterical and rather inadequately equipped desecrator of graves, as well as a caricature of epic Aeneas drawing his sword against the ghosts in Hades (Virg. *A.* 6.290–4). The scene is certainly set for derision of the persona, both for his real faults (cowardice, blasphemy) and because of his ridiculous appearance. Much more than in Persius, this programme joke opens up for humour directed at the persona in the satiric opus

---

[107] Griffith, starting from the technical meaning of 'experiar' as 'put to the test of a legal issue', and the rhetorical patterns of *apologiae* in general, argues that the satirist's last words spell out what line of defence he might take if challenged. The lines can then be paraphrased as 'If pressed, I shall rely on the defence that I shall test by legal process how far liberties may be taken against the dead' (Griffith, 'Juvenal's First Satire and Lucilius', 62–4, citation from 63). While explaining the forensic flavour of Juvenal's *apologia*, this argument does not solve the problem of the persona's frustrating metamorphosis from warrior to chicken.

to follow. This, again, threatens dire consequences for the persona's moral and/ or intellectual authority. As will become clear in my second chapter, these consequences do not fail to materialize in Juvenal.

Furthermore, the explicit proposal to attack the dead ostensibly flouts the popular notion *de mortuis nil nisi bene* ('nothing but good about the dead')[108] with its overtones of superstition, and so challenges norms of piety and polish. The outrage implied in the final image indicates that there will be coarseness and taboo-breaking in the poems to come, and this is certainly proved true. The improper intention to attack the dead was one of the few features of Juvenal's satire to attract a comment from Bakhtin. In an essay entitled 'Satire' he writes that this formulation in Juvenal has a twofold aim. First, it will protect the author from political disgrace. Secondly, it claims for his writings the 'folkloric-festive derision and abuse of the dying, receding, old (winter, the old year, the Old King) and the traditional freedom associated with such derision and abuse'. Bakhtin goes on to say that this is also how Juvenal's obscenities should be understood, as exploiting the traditional connection between laughter and on the one hand death, on the other hand rebirth, the creative force of the bodily lower stratum.[109] It is easy to see that rebirth does not play a major role in this satirist, and it seems at least questionable whether his foul-mouthing can be called 'festive' in any reasonable sense of the word, even though it is often comic. An interpretation of Juvenal's satire in terms of carnival seems inapposite, and it is symptomatic that Bakhtin does not return to Juvenal in his writings on carnivalesque literature. Nevertheless, as I try to show below in my analysis of the Naevolus satire (J. 9), a sort of grotesque and negative fecundity is occasionally part of Juvenal's imagery, though such 'rebirth' is more like The Second Coming than like festive renewal. The 'Saturnalian' phenomena of abuse, death, obscenity, and fertility tend to go together even when this is not done under the sign of

---

108 See Otto, s.v. *mortuus*, with *Nachträge* 42, 189 (A. Otto, *Die Sprichwörter und sprichwörtlichen Redensarten der Römer* (Leipzig: Teubner, 1890)); Courtney, *Commentary on Juvenal*, ad loc., paraphrases: 'So the rule to Juvenal is *de mortuis nil nisi malum* ...!'.

109 M. M. Bakhtin, *Sobranije Sočinenij*, ('Collected works'), v (Moscow: Russkije Slovari, 1997), 24; my translation.

joy—after all Saturn had two aspects, and apart from ruling over the Golden Age and the Saturnalia, he also devoured his children. In connection with Juvenal's joke about turning on the dead it is perhaps enough to say that this suggests that he will use uncouth, taboo-breaking humour.

'Juvenal' 's statement that he will satirize the dead is not only impolite, but also very strange. If we follow the most obvious interpretation that he does so in order to avoid the wrath of today's rulers, we must conclude that he will satirize the living under the names of previous generations, for it would be merely irrelevant to attack the dead if they were wholly different from the living, and in fact 'Juvenal' has already derided the present earlier in *Satire* 1, as when he said that all sins have today reached their apogee (1.147–9). As part of such a conclusion it is helpful to note that rich and mighty people were buried under the Flaminia and the Latina, as the scholiast points out—Juvenal will thus attack the mighty especially.[110] Perhaps he is lying about them being dead, and perhaps he will attack the mighty of the present?[111] A similar solution is to claim that the vices are what is satirized, while the persons carrying them are exchangeable: the dead will be used as rhetorical *exempla* for timeless points.[112] It has also been suggested that the satirist is really out to ridicule the dead, in the transferred sense that he is out to deride untenable archaic ideals and sentimental longing for an idealized past.[113] On the other hand, the opposite interpretation has also been advanced, namely that so far from blaming the living through blaming the dead, Juvenal praises the living by implying a contrast between them and their predecessors on earth. This thesis has particularly been developed as regards the rulers: by mocking Domitian the author flatters Hadrian, for example.[114] It seems to me that these

[110] P. Wessner (ed.), *Scholia in Juvenalem vetustiora* (Leipzig: Teubner, 1931), 17. This interpretation has however been questioned, since a good many poor people were buried there too (Courtney, *Commentary on Juvenal*, ad loc.).

[111] So Highet, *Juvenal the Satirist*, 57, 289–94. An extra twist is added to this argument in Freudenburg, *Satires of Rome*, where it is argued that Juvenal is out to parody the over-critical *authors* of his time, who had been silent enough under Domitian, but now spared no vehemence in attacking the dead.

[112] e.g. Kenney, 'The First Satire of Juvenal', 37–8.

[113] S. C. Fredericks, 'Irony of Overstatement in the Satires of Juvenal', *ICS* 4 (1979), 190.

[114] e.g. Braund, 'Paradigms of Power'; Hardie, 'Domitian'.

interpretations are built on taking into account not only the programme, but also the bulk of Juvenal's satire; the meaning of the proposal is decided by looking at the result. At the site of the programmatic statement, the choice between these different interpretations cannot be made, the exact meaning of the programme cannot be decided from the programme alone. But what is most important to notice is that it is precisely the joke that allows for the different readings, that it multiplies meanings and above all indicates that there are hidden meanings present (under ground?). The satires cannot be read at face value. Juvenal's programmatic joke tells the reader that the satirist intends to cheat.

Lucilius

The discussion of the first Roman satirist is placed last, since any inquiry as to a satiric apology in Lucilius must be based on the *apologiae* of Horace, Persius, and Juvenal, which have come down to us in their entirety. It has been suggested that Juvenal in particular imitates the apology of the great son of Aurunca. Juvenal's formulation at vv. 168–9 ('tecum prius ergo voluta | haec animo ante tubas' ('think it over in your mind before the trumpet blows')) in his programme has been seen to hark back to a fragment in Lucilius, 'haec tu me insimulas? nonne ante in corde volutas?' ('Do you hurl these false accusations against me? Shouldn't you think it over in your mind first?', 1017 M).[115] Together with the clear pattern of satiric programmes in the other three verse satirists, this allusion has inspired an interesting reconstruction of a programmatic satire for Lucilius' Book 30.[116] This book is a reasonable place for a

---

[115] Griffith, 'Juvenal's First Satire and Lucilius', 64–5.

[116] Ibid. 65–72. L. R. Shero, 'The Satirist's Apologia', *University of Wisconsin Studies in Language and Literature. Classical series II*, xv (1922), 165–7, attempted to reconstruct an *apologia* for Book 1, arguing that this book would be the first in the second collection, and so occupy relatively the same position as Horace's programmatic 2.1. The three fragments which he puts together (frs. 1, 2, and 9 M), however, have less recognizable similarity with the programmes found in the other satirists than Griffith's reconstruction, and contain no element of humour. This does not exclude the possibility that they may still have been part of a satiric programme, but makes it irrelevant for my interests here.

programme, for it is the last book in Lucilius' first collection of satires,[117] and the first to consist wholly of hexameters, the metre that became canonical for Roman verse satire from then on. A section of fragments from the book (1008–38 M) seem to tell of an altercation between Lucilius and one or two interlocutors, offended by some harsh remark in his satires, referred to as *sermones* ('discourses'). Griffith proposes the following core of apparently cohering fragments as part of a satirist's *apologia* by Lucilius:

1014 idque tuis factis saevis et tristibu' dictis
1015 gaudes, cum de me ista foris sermonibu' differs
1016 et male dicendo in multis sermonibu' differs
1017 haec tu me insimulas? nonne ante in corde volutas ...?
1033 quem scis scire tuas omnes maculasque notasque
1034 quem sumptum facis in lustris, circum oppida lustrans
1035 nunc, Gai, quoniam incilans nos laedi', vicissim ...

1014 and this with your cruel actions and stern words
1015 You're glad to spread abroad those things about me in your discourses
1016 you slice me up and spread the pieces, by libelling me in many discourses
1017 Do you hurl these false accusations against me? Shouldn't you think it over in your mind first ...?
1033 who, as you know, knows all your blots and brands
1034 how much you spend on call-girls, calling at the race-track with its barriers
1035 Now, Gaius, since you in your turn attack by lashing out against us ...

Among these, Griffith takes frs. 1017, 1033, and 1034 as being directed to Lucilius by an opponent rather than being uttered by Lucilius himself. His arguments are that Lucilius' morality was indeed less than perfect, that such self-revelation would be in line with Horace's description of Lucilius as fully revealed in his satires (Hor. *S.* 2.1.32–4), and that the subject of 'voluta' ('turn over', i.e. 'contemplate') in Juvenal (1.168) is 'Juvenal' himself, which makes it likely that the subject of Lucilius' 'volutas' was also the satirist himself.[118] As Lucilius' unexpected answer to these accusations Griffith proposes fr. 1037–8, 'quin totum purges, devellas atque

[117] Books 26–30 appeared first, followed by those now numbered 1–25.

[118] Griffith, 'Juvenal's First Satire and Lucilius', 67–8. A persuasive, but necessarily somewhat uncertain line of reasoning.

deuras | exultes'. The import of the satirist's line will be something like '("if that's how you feel") why not hurt me and singe me and pluck me?', and so he would seem 'to have parried an attack by an aggrieved opponent with the surprise counterstroke of inviting him to do his worst'. According to Griffith, this counterstroke may be the prototype of what subsequently grew into a necessary element in the satiric *apologia*, what I have here called *the programmatic joke*: 'This novel twist may be the germ of the culminating element of surprise in what later became the set pattern of the satirist's apology, as developed by Horace, Persius, and Juvenal.'[119]

If this reconstruction is close to the original, then Lucilius' programmatic joke looked somewhat different from those in his followers, in that he directly challenged his opponent(s), without pretending that he was a peaceful poet writing in an innocuous genre. Nevertheless, through its exaggerated and clearly comical form the joke still allows different interpretations of it. Instead of representing a bold challenge, it may be taken as painting the speaker in the role of an innocent joker, a good sport in not replying angrily to attacks on his satire. In this way Lucilius' line resembles the later programmatic joke with their function of multiplying meaning.

Both the reconstruction and my speculations about the nature of Lucilius' joke must remain just that, speculations, though not completely unfounded ones. It is, however, worthwhile to consider the possibility that the first programmatic joke appeared in Lucilius, passing on its pattern to his followers—to mould for their own purposes, but to keep in place so as to identify their genre, just as is done with other generic elements. In that case, the jokes in Horace, Persius, and Juvenal can no longer be seen as mere expressions of their 'Lucilius problem', i.e. their failure to write satire that named its targets (*onomasti kōmōdein*), and with the same boldness as Lucilius.[120] Rather the 'problem', an overarching paradox of combining humour with criticism, is traced to the *primus inventor* himself, and the programmatic joke which negotiates that problem is seen to be part of the generic pattern from the very beginning.

---

[119] Griffith, 'Juvenal's First Satire and Lucilius', 69, 70.
[120] Freudenburg, *Satires of Rome*, 2 *et passim*.

1

Object-Oriented Humour

THE PRINCIPLE OF MOCKERY FROM BELOW

In the field of mocking humour there is a widespread pattern of someone without power suddenly daring to deride a very powerful target. This is a model which in later literary history emerges as typical of the satiric mode,[1] but it germinates in antiquity. We meet it in the Greek diatribe, where it is a particular favourite with the Cynics. The Cynic, as a type, assumes a low role in society, and will deliberately refuse wealth and political position. Yet his free speech, *parrhēsia*, allows him to laugh at the rich and mighty. He may do this directly, as in the story where Diogenes, with a cheeky jocular formulation, answers Alexander that his best help will consist in stepping aside and clear Diogenes' view.[2] The Cynics may also make use of the model in a transferred sense, as in their master metaphor of the dog, a low creature which nevertheless has the freedom to bark at, and occasionally bite, anyone it sees fit. The model of someone powerless deriding the powerful may thus be translated into imagery such as low against high, small against big, physically weak against physically strong. Mostly these transferred terms remain formal, almost physical (as in the case of the dog) and do not include mental qualities such as stupidity/cleverness, the lack/presence of talent, or moral depravity/goodness. The positive mental qualities stay firmly on the side of the aggressor, no matter how

---

[1] See the discussion in N. Frye, *The Anatomy of Criticism* (Princeton: Princeton University Press, 1957), 226–9.

[2] D.L. 6.38; cf. the discussion of *parrhēsia* in this exchange in Branham and Goulet-Cazé, *Cynics*, 88.

inferior he may be in formal power. Diogenes is morally and intellectually superior to Alexander in the anecdote, and so is the Cynic dog to the humans he bites. Since uninhibited free speech is also a treasured characteristic of Old Comedy, the model occurs there as well. We see variants of it when Peithetairos and Euelpides overpower both humans and gods in Aristophanes' *Birds*, or when Lysistrata and her friends get the better of the magistrate.

This model of mockery from below has several features to recommend it to its user. It effectively combines an element of supposedly rightful opposition with an element of merriment, the latter built into the very incongruity of the powerless overcoming the powerful. Furthermore, the very structure of low against high suggests that it is a matter of self-defence, of *hitting back* rather than hitting first. This, in turn, strengthens the audience's sympathy with the lowly attacker,[3] as does the feeling of liberation inherent in the act of striking out against those on top. I would like to argue that the Roman satirists, like later satirists, make frequent use of this model, which grants them several advantages in an irrational way, simply by force of the positive connotations of the structure: fearlessness, intelligence, righteousness.

Yet it would be obviously naïve to claim that mocking humour in antiquity is essentially subversive, directed against the powerful by advocates of the powerless. Several studies have amply shown that it is often the other way around.[4] Still, I believe that the model presented here can be helpful if it is combined with insights such as those outlined by Mary Douglas in her article on joke perception.[5] According to Douglas's analysis, the essence of all jokes lies in the

---

[3] This mechanism seems to be recognized in Cicero's treatment of the laughable in *De Oratore*. At *De Or.* 2.236, Cicero states that wit is more commonly admired in the defence than on the accuser's side. Further on, he warns against unprovoked mockery, which may become scurrilous ('scurrile ... quod sine causa lacessivit' ('it was scurrilous ... because he attacked without any reason')), and which is generally unworthy of the orator, 246–7. Throughout the discussion he also gives examples of altercations where what is said in repartee is praised as both funnier and more decorous than the original attack: 246, 255, 263, 276–7.

[4] Notably Richlin, *Garden*; Henderson, 'Satire Writes Woman'; and id., *Writing Down Rome*, Gold; 'Humor in J. 6', Miller, 'Grotesque in Roman Satire'; and Walters, 'Making a Spectacle'.

[5] M. Douglas, 'The Social Control of Cognition: Some Factors in Joke Perception,' *Man. The journal of the Royal Anthropological Institute*, 3/3 (1968), 361–76.

challenge to an accepted pattern, and so all jokes have a 'subversive effect on the dominant structure of ideas'. What is new in her discussion, however, is that she introduces potential mobility into the structure, as she submits that the dominance may be of a temporary kind. One of her examples is the Thersites episode in the second book of the *Iliad* (2.212–77), in which Odysseus abuses and beats Thersites in answer to his suggestion of mutiny, whereupon the men of the Greek army laugh. In this connection Douglas argues that although the humour of Odysseus and the laughers may seem to reinforce an already existing power hierarchy in crushing its challenger, this is to describe the story out of context. Within the narrative of the *Iliad*, the anecdote follows directly upon Thersites' attempt to persuade the war-weary soldiers to make a dash for the ships and sail off, and Odysseus' reaction checks him on the brink of success. Thus in the text, the hierarchic roles have been momentarily reversed, and the beating is not the humiliation of the weaker by the stronger, but a reinstatement of power that seemed, albeit for an instant, lost:

In the context of threatened mob rule, the leaders are not the dominant element in the pattern, but the weak, endangered element. One could say that everyone laughs with relief that their scramble for home is not allowed to overwhelm the delicate balance of power between a handful of leaders and a mass of followers.[6]

The gains of this analysis in comparison with an explanation of the episode as simply an instance of superiority humour are considerable.[7] Douglas accounts for the dynamics of the story, the swift changes in balance between the rulers and the rebel, and the important element of relief when the sudden danger is over. This interpretation gives a satisfactory explanation of how this story differs from one where someone would make an unprovoked attack. Note that we may still speak of superiority humour—the difference is that the superiority is created, as it were (or re-created), at the moment of the victim's humiliation, rather than being present all the time. Such

---

[6] Douglas, 'Joke Perception', 367.

[7] For such readings, see S.Jäkel, 'The Phenomenon of Laughter in the Iliad', 23–7, and R. Garland, 'The Mockery of the Deformed and the Disabled in Greco-Roman Culture', 77–8, both in S. Jäkel and A. Timonen (eds.), *Laughter down the Centuries*, i (Turku: Annales Universitatis Turkuensis, 1994). Garland comments on Douglas's interpretation dismissingly, but does not really argue against it.

a description is in fact in line with one of the most famous statements of the Superiority theory, Hobbes' suggestion that '*Sudden glory*, is the passion which maketh those grimaces called LAUGHTER.'[8]

The greatest advantage of Douglas's approach to this passage is that it shows how a well-established hierarchy, which is *momentarily threatened*, may exploit this situation to take up the effective weapon of ridicule. This can easily be expanded to include mere posing: an author may choose to represent an established institution as threatened by some challenge in order to mock the challenge *as if* attacking something dangerous from a lowly position. He will then be able to create a sudden superiority for his hero, as well as draw upon the powerful effects of relief and liberation which accompany the model.

A theorist of satire, Northrop Frye, also hints in this direction in his *Anatomy of Criticism*, when he says that 'Dryden transforms his victims into fantastic dinosaurs of bulging flesh and peanut brains.'[9] If Dryden performs such a transformation, this means that he is deliberately enlarging the objects of his attack before slaying them, that he is pretending to challenge the mighty while not necessarily doing so. Once we allow for movement and pretence within the paradigm of mockery from below, it becomes very elastic, and useful for discussion of both radical and conservative satire. It is precisely this kind of humorous attack, which pretends to be issued from a lowly position upwards, that I believe to be typical of object-oriented humour in Roman satire.

Simulated mockery from below in Roman satire

In order to create a situation where the satiric persona may shoot at an upraised target, the satirist may artificially (i.e. through imagery,

---

[8] *Leviathan* (1651), ch. 6; original emphasis.

[9] Frye, *Anatomy of Criticism*, 228. Purdie argues that a process of this kind underlines all humour that has a butt: 'Laughing at someone involves our constructing them as discursively powerful, and then denying them that construction.' An accompanying element of this is often resistance on the part of the victim, reinforcing their 'perceived oscillation between having and not-having power—i.e. their *degradation*' (Purdie, *Comedy*, 59, 64–5; citation from 64). I would still claim that satire spells out the up-and-down pattern more obviously than other humour genres, since the satirist is not simply interested in deriding a particular object, but also has a separate interest in painting himself as a knight of justice.

allusion, or other literary devices) heighten/enlarge his object. Alternatively, he may artificially lower/diminish his persona. In some cases he may do both. As Roman satire develops into an increasingly less personal genre, the preoccupation with the objects takes over after the focus on the persona. Thus we will encounter more instances of the heightening of objects and less lowering of the persona in Juvenal, while the reverse picture is seen in Horace, where drawing a portrait of the persona is still a major interest, in Lucilius' wake. At closer examination, Horace, Persius, and Juvenal all hold examples of both procedures. Still, the category of 'lowered subject' will not be separately discussed in Juvenal's case, where it largely coincides with the heightening of objects. In the section on Juvenal I include a separate discussion of concrete images in which the targets are raised. I argue that this is a recurring metaphor for the device of lifting the object to mock it from below, and entitle the discussion 'The device as image'.

HORACE

Raised objects

In Horace's satires, both major and minor personages are time and again heightened in order to be brought down all the heavier. This heightening is achieved by way of literary allusions, or sometimes other imagery.

Punning on 'reges'—how to kill kings without hurting anyone (1.2; 1.3; 1.7)

One way of heightening, punning on the word *rex*, occurs several times in the first book of Horace's satires, with the maximum exploitation found in *S.* 1.7, where a pun of this kind is made the very point of the whole poem.

The first joke pertaining to kings appears in 1.2, the aggressive youngish diatribe on how a man should arrange his sexual life. After having praised prostitutes' open exhibition of their wares, the satirist

rather suddenly remembers the practice of an unspecified category of
kings:

> regibus hic mos est: ubi equos mercantur opertos
> inspiciunt, ne si facies ut saepe decora
> molli fulta pede est emptorem inducat hiantem,
> quod pulchrae clunes, breve quod caput, ardua cervix.
> hoc illi recte ...   (1.2.86–90)

Kings have this habit, that when buying horses they inspect them after
covering them up. This is in order that a handsome shape supported on a
soft hoof—as often happens—may not fool the buyer as he gapes at the
beautiful haunches, the small head, the fiery neck. They are right in this ...

The facts that the *reges* are presented without further qualification,
and that they appear out of the blue, have puzzled commentators so
much that Adolf Kießling even suggested the emendation 'Thracibus'
for 'regibus' to solve the problem.[10] Furthermore, although the kings'
practice of buying horses is explicitly applauded (90), it is not
altogether in line with the rest of the satire, and especially not with
the immediately preceding passage. These kings first cover up the
horse and then examine it, whereas the prostitutes were praised for
showing what they have openly.[11] The hooves of a horse are admit-
tedly important, but so are many other parts that would be covered,
such as e.g. teeth, eyes, and back. In addition, the paradox of 'oper-
tos|inspiciunt' is conspicuously flashed over a line break. This makes
the good example of the kings if not decidedly ambivalent, at least
related tongue in cheek.

The comic ambivalence of the passage, in turn, strengthens a
solution like that suggested by William Turpin, that the *reges* are
brought in for the pun latent in the word. Turpin's further claim that
the pun turns on *rex* as the patron of a parasite, with a specific
reference to Horace's own *rex*, Maecenas,[12] is too far-fetched. However, I believe that he is right to say that the word *reges* is used slightly
out of context in order for its multiple meanings to resound freely. It

---

[10] See Kießling and Heinze, *Satiren*, ad loc., where the problem is summarized in
the sentence: 'Bedenklich bleibt, daß hier weder der Zusammenhang auf bestimmte
reges hinweist noch die Sitte sich aus dem Wesen des Königtums erklärt.'

[11] The logical problem of the comparison is noted in W. Turpin, 'The Epicurean
Parasite: Horace, Satires 1.1–3,' *Ramus* 27 (1998), 136.

[12] Turpin paraphrases: 'here's what you big-shots do'; ibid.

seems to me that there is a pun involved here, but of a deliberately vague kind: *reges* can be foreign kings, they can be tyrants, they can be parasites' patrons. The statement about them is basically a compliment, but their behaviour looks somewhat ridiculous. Of course if we follow the line of the patron and his parasite-poet, the feet of the horse could be seen as standing in for metrical feet, essential to good poetry,[13] but the covered parts are still problematic. The joke is *not necessarily altogether* complimentary, and since some of the possible references are close to home, Horace keeps his humour elusive. What I would like to underline here is that the word *rex* is perfect for the occasion: polysemic, evocative, and repeatedly used for puns in the Roman literary tradition.[14] In addition, it also achieves—in a purely formal, yet effective manner—a heightening of the narrative before throwing it down to the lowly level of sex-trade with its petty inconveniences.

The next time *reges* appear is in a more developed, explicit joke on Stoics, at the end of the next satire, 1.3. In this case the Stoic idea that the wise man alone is 'king' is thoroughly ridiculed, in good Epicurean tradition.[15] Not only is the notion a favourite target of Epicurean derision, but punning is also a fitting method for Epicureans,[16] since it undermines the Stoic idea of a natural language with a non-arbitrary connection between referent and reference, and stresses the importance of arrangement and context, essential features in an atomistic world-view. The coda of satire 1.3 depends on the word *rex*, which, having been foreshadowed in 'regnum' at v. 123, is hammered in five times before the final instance in the last line (142). The heightening effect of the word is fully exploited as 'Horace' keeps purposefully 'misunderstanding' the abstract nature of the Stoic sage's 'kingship', whereby he can throw down his opponent from

---

[13] Cf. Freudenburg, *Walking Muse*, 195, on the feet of the prostitutes compared to the kings' horses at *S.* 1.2.102.

[14] e.g. by Cicero (*Att.* 1.16.10) and Caesar (Dio 44.10), mentioned in Brown, *Horace: Satires I*, to *S.* 1.7.35.

[15] Cf. Lucil, 1225–6 Varro, *Men.* 245 (Cèbe); and Brown, *Horace: Satires I*, ad loc. Sack (*Ironie*, 48–9) discusses the ironies at work in the punning ending of 1.3.

[16] For Epicurean humour, see P. Kragelund, 'Epicurus, Priapus and the dreams in Petronius', *CQ* 39 (1989), 436–50; Freudenburg, *Walking Muse*; Stewart, 'Laughter in the Greek Philosophers'; and Turpin, 'The Epicurean Parasite', 137, who also points out that *S.* 1.3 'contains an invocation of the Epicurean theory of language'.

his regal height time and again. First, the satirist says that if the wise man is rich, a good craftsman, and *king* (125), it is surprising that he should want what he already has—taking the words literally. The poor Stoic is allowed to answer, and muddily tries to explain what his master Chrysippus teaches: Hermogenes will be a singer even if silent, Alfenus a barber even outside his shop, in the same manner the sage is a craftsman and a king (133). In response 'Horace' presents the Stoic with the following scenario:

> vellunt tibi barbam
> lascivi pueri; quos tu nisi fuste coerces,
> urgeris turba circum te stante miserque
> rumperis et latras, magnorum maxime regum.　(1.3.134–6)

cheeky boys pull your beard, and if you do not keep them at bay with your stick, you'll be mobbed by the throng, and you'll miserably burst with angry barking, O greatest of Kings!

Again, 'king' is understood literally, even strengthened by being called *the greatest*, 'magnorum maxime regum'. The great monarch is then degraded from that level by being shown as physically humiliated by small boys who tear at his philosopher's attribute, the beard. This effect is paralleled in the next move of the joke, where the Stoic is said to go to bathe for a quarter of an *as*, king that he is (138), with his retinue of Chrysippus alone. At the end the thematic threads of this satire are drawn together:[17]

> et mihi dulces
> ignoscent, si quid peccaro stultus, amici
> inque vicem illorum patiar delicta libenter
> privatusque magis vivam te rege beatus.　(1.3.139–42)

and my kind friends will forgive me if, foolishly, I make some mistake. I, in turn, will gladly tolerate their transgressions, and as a commoner I will live happier than you as King.

In the last line, the pun on *rex* is elegantly used for multiple purposes. It plays off Epicureanism against Stoicism, as *rex* stands for Stoic doctrine, while 'privatus . . . magis vivam . . . beatus' must be seen as a

---

[17] Both Kießling and Heinze (*Satiren*) and Brown (*Horace: Satires I*), ad loc., point out that the central theme is reintroduced, but do not stress the economic use of the pun for thematic ends.

paraphrase of Epicurus' maxim λάθη βιώσας ('live hidden'). It plays off the happiness of the private citizen with no particular powers, equal among friends, against the unforgiving Stoic, whose sternness has turned him into a lonely tyrant (*rex*). Finally, it excellently illustrates the heightening of the target of ridicule and the lowering of the speaking subject in order to achieve the right proportions of satiric humour.

Interestingly, it has been noticed that with entering the coda of 1.3 (vv. 120–42), Horace modifies his metre. Where the main, middle part of the satire had a freer metre, the ending uses a stricter metre with fewer elisions.[18] It would seem that the final punch against the absurd Stoic is marked by the most programmatic style of humour in satire—'fair' derision of grand objects from below—as well as by a smoother metre. Both of these place the poem firmly within the genre, close to satire's ideal image of itself. With the help of nothing more than a pun, 'Horace' has become a private citizen attacking a king.

We have now reached *Satire* 1.7, the short piece so differently evaluated—as 'refined' or 'trivial'—by two eminent Horatians.[19] Before discussing the effect of its punchline use of the pun on *rex*, however, it is instructive to look at some other instances of comic heightening in the poem. These precede the final pun, and may be said to lead up to it by rehearsing the pattern of lifting up and shooting down by derision. The story in 1.7 is a prolonged anecdote about two characters, Rupilius Rex and Persius, insulting each other in a litigation before Brutus' court in Asia. At the end of the poem Persius wins by appealing to Brutus, the killer of kings, to do away with this Rex (= King). The two main personages are in themselves neither oppressive nor vicious, and to deride them would be idle if they were not magnified for the occasion. Everything that makes them worth laughing at is purely formal: there is the matter of the name Rex, and there is the elaborately epic description of the antagonists and their appearance before Brutus' tribunal.

---

[18] N.-O. Nilsson, *Metrische Stildifferenzen in den Satiren des Horaz* (Uppsala: Almqvist & Wiksell, 1952), 170–1.

[19] E. Fraenkel, *Horace* (Oxford: Oxford University Press, 1957), 120; Rudd, *Satires of Horace*, 160.

The epic allusions (primarily to Homer) have been amply discussed in three consecutive studies of this satire.[20] Here I will content myself with repeating some of the most striking examples, in order to describe their humorous function. Fortunately, the allusions all go together with humour, since the contrast between the sublime intertext and the banal characters creates simultaneously derision of the characters and parody on the intertext.

So the very first line introduces Rupilius Rex with a Homeric formula, 'Rupili pus atque venenum' ('Rupilius' pus and poison'), parodically reminiscent of such expressions as βίη Διομήδεος, ἱερὴ ἲς Τηλεμάχοιο ('the force of Diomedes; the divine strength of Telemachos'). His adversary Persius is given an epithet to match Rex— *hybrida* ('half-breed'). Here the raising of the characters is almost simultaneous with their subversion, since on the one hand they are raised by being described like epic heroes, on the other hand derided by the unflattering qualities ascribed to them. Yet even this flawed epic tone is not allowed to reign for long, but immediately crushed against the low-life description of those who have heard the story: 'opinor | omnibus et lippis notum et tonsoribus esse' ('I believe that all the bleary-eyed people and all the barbers know it'), 2–3. This is a company of personages familiar from the world of satire,[21] and perhaps containing an ironic reference to Horace himself in *lippis*.[22] After this plunge, the tone climbs again with the exaggerated description of Persius' riches (4–5), drawing on an association between his name and the proverbially wealthy inhabitants of Persia. Martial terms follow, in 'posset vincere Regem' ('he could overcome the King'), 6, as well as in the ensuing heroic simile. The simile is worth quoting in full:

> hoc etenim sunt iure molesti
> quo fortes quibus adversum bellum incidit; inter
> Hectora Priamiden animosum atque inter Achillem

---

[20] R. Schröter, 'Horazens Satire 1.7 und die antike Eposparodie,' *Poetica*, 1 (1967), 8–23; V. Buchheit, 'Homerparodie und Literaturkritik in Horazens Satiren I,7 und I,9,' *Gymnasium* 75 (1968), 519–55; G. Bernardi Perini, 'Aceto italico e poesia Luciliana: Hor. *Sat.* I.7,' in *Scritti in onore di Carlo Diano.* (Bologna, 1975).

[21] Cf. *S.* 1.5.30, 49; 1.3.132; 2.3.17.

[22] Cf. 1.3.25; 1.5.30 and 49. Bernardi Perini ('Aceto italico', 7) takes 'lippis' here as an allusion to Horace.

ira fuit capitalis, ut ultima divideret mors,
non aliam ob causam nisi quod virtus in utroque
summa fuit: duo si discordia vexet inertis
aut si disparibus bellum incidat, ut Diomedi
cum Lycio Glauco, discedat pigrior ultro
muneribus missis: Bruto praetore tenente
ditem Asiam Rupili et Persi par pugnat, uti non
compositum melius cum Bitho Bacchius. in ius
acres procurrunt, magnum spectaculum uterque. (1.7.10–21)

for men who meet in head-on battle are fierce in proportion to their bravery; between Hector, son of Priam, and fiery Achilles the wrath was deadly, so that only death could part them, for the very reason that both possessed consummate valour. If there is conflict between two cowards, or if it comes to battle between two unequal men, as happened between Diomedes and the Lycian Glaucus, the fainter-hearted voluntarily withdraws, offering gifts, but when, under Brutus' praetorship over rich Asia, Rupilius faced his match Persius in battle, not even Bithus and Bacchius could be considered better matched. They rushed fiercely into court, each of them a great sight.

The heroic terms proliferate: *fortes* ('brave'), *bellum* ('war'), *discedere* ('withdraw'), *pugnare* ('join battle'), *acres procurrere* ('rush fiercely'); a little further on there is *invictus* ('unconquered') (30). Not only is the diction Homeric and Horace's two litigants explicitly likened to Homeric heroes, but they are likened to the two most outstanding warriors in martial epic, Achilles and Hector. Horace takes care to point out that they are *not* like the mismatched Diomedes and Glaucus.[23] The satirist further heightens the status of his characters by calling their battle a matter of life and death ('ira ... capitalis', 'ultima divideret mors'), and the characters utterly brave ('animosum', 'fortes', 'virtus in utroque|summa'). The scene is thus set for satiric degradation, and this is achieved in the poem's second comic downfall, which is performed in two steps.

First, still within the imagery of a capital battle, the Greek warriors from Homer are suddenly replaced with two gladiators from Rome. As with the introductory plunge from the presentation of the heroes to that of the bleary-eyed audience, the fall involves at least the following aspects: from high literature to real life, from mythic to

[23] Cf. *Il.* 6.236.

contemporary, and from Greek to Roman. When Horace comically smashes his objects down from the level of Achilles and Hector to that of low-life entertainers, we feel a whiff of the satirist's 'solvent of reality',[24] of that laughing truth he has promised us. We begin to forget that he has not actually revealed anything, only shot down those whom he himself had hoisted.

The lowering continues when, after the gladiators, the actual context is bluntly spelled out—'in ius' ('into court'). The effect is that of a retake, a second step in the degradation. As Persius begins, at long last, to address the court, the reaction of his audience, unanimous laughter ('ridetur ab omni| conventu', 22), is surely meant to encourage the same reaction in Horace's reader at this point.[25] In the rest of this satire, the tone never rises as high as at the outset, and although some words connoting warfare and epic are scattered in the final section,[26] the imagery stays at a lower level, that of agriculture.

The concluding attraction in 1.7, the pun on *rex*, appears as the splendidly inane climax of a tale of the Emperor without clothes. Persius wins over Rupilius Rex with this joke, flattering to Brutus, killing to his opponent:

> '... per magnos, Brute, deos te
> oro, qui reges consueris tollere, cur non
> hunc Regem iugulas? operum hoc, mihi crede, tuorum
> est.' (33–5)

in the name of the mighty gods, Brutus, I ask you: why don't you, who are used to getting rid of kings, slit this King's throat? Believe me, this is your line of business!

We may now remember that Rupilius' regal name has resounded throughout the poem, from the first parodic line, and repeatedly (5, 6, 9, 25), while Persius was identified as a mere hybrid in the second line. Here, in the finale, we get the solution to this name game, and,

---

[24] Hendrickson, 'Satura Tota Nostra', 52.

[25] I take 'ridetur' in the impersonal sense defended by Bernardi Perini ('Aceto italico', 22), 'is greeted with laughter', *contra* Buchheit, 'Homerparodie', 543, E. Kraggerud, 'Die Satire I.7 des Horaz,' *SO* 54 (1979), 91–109; p.101.

[26] E.g. 'invictus' ('unconquered'), 30; 'cessisset' ('he would have withdrawn'), 31; 'per magnos ... deos' ('in the name of the mighty gods'), 33; see Bernardi Perini 'Aceto italico', 6, for a detailed exposition.

as it were, the naked structure of the workings of exemplary satire: a nobody mocking a tyrant with the help of traditional Justice. In this case Justice appears in the shape of Brutus and his glorious ancestor, Iunius Brutus. Here, a pun on rex in Cicero, *Ep. ad Att.* 1.16.10, is often adduced as a parallel:

'Quousque,' inquit [*sc.* Clodius], hunc regem feremus?' 'Regem appellas,' inquam, 'cum Rex tui mentionem nullam fecerit?'; ille autem Regis hered-itatem spe devorarat.

'How long,' said he, 'are we to tolerate this king?!' 'You speak of a king,' said I, 'when Mr. King didn't even mention you in his testament?' For he had squandered the money he hoped to inherit from Mr. King, before getting it.[27]

The resemblance, however, is rather superficial. In Cicero it is a question of repartee within a conflict that does not hinge on the pun on *rex*, and after the joke the quarrel continues with other arguments. In Horace it is, instead, the climax of a carefully built tension—a culmination of a serious conflict and a reversal to the comic at the same time.[28]

The heightening of the target (Rupilius Rex), his comic degrad-ation,[29] even this satire as a whole, are, on the face of it, nothing but a game with words, and this the author could plead if criticized. Yet this is not the whole truth, for we must remember that words are the material of literature, and in this case, there is also the additional feature of a pun, which wrecks the unproblematic connection be-tween things (or people) and their names. If 'Rex' need not mean only Rupilius Rex, but can mean any king, whom else can it mean? At this time, it was hardly possible to mention a *rex* (which can mean

[27] Cicero is reporting an altercation between his enemy Clodius and himself. Here he parries an attack in which Clodius calls Cicero a tyrant (*hunc regem*). Cicero retorts by alluding to the fact that Q. Marcius Rex (Rex = *Mr. King*), though Clodius' relative, had not let Clodius inherit him.

[28] Kraggerud, 'Satire I.7', 103. Yet unlike Kraggerud, I cannot help but see this pun as very aggressive, and I do not understand his argument that it points to the overcoming of tensions and connotes Horace's compromising attitude to Augustus.

[29] Cf. the Gowers' comment on this feature of the satire: 'Kings in the poem are underdogs who go on rearing their ugly heads and being suppressed; see lines 1 (*Proscripti Regis*), 6 (*vincere Regem*), 25 (*excepto Rege* [king as a scapegoat]), and 35 (*Regem iugulas* [king as a sacrificial victim])' (E. Gowers, 'Blind Eyes and Cut Throats: Amnesia and Silence in Horace *Satires* 1.7', *CP* 97 (2002), 149).

'tyrant', 'patron' etc.), proscription, and Brutus, without creating a hint at the political conflicts of the day.[30] Does not Persius the *hybrida* remind us of 'Horace' himself—another mocker, who later described himself as 'something in between a Lucanian and an Apulian' (*S.* 2.1.34), a kind of hybrid?[31] Precisely by being non-literal, and non-serious, the pun reverberates in meaning, and the satirical probing potentially spreads to all the mighty of this world. This is only a shadow of a meaning, it has no substantial references, and the satire remains an essentially inoffensive sketch, but a shadow of a meaning inherent in the words will still *de facto* be present in the poem. Something of the fearless and humorous barking at kings, almost a meta-literary illustration of satire as a genre, lingers in the reader's mind.

It has been claimed that the pun on *rex* is a bad one,[32] but it seems unlikely that Horace should have thought so himself, given how much he exploited it in several satires, and it must at least be admitted that the uses to which he puts it are both varied and complex. Horace knew how to do things with words.

Deconstructing the enemy you have built up (1.8)

In the following poem, 1.8, the hilarious tale of Priapus and the witches, there is again a tendency to replace real attack with the mere image of attack. As has been recognized, Priapus is a comic version of the satirist himself,[33] but it remains to see who his opponents are. In the sober, realistic world of satire witches can hardly exist as truly magical fairy-tale creatures, the way they appear in Apuleius' *Metamorphoses* or Trimalchio's ghost story in Petronius. The end of *S.* 1.8, where Canidia and Sagana are revealed as frauds, indeed indicates that they are not to be taken as literal witches. Depending on what

---

[30] Gowers, 'Amnesia and Silence', presents an excellent analysis of the political implications of 1.7, with further references.

[31] 'Lucanus an Apulus anceps', *S.* 2.1.34.

[32] Turpin, 'The Epicurean Parasite', 137.

[33] W. S. Anderson, 'The Form, Purpose, and Position of Horace's Satire I,8,' *AJP* 93 (1972), 4–13, repr. in *Essays on Roman Satire* (Princeton: Princeton University Press, 1982); M. Habash, 'Priapus: Horace in Disguise?,' *CJ* 94, 3 (1999), 285–97.

attributes the reader focuses on, the hags could be differently interpreted.

They could be seen as standing in for women in general,[34] since the
hags are not only female themselves, but also linked to the female
divinities Hecate, Tisiphone, and the moon.

They could be taken as competing fellow poets, unwelcome to
Maecenas' garden, guarded by Horace-Priapus. The strongest argument for this interpretation is that the witches, just like poets, are
creators of *carmina*. In fact, they are first introduced with the phrase
'carminibus quae versant... humanos animos' ('those who turn
human minds with their spells [*lit.* songs]') (1.8.19–20).[35] Another
argument in favour of this reading is their invasion of *Maecenas'
garden*, i.e. that particular territory which Horace–Priapus regarded
as his. Horace the persona, like Horace the poet, had once entered
Maecenas' realm from outside, and he was only too conscious of the
fact that other poets might want to do the same. In his satires, he
fiercely defended this territory under his patron's wing, as, for instance, against the 'bore' in *S.* 1.9.

There may be a socio-hierarchical aspect in their unearthing of the
social underworld[36] of slaves and criminals that literally lies buried
under the feet of Priapus. Close to the beginning of the poem we are
told that the garden where the statue stands used to be a cemetery for
disrespectable people. A slave would carry the corpses of his co-slaves
to this place in a coffin (vv. 8–9); this was the common grave of the
wretched poor (10–11); the field was a sorry sight, full of white bones
(15–16). Although the territory is now covered by a layer which has
transformed it into a healthy, sunny area for living and leisure, the
hags who come at night easily bore through this upper layer: they
collect bones (22) and dig the ground (26–8). Their aim is expressly
to raise the dead (28–9). In this place, raising the dead will mean

[34] So taken in Richlin, *Garden*, 66–7; Henderson, 'Satire Writes Woman'; and id.,
Writing down Rome.

[35] See Oliensis, 'Canidia, Canicula, and Horace's *Epodes*', 109–10. The ambivalence
of the word *carmen* is later fully exploited in *S.* 2.1. See discussion above, under
'Programmatic jokes—the hidden agenda of ambiguity'.

[36] For the concept of the 'social underworld', developed by John Bodel in an
analysis of Petronius' *Cena Trimalchionis*, see J. Bodel, 'Trimalchio's Underworld',
in J. Tatum (ed.), *The Search for the Ancient Novel* (Baltimore and London: Johns
Hopkins University Press, 1994), 251.

raising those wretched paupers buried under the ground trodden by those promenading on the now-fashionable Esquiline.

Perhaps we may also imagine that Horace's antagonists are a rather vague fusion of these groups (women, poets, slaves, the plebs), so that his aggression in this satire will hit all of them, but will not be easily tied down in reference. On whatever interpretation, the threat that the opponents represent seems to come from beneath rather than from above. Horace the satirist could of course harbour secret fears of the stealthy danger presented by women, fellow poets, or slaves, but none of these groups had any realistic power to hurt him. To attack such enemies makes perfect sense, but it is neither noble nor bold. Since such a charge in itself would hardly constitute satire, Horace transforms his enemies, empowers them and makes them dangerous in a direct, physical way. The persona he takes, Priapus, is a double character: a god hidden in the shape of a wooden scarecrow.[37] This allows him to switch suddenly from power to powerlessness and back again. In the main, middle part of the satire the antagonists are empowered, or in my terminology 'heightened', by being seen from the perspective of Priapus; and by allusions to high literature. This artificial empowerment, in turn, makes it possible for Priapus to assault his enemies—by the comic move of a loud fart—as if from a weak position, creating the favoured satirical structure of 'shooting from below'.

Looking more closely at how the hags are heightened, we may note that when they are introduced they are invested with the ultimate power over life and death, which can be done through the naïve point of view of the speaking garden statue. The Priapus statue exaggerates their might, and the reader is first made to view them through his horrified eyes. The hags are presented as much worse than thieves and wild beasts (*furesque feraeque*), and described as those 'who turn human minds with their spells and potions'. The speaker complains that he is completely helpless when faced with these women, and cannot stop their activities ('has nullo perdere possum| nec prohibere modo' ('there's no way I can get rid of them or stop them'), 20–1), which is very much at odds with the usually forceful

---

[37] For the mild humour against the persona involved here, see my discussion below, Ch. 2, under 'Horace', § 'Wearing the satyric mask of Socrates'.

role of Priapus in literature. The witches are terrible (*horrendas*, 26) and the statue is terrified (*horruerim*, 45). He conceives of them as superhuman beings, Furies, and above all, he actually believes that he sees the manifestation of their power to communicate with deities and open the gates of Hades:

> Hecaten vocat altera, saevam
> altera Tisiphonen; serpentis atque videres
> infernas errare canis, Lunamque rubentem,
> ne foret his testis, post magna latere sepulchra.
>
> . . . .
>
> singula quid memorem, quo pacto alterna loquentes
> umbrae cum Sagana resonarint triste et acutum   (1.8.33–6; 40–1)

one of them called on Hecate, the other on cruel Tisiphone. You could see snakes and hell-hounds roaming about, and the moon, with a blush, hiding behind the big tombs, to avoid witnessing this scene. . . . Why should I go through the details, how the spirits answered Sagana in mournful, shrill shrieks

In addition to the awesome picture achieved by the focalization through the eyes of Priapus, there is also the device of heightening through pointers to established literature. The most visible is the specific allusion to the *Odyssey* at vv.28–9, where the witches pour blood for the ghosts into a trench in the ground just as Odysseus himself had done to good effect (*Od.* 11.34–7). There is a continuous intertextual connection to Virgil's eighth *Eclogue*, where a serious and lyric version of magic is presented. Beyond that lurks the prototype of the *Eclogues*, Theocritus' *Idylls*.[38] Moreover, it has convincingly been shown that our satire can be regarded as a parody of a hymn, a high religious genre.[39]

---

[38] The second and the third *Idyll*, the former of which, like Horace's satire, features a woman exercising magic. See further W. Clausen, *A Commentary on Virgil, Eclogues* (Oxford: Oxford University Press, 1994), 237–8. For the connection between Horace's first book of satires and the *Eclogues*, see J. E. G. Zetzel, 'Dreaming about Quirinus: Horace's Satires and the development of Augustan poetry,' in T. Woodman and D. Feeney (eds.), *Traditions and Contexts in the Poetry of Horace* (Cambridge: Cambridge University Press, 2002).

[39] Habash, 'Horace in Disguise?'.

Yet the frame of the poem allows us to glimpse the real power structure between the persona and his opponents—that he is a god, while the hags are mere pretenders, without actual magical powers. When frightened, the fake witches scurry off, literally *falling apart*. Here are the satire's beginning and end:

> Olim truncus eram ficulnus, inutile lignum,
> cum faber, incertus scamnum faceretne Priapum,
> maluit esse deum. deus inde ego, furum aviumque
> maxima formido (1.8.1–4)

Once I was a trunk of a fig-tree, a useless piece of wood, when a carpenter, hesitating whether to make a bench or a Priapus, preferred me to be a god. A god I am since then, a great terror for birds and thieves

> et ut not testis inultus
> horruerim voces Furiarum et facta duarum?
> nam displosa sonat quantum vesica pepedi
> diffissa nate ficus. at illae currere in urbem.
> Canidiae dentis, altum Saganae caliendrum
> excidere atque herbas atque incantata lacertis
> vincula cum magno risuque iocoque videres.   (1.8.44–50)

how my shuddering, as a witness to the two Furies' voices and deeds, did not go unavenged? With all the noise of a balloon bursting I farted, and, made of fig-wood as I am, split my butt in two. They scurried off for the city. If you'd have seen Canidia's teeth, and Sagana's tall wig falling off, and the herbs and enchanted bonds dropping from their arms—you'd have had a lot of fun and a good laugh!

Priapus' fart, the climax of the satire, is a comic literary device, whose humour is underlined by the explicit invitation to laugh in the last verse. The persona's revenge disperses all horror and breaks down the witches with its lowly, 'indecent' materiality, with its connection to the body and its functions. This is a connection to that laughter-generating area which Bakhtin called 'the material bodily stratum'.[40] As Freudenburg has put it in commenting on this passage, when the statue breaks wind, this is 'an obvious injection of Bakhtin's "material grotesque " '.[41] It is the triumph of the ugly, open, and unfinished

---

[40] See Bakhtin, *Rabelais*, esp. 303–436.
[41] Freudenburg, *Walking Muse*, 230.

side of Priapus' nature; it is also the triumph of his power. His victims are exposed as overwhelmingly human, and all attention is focused on their old age, nakedness, and fear—degrading and levelling phenomena.[42]

As already indicated, there are good reasons for seeing the role pattern before the unmasking, i.e. the threatening superiority of the witches to the wretched god, as a temporary role reversal, and the change at the end as a *reinstatement* of the normal state of affairs.[43] The speaker's terror before the witches is unexpected, not in line with the normal conditions. When Priapus appears in other literature, such as the *Priapea*, he is always in full control of his garden and his physique, and often threatens to rape and humiliate any intruders in his realm, male or female.[44] He is usually aggressive, always potent, and never afraid. When witches or lecherous women turn up in connection with Priapus, which is rarely, they are not pitched against him.[45] The Priapus of 1.8, on the other hand, although mentioning his conventionally huge member (5), is curiously unwilling or unable to use it for raping the hags. His revenge, which is here neither aggressive nor sexual in nature, must surely be seen as an inversion of his usual attacks. The attacking phallus in front is even formally replaced with the farting backside. The witches, on their side, are not really invested with supernatural powers, as can be surmised from

[42] Freudenburg, ibid., comments on the levelling effects of old age, and points out that this is also a theme in Juvenal, 10.198–202. M. Hodgart, *Satire* (London: Weidenfeld & Nicolson, 1969), 30, claims that the levelling stress of the naked body is an essential technique of satire in general: 'The satirist's aim is to strip men bare, and apart from physique one naked man is much like another.'

[43] The humorous nature of Priapus' revenge and the explicit invitation to laugh that follows it have been especially commented upon by Habash ('Horace in Disguise?'), who has likened this strategy of comic unmasking to the basic mechanism of Horatian satire, which she sees as the revelation of hidden vice. Her analysis differs from mine in that she believes that Priapus' revenge at the end brings about 'a temporary reversal of roles where the victim becomes the avenged' (p. 294), whereas I see this final reversal as a return to the norm. Rather, I regard the magnification of the witches that precedes the fart as the temporary role reversal.

[44] Discussions of Priapus as a literary figure may be found e.g. in Rudd, *Satires of Horace*, 68; E. M. O'Connor, *Symbolum Salacitatis: A Study of the God Priapus as a Literary Character* (Frankfurt am Main: Lang, 1989); and Richlin, *Garden*, 57–70.

[45] e.g. in the *Priapea* 4, 19, 27, 34, 40; or in the Quartilla episode in Petronius (*Sat.* 16.1–26.6), where lewd women and male prostitutes perform the role of Priapus' priestess-with-retinue. Note also that the orgiastic females in Juvenal's *S.* 6 are called 'Priapi | maenades' ('the maenads of Priapus') (6.316–17).

their fright, and from their dismemberment when they are stripped of their false attributes. Yet from the beginning and until the statue's revenge, they are presented as magnificently terrifying creatures with mastery over life and death. I would regard this magnification, expressly revealed as false in the end, as a temporary reversal. It is curious that Priapus, who is both a god and the guardian of this garden, should be so afraid of the witches, but if he were not, he would not be able to shoot them down from their authority and triumph so hilariously over them at the end.

The closeness of the witches' sudden terror to Priapus' own fear makes the grotesque revenge look very bold as well as laughable. Laughter and the 'naked' truth have conquered the dark powers of evil, night, and death. Horace has not attacked anyone powerful, and yet the effect is one of fearless exposition of the mighty. His opponents have been put back in place from a height to which he himself had momentarily raised them. This is the skeleton of satire, and the humour and laughter in this poem help to create this structure from, as it were, thin air.[46]

The satirical sequel to the epic conversation between Odysseus and Teiresias (2.5)

A poem in the second book, 2.5, offers what is perhaps the most striking example of epic imagery among Horace's satires. The topic is legacy-hunting. In order to give more serious resonance to his humour, so as to create satire not comedy, Horace casts his characters in the shape of two important, refined characters from epic: Ulysses and Teiresias. The satirist's persona is not on stage at all in this satire. The targets are allowed to reveal and disgrace themselves with no explicit interference from the judging and ridiculing 'I'. This is an unusual device in Roman satire, though it is common in the later history of satire.

The poem consciously begins on a high note: at the very point where the *Odyssey* ends the conversation between Ulysses and

---

[46] Heightening through imagery, style, and epic allusion, is also found in 1.9, where it has been well analysed by Anderson (1956, repr. in Anderson, *Essays*, 84–102) and Henderson (*Writing down Rome*, 202–27).

Teiresias in the underworld (*Od.* 11.90–151). In Homer, the seer has foretold the Ithacian hero's journey home, and has instructed him on how to slay the suitors and appease the gods upon his arrival. He then answers the Ithacian's question about how to speak to his mother's ghost, and withdraws. In Horace's satire, we get to read the unknown, and scandalous, sequel to the conversation. The satire opens thus:

> 'Hoc quoque, Teresia, praeter narrata petenti
> responde, quibus amissas reparare queam res
> artibus atque modis. quid rides?' 'Iamne doloso
> non satis est Ithacam revehi patriosque Penatis
> aspicere?' (2.5.1–5)

'Answer me this question too, Teiresias, besides what you've told me: by what arts and means I may regain the wealth I have lost. What are you laughing at?' 'So it's not enough for the man of many wiles to return to Ithaca and look on his household gods?'

Yet a sequel to Homer is not in itself necessarily either lowly or comic, as witness Greek tragedy. The first line of this satire does not prepare us for what is to come, but keeps a high tone, drawing on the useful camouflage of the dactylic hexameter, the metre that Roman satire has in common with epic. With the next line, when the new question of the hero turns out to be of a monetary and dishonest nature, the tone is comically dashed down to the ground. The lowering in theme and genre is marked by Ulysses' comment to Teiresias' reaction: 'Quid rides?' which could mean both 'What are you laughing at?' and 'Why are you laughing?'. The seriousness of the epic underworld is subverted with this question, which clearly signals satire. It not only underlines the humour, but also connects to the very first of Horace's satires (1.1.69), where the same question had referred to the reader's reaction. Another hallmark of the genre, the phrase 'non satis est' ('it is not enough'),[47] appears in the next line. With this description of the Homeric hero as a man not satisfied with his lot we are

---

[47] Cf. the instances of 'satis' at *S.* 1.1.62 and 120; 1.2.52; 1.4.41, 54, and 116; 1.10.7 and 76; 2.3.127; 2.4.37 and 48; 2.5.4. See further the discussions in Freudenburg, *Walking Muse*, 110–14 and id., *Satires of Rome*, 15–16, 27; D. J. Coffta, *The Influence of Callimachean Aesthetics on the Satires and Odes of Horace* (Lewiston, NY: The Edwin Mellen Press, 2001), 21–2.

clearly brought down to the realm of Horatian satire, where the
target of derision is no more than a dissatisfied, greedy fool. In
commenting on this satire, Oesterlen has claimed that the deviation
from the Homeric intertext, and so the satire proper, begin in verse
10, where Teiresias gives concrete examples of appropriate presents to
rich and childless old men.[48] It is difficult to agree with Oesterlen's
contention, because of the early reference to Teiresias' laughter and
the genre-signalling phrases 'quid rides?' and 'non satis est'. Rather,
I would say that the lowering, the humour, and the satire break loose
in the third verse, and are already foreshadowed in the second.

This pattern of first mimicking an ascent in tone and imagery, as if
entering the world of the *Odyssey*, and then plunging the depths of
sordid but comic cynicism, is repeated several times throughout the
satire. So in vv. 5–6 Ulysses addresses the seer 'O nulli quidquam
mentite' ('o, you who have never lied to anyone'), and refers to his
prophesy that Ulysses will return to Ithaca destitute—both points
that are allusions to passages in the *Odyssey*.[49] From this high note
Ulysses is brought down with the slightly off-key word choice in
apotheca ('cellar', 7) of the empty cupboard, and completely humiliated with his next utterance that neither high birth nor *virtus* ('manly
virtue') are any good without money. It has been noticed that Horace
is making fun of Ulysses' role as the Stoic hero with his patient
heart,[50] but in fact the satirist goes further, attacking the hallowed
concept of *virtus*, another central element in Stoicism.[51] The squalor
of Ulysses' cynical statement is rubbed in as Teiresias, among the
concrete advice on how to court rich men, describes the potential
giver as an inversion of the noble man: 'quamvis periurus erit, sine
gente, cruentus | sanguine fraterno, fugitivus' ('even if he is a per-
jurer, lowborn, an escaped convict stained with his own brother's
blood'), 15–16. Nevertheless, this immoral man must be fawned
upon, and Ulysses the *captator* must not refuse to escort him. At
this point Ulysses suddenly remembers his old noble self, and protests, contrasting his role in Roman satire to that in Homer's epic:

---

[48] Oesterlen, *Humor bei Horaz*, 81–2.
[49] *Od.* 11.137 and 11.113–16 respectively.
[50] Kießling and Heinze, *Satiren*, 280.
[51] Cf. also the mocking use of *virtus* again in v. 33.

'Utne tegam spurco Damae latus? Haud ita Troiae
me gessi certans semper melioribus.'   (18–19)

What? Am I to be dirty Dama's servant? This wasn't the way I behaved at
Troy, where I always competed with better men.

This time the degradation of the Homeric hero, and of the thematic
level of the text, is promptly furnished by the interlocutor: 'then you
will be poor' (19–20). In the world of Rome not Greece, contemporary time not semi-mythical past, satire not epic, noble behaviour has
no place, and can only be regarded as a quixotic path to destitution.
The humour continues in Ulysses' answer, 'Fortem hoc animum
tolerare iubebo; | et quondam maiora tuli' ('I shall order my heart
to endure this. I have borne worse things in the past'), a perfect
parody in the sense that he speaks exactly what he had spoken in the
Odyssey, but with the reference of his words shifted down the scale of
respectability.[52] In the *Odyssey*, Ulysses' words had referred to his
endurance of the shameless behaviour he found in his house on
returning to Ithaca, i.e. the behaviour of the suitors and the maids
who slept with them. Here, in Horace's satire, his words refer to his
own shameless behaviour, which he plans after his return—in order
to win some rich legacies. He will have to endure the inconveniences
of legacy-hunting, even the humiliation of escorting filthy Dama
down the street. In this case, as often with allusions to high literature
in lowly contexts for comic effect, the heightening and the degradation are almost simultaneous, but it is the degradation that lingers
with the reader. The low situation conquers the high tone of the
allusion, and we get the feeling that someone or something grand has
been attacked and subdued with the weapon of satiric humour. Here,
the triumphant degradation is further enforced when Ulysses bluntly
expresses his greed, the satirical topic *avaritia*, in the explicit terms of
divitiae, *ruere*, and *aeris acervi* ('riches', 'shovel up', 'piles of cash').[53]
The hero then gives up on his own dignity, but he still defends that of
his wife, Penelope, when Teiresias suggests that she should be handed
over to the rich patron should he be a womanizer:

[52] *Od.* 20.18—Hor., *S.* 2.5.20–1. For this kind of parody, cf. G. Genette, *Palimpsestes: la littérature au second degré* (Paris: Seuil, 1982), 19–31.
[53] For the branching significance of *acervus* in Roman satire, see discussion in
Freudenburg, *Satires of Rome*, 183–8.

'Putasne
perduci poterit tam frugi tamque pudica,
quam nequiere proci recto depellere cursu?'   (76–8)

Do you think she can be brought to this, so proper and so chaste, she, who
could not be seduced from the right path by the suitors?

Again, the role of the epic Penelope is brought in for contrast with
her satiric role, and, as in the case of Ulysses himself, it is smashed
against the reality of satire at Rome. He need not worry, Teiresias
answers, that was because the suitors were young men not really
generous in love, but as soon as she gets a taste of the gain to be had
from the old womanizer, she will not be torn from him, like a dog
from a greasy hide (79–83). Stoic Ulysses had turned into a miser,
faithful Penelope is transformed into a bitch. These are the actors of
satire, yet simply attacking misers, legacy-hunters, and immoral
women would not have looked either aggressive or noble enough,
and so these petty villains have momentarily been dressed into the
larger-than-life costumes of epic heroes, only to be 'exposed' and
dragged into the dirt. To fit in at Rome Ulysses must be debased not
only morally, but also generically, as Teiresias explicitly tells him. He
must become the ridiculous slave of comedy, 'Davus sis comicus' ('Be
the "Davus" of comedy'), 91. His metamorphosis is complete when
he is told how to behave when he has reached his goal. As his name is
recited among Dama's heirs, he must wail for the loss of the legacy-
giver, 'Dama sodalis' ('Dama, my old friend!'), 101, and insist that he
will never again find anyone so brave and faithful. Bidding his heart
to be patient, the Ithacian has exchanged his brave comrades for
Dama, and endured all for the sake of money. The satirist's derision is
precise and mimics boldness, even imitating the classical satiric
principle of naming and shaming (*onomasti kōmōdein*), only the
name in question is from literature—'Ulixes'.

The other party of the conversation, Teiresias, is not as drastically
lowered as Ulysses, never having been depicted as particularly venerable in this satire. His character is cynical throughout the text.
However, it holds another kind of ironic twist, since he is the main
speaker, and so a kind of persona in this poem, as well as a *vates* (both
'poet' and 'prophet'), like Horace himself. His authority is thoroughly subverted when, in addition to giving vulgar advice, he

admits that what he prophesies will 'either come true or not' (vv. 59–60).[54] When the satire closes, the discredited seer is dragged back into the realm of the dead, which is also the realm of the Homeric underworld. The scandalous sequel 'Homer never told you' has been told, and the narrative dives back into the *Odyssey* at the same point where it began. Concretely, the dragging back of Teiresias is performed by a less than gentle Proserpina, somewhat reminiscent of the bossy, breadstick-armed wives in comedy.

It may also be noted that the whole satire is on how to court rich men in order to win their favour, a topic dangerously close to home in Horace's case. Just as he has ridiculed potential competitors for his role as Maecenas' 'private poet' in 1.9, here we see the favourite parasite[55] disgracing fellow parasites. Humour hoists them, and shoots them down, which makes the impression of fearless attack and candid boldness, as well as performing the important function of obscuring their likeness to the satirist himself.

Satire's metaphor: the spectacle of a falling curtain (2.8)

Before we leave the row of characters that are heightened for derisive attack, some observations should be made about the target of the last satire in the second book, 2.8, the so called *Cena Nasidieni*. Nasidienus, Horace's contribution to the satiric tradition of the 'vulgar host', is not as consistently enlarged as, for instance, Ulysses and Teiresias in 2.5, and a considerable part of the humour against him is simply abusive, not bothering to pretend that someone mighty is being attacked.[56] Such is the mockery of the dishes Nasidienus serves and of his fear of abuse from drunk guests. Nevertheless, in addition to

[54] Oesterlen, *Humor bei Horaz*, 83, notes the humour of the passage, and calls it 'eine köstliche Parodie der Seherkunst,' but does not develop the observation further. For the implications of such an admission by a speaker in satire, see my discussion below, Ch. 3, § 'Mock-consultations: peace-loving violence and an unreliable seer'.

[55] Cf. Suetonius' famous story of Augustus' exhortation to Horace, to exchange his place as parasite at Maecenas' table for a place at his royal board: 'Horatium nostrum a te cupio abducere. veniet ergo ab ista parasitica mensa ad hanc regiam et nos in epistulis scribendis adiuvabit' ('I want to steal our friend Horace from you. Let him come from that parasitic table of yours to this royal one, and help us with our correspondence'), *Vita Horatii*, 3. Cf. Fraenkel, *Horace*, 17–18.

[56] Rudd (*Satires of Horace*, 222) has correctly cautioned us against feeling sorry for Nasidienus. From parallel instances of rough treatment of essentially innocuous

attacks of this kind, there are also a few carefully placed strokes that suggest a pathetically grandiose setting, and thus offer occasions for feigned 'attacks from below'. The first such stroke is applied in the very first line, where Nasidienus is called *beatus*, a word implying both wealth and happiness.[57] This epithet, used by Horace's own persona, who, unlike his interlocutor Fundanius, does not speak many lines in the dialogue, places the poem in the symposium tradition,[58] and sets up expectations of a splendid dinner in a splendid house. These are soon confirmed by the information that the dinner smartly began at an early hour and that Fundanius enjoyed himself immensely (the latter statement is ironic, but the reader cannot yet be sure it is). Degradation and derision begin with Fundanius' report of the first items of food, all comically inept, and accompanied by tedious explanations from the host.[59]

The next mock-elevated reference is the description of the wine-serving slave, a dark-skinned boy named Hydaspes, whose affected gait is sarcastically likened to that of an Attic maiden in a religious procession: 'ut Attica virgo| cum sacris Cereris' ('like an Attic maiden with the holy vessels of Ceres'), 13–14. The pretentiousness of Nasidienus' arrangements is given outer form in the simile, and soon dashed to pieces with the words 'fuscus Hydaspes' ('swarthy Hydaspes'), at the end of the same line 14. The slave is the very opposite of the presumably pale-skinned stately maiden. His companion, the Greek slave serving Greek wine, is, on the contrary, comically close to the Attic virgin, for in addition to his origin there is also a joke on his femininity, as 'maris expers' in 'Alcon Chium, maris expers' (15) can be taken as a pun on *mas*, male, to

characters in Horace's satires, I would agree that Nasidienus is indeed the butt of 2.8, and that the abusive humour was there to speak to the less refined feelings of the audience.

[57] As witness the famous opening line of *Epod.* 2, 'Beatus ille qui procul negotiis...' ('Happy he, who far from troubles ...').

[58] Cf. Plato, *Symp.* 173–4; Lucian, *Symp.* 1. See further F. Muecke, *Horace: Satires II*, 229.

[59] Towards the end of the satire, Fundanius says that most of the food was spoiled by Nasidienus' boring descriptions: 'suavis res, si non causas narraret earum et/ naturas dominus' ('wonderful things, if only the host had not discoursed on their causes and natures'), 92–3.

Alcon ('emasculate', 'effeminate') and *mare*, sea, to the wine ('un-mixed with sea-water').[60]

After this, the other heightening passages come at about twenty lines' intervals. First, Vibidius is quoted as saying 'nos nisi damnose bibimus, moriemur inulti' ('if we don't drink him bankrupt, we shall die unavenged'), 34, which combines a suggestion of crude offen-siveness ('drink him bankrupt') with a high-styled motivation, liken-ing the tension between host and guests to a tragic or epic battle.[61] This is immediately followed by his asking for larger cups—a deg-radation to the banal level of drinking. Then comes an epic descrip-tion of Nasidienus' terrified reaction, 'vertere pallor | tum parochi faciem' ('at this, pallor spread over the host's face'), 35-6,[62] which is in turn punctured by the aggressively comic explanation that this is because he dreads drunk, freely abusing guests. Oesterlen well ob-serves that this passage exhibits a 'Mischung von Pathos und Komik'.[63] We can add more precisely that it is not a random mixture, but a roller-coaster of two high allusions immediately followed by degrading touches, which smash the allusions against the culinary context of the larger cups. All is arranged in a parallel pattern and condensed to four lines (34–7). Towards the end, in verse 93, the reference to solemn revenge is taken up by the information that the guests were indeed avenged, 'sic fugimus ulti' ('thus we fled avenged')—by not touching the dishes.

Symmetrically arranged between these two mentions of revenge is a mock-epic disaster that befalls the 'hero' Nasidienus, complete with the quasi-philosophical comments on this by the clownish guest Balatro. The grave catastrophe, the fall of a curtain, is described in elaborately heroic language, punctured by the unpoetic expression 'in patinam':

---

[60] A. E. Housman, 'Notes on Persius,' *CQ* 7 (1913), 28, argued that the meaning from *mas* is the only one intended, on the basis of the chiastic structure thus achieved ('fuscus Hydaspes ... Alcon ... maris expers'), but a pun seems more in line with Horace's practice, and with the ambiguous placement of the epithet. See also E. Gowers, *The Loaded Table: Representations of Food in Roman Literature* (Oxford: Oxford University Press , 1993b); Muecke, *Horace: Satires II*, ad loc.

[61] Cf. Aesch. *Ag.* 1234; Virg., *A.* 2.670, 4.659.

[62] Cf. Hom. *Il.* 7.479, *Od.* 11.43; see further F. Muecke, *Horace: Satires II*, ad loc.

[63] Oesterlen, *Humor bei Horaz*, 98.

Interea suspensa gravis aulaea ruinas
in patinam fecere, trahentia pulveris atri
quantum non Aquilo Campanis excitat agris   (54–6)

In the mean time the tapestry suspended above fell heavily onto the dish,
trailing more black dust than the North Wind raises on the fields of
Campania

This may further be read as a meta-literary comment on the effect of
heightening the object of satire and then dashing it down. Just as the
tapestry is hung high ('suspensa') before its heavy fall ('gravis ... ruinas'), so is Nasidienus here, and throughout the poem. The hanging
up is repeated in the description of Balatro's mockery, when he is said
to hang everything from his nose ('*suspendens* omnia naso', 64). To
'hang something from one's nose' in the sense of 'make fun of something' seems to be a comic metaphor invented by Horace, used by him
also at 1.6.5.[64] It should be noted that this mockery of the host,
together with Varius', another guest's, explicit laughter just before, is
exactly parallel to the derisive direction of this satire as a whole. The
punchline of Balatro's speech, his likening of Nasidienus' trouble to
the character-proving difficulties of a general (73–4), is placed approximately twenty lines after the epic fall of the curtain that first
provoked this harangue, and connects to that passage through the
military-heroic imagery. When Nasidienus answers his mocker with
praise, completely swallowing his irony (75–6), he is again falling
heavily not only from Balatro's nose, but from the author's.

In conclusion, after the guests have fled without eating, and so
avenged themselves, Horace's literary arch-enemy, Canidia, is evoked
in the last line, as Nasidienus' dishes are said to have seemed foul to
his guests, as if they had been blown upon by Canidia's poisonous
breath:

quem nos sic fugimus ulti
ut nihil omnino gustaremus, velut illis
Canidia afflasset peior serpentibus Afris.   (2.8.93–5)

---

[64] See the excellent discussion of this Horatian metaphor in G. Bernardi Perini,
'Suspendere naso. Storia di una metafora,' *Atti e Memorie dell'Accademia Patavina di
Scienze, Lettere ed Arti*. Classe di Scienze morali, Lettere ed Arti 79, parte III (1966–7),
233–64. Bernardi Perini argues persuasively that the similar expression in Persius
1.118 is not, in fact, identical.

we fled him, taking our revenge by not tasting any of the dishes at all, as though Canidia, worse than African snakes, had breathed over them.

The last verse (95), which is simultaneously the last in Horace's satiric opus, is very rich in allusion,[65] but I would particularly like to underline two points here. First, there is a connection between Canidia and Nasidienus: Nasidienus' spoiling of the dishes with his explanations is paralleled by Canidia's spoiling of them with her breath. This suggests that they are somehow in collusion, approaching Maecenas, the guest of honour (cf. 16–17). Horace will not accept this, and takes his revenge with aggressive humour, here as well as in 1.8, where Canidia first intruded upon Maecenas' garden. Secondly, Canidia is again larger than life, just as she initially was in the Priapus satire—she has more poison in her breath than the snakes of Africa. She is unflatteringly described, but nevertheless pictured as very powerful, and so 'hung up' for derision, thus closing the line of derisive hoistings and degradations that began with Nasidienus *beatus* in the first verse.

The rhythm of humorous raising and falling has helped to structure the poem. Yet in this last line we also perceive some of the danger involved in this strategy, for as the satirist blows up his target, some of the resulting size may linger ambivalently in the reader's mind. This time, Canidia's poisonous power is not as thoroughly degraded as it was in 1.8. Although she has been shown as foul, and although it is explicitly said that the other side, the mockers, *did* get their revenge, it is not triumphant. The mockers could only get it by fleeing, just as Horace flees satire after this line, and this, after all, is a questionable revenge.

Lowered subject

In turning from the objects of attack to the speaking subject in Horace's satires one enters a vast topic, for the description, or, on the perspective adopted here, the *creation* of a poetic self is a major preoccupation in the *Sermones*. The profile of 'Horace', i.e. his

---

[65] See the discussions in Freudenburg, *Walking Muse*, 235; and Oliensis, 'Canidia, Canicula, and Horace's *Epodes*', 109–10, and *ead.* 'Horace, Nasidienus', 100–1.

persona, emerges complete with a biography, a physical appearance, a moral and artistic character.[66] He is a charming personality, coming from humble beginnings, but with a great talent and wisdom harboured within his short, fragile body. This image is shaped throughout the satires of Book 1 and rerun, at another level, through most of the satires in Book 2, with the notable exception of 2.5, from which 'Horace' is absent. Horace's persona is full of potentially comic inconsistencies, such as the great within the small and the diamond suddenly found in the mud, but these are not uniformly employed. Sometimes the small and lowly side is stressed, and the explicit insistence on the great poetic gift left aside for a while, sometimes the contrast is played in the other direction, and what was introduced as modest turns out to be glorious in essence, with an effect of gentler humour.

Those satires where the description of the persona and/or his satiric art are central, such as 1.4–1.6, 1.10, and 2.1, are the ones to display the Aristotelian ideal of 'the liberal jest' most insistently. The recognition of the Aristotelian influence on both the theory and practice of Horace's humour is now more than a century old and sufficiently well established.[67] There is, however, also another, less decorous and more aggressive approach to humour in Horace's *Satires*—humour in the tradition of the Cynics. This has only recently been analysed, first in Freudenburg's study of 1993. The satirist's complex and latently incongruous persona is excellently adapted for deployment in both approaches, and I would like to suggest that it is sketched in slightly different ways in the softer, self-centred satires and in the fiercer ones, where derision of a specific object is uppermost, such as 1.2, 1.3, 1.7–1.9, and 2.8. The portrait of

---

[66] This interest, traditionally taken as 'biographical', but in recent times more and more often as the conscious shaping of a persona, has been much discussed. Fraenkel, *Horace*, and D. R. Shackleton Bailey, *Profile of Horace* (Cambridge, Mass.: Harvard University Press , 1982), may be mentioned as examples of the traditional approach; J. E. G. Zetzel, 'Horace's Liber Sermonum: the Structure of Ambiguity,' *Arethusa* 13 (1980), 59–77; and Freudenburg, *Walking Muse*, as examples of the more formalistic (New-Critical) approach; Gowers, 'Fragments of Autobiography', is to my mind the most convincing attempt at synthesis between the two positions. Cf. also 'A note on author and persona' in the Introduction above.

[67] First suggested in Hendrickson, 'Horace 1.4'; thoroughly treated by A. Parker, 'Comic Theory in the Satires'. Cf. the exposition in the survey of critical literature above, under 'Developing meta-literary comments in the satires'.

'Horace' spans over different kinds of satires, building up cumulatively as the audience makes its way through the work. Still, I would like to treat the speaking subject under two headings, that of object-oriented attack and that of persona-oriented humour. Under 'Object-oriented humour', I will discuss how the persona is lowered for efficient use in the satires with aggressive humour, below, under 'Humour directed at the persona',[68] I will analyse the persona's role in the milder, more decorous humour.

It is as if Horace were polarizing the contradictory aspects of the satirist's persona recognized by Kernan—the persona's bluntness versus his sophisticated craftsmanship as poet and rhetorician[69]—and stressing one or the other pole in alternating satires. The 'tension' that Kernan speaks of is still present, but Horace's spreading dilutes it and makes it less visible than it is in the other satirists.

The voice from the groin (1.2)

In 1.2, the boldest of Horace's satires in diction and sexual subject matter, the direct object of derision, *moechi* ('adulterers'), are slyly heightened in the text by association with their mistresses' high birth, with (their own) big money, and with occasional references to real contemporaries of high position. The persona, by contrast, is drawn as a simple and honest man, happy with 'the wares of the second class', 47, (i.e. freedwomen), and not afraid of calling a spade a spade, or even a bloody shovel.[70] He is close to what Douglas Muecke, in his study of literary irony, has termed the 'ingénu' commentator in ironic works.[71] Such a commentator is too simple to understand clever lies and sophisticated depravation, and his baffled misunderstanding of these vices allows the author to ridicule them in an indirect and elegant manner. Although the author has another intellectual level, he is of the same moral opinion as his naïve speaker.

In *Satire* 1.2, the persona's ingénu-like character is particularly cast in relief at the end, where a description of what the speaker does *not*

---

[68] Ch. 2.   [69] Kernan, *Cankered Muse*, 14–30.
[70] Cf. 1.2.35–6; 68–71; 116–18; 127. See the discussion in Henderson, 'Satire Writes Woman'.
[71] D. C. Muecke, *Compass of Irony*, 91–2.

have to fear (since he does not get involved with matrons) glides into a very real sketch with him at the centre:

> nec vereor ne dum futuo vir rure recurrat,
> ianua frangatur, latret canis, undique magno
> pulsa domus strepitu resonet, vepallida lecto
> desiliat mulier, miseram se conscia clamet,
> cruribus haec metuat, doti deprensa, egomet mi,
> discincta tunica fugiendum sit, pede nudo,
> ne nummi pereant aut puga aut denique fama.
> deprendi miserum est; Fabio vel iudice vincam.   (1.2.127–34)

and I'm not afraid that while I'm fucking, her husband should come rushing home from the country, the door be broken down, the dog bark, and the house, assaulted, resound on all sides with a tremendous din. The woman would jump out of bed, pale as death, and her helpful maid would loudly declare herself wretched. The maid would fear for her legs, the lady-caught-in-the-act for her dowry, and I for my own person. I have to flee barefoot, with my tunic undone, in order to save my money, my arse, or at least my good name. It is wretched to be caught—I could prove that even if Fabius were the judge!

The scene is cut off with the confident reference to Fabius, the wordy Stoic who had already appeared in satire 1 (v. 14). Before that, however, the whole scene has been in the first person. The negation at the beginning of the passage is forgotten as the vivid scene develops with one staccato clause after the other, and at its end the non-adventures of the 'speaking I' certainly seem real enough. This scene is the last of three scenes showing the punishments eventually bound to befall the adulterer (the other two being 41–6 and 65–7).[72] It is all the more remarkable that the persona himself is placed as the protagonist of this situation, so important both thematically and structurally.

As Michael Brown notes in his commentary on the first book of the *Sermones*, the irony of the final scene in 1.2 is partly at the persona's expense, and constitutes a 'disarming and engaging touch to conclude the poem'. Brown is also quite right in saying that the expression 'deprendi miserum est' followed by the depiction of the poet himself escaping after being caught in the act, 'is tantamount to

---

[72] Oesterlen, *Humor bei Horaz*, 19.

an *experto crede*.[73] This is what I would like to develop: the humour of this scene serves to lower the persona, so as to disarm any criticism along the lines that it is unfair to attack the ridiculous sin of adultery from a secure, proud position of a detached poet. His knowledge of 'real life' gives him the moral right to preach, the caricature of himself at the end grants him the authority to ridicule others, and protection against ridicule of him. Self-irony here becomes a protection against irony from the outside.[74] The image is constructed to lower the persona in just the right measure: note, first, that he is the only one of the adulterers to get off with no more than a fright. Secondly, unlike the other two descriptions of punishment, this one contains a pronounced element of comedy in the chaos of sound and movement: the broken door, the barking dog, the presence of a helpful, but at this moment terrified maid.[75] Thirdly, there is the appearance of the delinquent himself, expressed in a near-golden line: 'discincta tunica fugiendum sit, pede nudo' ('I have to flee barefoot, with my tunic undone'), 132. This verse points forward to the nameless caricature in 1.3, where that personage's sloppy dress is described as 'toga diffluit et male laxus | in pede calceus haeret' ('his toga is loose, and his oversized shoes barely stay on his feet'), 1.3.31–2.[76] There, we are told that although this man dresses badly, he has a golden heart and a great talent beneath his uncouth body, and something similar may be suggested in 1.2. Horace keeps returning to this portrait of his persona hobbling along barefoot, with his clothes fitting badly, because it is an important image: that of the great genius with his great soul hidden underneath loose rags. This image lowers the persona to just the right position. He is low enough to be an ordinary fellow, even a little funny, 'in the know' about the sins he criticizes in others—and yet his ridiculousness is carefully limited to the surface, while his essence remains impeccable. He is, in fact, all the more sympathetic because of his faulty exterior.

[73] Brown, *Horace: Satires I*, 114.

[74] D. C. Muecke (*Compass of Irony*, 31) has correctly pointed out that the only true protection against all irony would be absolute circumspection, 'a shield no man can lift.' Yet self-irony is a good substitution, and Horace knows how to use it.

[75] In this connection Kießling and Heinze, *Satiren*, 44, note that *crurifragium* is referred to as a slave punishment at Plaut. *Poen.* 886; Brown, *Horace: Satires I*, 114, adds *Truc.* 638.

[76] Cf. also *S.* 1.3.63–6. See my discussion of these passages below, Ch. 2, 192–8.

The use of the forms of comedy in the scene at 1.2.127–34 is well calculated, for in that genre, the fleeing lover is not only a victim, but ultimately the comic hero, with whom the sympathy of the audience lies.[77] True, 'Horace' did get himself into an unpleasant, even laughable situation, but, like the *adulescens* of comedy, he managed to save all the important things he was at pains to save: his money, his backside, and his good name (133). Most importantly, he has learned from his bitter experience, turned his interest to freedwomen, and is now in a position to mock those who are similarly mistreated, yet never learn.

By giving up the outward dignity of his persona, Horace has endeared him to his audience. He has strengthened his moral authority by making him a reformed sinner rather than a saint, and lowered him to the position from which it is all the more effective to fire ridicule at his real targets. The final line is exactly such ridicule: from his lowly experience 'Horace' knows that it is miserable to be caught *in flagranti*, and it only remains to tear down Fabius from his high horses. Fabius is elevated by just one word here, *iudice*, because he is invited to sit in judgement when 'Horace' proves his case— simply the *mot juste*, but also with connotations of grandness, and of the Stoic's implicit claim to be the judge of the whole world. The speaker is sure of his cause. He will prove that even the Stoic sage would be miserable in this situation, despite the Stoic maxim that the *sapiens* never feels pain.[78] Thus the last verse mocks not only Fabius, but all Stoics, and generally people willing to play judges, and this can be done because the satirist's persona has just been brought down so low. 'Horace' is the clown who dares laugh at the judges of this world, and he makes us forget that a satirist is actually the most presumptuous moral judge of all.

Before leaving this satire, I would like to look briefly at another passage, where not the actual persona, but his opinions—the

---

[77] I would thus not agree with the interpretation of this passage in Freudenburg's sophisticated reading of the whole of 1.2 as a discussion of poetics. Freudenburg (*Walking Muse*, 197) regards the hectic hobbling of the barefoot adulterer as an image of the bad, limping verse of Horace's incompetent colleagues, but I cannot see how a scene beginning and ending with the first person singular (vv. 127, 134), and with the pronouns 'egomet mi' in between (131), can be separated from the speaking persona.

[78] See Kießling and Heinze, *Satiren*, 44.

message of the satire—are degraded to the level of a speaking penis, 68–71. The *mutto* speaks what 'Horace' might have spoken, and apart from enlivening the text at this point, the humour of this unexpected prosopopoeia degrades the accusing voice and makes it emanate literally from underneath.[79] We have just heard a sarcastic account of the humiliations of a certain Villius, who is infatuated with Sulla's daughter Fausta, or rather with her glorious lineage, when the elaborate speech situation is introduced. What if, says Horace, Villius' *mind* would speak to *Villius himself*, who had seen so many indignities, in the words of his *prick*? When the lines are then presented in direct speech, there can be no doubt that the words truly belong to Villius' member:

> 'quid vis tibi? numquid ego a te
> magno prognatum deposco consule cunnum
> velatumque stola, mea cum conferbuit ira?'   (69–71)

'What are you up to? Do I ask you for a cunt descended from a great consul, and draped in a matron's robe, when my fury flares up?'

The utterance is direct, obscene, and comic. As can be expected from the point of view of the *mutto*, any kind of woman is reduced to a *cunnus*, which reveals, in a vulgar manner, the essential exchangeability of all women, a point that the satirist insists on throughout the satire. The lines can be said to have two targets: proud ladies and the fool Villius. The ladies are hoisted by the stately words and rhythm at the beginning of v. 70, and shot down by the last word of that line, sarcastically recalling 'consule' through the c-alliteration. Villius, after listening to the words of his member, is at a loss for an answer (72). The *mutto* may be lowly and undignified, but his essence is morally upright, for it is equivalent to that of Nature herself, whose high authority is brought in immediately afterwards, in 73–9. On a small scale, the transformation of the satiric voice in this passage is parallel to the lowering of the persona at the end of the whole satire, and makes use of the same pattern, that of mockery from below.

[79] The commentators suggest that this striking use could have been inspired by a personification of the organ in Lucilius, (307 M), but there it does not speak.

Passing down the megaphone—the role of secondary personae

Something should be said about the lowering of the persona/perso-
nae in the second book. It is only in 2.1 and 2.6 that 'Horace' himself
appears as a primary persona, i.e. both as the protagonist and the
narrator. In 2.5, the dialogue between Ulysses and Teiresias, he makes
no appearance at all, and in the rest of the book he plays the
secondary role of part-interlocutor, part-object. The latter may be
called 'subdued persona', for the very name 'Horace' still carries some
of the real persona's authority, even though the roles be reversed. In
the satires where 'Horace' plays second fiddle, the lead is always
granted to personages who are lower on the social/philosophical/
aesthetical ladder than the satirist. These I call 'secondary personae'.[80]
Although they have the traditional space and limelight of the main
first-person speaker, they function in dialogue with 'Horace', who
retains much of his importance, and of the claim to being the
persona *par excellence*.

For the satires with a secondary persona (2.2–2.4; 2.7 and 2.8),
Oliensis has correctly observed that the satiric megaphone is passed
downwards on the social scale.[81] She has reasonably argued that this
is the result of the real Horace's journey upwards in society, and from
being a new arrival to Maecenas' circle (with preceding outsidership
still fresh in his memory) to being a full-blown, perhaps even privileged member of it. Except for Fundanius in 2.8, the low status of all
these secondary personae is spelled out in the text.[82]

As often, there is also an aesthetical reason paired with the socio-
psychological one: the device of using a secondary persona with the
satirist as interlocutor destabilizes the moral perspective by upsetting
the stereotype of the righteous, truth-telling I-figure, and so makes
for a more ironical, open satire. In re-running satirically the material
of his own first book of *Sermones* in such satires as 2.3 and 2.7, where
dubious secondary personae voice the sentiments of the satirist of
Book 1, Horace developed his verbal art, making it multifaceted, and
morally more complex. But in doing this, he also journeyed to the
end of satire. Without the skeleton of object-oriented derision, with

---

[80] See above, section 'A note on author and persona' in the Introduction.
[81] Oliensis, 'Horace, Nasidienus', 96.
[82] 2.2.1–3; 2.3.18–26; 2.4.1 and 11, cf. vv. 88–95; 2.7.1–4.

at least fairly firm moral accents, satire could not stand, and he left it there. Perhaps it is no coincidence that 2.5, the poem that *opens the second half of the second book,* has no persona at all. Furthermore, its main speaker, the traditionally trustworthy seer Teiresias, placed in the traditionally authoritative speech context of a literary under-world, is made to say the comically confusing lines about his proph-ecies being either true or false (2.5.59–60)—lines neatly placed at the *opening of the second half of this poem.*[83] We have come a long way from 'ridentem dicere verum' in Horace's first satire.

Finally, the hungry flight from the table of the less-than-philosophical *convivae,* performed by the secondary persona and his friends at the end of the last satire (2.8.93–5) embodies, but inverts, the noble Epicurean metaphor at the conclusion of the first satire. There, in the first satire, the satirist had claimed the metaphor for himself by connecting it to the genre's name, *satura*:

> qui se vixisse beatum
> dicat et exacto contentus tempore vita
> cedat, *uti conviva satur*   (1.1.117–19)

who would say he has lived a happy life, and when his time was up would leave life contentedly, as a dinner guest that has had his fill[84]

Now, in the last satire, there are again dinner guests leaving the table, but their manner is the opposite of Epicurean bliss. They flee, so far

---

[83] See below, Ch. 3, § 'Mock-consultations: peace-loving violence and an unreli-able seer'.

[84] As commentators note, the image is borrowed from Lucretius 3.935–9, 'nam si grata fuit tibi vita anteacta priorque| ... |cur non ut plenus vitae conviva recedis| aequo animoque capis securam, stulte, quietem?' ('For if you liked the life you have lived, now past, ... why don't you, you fool, retire like a dinner-guest sated with life, and calmly enjoy a secure peace?'), and 3.959–60: 'et nec opinanti mors ad caput adstitit ante| quam satur ac plenus possis discedere rerum' ('and unexpectedly, death stands by your head| before you can retire, stuffed and sated with everything?'). While Horace thus has a Lucretian precedent for 'satur' as well as the rest of the image, his emphatic inclusion of the adjective (in the middle of the verse, before hephthemi-meres) is certainly also meant to recall his genre, 'satura'. There may also be influence from Bion (fr. 68 Kindstrand); see further Kießling and Heinze, *Satiren,* ad loc. For a short treatment of Epicurean food symbolism in the *Sermones,* in this case and others, see J. Glazewski, *'Plenus Vitae Conviva*: a Lucretian Concept in Horace's *Satires,' CB* 47 (1971), 85–8.

from being satisfied or sated (*satur*), that they have actually not even tasted the food, as if it were poisonous:

> 'nos sic fugimus ulti
> ut nihil omnino gustaremus, velut illis
> Canidia afflasset peior serpentibus Afris.'   (2.8.93–5)

'we fled him, take our revenge by not tasting any of the dishes at all, as though Canidia, worse than African snakes, had breathed over them.'

Likewise, Horace now fled from the table of *satura* to other genres with more room for his growing complexity.

PERSIUS

Swollen objects

Persius' satire begins with a humorous attack on the decadent and imitative poetasters of his day, connected to the height of Parnassus through their pretensions. In the second part of the *Prologue* (vv. 8–14) these poets are revealed to write out of a wish to satisfy their greed for food and money:

> quis expedivit psittaco suum 'chaere'
> picamque docuit nostra verba conari?
> magister artis ingenique largitor
> venter, negatas artifex sequi voces.
> quod si dolosi spes refulserit nummi,
> corvos poetas et poetridas picas
> cantare credas Pegaseium nectar.   (*Prol.* 8–14)

Who coached the parrot to say his 'Bonjour!', and who taught the magpie to have a go at human words? Teacher of art, generous bestower of talent— Belly, you master at imitating words denied by nature. If there should be a gleam of hope for deceitful cash, then you'd think that the crow poets and magpie poetesses were singing Pegasean nectar.

Such poets, Persius tells us, are nothing but trained birds singing for rewards, but still laying claim to the nectar of heavenly song inspired by Pegasus' fount. The satirist smashes the haughty pride of their pretensions to Parnassus and Hippocrene against the lowering belly, and the subhuman images of crows and magpies in which these Graecizing Roman poets are clad. The typical humorous device of mocking from below functions as a business card to introduce satire.

Yet as we move from the *Prologue* into the body of Persius' satire, the imagery of elevation is almost everywhere replaced by *inflation*, seen in the absurdly big men, fat bodies, and big poems that fill these satires.[85] Persius, however, also has a disquieting tendency to make sudden reversals and apply the same images to his friends or to himself. So it is with size, paleness, and even with laughter. Although we learn that laughter is Persius' most treasured possession (1.122–3), it is occasionally granted to his enemies, to whom the satirist's moral prescriptions are said to seem ridiculous (3.86–7; 5.189–99). Sometimes Persius lets go of the heightening/inflating device and attacks his target head on, but this is not the rule.

Even when he does use his version of humorous heightening, Persius poses other problems than Horace and Juvenal in his object-oriented humour. Most important, there is rather less of it. While the old, prejudiced notion that Persius completely lacks humour is certainly false (as I hope to show below), it may well be claimed that he is the most earnest of the Roman satirists. He often makes non-humorous statements, e.g. in the form of bursts of moral preaching and in the form of angry exclamations, branding immoral behaviour. In this latter form, what could have been sarcasm is stripped of its hilarity: it is so firmly tied to the negative meaning, and the innate ambivalence of humour so tightly muted, that what is left can hardly be called humour. There is rarely any doubt about what ideological position Persius wishes to propound, or which side he supports. This gains his moral message greater clarity, but it reduces the comic aspect of his poems. In Horace and Juvenal, humour rejoices in its own ambivalence, and one of the most delightful aspects of Roman satire is its oscillation between pathos and fun. Since I will concentrate on the humorous devices in Persius' satire, the fact that these devices are *rarer* in Persius than in Horace and Juvenal will necessarily be obscured in my discussion.

---

[85] For Persius' metaphor of swelling and fatness, see K. Reckford, 'Studies in Persius,' *Hermes* 90 (1962), 476–504; p. 490; Henderson, *Writing down Rome*, 243.

Inflating the bodies of men and poems (P. 1)

The swollen bodies of men and poems are interchangeably pictured as suffering from an illness with a lethal outcome already within sight. With the change of imagery used of the objects—as compared to Horace, and to Persius' own *Prologue*—there is also a change in the view of the satirist's role. Adopting for his uses the metaphor of medicine sweetened with honey, Horace had changed his role from moral doctor to moral teacher (Hor. *S.* 1.1.25–6),[86] but with Persius we are certainly back to the doctor, even a surgeon. He will scrape people's morals with a scalpel (5.15), will tear out prejudices from their lungs (5.92), and clean their ears with an acrid decoction (1.125, cf. 5.86). Some cases are beyond help, and these he will explode, or sink in deep water (3.94–106; 3.33–4)—a grim version of the satirist's metaphorical lowering.

The imagery of 'great' poems and poetasters is particularly elaborated in satires 1 and 5. The first satire, after beginning with a short reference to its own genre by way of a quotation from Lucilius, immediately turns to making fun of the contemporary poet Attius Labeo. For this occasion, the mocking comparison between Labeo and the satirist himself is heightened with the incongruous reminiscence of Polydamas and the Trojan women, whose censure Hector feared in *Il.* 22.99–107. 'Should I fear,' Persius says, 'that Polydamas and the Trojan women may prefer Labeo to me?' This high level of association is crashed with the axe-blow of *nugae* ('rubbish!') (1.5). In the next bout of attack, the images become more physical, and they are to stay that way. We learn that everybody nowadays writes something 'grand', which his lungs will wheeze out in performing, inflated to the point of bursting (1.14). Bramble has analysed the following description of a recital, 1.15–21, in rich detail (Bramble, *Persius and the Programmatic Satire* 73–9), showing the exchangeability of corrupted morals, corrupted style, and corrupted physique in Persius' universe.[87] The images of greatness are interspersed with

---

[86] Cf. above, Introduction, p. 28 and n. 66.

[87] For the ancient ideas on the exchangeability of literary style and life, perhaps most poignantly expressed in Seneca's *Ep.* 114, see C. S. Dessen, *Iunctura Callidus Acri: a Study of Persius' Satires* (Urbana: University of Illinois Press, 1968), 23–4, and Bramble, *Persius and the Programmatic Satire*, 23–5.

derisive references to debility, physical and moral. So, the reciter is dressed in his finest, and hoisted onto a high platform, 'sede leges celsa' ('you will read from a high platform'), 17, only to be humiliated with the disgusting, but nevertheless comic images of his 'flossing' recital and ejaculating eye:

> sede leges celsa, liquido cum plasmate guttur
> mobile conlueris, patranti fractus ocello.   (1.17–18)

You'll read from a high platform, having rinsed your supple throat with a liquid trill, languishing with your ejaculating eye.

The listeners' bodies are enormous, and they are called 'Tituses', the flower of the aristocracy, but sandwiched between these two grand words ('enormous' and 'Tituses') is their revealing shaking with excitement: 'ingentis *trepidare* Titos' (20). The only greatness left in the new Romans is their full, bulging flesh, beneath which there is only effeminacy and slackness. The ageing, sickly poets actually look forward to the bursting of their livers, swelling with the yeast of inspiration, and the birth of a fig-tree (23–4)—again a traditional sexual symbol (Bramble, *Persius and the Programmatic Satire* 91–9). The satirist will help to burst their inflated natures, yet the result will not be a fig-tree, but dead bodies.

At 1.30–1 the effeminate sons of Romulus are displayed as taking a mild interest in 'divinest Poesy' between their drinks, themselves full of food, 'saturi'—a word with a rather negative sound to it in Persius. When we next encounter the well-born Romans, they are 'crudi ... proceres' ('dyspeptic nobles'), 51–2. Just as the great Tituses were revealed with the one word 'trepidare' ('shake'), so these nobles are shot down with the qualification of them as 'crudi', dyspeptic.

To the vain gentleman who 'likes to hear the truth' about himself 'Persius' answers with a merciless description of his outer appearance (56–7), applying the metaphorical to the concrete in answering about his body to a question about his moral character. This is a classical comic device, described in Cicero's *De Oratore* 2 (250, cf. 253–5). The roller-coaster journey of up and down continues at 1.61 as the 'great' poets are lifted with the appeal 'o patricius sanguis' ('O patrician blood') and taken down with the admonition to face the grimace behind their backs (62). They are then ironically described as receiving inspiration (68–9), only to be shown as unable to describe a rural scene in humble style (70–5). At 87 the lowering attack is presented in maximally concise form: 'an, Romule, ceves?' ('Are you waving your ass, Romulus?'). The target of the satire is called 'Romulus', no longer only his descendant as at v. 31, but the highest of the high himself, the great ancestor of all Romans. His behaviour, in contrast, is the lowest of the low: he is said to be waving his butt as a male prostitute.[88]

'Podgy exploding' and other horror humour (P. 3)

Elsewhere, when morals, not letters, are under direct attack, telling images of vicious characters in the shape of fat men pop up time and again. Two particularly lucid examples of such villains, both killed off by the satirist, appear in P. 3, at vv. 32–4 and 94–106 respectively. Into the first of these portraits Persius glides gradually, shifting from an appeal to an entity addressed as 'you', which actually seems to be one part of his own self.[89] To this 'you' the satirist had said: 'I know you, even under your skin' (3.30), and then mentioned the example of Natta, a villain from Horace's satires (3.31; Hor. *S.* 1.6.124). When he turns to his concrete picture of a villain, he does indeed bore under the skin:

> sed stupet hic vitio et fibris increvit opimum
> pingue, caret culpa, nescit quid perdat, et alto
> demersus summa rursus non bullit in unda.   (32–4)

but he is numb with vice, prime fat has overgrown his heart, he's beyond blame, because ignorant of his loss. Deep submerged, he sends no more bubbles to the surface.

Under the skin there is vice, fat, and lack of self-knowledge, all apparently depending on each other and, as it were, signifying the same state of perdition. Metonymically, the fat is said to have grown

---

[88] Yet it must be noted that Persius occasionally uses much the same imagery of size and swelling for entities he seems to admire, and which he definitely does not wish to deride. Thus such metaphors are used of Virgil's *Aeneid* at P. 1.96–7, and of Old Comedy in 1.123–5. It would seem, then, that there are different kinds of greatness, one false deserving puncture, and one worthy, deserving admiration. With the latter kind, however, we have reached the limit of humour, and it only remains to ask (nastily, and parenthetically) whether Persius was not perhaps himself somewhat affected by that disease of bombast which so plagued his age, and which he was so eager to mock.

[89] On the actors of this satire, see below, Ch. 2, 'Persius' splitting self'.

deeply into the internal organs (*fibris*). Almost as if by his own weight, but actually through the satirist's device of shooting down the object of mockery, this inflated character sinks down deep and breathes the air no more.

In the more developed second vignette, Persius' miniature version of the satiric *cena*,[90] the object is exploded rather than sunk down. The first symptoms in this eater are a trepidation in the chest and bad breath (88–9), but ignoring the doctor's advice he continues walking the road to perdition, i.e. drinking and eating before his bath, stuffing himself with vice. His gradual inflation is menacingly worded in his interlocutor's warning, 'surgit tacite tibi lutea pellis' ('your skin is yellow and quietly swelling'), 95.

To this the villain answers with a threat to bury his adviser as he previously buried his tutor (96–7)—lines that constitute a twisted allusion to Horace's encounter with the bore, S. 1.9.26–8.[91] There the bore had only said that he had buried his relatives, and the threat to 'Horace' was at most implicit, perhaps non-existent; 'nunc ego resto' ('now I'm the only one left') is 'Horace' 's own ironic clipping. In Persius, the relatives are replaced by a tutor, the paradigmatic giver of advice, and the threat is unambiguously spelled out in the villain's line, 'iam pridem hunc sepeli; tu restas' ('I buried him long ago, now you're the only one left'), 97. A deeper difference is that Horace's antagonist had been magnified by being clad in epic images of martial attack, while Persius' man is *physically* swelling with vice. The touch of his threat to his adviser is significant, for as in Horace, it gives the satirist's ultimate blow of derision the tinge of a counter-attack rather than an unprovoked attack. Yet in Persius the aggressiveness of the villain is considerably smaller, and even his refusal to listen to good advice ultimately falls back on himself, which makes his death at the satirist's hands seem rather grimmer humour than that in Horace's bore satire.

---

[90] For the theme of the satirical dinner, see L. R. Shero, 'The Cena in Roman Satire', *CP* 18 (1923), 126–43; G. Highet, *The Anatomy of Satire* (Princeton: Princeton University Press, 1962), 221–4; W. Pabst, 'Zur Satire vom lächerlichen Mahl', *A&A* 32 (1986), 136–58; Rudd, *Themes*, 129, 137, 157–60; Gowers, *Loaded Table*, 109–219. More specifically, the image of a hidden illness (as a symbol of moral decadence), revealed at meal-time, alludes to Horace's *Ep.* 1.16.21–3; see discussion in Reckford, 'Reading the Sick Body', 347.

[91] On this allusion, see Kißel, *Persius*, 474.

After the Horatian allusion, Persius' sinner, still growing in size from another meal ('turgidus hic epulis', 98), goes to the baths, and the end is near, as the return of bad breath signals (99). Then follow the horrid lines describing his death:

> sed tremor inter vina subit calidumque trientem
> excutit e manibus, dentes crepuere retecti,
> uncta cadunt laxis tunc pulmentaria labris.   (100–2)

But as he's drinking his wine, shaking overcomes him and knocks the hot goblet from his hands; his bared teeth chatter; then greasy morsels fall from his loose lips.

Peter Connor ('The Satires of Persius', 74) comments that this scene is permeated by a 'grim and breathtaking humour'. This humour, I suggest, arises from a metaphorical explosion of the target of satire, for when the vicious man has eaten more than he can hold of food and vice, not only bad breath squirts out from his body. While still drinking he begins to shake, and the goblet shoots out of his hands, then the teeth, since Homer the gate to a man's inner self, start chattering, 'retecti', open to view. Finally, the rip in his surface is complete, and almost surreally, fat savouries start falling out, completing the lethal explosion. To rub in his point, the satirist haunts the sinner with fat and magnification even after his death, by having him anointed with smeary balms and carried out shoulder-high by yesterday's slaves, now fabulously grown into noble Romans, *Quirites* (106):

> hinc tuba, candelae, tandemque beatulus alto
> conpositus lecto crassisque lutatus amomis
> in portam rigidas calces extendit. at illum
> hesterni capite induto subiere Quirites.   (3.103–6)

Then there is the sound of the trumpet, the candles, and at last the dear departed is laid out on a high bed. All anointed with fatty balms, he stretches his stiff heels towards the door. But Roman citizens—as of yesterday—lift him up, their caps still on their heads.

Enlargement and multiplication of the enemy in P. 5 and P. 6

Persius' version of satiric heightening—inflation—is also abundantly present in *Satire* 5, where it is coupled with multiplication. As has been shown in Anderson's analysis of this poem, the introduction (1–51) is tied to the bulk of the satire precisely by imagery, that of a hundred voices, i.e. unrestrained multiplicity. This multiplicity is contrasted with noble philosophical oneness, the singularity of the right way.[92] In the introduction, Persius fuses the high genres of epic and tragedy into one overconfident whole, and mocks them both through reducing their powerful hundred voices to a hundred throats, for eating. He carefully avoids any carnivalesque merriment at the big feast[93] by making it a cannibalistic one, that of Procne or Thyestes, and by serving the reader revoltingly concrete images of a boiling pot (8–9) and a table laid out with hands and feet (18). The picture of the grandiose swelling of thin air also appears here, once dangerously close to bursting a reciter's cheeks (11–13), later inflating the written page (20). Further on in the satire, where the criticism of letters gives way to criticism of manners, we encounter among the many faces of vice another swelling character (5.56). This character is simply swelling with food, drink and sleep, and we may note that he is called 'satur', again showing that this adjective is used of the objects of satire by Persius, rather than of its speaking subject.

There are various other minor movements of inflation spread throughout *Satire* 5, such as the personification of avarice (132–9), luxury (142–53), and ambition (176–7) into semi-divine creatures with the power to command people, but we may limit ourselves to mentioning the images in the coda, the last three lines. This ending plays on the pattern of Horace's subversive codas, in that it presents a view opposite to that expounded in the rest of the satire. Yet far from subverting or even questioning what has gone before, Persius' last lines seem only to brand the sentiment expressed in them all the more by the emphatic final position:

> dixeris haec inter varicosos centuriones,
> continuo crassum ridet Pulfenius ingens
> et centum Graecos curto centusse licetur.   (5.189–91)

---

[92] 'Part versus Whole in Persius' Fifth Satire', 1960, reprinted in Anderson, *Essays*, 153–68.

[93] For the notion of 'carnival', see Bakhtin, *Rabelais*, esp. the introduction and the first chapter of his book, 'Rabelais in the History of Laughter', 1–144.

If you say this among the varicose centurions, then huge Pulfenius will immediately emit a fat laugh, and bid a chipped hundred-*as*-piece for a hundred Greeks.

As Anderson has pointed out, the imagery of 'one hundred', which introduced the poem, turns up again here, not only in 'centum Graecos' and 'centusse', but also half-hidden in the word '*centuriones*'. The centurions and their ideas are thus marked as belonging to the pole of vicious, confused, and unfree plurality.[94] To this I would like to add that combined with the negative imagery of multiplication there is also the imagery of huge body volume and grossness: Pulfenius is himself enormous, *ingens*, and even his laugh is fat, *crassum*.[95] The satirist's own laughter, we learned in P. 1, is small in all respects, 'tam nil' ('so nil') (1.122), while the centurion's is thick and gross, like himself, and thus, in Persius' imaginary universe, tagged as an object of derision. Thus I find it difficult to agree with Kenneth Reckford's thesis that Pulfenius' laughter is also an invitation to the reader to join in this laughter against philosophers.[96] There are enough signs of Pulfenius' (and his laugh's) badness and ridiculousness to counteract even the strong appeal of laughter in a comic genre often using explicit laughter as its generic emblem. Pulfenius' laugh is not needle-like, piercing the grand pretensions of others, as Persius' guffaw had done in the first satire, but itself constitutes a big fat pretension. In the last line, it is in fact the Greek philosophers who end up with the healthy 'oneness' of a chipped one-*as*-piece.[97]

Some details in the sixth satire also deserve comment. In this, the most Horatian of Persius' satires, we encounter the satirical person-

---

[94] Anderson, *Essays*, 167.

[95] *Crassus* is an adjective that is used negatively elsewhere in Persius, e.g. 2.42.

[96] Reckford, 'Studies in Persius', 494; similarly Henderson, *Writing down Rome*, 245.

[97] The same argument may be made for 3.86–7, 'his populus ridet, *multum*que *torosa* iuventus/ *ingeminat* tremulos naso crispante *cachinnos*' ('the crowd laughs at this, and the brawny youths guffaw over and over again, cringing their nostrils.'), where the *torosa iuventus* are surely the descendants of Horace's enemies in *S.* 1.6.72–3, 'magni |... pueri magnis e centurionibus orti' ('great ... boys born of great centurions'). Again, I disagree with Reckford's claim that 'we must agree' that philosophers are funny (Reckford, 'Reading the Sick Body', 347, foreshadowed in id., 'Studies in Persius', 496–7, in a milder version).

age of the impatient inheritor, in this version characteristically stuffed with food. Should I eat poor meals even on festive days, Persius exclaims, so that this grandson may be all the more well-fed:

> ut tuus iste nepos olim satur anseris extis,
> cum morosa vago singultiet inguine vena,
> patriciae inmeiat volvae? mihi trama figurae
> sit reliqua, ast illi tremat omento popa venter? (6.71–4)

so that one day this grandson of yours, crammed full with goose innards, may piss into a noble vagina whenever that capricious vein hiccups in his wide-roaming groin? Am I to be left with a woof of a figure, while his priest-belly wobbles with fat?

After the caesura in verse 71 the inheritor is qualified with 'satur anseris extis'. Note again the negative, derisive use of *satur*, and the choice of food: the particularly fat and luxurious item of goose innards. From the stomach the focus moves down to the member, and there follows the coarse, lowering joke of 'pissing' into a high-born vagina.[98] Yet remarkably enough, this is not allowed to stand as the climax of the description of the vicious *nepos*, and Persius instead returns to the contrast between thick and thin. The respective figures are placed as the grammatical subjects, and the inflated belly of the antagonist is even personified with the apposition *popa*, the luxuriant servant of a temple.

In the coda of P. 6, which follows immediately upon this image, the language becomes more abstract, but here again the device of magnification turns up, in the antagonist's restless multiplication of his riches. In vv.78–9 the object of derision manages to double, triple, multiply his possessions by four, and finally by ten, before he is degraded in the sarcastic final line (80), where he is allowed to make a fool of himself by comparing his multiplied riches to Chrysippus' philosophic problem of the heap:[99]

---

[98] See comments in Richlin, *Garden*, 189–90.

[99] Chrysippus, head of the Stoic school in the second half of the 3rd cent. BC, set up his puzzle of the heap by adding one grain after another and asking his interlocutor to call a halt when there was a heap before him. When the interlocutor did call a stop and said 'yes, now it is a heap', Chrysippus would take off one grain and say: 'Do you mean that this one grain makes the difference?' The puzzle also functions in reverse—when does a heap stop being a heap? For an excellent discussion of the heap-metaphor in Persius, see Freudenburg, *Satires of Rome*, 183–8.

'rem duplica.' 'feci; iam triplex, iam mihi quarto,
iam decies redit in rugam, depunge ubi sistam,
inventus, Chrysippe, tui finitor acervi.' (6.78–80)

'double your wealth.' 'I have, and I've trebled it, and quadrupled it; it now goes down my pocket multiplied by ten. Tell me at what point to stop—and we've found a man to check your heap, Chrysippus!'

Laying it on thick: detached fat in P. 2

In P. 2, on the vanity of human prayers, the rich, ridiculous fat seems to have been detached from human bodies and appear in pure form. Still on the side of the target of the satire, the fat, in the form of offerings to the gods, serves to make the people criticized not only egoistic and superstitious, but also luxurious. They are said to try to buy the favour of the gods 'pulmone et lactibus unctis' ('with offal and greasy chitterlings'), 30, and somewhat further on we hear that great plates and the fat meat on them actually hinder the gods from hearing the offerer's prayers (42–3). Wishing to obtain great gifts from Mercury with great gifts to him, one of the satirist's victims builds a pile containing a slaughtered ox, and the fat (*omenta*) of so many young cows (44–7). The next example asks for increasing riches simply with 'extis et opimo...ferto' ('innards and fat cakes'), 48, looking forward to the description of the last villain in Persius, the inheriting relative of *Satire* 6, who is 'satur...extis' and whose belly shakes with fat (6.71, 74). In P. 2 the dripping innards, significantly, metamorphose into *fat gold* over a line-break: 'incusaque *pingui* |*auro* dona' ('embossed with fat gold'), 2.52–3.[100] The imagery of gold for the gods then continues until v. 69.

---

[100] A similar effect is achieved at 5.179–88, where superstition is again under attack: 'cum | Herodis venere dies *uncta*que fenestra | dispositae *pinguem* nebulam vomuere lucernae | portantes violas rubrumque amplexa catinum | cauda natat thynni, *tumet* alba fidelia vino | labra moves tacitus recutitaque sabbata palles. | tum nigri lemures ovoque pericula rupto, | tum *grandes* galli et cum sistro lusca sacerdos | incussere deos *inflantes corpora*, si non | praedictum ter mane caput gustaveris ali' ('When, on Herod's day, the violet-adorned lamps placed on *greasy* window-ledges spew out bursts of *fatty* fog, when coiled around its red dish a tunny's tail swims about, and the white pot *swells* with wine, then you silently move your lips, and blanch before the Sabbath of the circumcised. And then we have the black ghosts and the danger signalled by a broken egg, the *big* eunuchs and the one-eyed priestess with her rattle, scaring you with gods who *inflate your body* unless you chew garlic thrice in the morning, as prescribed.')

The heightening images are finally summed up and dismissed in 2.71–2, with an appeal to give the gods what the descendants of great Messalla cannot give on their great plates. Rather, the gods should be presented with the very opposite of fat men's fat offerings, the satirist's concentrated, dry virtue (73–5), but to this we will return below.

Persius' recipe for satura—fatter and heavier

The more traditional heightening device of importing a grand personage from myth or history, which we have seen in Horace and will see again in Juvenal, is found (on any considerable scale) only in Persius' short fourth satire. Here the object of mockery, a vain and hypocritically effeminate man, is clad in the mask of Alcibiades, while the satirist's sentiments and derisive criticism are voiced through the figure of Socrates, again a reminiscence of Horace, who liked to cast his satirical self in the image of Socrates. The contrast between *Sein und Schein* is played off on Alcibiades high birth (vv. 3, 20, 46–7), his decorous surface appearance (14, 35, 43–5) and his grand life-style (4–14, 17–8) vs. his actual vanity and effeminacy (20, 35–41, 43–5, 47–50), and his foolishness (16). Nevertheless, even when armed with the powerful device of a high historical personage, Persius cannot refrain from providing him with a greased plate, 'uncta...patella' (16–17), and making his skin glisten with unguents, 'unctus cesses' ('you walk with your skin all greasy'), 33!

In summary, it may be said that Persius' version of the heightening device (inflation and fat) and his remedy (puncturing or sinking his adversary) are better suited to his stern moral opinions than the swings and tumblings found in Horatian satire. The difference between Horace's and Persius' use of the adjective 'satur', with its obvious connection to the name of the genre, *satura*, is significant here. It had been used by Epicurean, Augustan Horace of well-tempered satisfaction, an ideal moral and physical condition (e.g. of the moderate guest *S*. 1.1.119). In the Stoic and Neronian Persius, such a state is no longer possible, just as it is no longer possible for the degenerate aristocrats to eat healthy peasant food (3.113–14), and 'satur' now indicates the condition of having *overeaten*, and of being ripe for satiric derision, rather than representing satire's ideal.[101] Persius adapts the word for the description of satire's objects, while Horace had employed it for satire's subject (= the persona), or for moral heroes parallel to that subject. In this, as well as generally, Persius needs a harsher, crueller, more negative satire than that written by Lucilius and Horace. As a Stoic Persius would take seriously the paradox of all sins being equal (and thus equally blameworthy), and as an intellectual under Nero, he would see cruel punishment as an inescapable fact of life.

Persius' earnestness, however, creates problems for writing satire. At the beginning of this discussion of Persius' object-oriented humour I mentioned that it interferes with the mission of being funny. In addition, the 'real targets' behind this Stoic satirist's metaphors of heightening and inflation are different from those of his fellow satirists. Horace's anger was mostly directed against competing poets, and/or competing pretenders to Maecenas' patronage; occasionally he turned against groups that could (potentially) threaten his status as an elite Roman male, such as the women lurking behind his witches. For Juvenal, this latter group of threatening social elements will become dominant—with him, it is almost always women, foreigners and *cinaedi* that are metaphorically hoisted to great power. In Persius, the 'real enemy' behind the images seems to consist of qualities, not people or groups of people. The qualities he turns against—greed, gluttony, vanity, laziness etc.—are all abstract moral traits. This affects the metaphors in which they are clad: despite a seeming engagement with the corporeal, Persius often serves us bloodless, essentially impersonal fat men. Unlike the characters who people the work of the other satirists, Persius' villains are exchangeable, and his battles with them never take on that vivid fierceness, blazing with aggression and humour, which we meet in Horace's conflict with Canidia or Juvenal's attack on women in his sixth satire.

Connected to this problem of impersonality both in the imagery and in the real antagonists peeping out from behind the images, is a certain monotony in the metaphors. As seen in the above analyses, the forceful image of fat—in obese men, and in detached pure form—is used to the very limit of its possibilities. The question is

---

[101] As we have seen from the examples mentioned above, at 1.31, 5.56, and 6.71.

whether Persius' seriousness does not make his poetic dish too heavy for the genre of *satura*.

Piercing subject

Persius does not offer us many images of the mocking persona in connection with focused humorous attacks, he is much more often a detached voice pouring forth from a vaguely defined source. There is nothing here like Horace's vivid mocker in the shape of a small, round figure, harmless and jovial while undisturbed, quick to draw his weapon of derision when provoked.[102] Nevertheless, in the few glimpses that Persius affords of the laughing speaker, his imagery is remarkably consistent with that applied to the targets laughed at. The master metaphors for Persius' objects of derision were swelling and fat, and the metaphors for the derider are things that will cure swelling and dissolve fat: decoctions, vapour, and acid.

So in the famous image of his own satires as 'aliquid decoctius' ('something more boiled-down', i.e. 'concentrated'), 1.125, Persius presents the opposite not only of the grand and outsized contemporary poems, but also of the big bellies of bad poets and immoral men. In the following verse, 'inde vaporata lector mihi ferveat aure' ('my reader should have an ear steamed by that, and all warmed up for me'), 1.126, I find it difficult to take *inde* as a reference to his own boiled-down poetry.[103] Rather, it seems that *inde* goes back to the writers of Old Comedy (Cratinus, Eupolides, and Aristophanes), of whom 'Persius' had said that they were his inspiration (123–5). The same movement from them to 'Persius' that was performed in vv. 123–5 is made again in this one verse (126). These two parallel statements, meaning 'if you liked them [sc. the authors of Old Comedy], you'll like me too', are further bound together by the image of the ear. Persius' decoct is to be taken through the ear (*audis* [you hear], 125), and those will be receptive to it who have

---

[102] Persius, however, saw through this pretence at peacefulness in Horace, and in his ingenious description of the earlier Flaccus' persona he adds a touch of wiliness: according to Persius, 'Horace' would get himself admitted to the inner soul of his friends, and then make fun of them from that privileged position (P. 1.116–18).

[103] Freudenburg, *Satires of Rome*, 181–2.

already had their ears cleaned with the steam of Old Comedy ('inde vaporata . . . aure', 126). The scandalous revelation of the first satire is that everyone at Rome has asinine (8, 121), effeminate (107–8) ears, dumb with listening to recitals of soft, oversized literature.

Above, we have seen the interchangeability between a man's physique, his poetry and his morals, and the same semiotic interchangeability is at work in the imagery of ears. From soft poetry the ears become soft (*teneras*), and need to be scraped with the mordant truth of satire ('mordaci radere vero', 107). From swelling poetry the ears presumably become overgrown with fat wax, which needs to be dissolved by the hot vapour of Old Comedy, and then by the decoction of Persius' satire.[104] Beyond the ears, good morals should be poured into the heart and boiled down into its fibres,[105] as we learn from 2.73–4:

> compositum ius fasque animo sanctosque recessus
> mentis et *incoctum* generoso pectus honesto.

a spirit at peace with human and divine law, a mind pure to its very depths, a heart steeped in noble honour ('literally: a heart with noble honour boiled into it')

In the immediate context of P. 2, the image is opposed to the big and fat gifts of insincere grandees. The satirist, unlike the villains with their fat gifts, will make an offering in (dry) emmer, 'farre litabo' (2.75). But we may also contrast this image of noble honour 'boiled into' the heart with the picture of the immoral heart, overgrown with fat, in the third satire: 'fibris increvit opimum | pingue' (3.32–3). The small concentrated size and the mordant essence ascribed to Persius' satiric poetry in these pictures combine into his version of the lowly mocker laughing at mighty men. The thin jet of his satirical laughter will eat away at the thick layer of fat which has overgrown Rome's hearts and ears, and so help to cure the universal disease.

---

[104] Cf. 'fruge Cleanthea' ('the seeds of Cleanthes') 5.63–4; 'aurem mordaci lotus aceto' ('with his ear washed by sharp vinegar') 5.86. For the difference between 'auris' (positive) and 'auricula' (negative) in Persius, see Reckford, 'Studies in Persius', 477–83, and Kißel, *Persius*, 268.

[105] Moral teaching in the form of medicine poured into the ear had a satiric precedent in Lucilius, fr.610 M, 'haec tu si voles per auris pectus inrigarier'; the image is also used by Horace in *Ep*. 1.1.7 and *Ep*. 1.8.16. For the ancient medical use of aural infusions, cf. *TLL*, under 'auris', 1505, and Reckford, 'Studies in Persius', 478 and 482.

JUVENAL

In Juvenal's work, the device of heightening or magnifying the object of satire before shooting it down with derision is used extensively. This corresponds to his tendency to adopt a rougher, angrier tone, and to concentrate his focus on the targets, with less space for (pseudo-)biographical depiction of the persona. He makes heavy use of the import of grand and terrifying historical personages as examples of greater and smaller vices, he gives his targets high social status, shaping them into ministers, senators, aristocrats. Nor is he averse to occasionally drawing them as physically huge, brawny or fat men and women, somewhat reminiscent of Persius' inflated villains discussed in the preceding sections.

The device as image: depictions of looking up at the satiric object

What I would like to look at first, however, are Juvenal's remarkable pictures of the *literal* hoisting of the object of derision. In these cases the satirical persona is gazing up at the object from below. The image becomes an emblem of object-oriented derision, satire's hallmark. At the same time, the artificiality inherent in hoisting an otherwise rather insignificant object for the show of satiric attack becomes apparent, and makes the images self-conscious, almost self-ironic, in their explicitness.

While these pictures are not frequent, they nevertheless appear at significant points in the satirist's opus, such as the first, the third, and the last satire (*S.* 16). In the first satire, where 'Juvenal' is presented as being under attack, and eager to take his satirical revenge, an instance of his looking up comes in the celebrated passage about filling his notebooks in the street corner (1.63–80). As has been noted, the urban scene itself is the main actor here, and 'Juvenal' only has to stand still and record what comes rushing at him in order to create sizeable satires.[106] As soon as he has placed himself in the street, pen in hand, a suitable object, ripe for satire, floats by:

---

[106] Kernan, *Cankered Muse*, 8, and 7–14 on the (urban) scenes of satire in general; for this general observation cf. also Hodgart, *Satire*, 129, 135–7; Braund, *Roman Satire*, 2–4.

nonne libet medio ceras inplere capaces
quadrivio, cum iam sexta cervice feratur
hinc atque inde patens ac nuda paene cathedra
et multum referens de Maecenate supino
signator falsi, qui se lautum atque beatum
exiguis tabulis et gemma fecerit uda?   (1.63–8)

who doesn't want to fill sizeable notebooks with satires in the middle of the crossroads, when a person is carried on six necks, in an almost bare litter, exposed on this side and that, and he (looking much like Maecenas lying on his back)—a forger, who has made himself rich and happy with the help of little writing tablets and a moist signet-ring?

The form of this arrival is almost that of a dish being carried in at dinner, a tasty *lanx satura* for our mocker. This nameless swindler is lifted onto six porters' necks, a physical heightening and multiplication to mirror the social grandness he has achieved by means of forgery. Moreover, still like a grotesque dish, the forger is placed on a very broad but empty, naked-looking litter, whose absurdly stretching sides ('hinc atque inde patens') function to stress the object's laughable, hollow ('naked') pretensions to greatness. After a final, rather dubious, compliment of likening the villain to Maecenas, a notoriously ridiculous-looking and effeminate great man,[107] the satirist shoots his object down with the sudden revelation of his true identity, 'signator falsi' ('one who signs false documents'). The revelation is made all the more mocking by its emphatic position at the beginning of a line, with nothing to foreshadow it before the line-break. The movement of raising-up and toppling-down is then repeated in verses 67–8, where the object is said to have grown rich and fancy with the help of—minute notes and the moist stone of his signet-ring. The implication is of course that the man has hoisted himself up onto this undeserved height, and so the device used by the satirist is, characteristically, blamed upon the victim instead. The image of this uplifted object being served to the satirist's derisive gaze, as soon as he has got himself into position at the crossing, is an excruciatingly neat emblem of what Juvenal and the other Roman satirists do all the time, though mostly in less explicit form. Naturally 'Juvenal' has the right to defend himself by exposing this object with a laugh: he is being looked down upon, almost run down! We forget,

[107] Cf. Seneca, *Ep.* 114.

as we are meant to, that this object is not really one of the mighty men of Rome, that he has no identity, rank, or status. We forget that it is none other than the satirist who has lifted this nameless voodoo-doll onto the height of six fictitious bodyguards, made him up as Maecenas with his nose in the air (*supino*), and placed himself underneath, so that his vicarious attack might not look ignoble.

The next image of the same kind turns up towards the end of the first satire, where the argument between the persona, intent on writing satire, and his protesting interlocutor has grown thicker, with both sides becoming more animated. The interlocutor has just warned 'Juvenal' that the times have changed since Lucilius mocked Mucius, and that the satirist of today may expect gruesome death as punishment for *nominatim* attacks on real, mighty men at Rome. 'Juvenal' retorts by exclaiming that murderers will then go unpunished, looking down on the satirist and his friends:

> qui dedit ergo tribus patruis aconita, vehatur
> pensilibus plumis atque illinc despiciat nos? (1.158–9)

so he who has served poison to three of his uncles should be carried by on his hanging cushions and look down on us from there?

The satirist weasels his way out by seemingly protesting against the interlocutor's admonition to cowardice. Yet although 'Juvenal' parades his indignation over such advice, mentioning a criminal whom he would like to brand, he tacitly accepts the advice in that he does not mention any named individual. There is also minor cheating here: while the real offence of the man in 'Juvenal' 's utterance is his propensity for murder, the hoisting of him onto a litter and his despising *von oben* glance are more essential for raising *indignatio* in both speaker and reader. The villain's position does not simply add insult to injury, it insults the satiric persona directly, and gives him a clear, righteous reason for self-defence by derision. Furthermore, it adds status and dignity to yet another nameless object by the simple device of making him *physically* look down on the satirist. Even the downy cushions of his couch hang dangling,[108] as if pointing

---

[108] For this explanation of 'pensilibus plumis' see Courtney, *Commentary on Juvenal*, ad loc., where he compares Sen. *Ep.* 80.8, 'quos supra capita hominum supraque turbam delicatos lectica suspendit' ('those effeminates, suspended by the litter above the heads of men, above the crowd').

contemptuously downwards at the speaker, and through the words
pensilibus, plumis, despiciat, and *nos* the harsh p-s alliteration makes a
sound as of spitting or hissing with contempt. It is, I believe, no
coincidence that Juvenal chooses the first person plural here. It is a
clever move to include, by implication, both the audience and all
decent Romans among those looked down upon by the murderer.
As readers, we naturally identify with a first-person speaker as long as
it is not signalled that we should not. Here we are made to look up
at the villain through the speaker's eyes. As we are expressly
told that the villain presumes to look down on *us* (*nos*), we are
literally subsumed in the satirist's point of view, and feel that the
object deserves all the derision he can get from the mob we form
together with the satirist.

The satiric device of heightening the object of mockery has grown
into a metaphor, on the verge of becoming too obvious. Yet it still
works effectively precisely because of the vivid, exact contours of the
picture. Though the image is a relative of Horace's intellectual puns
on *rex* and Persius' nightmarish fat men,[109] it is the most explicit
instance of the device, barely concealing its artificiality. Juvenal only
gets away with it because his show is so racy. There is the high
emotional tension induced by the horrible crime, but tempered
with the humorous incongruity of transcribing it as 'serving aconite',
the pithy, alliterative language, the engaging stroke of the pronoun
us, and, as everywhere in this satirist, there is movement—and we are
swept along by the swinging cushions.

A strikingly similar image, in miniature, is used in the fifth satire,
Juvenal's variant of that satiric stock theme, the horrible dinner.[110]
A poor and dependent client, Trebius, is dining at the table of his
patron, a disgusting and cruel nabob by the name Virro, who goes
out of his way to humiliate his guest in every possible manner, simply
for his own amusement. The whole poem is arranged around the

---

[109] See the discussions above, in the sections ' Punning on 'reges'—how to kill
kings without hurting anyone (1.2; 1.3; 1.7)' and 'Persius: swollen objects' respectively.

[110] To the motif of the dinner-party Horace and Juvenal devote whole satires (Hor.
S. 2.8; J. 5); before them, Lucilius seems to have used it for at least one book (Book
20). There is no full dinner satire in Persius, but we have the grotesque vignette in
3.88–106, which we can possibly regard as his (miniature) version of the topos. For
secondary literature on satirical dinners, see Ch. 1, n. 90 above.

contraposition of the food served the host and that served Trebius. The former is fabulously exquisite, and described in mythical terms, the latter inedible and repulsive. It has been correctly noted that the satirist does not sympathize with Trebius, who allows himself to be too much humiliated out of material greed, and rather satirizes both extremes.[111] Still, it is reasonable to claim that the main object of this satire is the rich and sadistic host, in line with the literary tradition of satiric dinners. The beautiful dishes served to Virro are heightened in various ways, mostly by means of parodically high style and references to myth. Trebius' dishes, on the other hand, are lowered, creating a sharp, comic contrast.[112] In the middle of the satire a highly symbolic dish is carried in:

> aspice quam longo distinguat pectore lancem
> quae fertur domino squilla, et quibus undique saepta
> asparagis qua despiciat convivia cauda,
> dum venit excelsi manibus sublata ministri.   (5.80–3)

look at the lobster carried in for the host: how it adorns the dish with its long body, and what asparagus surround it on all sides, as it looks down its tail on the dinner party on its way in, lifted high in the hands of the tall servant.

It has been noted that the lobster looks down on the guests, as an emphasis and exaggeration of the host's contempt for them,[113] but the details of this image deserve further examination. The passage begins with an imperative, 'look!', and though the appeal is formally directed at Trebius, the reader is in effect urged to gaze up at the haughty dish. The lobster is literally served on a *lanx* ('dish'), with its association to the genre name (*lanx satura*),[114] and it is said to 'set off' that plate with its great size, 'longo pectore'. Just as the forgerer in

---

[111] Highet, *Juvenal the Satirist*, 83–8; Anderson, *Essays*, 244–50.

[112] It may be added that in the main passage of direct mockery of the poorer man (5.6–11), the satirist compares Trebius' position with one that is materially even lower, though more honourable—that of living in the street like a dog. In this way the satirist thus tries to create a situation of barking upwards even here. In addition, this may well be a hint at the honourable but threadbare Cynics, who called themselves 'Dogs'.

[113] Courtney, *Commentary on Juvenal*, ad loc.

[114] For the Roman associations of 'satura' with mixed food offered on a dish ('lanx'), see van Rooy, *Classical Satire and Literary Theory*; cf. Gowers, *Loaded Table*, 110-17.

Satire 1 had been lifted up on the shoulders of six men, so this fish, firmly associated with the master by its position in the verse ('fertur *domino* squilla') is raised high in the hands of a tall slave, and ceremoniously carried in, just as the forgerer was ('fertur', 5.81; 'feratur', 1.64). The *squilla* is embedded in luxury on all sides, 'quibus undique saepta | asparagis', like that second litter-riding villain in J. 1, the murderer who travelled surrounded by 'pensilibus plumis' (1.159). Finally, the lobster's position on the platter is a kind of combination between the positions of those two villains in the first satire: like the forgerer, she must have her nose in the air, for she sets off the dish with her breast (cf. 1.66); like the murderer, she looks down on people in every sense, 'despiciat' (the same form as was used of the murderer, 1.159). To make things worse, she looks down her tail at the guests. There is even an echo of the spitting alliteration that was found in the description of the contemptuous murderer, here in the words 'a*s*paragi*s* qua de*s*piciat'.[115]

The proud lobster despises us, the guests at the satirist's dinner, and therefore deserves derision, and so does, by association, her master and his house. The passage works as satiric humour, for the lobster is only a lobster, and so laughable in her pride—she is therefore revealed as a fraud, with the weapon of ridicule. Yet the same passage also comes curiously close to being a meta-literary comment on the typical fraud of the Roman satirists, who hoist an insignificant object, by means of imagery, into a high, grand position, then smash it down with their 'fearless', upward-directed mockery, and serve it to us as satire, though the *lanx satura* may hold nothing bigger than a piece of fish.

There is an extreme variant of the image, where the mocking subject is literally trampled underfoot by the hoisted, magnified object of his mockery. One instance is found in J. 3, the famous jeremiad on the difficulties and dangers of life in contemporary Rome. The overwhelming part of this satire is spoken by 'Juvenal's' friend Umbricius, who explains why he has decided to leave Rome for good. According to the terminology suggested above,[116]

---

[115] This glorious lobster is then contrasted with Trebius' tiny shrimp, uncomfortably stuck between two egg-halves on a narrow plate, reminiscent of the meals presented to the dead nine days after burial (5.84-5).

[116] Introduction, under 'A note on author and persona'.

Umbricius is a 'secondary persona', and although his point of view cannot simply be identified with that of 'Juvenal', many of his bitter sentiments are obviously close to the main persona's.[117] However Umbricius' judgement is interpreted, it is an undeniable fact that we are made to look at the big city from his point of view for most of the narrative. Umbricius' powerful enemies, such as the brazen Greeks, the filthy rich, and the drunken bullies, are directly, forcefully ridiculed by him in a speech which is linguistically and stylistically very close to those delivered by the primary persona elsewhere. About two thirds through the satire Umbricius describes the bustle of the morning in Rome. The description includes Juvenal's favourite image of the litter of the rich man, here gliding by swiftly as a warship, above the (upturned?) faces of the crowd, *super ora* (3.240). By contrast, Umbricius, who cannot not afford a litter, has to walk by foot. He is bound to arrive later though he hurries on his way, for he will be hindered by the waves of people, then pushed, hit, smashed on the head, trampled upon, and finally impaled with the nail of a military boot:

> nobis properantibus *obstat*
> unda prior, magno populus *premit* agmine lumbos
> qui sequitur; *ferit* hic cubito, *ferit* assere duro
> alter, at hic tignum capiti *incutit*, ille metretam.
> pinguia crura luto, planta mox undique magna
> *calcor*, et in digito clavus mihi militis *haeret*. (3.243–8)

as we hurry on we are blocked by a wave in front; a great throng of people presses down on our loins from behind. Someone hits me with his elbow, another one hits me with a pole; this one crashes into my head with a beam, that one with a wine-jar. My legs are smeared with mud, I am trampled by big feet from every side, and my toe is transfixed by a soldier's hob-nail.

---

[117] There is no agreement about what intellectual and moral status Umbricius should be seen as having in the satire. Opinions range from the more traditional understanding of him as Juvenal's alter ego (so Highet, *Juvenal the Satirist*; C. Witke, *Latin Satire. The Structure of Persuasion* (Leiden: Brill, 1970)) to the radical view of him as almost a target of Juvenal's satire (foreshadowed in Anderson's 'Lascivia vs. ira: Martial and Juvenal', 1970, repr. in Anderson, *Essays*, 362–95; developed by R. A. LaFleur, '*Amicitia* and the Unity of Juvenal's First Book,' *ICS* 4 (1979), 158–77; B. Fruelund Jensen, 'Martyred and Beleaguered Virtue: Juvenal's Portrait of Umbricius,' *CM* 37 (1986), 185–97; Braund, *Roman Satire*). I will return to this problem in Ch. 3.

As can readily be seen from the italicized verbs in the passage, the scene moves rapidly and straightforwardly towards its painful climax. It is briskly comic both simply as vivid farce and as satiric derision of uncultivated bullies, especially soldiers.[118] At the beginning of this description, the pronoun used is in the plural, *nobis* ('us'), so that the audience is invited to identify with the group of the undeservedly oppressed. As the rough crowd grows more aggressive, a storm of city dwellers hits against the head of the speaker. Then suddenly legs and feet snap into focus. With 'planta mox undique magna' the aggressors have grown larger than life, and have all melted into one giant aggressor, a trampling foot. The objects of the satire have been heightened by being placed on a litter, by being armed with clumsy baggage, and finally by a fall in perspective, in which Umbricius, the secondary persona, has dragged us down to a worm's-eye view of the situation. In the last clause, although Umbricius is hurt, he still gets a laugh out of giving the aggressor the characteristically uncouth shape of the soldier, with nails coming out of his inelegant shoes, and, to use Edward Courtney's formulation, 'all brawn and no brain'.[119]

Umbricius' suffering under the soldier's shoe-nail, in fact, looks forward to a more elaborate repetition of this image in the sixteenth satire,[120] the last, unfinished poem which is wholly about soldiers and the ills they inflict on ordinary people. Near the beginning of that satire, which is spoken by the primary persona, it is said that if a civilian who has been beaten into a pulp by soldiers wants redress, he will be given a hobnailed boot for a judge (16.13–14) and a benchful of giant legs for a jury, 'grandes magna ad subsellia surae' ('great legs on the big benches'), 14. The image recurs somewhat further on, when a naïve, nameless interlocutor who believes in centurion justice is told that, since he only has two legs, it would be madness to offend so many boots:

---

[118] In his article on Juvenal as a humorist, Dunn (1911, 53) lists this passage as funny, but does not do much more. On the image of the soldier in Roman thinking, see N. Horsfall, 'The Legionary as his own Historian,' *Ancient History*, 29/9 (1999), 107–17.

[119] Courtney, *Commentary on Juvenal*, 616: this is on another (though similar) group, namely the judges allied with the soldiers in J. 16 (vv. 13–14).

[120] As pointed out in Mayor, *Juvenal, with Commentary*, vol. I, in the note on 3.248.

> cum duo crura habeas, offendere tot caligas, tot
> milia clavorum. (16.24–5)

to offend so many boots, so many thousands of hob-nails, when you yourself have only two legs.

As in J. 3, the speaker gazes up at the objects of his satire as if from the ground, expecting to be kicked again. The situation is approximately the same as it was for Umbricius—he too had naked, unprotected legs, *crura*, against the soldier's boots with sharp nails—only here there is more than one boot, and the amount of nails has reached several thousand, *tot milia*.

Yet by placing himself so low that he only sees his enemies' aggressive boots, the satirist has not only made them powerful and placed them above himself in the extreme, so that his mockery seems a fully justified, and brave, counter-attack. He has also, by that very move of hoisting them, made them look foolish and laughable, for while he is still a clever, witty human being, they are nothing but enormous shoes with sharp thorns, and no head in sight anywhere: an ancient form of killer robots. Called on to play the role of judges and jurors, the shoes may be dangerous, but they are also ludicrous. Thus, in his last poem Juvenal serves the reader the satirical dessert of a whole army fearlessly mocked - without giving a single name or any concrete allusion. This is Roman satire's mechanism of object-oriented humour in a nutshell.

It is perhaps no coincidence that the whole of Juvenal's satiric opus begins with the line:

> Semper ego auditor tantum? numquamne reponam...   (J. 1.1)

Should I always only be a listener? Will I never be able to hit back...

so reminiscent of the first line in Horace's *S.* 2.7:[121]

> Iamdudum ausculto et cupiens tibi dicere servus...   (Hor. *S.*2.7.1)

I have been listening for a long time, and I'd like to tell you—but since I'm a slave...

In Horace, the slave Davus had taken the opportunity offered by the Saturnalia to 'talk back' to his master with all the satirical rhetoric he

---

[121] As observed by F. Muecke, *Horace: Satires II*, 214.

had been listening to for so long. Juvenal borrows the profitable position of the low, endlessly hushed listener who will now finally get his revenge. In a more radical way than Horace, who only used the device of a speaker lowered at the outset for one satire, Juvenal uses it for his whole work. Furthermore, where Horace only lowered a secondary persona thus, Juvenal does it to his primary persona. The battered, tired, and—by allusion to Horace's slave-speaker—lowered 'Juvenal' will be able to attack his enemies all the more fiercely since he is only *paying back.*

Raised objects

'Vincant divitiae'—money conquers aristocracy

After this digression to Juvenal's visual images of the heightening device, I will now return to the device itself, and discuss this last Roman satirist's use of the false (and half-false) raising of his objects. The trio of money, women, and pathics are among Juvenal's favourite objects, and with all of these he employs the device more boldly than his satiric predecessors. He lifts his targets higher, and makes fiercer from-below attacks on them, thus creating lively but risky satire, and exploring the limits of his genre.

Money occupies a special position in Juvenal's satire. Money is connected to everything he finds wrong with Rome, and so with the world: the prevalence of bad poetry written for pay, the visibility of shameless women and ditto *cinaedi*, the progress of freedmen and non-Romans, general corruption and the humiliation of the penniless, beatings and even murders. As regards the pattern of elevating the objects of satirical attack before smashing them down, however, the motif of money poses certain specific problems. Unlike most of the other objects of the Roman satirists' derision, money is not in reality far from power, nor from the mighty of this world. On the other hand, it must not be forgotten that the emperor and others who really mattered in Rome did not own their power exclusively to money, perhaps not even primarily to it. As regards Juvenal, it soon becomes apparent that there is one aspect in particular which he loathes about money: its ability to stir social and gender hierarchies.

New money, money suddenly gained in large amounts, will advance its owner beyond honourable aristocrats, indigenous Romans, and heterosexual men. Members of these groups, in turn, may lose their money and fall into unheard-of humiliation, almost as horrifying to the satirist as the triumphs of the *nouveux-riches*. Juvenal apparently does not mind richness that people are born with (rather, what comes under attack in such cases is the *squandering* of rightfully inherited fortunes, as in, for instance, the eighth satire). The gain of money during one's lifetime, however, is something that cannot, in this author's satiric universe, be decent.[122]

The very fact that someone who was recently a nobody (or worse, a slave) is now prosperous and respected is an outrageous incongruity in itself, held up to ridicule time and again—there are thirteen images of this kind in the first satire alone.[123] Most of these ridiculous images, throughout the satires, are accompanied by a reference to the criminal ways the money was earned: deceit in business and love, nepotism and robbery, outright murder. In the universe of Juvenal's *Satires*, what can be exchanged for coins is crime. The ready money, in turn, is promptly exchanged for an undeservedly high position, a platform from where to look down on those who have no part in these filthy dealings. Standing below in his moral purity (for he is one of those who will take no part in the filthy monetary dealings), the satirist laughs upwards at his targets. What Juvenal and the other Roman satirists perform with imagery, i.e. the undeserved and ridiculous hoisting of objects ripe for derision, is paralleled by the workings of new money.

Although wealth was always important in Rome, on the socio-moral plane upper-class Romans often tried to cover the bare reality of money with ethically more acceptable exchanges such as gifts, patronage, and *amicitia* (which, in turn, were connected to the

---

[122] The *abuse* of money was a commonplace of Roman moralistic discourse from Cato on; see D. Earl, *The Moral and Political Tradition of Rome* (London: Thames & Hudson, 1967), 31–2, 45. However, as Earl points out (p.32), 'seemly' acquisition of money—such as inheritance or income off land—was not considered wrong. Here Juvenal goes further, not recognising *any* means of becoming rich.

[123] Lines 1.24–5, 26–9, 31–3, 33–6, 37–42, 46–7, 55–7, 64–8, 69–72, 75–6, 77, 102–12, 129–31. Two images in the same satire deal with aristocrats squandering money: 1.58–62 and 88–93.

semi-religious concept of *pietas*.[124] Roman moralists worked hard to find a definition of 'nobility' that would be based on some more reliable ground than that of private wealth. In the aristocratic value system, high birth was felt to be a better criterion for power and glory than mere money, but some moralists went further and wished to show that nobility was an innate quality of high morals and intelligence.[125] If this kind of 'aristocracy of the soul' could be defined, this would have obvious advantages for those already in power. It would include certain worthy individuals who had unfortunately been born into the wrong environment. Most importantly, however, it would safely preclude unwanted persons from rising into importance simply through coming by a given amount of money. Needless to say, the innate traits required for membership of the aristocracy of the soul were carefully modelled on the traditional value code of the born and moneyed aristocracy.

Juvenal's approach to money and nobility differs from that of Horace and Persius. In the time of Horace, such moralistic arguments were still optimistically possible, and, in the case of his particular path in life, even more so. In the *Sermones*, Horace claims to be precisely an aristocrat of the soul. In Horace's presentation, even his father was one, or almost, in his devoted care of his son and the sound philosophy he passed on to Horace,[126] which suggests a quasi-aristocratic descent for the poet. His real installation, however, came with Maecenas, who, recognizing this humble man's inner worth, i.e. his great talent, agreed to become his patron and protector, in effect his father.[127] Horace of course repays this adoption, and its pleasant fruits, with the noble *pietas* of a model son. Substantial

---

[124] Cf., as a contrast, the explicitly money-obsessed behaviour of the most famous vulgar host of Roman literature, Trimalchio in Petronius' *Satyrica*. His portrait undoubtedly draws on the satiric tradition, though not in a straightforward way.

[125] See discussion in Earl, *Moral and Political Tradition*, 44–58. As he points out, *novi homines* could in this way be admitted to the Roman elite in a controlled manner. Catharine Edwards has persuasively argued that the most outstanding Roman moralists were interested in finding a moral definition of 'nobility' because their own social status was somehow open to question, in *The Politics of Immorality in Ancient Rome* (Cambridge: Cambridge University Press, 1993).

[126] Hor. *S.* 1.4.105–29.

[127] Cf. *S.* 1.6.61–2, 'revocas nono post mense iubesque| esse in amicorum numero' ('you call me back after nine months, and bid me be one of your friends'). See my discussion of this passage below, Ch. 3, 285–6.

amounts of money have passed to the poet from both his 'fathers', but this fact is carefully hidden behind more abstract, emotionally charged gifts: moral education, deserved appreciation based on good judgement, and friendship. For a satirist, Horace's metamorphosis from inner nobility to outer, with its elegant avoidance of money and central emphasis of literary talent, was a perfect paradigm: in some cases, he could exploit the 'smallness' into which he had been born, in others, the inner excellence that had caught the eye of Maecenas, and in still others, his powerful new position as Maecenas' friend.

By the time of Persius, the anxiety that Roman moralists felt about money's ability to stir the distinctions between different social strata had grown considerably. This may be surmised from the vital role of slaves and freedmen in contemporary works such as Petronius' *Satyrica* and Seneca's *Apocolocyntosis* (regarded as Menippean satires by some scholars).[128] Persius may have been safer through his high birth, and did not need patronage to make a living, but he still describes his relationship with the Stoic philosopher Cornutus in terms of moral guidance and friendship. This description sounds like his version of a young poet's 'discovery and success' story, corresponding to Horace's discovery by the Epicurean Maecenas. As in Horace, there is an insistence on intrinsic moral value and innate liberality (the noble devotion between Persius and Cornutus was even written in the stars, 5.45–51), which cannot be bought with money or manumission.

Unlike his predecessors, Juvenal does not hide money in connection with himself and ridicule it in connection with others; he directs all his powers to derision, not telling about his own case at all. The historical situation has moved further in the direction of social

---

[128] e.g. U. Knoche, *Die römische Satire* (2nd edn. 1949; Göttingen: Vandenhoeck u. Ruprecht, 1957); M. Coffey, *Roman Satire* (London and New York: Methuen & Co, 1976); E. S. Ramage, D. L. Sigsbee, and S. C. Fredericks, *Roman Satirists and their Satire* (Park Ridge, NJ: Noyes Press, 1974); J. Adamietz (ed.), *Die römische Satire* (Darmstadt: Wissenschaftlige Buchgesellschaft, 1986). My own opinion is that while the *Apocolocyntosis* is our best example of ancient Menippean satire, the *Satyrica* is better called a novel, since it shares certain traits not only with Roman satire but also with the Greek novel, and since it may reasonably be said to stand at the beginning of the history of the realistic novel. For the genre of the *Satyrica*, see G. Schmeling (ed.), *The Novel in the Ancient World* (1996; 2nd, rev. edn. Leiden: Brill, 2003), with further references.

mobility with the help of money gained or lost, and there is also an individually darker vision in this last Roman satirist. In Juvenal's universe money is always unfair, lifting undeserving villains to high positions whence they can be cast down with revealing derision, while the innate nobleness is only present as an implied opposite, a positive to the many negatives in the satires. It is hardly ever described in itself, because it presumably no longer exists. Thus while Horace and Persius show and imply examples of moneyed nobleness, Juvenal has no comparable instances. Both patronage and *amicitia* have been reduced to the mere exchanges of cash, as the eager queue of clients waiting for their sportula in the first satire (1.95–126) already tells us. The degeneracy of these institutions and their replacement by monetary transactions becomes a major theme in Juvenal's opus.[129] As a Roman poet and moralist, Juvenal is on the side of the aristocracy because they are his readers and protectors. But there is also more: while Horace and Persius combined the proclamation of an aristocratic value system with respect for wealth, Juvenal adapts this value system to his own uses, one of which is to fight against the power of wealth. Thus in Juvenal's satiric vision, the aristocratic value system ascribes an intrinsic value to the liberal arts (= the poet's own domain),[130] while the monetary system declares them worthless. In his vision, 'inner nobility' implies a denial of money, as it did not for Horace and Persius. Again, unlike the other Roman satirists, Juvenal is not willing to describe his own situation in idyllic terms, and even gives Horace a vicious kick with the observation that the latter was well-fed when composing, 'satur est cum dicit Horatius "euhoe" ' ('Horace says his "Euhoe!" on a full stomach'), 7.62. We are never told whether Juvenal had a helpful friend or how

---

129 In this connection it is interesting to recall the observation of Mary Douglas (*Purity and Danger: an Analysis of Concepts of Pollution and Taboo* (London: Routledge & Kegan Paul, 1966), 70–1) that from an anthropological point of view, money is a ritual. Like any ritual it works when the majority of the community trusts the worth of the ritual ingredients, in this case, the currency. Before money, the ritual of aristocratic hierarchy and power exertion had pervaded Roman society—but that ritual is in Juvenal's time giving way to the monetary one. The satirist is feeling the approaching end of the only system he could accept. Out of this fear and frustration comes his protest, a protest stating that the monetary ritual works with false currency, that it is void, a pseudo-ritual impossible to live by in a civilized society.

130 Cf. the appeal to the emperor's patronage at the beginning of J. 7—the ruler of the aristocratic system is the only one from whom the arts can expect help.

he made his living. His persona has no influential friends and seems to be starving in the name of poetry[131]—a clever 'low' position for the attack on money and those heightened by it, more straightforward than Horace's and Persius' ambiguously placed personae.

Once the vulgar motif of money is allowed to enter, it carries a carnivalesque liveliness with it, as we could already observe in e.g. Horace's satire 2.5, where the combination of mythological characters and the cynical conversation on successful legacy-hunting made for racy humour. Money may be avoided in the nobler genres and in the aristocratic value code, but in the low, humorous genres of comedy and mime it is a central attraction. It is often a catalyst for the plot, and the axis on which many hilarious adventures turn, including sudden changes in roles and fortune. It makes for merry transgression of what is allowed, and of who is who. In such lowly cultural contexts, money sides with food, sex, and the body in general (or, in the Bakhtinian term, with the material bodily stratum)[132] to make up the regenerative, triumphant core of life. Thus the motif of money is not only a convenient device to heighten undeserving *nouveaux-riches*, but also has a low, hilarious aspect to it, not least by its connection with fraud and fooling, and especially with the archetypal comic figure of the trickster. When satire, a genre with a double mission of humour and moral criticism, takes up such a charged motif, satire will try to exploit money's merry connotations to enhance the humour and quicken the pace of the show, but it will be careful to limit its transgressive power and in the end expel transgression in favour of the moral norm. Satire must beware lest it comes too close to the outlook of the merry trickster. This kind of transaction poses a difficulty and a risk, and is actually a special case of satire's big problem of being focused on precisely what it denounces. As regards the motif of money, Juvenal is certainly the

---

[131] As witness J. 7, a whole satire devoted to the poverty (and other trouble) of intellectuals.

[132] Though money is not associated with either 'the material bodily stratum' or 'carnival' by Bakhtin himself, who seems rather to connect it to official culture (e.g. in Bakhtin, *Rabelais*). This weakness in the semiotic system constructed by Bakhtin is discussed and corrected in P. Stallybrass and A. White, *The Politics and Poetics of Transgression* (London: Methuen, 1986).

most successful, and possibly also the most ambivalent, among the
Roman satirists, and we must now look closer at how he deals with it.

Juvenal's programme satire, J. 1, is the place where money is most
conspicuously hoisted to a position worthy of derisive attack. In this
poem, money is placed in heaven. At the beginning of the second half
of the poem, we are presented with a caricaturesque scene of a queue
of waiting clients (1.95–126)—this is a bitterly comic inversion of the
good relationship between patron and client. The first part of the
scene reads as follows:

> nunc sportula primo
> limine parva sedet turbae rapienda togatae.
> ille tamen faciem prius inspicit et trepidat ne
> suppositus uenias ac falso nomine poscas:
> agnitus accipies. iubet a praecone vocari
> ipsos Troiugenas, nam vexant limen et ipsi
> nobiscum. 'da praetori, da deinde tribuno.'
> sed libertinus prior est. 'prior' inquit 'ego adsum.
> cur timeam dubitemve locum defendere, quamvis
> natus ad Euphraten, molles quod in aure fenestrae
> arguerint, licet ipse negem? sed quinque tabernae
> quadringenta parant. quid confert purpura maior
> optandum, si Laurenti custodit in agro
> conductas Coruinus ovis, ego possideo plus
> Pallante et Licinis?'   (1.95–109)

Nowadays a little basket at the edge of the threshold stands waiting to be
snatched away by the toga-clad mob. But first he examines each face,
trembling at the thought that some impostor might turn up and claim a
dole under a false name. Once you're identified you'll get your ration. The
crier is ordered to call even the true-blue descendants of Troy, for they too
are infesting this threshold together with us. 'Now give his dole to the
praetor, then to the tribune.' But a freedman is first. 'I got here first;' he
says, 'why should I be afraid or hesitate to defend my place, though I was
born on the Euphrates—as the fancy slits in my ear-lobes testify, even if I
would deny it. Still, those five shops of mine, they bring in four hundred
thousand. What use is purple-decorated nobleness, if Corvinus looks after
leased sheep in the Laurentine country, while I have more money than Pallas
and Licinus?'

The sportula is ridiculously small (95–6), the queue long, impatient, and made up of the wrong participants, including both too high and too low people. 'Troiugenas' (the descendants of Troy, 100), 'praetori...tribuno' (to the pretor...to the tribune, 101), 'summus honor' (the highest magistrate, 117) are too high, while the freedman (102) is too low. At the threshold the clients are met by an anonymous *ille* ('he'), 97, presumably the patron,[133] who, so far from inviting them in, is nervous that he should pass the gift to someone who is not his client, appearing under a false name. As his own namelessness has already indicated, patron and clients are strangers to each other, and he only recognizes them with difficulty (97–9). A glimpse of the correct hierarchy passes by in his command to serve the praetor before the tribune at v. 101.

Yet even this flashing-by of the correct order is soon all the more brutally shattered as the freedman appears: 'sed libertinus prior est. "prior" inquit "ego adsum" ' ('But a freedman is first. "I got here first," he says'), 102. The adversative clause about the freedman's priority, with the words *prior est* framed by penthemimeres and hephthemimeres, is emphatically placed at the beginning of the verse, after the previous one had ended with *deinde tribuno* ('then to the tribune'). There can be no doubt of the new, inverted order of who should come at the end, and who should be first. The rest of v. 102 consists of the former slave's own repetition of this absurd fact in the first person. Unlike the sons of Trojans, unlike even the patron, he has a vivid presence and a personal voice with which to establish his position, based on wealth: 'ego possideo plus' (108). *I own more, therefore I am (first)*—it should not be forgotten that from the point of view of the Roman nobility the upsetting ridiculousness of this formula begins before the freedman's priority in the line, it begins with his insistence on being a man at all, hammered in through the emphatic inclusion of the personal pronoun *ego* in 102 and 108. We have now reached the climax of this sketch, the aphoristic explanation of the principle behind the new order:

---

[133] So Mayor, *Juvenal, with Commentary,* ii, ad loc., and the translation by P. Green, 1974. I do not feel convinced by Courtney's (*Commentary on Juvenal,* ad loc.) argument against thus identifying *ille* as the patron: 'even satiric exaggeration could hardly put the *patronus* himself in this position.'

> expectent ergo tribuni,
> uincant divitiae, sacro ne cedat honori
> nuper in hanc urbem pedibus qui uenerat albis,
> quandoquidem inter nos sanctissima diuitiarum
> maiestas, etsi funesta Pecunia templo
> nondum habitat, nullas nummorum ereximus aras,
> ut colitur Pax atque Fides, Victoria, Virtus
> quaeque salutato crepitat Concordia nido.   (109–16)

so let the tribunes wait, let riches prevail. There's no need for him who just arrived in the city with whitened feet to give way to the sacred office of magistrates, for the holiest majesty here is that of riches, even though accursed Money does not yet inhabit a temple, and though we have not yet raised an altar to Cash, the way we worship Peace and Loyalty, Victory, Valour, and Concord, who clatters in answer when her nest is saluted.

As in v. 101, the tribunes are placed last in the verse again (both 109 and 110), they will have to wait. The solemn heightening of wealth is presented in formulaic language: let money rule, let him not stand back for the holy tribunate, who only recently entered Rome as a slave, since for us, the majesty of money is most holy of all: 'sanctissima divitiarum | maiestas'. In his commentary, John Mayor correctly compares Horace's ironic hoisting of money, both in the *Sermones* (ambivalently placed within a moralistic utterance by the Stoic bore Damasippus in *S.* 2.3.94–7) and in the *Epistles* 1.6.36–8, including the expression 'regina Pecunia' ('Queen Money'), 1.6.37.[134] Juvenal, however, goes further than Horace in making money not only queen of things, but even a divinity, the highest possible position. From this height money is humiliated with the word *funesta* ('accursed'), and in the following two verses (114–15), we learn that Money does not as yet have an altar, and there seems to be some hope for the old deities of Rome—also representing, presumably, the implied positive of the speaker.

Yet in the next verse, this hope is annihilated in the comic, onomatopoeic image of a stork clattering its bill in the temple of Concord that is smothered with nests. The kind of worship that is paid to the old deities is something that Pecunia can well do without, for while she is a living, ruling presence in the city, the traditional

---

[134] Mayor, *Juvenal, with Commentary,* ii, to J. 1.110 and 1.113.

deities are nothing but dusty memories of days, and hierarchies, long gone. It is no coincidence that the image is chopped off with the humiliation of Concordia by the stork-nests. Concordia is the goddess of concord between the people, and traditionally between the orders of Roman society.[135] This deity represented the old system, where citizens of different rank, as well as slaves and freedmen, knew their place and did not transgress the limits of their rights. In Juvenal's sketch, we have just learnt about the total disintegration of that system, with the foreign freedman pushing his way through the *Troiugenae* with the right of his money—and so it is only fitting that we should then hear about the final fate of overridden Concordia. She has had her temple occupied by a foreign bird,[136] triumphantly clattering away in answer to those who greet the holy place, just as the freedman from Euphrates had rewritten the *concordia ordinum* with his loud and self-announced chatting. The clattering of the immigrant bird parallels the babble of the Egyptian. These are the new voices of the empire's capital, while the true masters of Rome have fallen silent.[137] This is the beginning of an important theme in Juvenal's satires, the lamented crumbling of social order—and with it of decent, human relations between men—because of the levelling and upsetting power of money.

As we have seen, Juvenal makes money a deity in the central tableau. This heavenly position is foreshadowed in the brief vignette on gigolos at 1.37–44. The selling of sex for money is a favourite object of Juvenal's derision, and it is interesting to see that in this first

---

[135] According to tradition, the foremost temple to Concordia in Rome was dedicated in 367 BC, in celebration of the end of civil strife over the Licinian rogations, and restored in 121 BC (after the death of C. Gracchus). The temple and its goddess were thus intimately connected to the regulation of social hierarchy at Rome.

[136] Cf. Petr. *Sat.* 55.6, vv. 5–6: 'ciconia etiam, grata peregrina hospita | pietaticultrix gracilipes crotalistria' ('even the stork, that welcome foreign guest, the pious, slender-legged player of rattles'). The idea that the clattering comes from the *ciconia* nesting had already occurred to the scholiasts: 'ciconia, quae contra templum Concordiae ex conlisio<ne> rostri sonitum facit' ('a stork which makes a noise by clattering its beak opposite the temple of Concord') (Wessner, *Scholia in Juvenalem*, 13); cf. Courtney, *Commentary on Juvenal*, 108–9.

[137] Cf. the situation in Petronius' *Cena Trimalchionis*, where the vulgar language of the freedmen dominates the table conversation; this battle over the discourse is excellently discussed in M. Bloomer, *Latinity and Literary Society at Rome* (Philadelphia: University of Pennsylvania Press, 1997), 235.

satire this activity is described as ascending to heaven. How can you hold back your rage, asks the satirist,

> cum te summoveant qui testamenta merentur
> noctibus, in caelum quos evehit optima summi
> nunc via processus, vetulae vesica beatae?   (37–9)

when you're shouldered aside by people who earn their legacies at night, who have reached heaven via what is now the best way to splendid success—a rich old hag's hole?

As in the greater picture analysed above, the outrage begins with the fact that decent people like the speaker are pushed aside by new money, i.e. by men who have made their way to heaven with the money that comes from the legacies of old women they have served sexually.[138] In this second case, the satirist avoids mentioning money outright, and it is rather those who have come by it that are placed in heaven. In v. 39 the way to heaven is revealed to be the 'vetulae vesica beatae', a comic lowering both in literally topographical, and in thematic terms. The tension of the potential scabrous merriment of this image is earthed with the negative word *vetula*,[139] and with the following description of the gigolos' pallor, likened to that painful pallor from fear experienced by those who have stepped on a snake or who have to speak in the humiliating rhetorical contests at Lugdunum (42–4).[140] The satirist fires the weapon of his derision from a suitably humiliated position, for these men have unfairly offended him first, by pushing him aside for room. Here as well, the reason for the satirist's attack on money is the disorder it creates on earth, smashing the old hierarchy and violently snatching for itself the primary place it has no right to.

---

[138] Cf. the other image of ascending to heaven, used in J. 3.77–8 of the Greek: 'omnia novit | Graeculus esuriens: in caelum iusseris ibit' ('A hungry Greekling knows how to do anything—if you tell him to climb the sky, he'll do it').

[139] See A. Richlin, 'Invective against Women in Roman Satire,' *Arethusa* 17 (1984), 67–80; and ead., *Garden*, 109–16.

[140] According to Suetonius (*Cal.* 20), Caligula had chosen the altar at Lugdunum as the spot for a contest of oratory where unsuccessful speakers had to clear the writing tablets with their tongues, unless they wanted to be whipped or thrown into the river. Courtney (*Commentary on Juvenal*, ad loc.) comments that Juvenal passes here 'from the sublime . . . to the ridiculous'.

Fortune, the enemy of order

It has already been noted above that the workings of suddenly acquired wealth parallel satire's device to heighten its objects before the attack, in that such new wealth raises 'undeserving' people to prominence. The persona is automatically placed in the position of gazing up at them. Another reason for the importance of money in Juvenal may be observed briefly, but I believe clearly, in the tenth satire. In this poem Democritus is introduced, and his laughing view of the world is drawn as an obvious parallel to 'Juvenal's approach, for they both laugh at all things human.[141] In the description of the laughing philosopher, however, a new element appears in the emphatic final position of the portrait, to wit that of 'Fortune':

> ridebat curas nec non et gaudia volgi,
> interdum et lacrimas, cum Fortunae ipse minaci
> mandaret laqueum mediumque ostenderet unguem.   (10.51–3)

he would laugh at the troubles and the joys of the crowd, and sometimes at their tears as well. For himself, he would tell threatening Fortune go hang, and give her the finger.

Thus Fortune, an important deity for the *vulgus*, is something most undesirable and laughable in the eyes of Democritus, Juvenal's model for how to view the world. Juvenal returns to Fortune at the very end of the satire, an even more emphatic position, which on a larger scale corresponds to the goddess' position at the end of the section on Democritus. We learn that 'Juvenal' has the same disdainful view of this goddess:

> nullum numen habes, si sit prudentia: nos te,
> nos facimus, Fortuna, deam caeloque
> locamus.   (10.365–6)

You have no divinity, Fortune, if people could have the sense to see that! It is we, we ourselves, who make you a goddess and place you in heaven

She is in fact no deity at all, only a harmful fantasy, fully deserving the 'up yours' of Democritus.[142] Now *Fortuna*, like money, is a force that moves people suddenly up and down on the scale of well-being and

---

[141] See Introduction, 'Programmatic statements on humour in Roman satire'.
[142] The same phrase (up to 'deam') is repeated at 14.315–16.

power, without taking account of their intrinsic merits. This is a function that Juvenal had spelled out plainly in the seventh satire, where he was describing the arbitrary rise to fame of some intellectuals (7.189–201). This function of Lady Luck is completely unacceptable to Juvenal. He dreams of a static world based on innate merit (moral–intellectual–aesthetic), a world that will not be disturbed and turned upside down by the workings of such fleeting and destabilizing forces as Fortune or Money.

In this connection, we may in fact observe that the Latin 'fortuna' denotes not only the principle, or godhead, of Luck, but also a person's private fortune, i.e. his money. In the first satire, Juvenal complained about the worship of *Pecunia* in Rome, at the expense of the traditional, and stability-bringing deities of Virtus and Concordia; in the tenth (a sort of second programme satire), he complains about the worship of *Fortuna* in Rome. She, like Money, does not deserve an altar in the satirist's view, and her worship, like that of Money, has only brought down disaster on the heads of the Romans, by allowing undeserving personages to come into power. What I suggest is that *Fortuna* with a capital F, and *fortuna* (i.e. wealth, money), neatly turn out to be the same disturbing principle in Juvenal's satires. Like Democritus, the satirist regards this principle of the unpredictable, and in his eyes unacceptable, changes in life, as the very queen of the wrongs of the world, and he strongly underlines this principle in both his programmatic satires, 1 and 10. It is her in particular that he would like to bring down from her undeserved place in heaven. Democritus held a deterministic world-view in tangible, materialistic terms; all could be explained by the movements of atoms, and there was naturally no place for Fortune—no wonder he laughed at her.

Juvenal held, I argue, a deterministic world-view in moral and social terms, desiring a world where all could be explained by every person's intrinsic value, which would lead to his fair advance or downfall with the same clear exactitude as in the movements of atoms. Instead he saw before him a world of flux (remember that he dismisses Heraclitus in the tenth satire, 10.28–32), and the rise of undeserving people, all due to Luck and Money, in short, to fortune/s. The world order was hopelessly out of joint and he could not mend it, could only laugh at it, and especially at that *Fortuna* whose worship had started the havoc.

Yet there is a hinge here, and this lies exactly in the parallel workings of Fortune and a satirist's prime trick of the trade—the haphazard, temporary lifting and smashing of his targets. Since Juvenal was a satirist, *Fortuna* was also his goddess, the Lady of tricks and cheating, and when he refused to worship her, his satire self-consumed in J. 15, and in J. 16 was brought to that stable stand-still which he had desired to his own, and his genre's, destruction.

A resisting reading of Juvenal's women

Apart from money, the biggest threat to order and stability in Juvenal's vision is unbridled sex, and especially the overwhelming lust he attributes to passive homosexuals and women. The two destabilizing forces of wealth and fornication are in fact explicitly connected in a *locus de saeculo* in the sixth satire, just before the infamous Bona Dea episode:

> nullum crimen abest facinusque libidinis ex quo
> paupertas Romana perit. hinc fluxit ad istos
> et Sybaris colles, hinc et Rhodos et Miletos
> atque coronatum et petulans madidumque Tarentum.
> prima peregrinos obscena pecunia mores
> intulit, et turpi fregerunt saecula luxu
> divitiae molles. quid enim venus ebria curat?   (6.294–300)

No crime or deed of lust is lacking here since the fall of Roman poverty. After that, these hills have been flooded by Sybaris, Rhodes, Miletus, and by drunken Tarentum, garlanded and shameless. It was filthy money that first brought foreign morals, and pansy riches crushed our time with foul luxury. When Venus is drunk, does she care about anything?

Although similar loci on how luxury, accompanied by moral decline, first entered Rome are not unusual in Latin literature, the particular focus on sexual morals is not self-evident.[143] In Sallust's famous analysis at *Bellum Catilinae* 10, for instance, lust for money brings lust for power not sex: 'primo pecuniae, deinde imperi cupido crevit' ('first the lust for money grew up, then the lust for power'). In Juvenal, wealth and lust are shown as arriving together to Rome,

---

[143] For comments on luxury in Roman moral thinking, see Earl, *Moral and Political Tradition*, 17–19.

where previously there had been place for neither: 'parva ... tecta' ('small houses'), 288–9; 'paupertas Romana' ('Roman poverty'), 295; 'castas ... Latinas' ('chaste Latian women'), 287; 'somnique ... breves' ('short hours of sleep'), 289; 'stantes Collina turri mariti' ('husbands standing on guard by the Colline Gate'), 291. Even on the verbal plane, wealth and lust are carefully intertwined in each of the three last verses of the passage: *obscena pecunia, turpis luxus,* and the condensed summary of *divitiae molles*. The arriving riches of foreign lands are effeminate, and bring the negative quality of *mollitia,* complete with vanity, perversity and Bacchic frenzy not only to Roman men, but also, and perhaps foremost, to the women. According to this vignette, before the arrival of wealth Roman women had been callous-handed from hard work, and had had no time for sex. With the fatal change, their femininity is unleashed, they become women pure and simple (*femina simplex,* 6.327), and the violent description of the Bona Dea orgy follows immediately to explain what that means.

Feminist studies have convincingly shown that the sixth satire leaves a woman no real alternative life-style by which she might please the satirist, and that it should thus be seen as a satire on women in general, not on female vices.[144] Nevertheless, this satire *masquerades* as an attack on vice, while actually attacking a whole category of human beings—women. This trick of attacking a potentially dangerous antagonist by associating him/her with obviously reprehensible qualities is typical of the genre, and worth further consideration in this case, for the manner in which a satirist makes a certain statement is far from negligible.

While accepting the feminist insistence that the sixth satire cannot be called a moral critique, I would like to argue against the feminists' tendency to take the satire as no more than an ideological statement. In such readings, the verbal form is usually regarded as something that confirms and intensifies the message. However, the form, and especially the humour, of Juvenal's satire often influences the general meaning of what is said, even to the extent of transforming it into its opposite. This is obvious in the case of irony, but there are also many

---

[144] Richlin, *Garden,* 65–70, 202–7, esp. 203.

other instances where questions can be raised about how, and in what degree, the humorous form alters the message.

The analyses of Richlin (*The garden of Priapus*), Henderson ('when Satire writes "Woman" ' and *Writing down Rome*), and Barbara Gold ('Humor in J.'s Sixth Satire') are of particular interest since they all discuss the aspect of humour. Gold methodically involves the reader in her analysis of how the humour functions. It is from her model, at the furthest remove from a Formalist close reading, that my discussion will take its beginning, in order to move gradually into more detail. Starting from a combination of Freud's and Bergson's humour theories, Gold sketches a model of A = speaker (of a joke/humour), B = object/butt (of the joke), and C = audience, supposed to side with A, and share his sense of the ridiculous, in order for the joke to be funny. Given that in Juvenal's sixth satire A is male and B are women, can female readers enjoy the humour? Structurally, they are placed in C, but by their gender they have more in common with B than with A, which of course destabilizes the necessary balance.[145] Gold answers this question with a firm no—conscious women readers, especially feminist readers should resist the humour, and not laugh at the satire.

It seems to me that both the negative answer and the question itself need some qualification. The first problem is whom we should call readers in this case. If we include all the centuries of Juvenal's readers from the first appearance of the book and up to ourselves (as Gold occasionally does, and as seems reasonable), then it becomes impossible to speak of 'Juvenal's stereotypical male reader'.[146]

Still, let us begin with the category of contemporary readers. Female readers contemporary to Juvenal would have been likely to be co-opted into the satirist's view, as Gold observes, simply because Roman women lived in a strict patriarchy, 'had little or no sense of

---

[145] Contrast Baumert who (to my mind reasonably) suggests that satire cannot function at all unless there is a 'satirical situation' which consists of the presence of three actors: satirist, object and audience. According to this view, the reader has to suspend her distrust and play the role of 'audience' in order for the satire to be realized in the first place (Baumert, 'Identifikation und Distanz', 735–6; the term 'satirical situation' ('satirische Situation') was first introduced by J. Schönert, *Roman und Satire im 18. Jahrhundert. Ein Beitrag zur Poetik.* Germanistische Abhandlungen, Bd. 27. Diss. (Stuttgart, 1969)).

[146] Gold, 'Humor in J. 6', 99.

belonging to a group, and might have given in to male stereotyping of women in order to gain admission to the men's club'.[147] It may be added that this also holds true for women readers in other patriarchal systems, up to our time. Where there is only one view of sexuality and gender relations—the male view—it will tend to be imposed on the oppressed group, women, and become their view too. What is essentially the view favourable to one side poses as neutral, and will be accepted as such even by the humiliated side. This is so not only because they have no alternative, but also because they hope (consciously or unconsciously) to gain at least some privileges from accepting what is 'normal'. An additional trick lies precisely in the fact that the oppressed group has no sense of belonging to a group. This is where the sixth satire's masquerading becomes useful: since the text claims to attack bad, misbehaving women, not women as such, a female reader can see B, the butt of the satire, as a group to which she does not belong, and happily laugh at B. Since she has little sense of women as a group, she will share with A the liking of decorous behaviour and a stable social hierarchy, and see herself as having nothing in common with B, which she regards as consisting of women who deviate from decorum and social order. This does not necessarily mean gaining admission to the men's club, the woman reader may see it as a 'decent people's club'.

If, on the other hand, all readers up to the present day are included in the category of the audience, C, then there may perhaps be other ways of reading this satire, which can be exercised precisely with the help of our ideological resistance to its misogynous tenor, combined with modern theoretical insights. The pessimistic reading of J. 6 as a poem that stereotypes and insults women is the inverse of the traditional reading. In this 'inverted' reading, the same act (the attack and ridicule of women) is evaluated in the opposite way (negative rather than positive), and avenges the butts of the satire, women, by doing to Juvenal what he did to them—attacking him verbally and branding him as morally inferior. Yet the satire might be read still more *against the grain* if the reader not only refuses to accept the explicit moral accents, but also questions the very categories and

---

[147] Ibid. I agree with Gold that it is quite possible that Juvenal could have had female readers at Rome.

contours set up by the text. A destabilizing factor may actually be found in the humour of the satire.

A major inspiration for such uncooperative readings of literature was provided by Judith Fetterley's influential study *The Resisting Reader: A Feminist Approach to American Fiction*, 1978. It is the last one of her sharp, provocative readings of eight fictional works—her analysis of Norman Mailer's *An American Dream*—that makes the best comparison to my reading of J. 6. Of this novel Fetterley says the following lines, which might also have described the starting point for my examination of Juvenal:

Mailer's work represents an end point beyond which sexism cannot go without becoming, in ironic fidelity to the logic of his own style, its opposite... Adherence to the patriarchal system and to the mythologies of male chauvinism becomes in Mailer's hands a kind of inverted feminism. At once the most blatantly and commitedly chauvinist... Mailer is also the most subintentionally feminist.... Through his relentless presentation of the nightmare content of the system of sexual politics and through his decision to embrace that content, to live it out to its ultimate conclusion, and to make it the stuff of moral courage, he provides nausea enough to clear out all our pipes.[148]

In the case of Juvenal's sixth satire, the uncooperative reader can, put simply, choose to focus on the recurring nightmare scenarios of female transgression, and read these scenarios as the triumphs of the women in them rather than as examples of inadmissible vice. Humour would be central to this procedure, because the transgressive character in a humorous scene is potentially a comic hero/ine. Even if his or her positive energy is suppressed at the end of the scene, the memory of it will linger on, for what is said in words, in poetry, is made real. To kill the positive energy completely the poet would have to abandon humour, and such a move is, significantly, made towards the end of the sixth satire, where the speaker says that the subject matter demands a diversion of his satire into tragedy (634–7). Yet it may be claimed that even this is not entirely seriously done. The reading outlined here would of course go against the expressed

---

[148] J. Fetterley, *The Resisting Reader: A Feminist Approach to American Fiction* (Bloomington: Indiana University Press, 1978), 156–7.

intention of the satire's speaker, but it would still highlight elements that are demonstrably present in the text.[149]

For the uncooperative reading it must first be noticed that J. 6 features freeborn, married upper-class *matronae* indulging in the most outrageous transgressions and role reversals, mostly of a sexual kind—a more active and comic role than this silent, decorous category of Romans had previously enjoyed in literature, not to mention social reality. In Roman comedy plots featured slaves playing masters and female slaves scheming transgressive tricks, but these plots had kept the matrons boring, nagging, and *in their proper place*—securely limited to their role of chastity and decorum.[150] Even in the orgiastic scenes in the Roman novel the misbehaving women are taken from the categories of prostitutes, slaves, or witches, not aristocratic wives and daughters. The vices of this class of women in previous specimens of verse satire, Horace's *S.* 1.2, 2.7 or Persius' 6.72-3, had consisted of hiding their corporeal blemishes behind clever clothes or, at most, capricious behaviour towards their lovers. In Horace's *S.* 1.2, for instance, adultery had been mentioned as a fact, but the role of the woman, when noticed, had not exceeded the elegiac touches of trying to hide the adultery from her husband or of occasional coquetry. The fact of the matrons' sexual licence was not painted in detailed, 'outrageous' scenes, and the focus was always on

---

[149] In addition to Fetterley, cf. Umberto Eco's notion of the 'Model Reader', who can be either obedient or disobedient (U. Eco, *Lector in fabula: la cooperazione interpretativa nei testi narrativi* (Milan: Bompiani, 1979), 50–66). An interesting feature in the system set up by Eco is his claim that a 'closed' text (i.e. a text engineered to arouse a precise response in a more or less precise group of empirical readers) is easier to read against the grain—read as a disobedient Model Reader—than an 'open' one. Juvenal's sixth satire is certianly a closed text in Eco's terms, since it is aimed at a well-defined goup of Roman elite males whose reactions are precisely guided throughout the poem. What I am attempting in this section is something like a disobedient reading of the closed text. In Postcolonialist studies some readings that want to redeem the silenced voices of oppressed groups make use of a similar approach: a fine example is Stephen Greenblatt's 'Learning to Curse' on Caliban in *The Tempest*, in his *Learning to Curse: Essays in Early Modern Culture* (New York: Routledge, 1990), 16–39.

[150] See A. Rei, 'Villains, Wives, and Slaves in the Comedies of Plautus,' in S. R. Joshel and S. Murnaghan (eds.), *Women and Slaves in Greco-Roman Culture. Differential Equations.* (London and New York: Routledge, 1998), who convincingly demonstrates 'the exclusion of honourable matrons from ludic agency' (101) in Plautus' plays.

the man. In J. 6 the focus is on the women, nor are they even *vetulae*, that stereotype of the old randy crone, who could more safely play a deviant role (as in Horace's *Epodes* 8 and 12), since she was past childbearing and thus in effect also outside the duties of a wife. Elite women in a fertile age—the pledge of Roman virtue and glory—had never been allowed so much fun as they were in Juvenal's sixth satire.

Furthermore, the transgression of these women is, from a patriarchal point of view, of the worst possible kinds: they bear their elite husbands no children or bastard children; they usurp typically and exclusively male roles; they attack the elite males, their husbands and sons, and kill them. For all of this, they are not punished in the narrative, for we never hear about them being taught a lesson, the way e.g. the greedy debauchee was in the first satire (1.142-6), when he died in the bath. The few times that the speaker directly addresses a female villain, she answers saucily, and shamelessly insists on the very behaviour she is being accused of (219–23; 281–4; 638–42).[151] It is far from obvious that these women's lines are, as Gold claims, scripted by the speaker and supportive of his case. The unabashed 'Yes, I'm bad!' in reaction to an accusation may be read as the very worst answer the chauvinistic speaker could get, since it puts an effective end to the shaming interrogation, and leaves him to splutter angry asides. Surely it would have been a better script from his point of view if the woman had begun to lose herself in excuses, showing that she did share his value code, but allowing him to get the last word. Also, it is easier to sympathize with this woman, who frankly opposes the ideology imposed on her, for unlike the shamed sinner, she shares certain traits with *comic heroes*. Such heroes delight in their transgression and insist on their 'badness',[152] thus offering the audience identification models for temporary freedom from the system they live in, and holding forth at least the momentary

[151] Thus I do not agree with Gold's claim that the speaker is free to 'vilify B without having to confront B directly and thus embarass or alienate his audience' (Gold, 'Humor in J. 6', 98, cf. 104–5).

[152] e.g. the slaves of Roman comedy, who have 'badness', *malitia*, as their main 'virtue'; see the discussions in W. S. Anderson, *Barbarian Play: Plautus' Roman Comedy* (Toronto: University of Toronto Press, 1993), 88–92; Rei, 'Villains, Wives, and Slaves in Plautus', 94.

realization that another world is possible.[153] The worse they are, the better, they are welcome to boast about it, and they must also be happy, quick-tongued, and funny. The matrons who talk back to 'Juvenal' have all these traits of the comic hero. The difference lies in the severity of their crimes, which would not pass in comedy. The persona cries hysterical comments about the effrontery of it, but a resisting reader does not have to agree with him, and may choose to stick with the direct dialogue rather than with the moralistic explanation, especially since the former is much funnier. The satirist's intended strategy is the device that we have seen throughout with object-oriented humour: the target is heightened and made more powerful before being derided. The satiric persona explicitly vilifies the women, and smashes them down with his mockery, but given the force of their 'vices', the question is whether that is really quite enough to neutralize the unsettling effect achieved by the comic staging of the central underlying anxieties of Roman patriarchy. As Braund has observed in an essay on this satire, the poem has a deep structure which charts the addressee's, Postumus', progress from his mad, death-associated wish to marry, at the beginning, to madness and death at the hands of a wife, with which the satire ends.[154] There is thus a ring-composition from madness to madness, and it may be added, from death to death, for 'Juvenal' begins his advice by suggesting several ways of committing suicide which Postumus can resort to rather than marrying (30–3), implying that marriage is a very painful form of death. Braund's further claim that this ring-structure supports the view that the satire is against marriage rather than against women in general seems less convincing.[155] It may rather be said that what surfaces here is the fear of the death of

---

[153] Cf. Douglas, 'Joke Perception', where jokes are analysed as the opposite of rites: 'The message of a standard rite is that the ordained patterns of social life are inescapable. The message of a joke is that they are escapable. A joke is by nature an anti-rite' and again, 'a joke implies that anything is possible' (370, 373).

[154] S. H. Braund, 'Juvenal—Misogynist or Misogamist?,' *JRS* 82 (1992), 85; she also points out a verbal echo between the initial madness, marked by 'caligantes . . . fenestrae' (v.31), 'vertiginous top-floor windows', and the final madness, 'animo caligo' (613), 'darkness of mind'.

[155] Ibid. The main argument of the article is connected to the question of the persona's unreliability, which will be discussed in Ch. 2, § 'The question of trust in Juvenal's speaker'.

men at the hands of women, the secret nightmare of a strict patri-archy. In this connection, it might also be remembered that one of the few ways a *pater familias* could lose his position was by being declared insane by his family. In this poem, woman robs man of his mind as well as his life, and in-between she takes his money and lays claim to the same sexual licence that he has. The satirist's device of empowering his object in order to mock it from below comes dangerously close to real fear.[156]

Moreover, the satirist's craft, and Juvenal's satire in particular, can be said to have characteristics similar to those the negative stereotype attributed to women: trickery, manipulation, doubleness, excite-ment, boldness, and inability to temper one's feelings, especially anger. In the case of the sixth satire, a formidable battle between the women and the satirist is staged; nowhere else is Juvenal as manipulative, as bold, and as angry. It could be said that what the women do to the persona at the level of imagery, this the persona does to them at the level of his appeal to the reader. Just as the women crowd 'Juvenal' with their terrible presence ('Clytemestram nullus non vicus habebit' ('there isn't a street without a Clytemnestra'), 656) and by implication threaten to kill him along with all men, so he, in turn, pacifies and dismisses all women by the sum of J. 6, inviting the reader to join him in the dismissal. Still, the persona's victory is not as clear as the satirist would have needed for a total branding of womankind, for the women are consistently cooler than the persona, and often funnier, since most of the comic incongruities are imbed-ded in the colourful scenes, the *showing*, while he is loaded with the hyperbolic, often hysterical commentary, the tedious *telling*.[157] The Romans considered anger and vindictiveness as typically female characteristics, as even 'Juvenal' himself tells us in *Satire* 13 (vv. 191–2). In the case of the sixth satire, a resisting reader might claim that 'Juvenal' not only discloses the anxiety about being killed by a woman, but also the anxiety of becoming one, while she usurps the active male role.

---

[156] Fear is taken as the rationale behind this satire by Richlin, *Garden*, 203: 'That the hostility towards women in *Satire* 6 stems from fear is easily seen.'

[157] We owe these useful terms of literary discussion originally to Booth, *Fiction*.

So, in the description of the female athlete at 6.246-67, we face an alternating rhythm, as Gold observes, of humour and aggressive comments from the persona.[158] Gold finds the beginning of the portrait hilarious, though its humour is built on the expectation that women should not be athletes. This woman with her shield and practising sword is, in the speaker's opinion, behaving so disgracefully as to be fit for the show combat of prostitutes at the Floralia.[159] Yet she is, shockingly enough, a matron, and the word is wedged into the meretrician context with jarring sarcasm: 'dignissima prorsus | Florali *matrona* tuba' ('in full measure worthy of the trumpet of the Floralia—though a lady'), 249–50. Still, she is not only as bad as a prostitute, she is actually worse, for she longs not for the staged battle, but for the real arena. The prostitute's profession gave her, together with the contempt she suffered, a certain freedom of movement. She was allowed to have a more active attitude than a married woman both in deeds and words, and thus in the dichotomy of male and female as active vs. passive, and speaking vs. silent, she fell somewhere in between, and was, significantly, marked off from 'decent' women by her male dress, the toga. This matron skips the middle stage of the prostitute, and goes directly to invade the athlete's equipment, the male outfit at the maximum remove from her matronly role.

What is presented in this portrait is a 'reverse stereotype', an expression which I shall use to understand an idea that has grown stereotypical, but which is originally the reversal of a norm-conforming stereotype. For example, the hen-pecked husband and the bossy wife have both grown into stereotypes by being repeated over and over, but they could not exist without the 'normal', primary stereotypes of the authoritative husband and the obedient wife, which correspond to the social and legal rules of a certain society. The *reverse stereotypes* are 'abnormal', secondary stereotypes that call for a response of laughter or outrage, not indifference. Unlike the norm-conforming stereotype, the reverse stereotype is not meant to be transparent, to pass unnoticed. There is the difference that the

---

[158] Gold, 'Humor in J. 6', 98–9; her discussion is made problematic by the fact that she does not include 'ridicule' in 'humour'.

[159] Courtney, *Commentary on Juvenal*, on 6.249–50.

reverse stereotype always carries its memory of disorder with it, even in the stalest joke or the most banal moralistic complaint. The reverse stereotype of the bossy wife has a whiff of the topsy-turvy about it, while the norm-complying stereotype of the obedient wife has not. Reverse stereotypes may perfectly well be used to dismiss what is inverted and defend the norm, but they are more dynamic than a plain insistence on the norm, for the inversion has the potential of two evaluations, negative or positive. In discussing satire, it is useful to differentiate between three categories: in addition to the stereotype and the reverse stereotype, there is also the *ad hoc* inversion of normal images and ideas, employed by the satirist as an original device and not (or not yet) a reverse stereotype confirmed by frequent usage.

The picture of the female athlete is a reverse stereotype in two ways: here is a woman indulging in a very male activity, gladiatorial training, and here is a matron more outrageously un-feminine than a prostitute. These are inversions of the real stereotypes of macho gladiators, physically daring courtesans, and decorous matrons. The idea of the matron-worse-than-the-prostitute, a notion which crops up repeatedly in the sixth satire, and which may be traced in Horace's *S.* 1.2, can be said to have passed into the category of accepted reverse stereotypes by this time. Still, reverse stereotypes and original inversions—both of which figure richly in J. 6—depend on norm-conforming stereotypes for their very existence. It thus seems strange to say, as Gold does, that the humour in the portrait discussed here is 'undercut (for less-than-sympathetic readers) by the ridicule and stereotyping',[160] for it is built on stereotyping. Without the knowledge of the stereotypes of decent matrons in stolae, and of dishonourable, male gladiators, we would not recognize the image of the *matrona* in an athlete's dress as humour in the first place. Conservative satire feeds on the energy generated by inverting stereotypes, but tries to tie down its own inversions by reverting to the norm and declaring the inversion unacceptable. The longer the inversion holds the stage the livelier the satire, but the reader must also be reminded of the need to dismiss this image. This is, I believe, what creates the

---

[160] Gold, 'Humor in J. 6', 98; original parenthesis.

alternating rhythm between theatrical showing and dismissive commentary in Juvenal's portraits of women.

It is hardly possible to *neutralize* the tendentiousness of the humour anywhere in the passage on the female athlete, either in the show or in the commentaries, but a resisting reading may *turn it in the opposite direction*, against the speaker. Such a reading may use two problems in the speaker's argument.

First, as in the case with money, the persona faces the problem of reality: the female monster he introduces is not only a product of his imagination. His move to give a Roman matron an aggressive part, and weapons to hold, for her role as the butt of this satiric scene, is in accordance with the satiric device we have observed throughout, that of heightening/empowering the target before the attack. Yet unlike the situation in e.g. Horace's battle with the bore (*S.* 1.9) the weapons of this woman are not merely verbal additions in the style of her description, and so cannot be dissolved into thin air at the end. Her equipment is an actual attribute in the scene, and what is worse, there were female gladiators and athletes in Rome, though they were of course not as common as 'Juvenal' exaggeratedly claims (6.247). In order to strip her of her power the persona has to describe the sale of her weapons (255–8), and, importantly, show her as putting them away when she needs to use a chamber-pot, as the woman she is. In this last case the persona even explicitly asks the addressee to laugh at this scene 'et ride positis scaphium cum sumitur armis' ('and laugh when she lays down her weapons to take up the pot'), 264. But whether the reader laughs at the scene or not, the woman's weapons are still there, laid down on both sides of the lowering word, and image: '*positis* scaphium cum sumitur *armis*'. The picture of the removal of aggressive attributes, and the showing of nakedness and bodily needs, is meant to bring her down from her high horses, and humiliate her. Yet she cannot be said to have been disclosed as a fraud, for she never pretended to be a man. She has practised with male arms, she has kept her lustful sex, she has embarrassed her husband when the equipment was sold, and she has presumably unashamedly taken a pause to use the pot—she has had it all, and has not been punished within the scene. The husband/addressee is, somewhat clumsily, asked to laugh, for he is dangerously close to being the fool here. He might perhaps have wept if he had not been instructed. Given the facts that this androgynous woman athlete corresponded to an actual Roman reality, and that she triumphs in the scene, while the man is humiliated (he is ashamed when her tools are sold), it would perhaps have been a better strategy to be silent about her existence. Looming symbolically huge over patriarchal anxieties about boundary-crossing, she has grown even bigger by being on stage for so long, and in such hilarious detail.

Secondly, in order for the woman's role reversal not to be complete, so as to stay comic and not too threatening, the reader must be reminded that she is actually still a woman. Thus the false note in this gladiator is there from the very first line of the passage: 'endromidas Tyrias et femineum ceroma' ('purple track-suits and ladies' mud'), 246, are images that combine male and female excesses of dress in an unexpected manner. She is meant to be a monster, neither male nor female, but the imagery in fact suggests that she is both. The idea that women derive more pleasure from sex than men (254), a reverse stereotype in relation to the norm of sexually passive women, further invokes the image of a powerful, two-sexed creature by alluding to the seer Teiresias. According to legend, Teiresias had been a woman for a time of his life, and so knew about the greater sexual satisfaction of women. The persona screams that she can have no sense of shame, this woman in a helmet, but the joke is that she does not want any shame, she wants sex. She keeps the combat equipment she has claimed from the men, along with her lustful, female body underneath, again alluded to in the toilet scene. Some of the shame she ought to feel, but does not, seems to fall on her husband when her athletic attributes are sold (255–8). When a happy personage faces a humiliated one, more clues will have to be included in order to steer the reader's sympathies to the side of the loser. The androgynous woman, monstrously equipped and fully satisfied, also becomes monstrously powerful. It is doubtful whether the lowering derision engineered through the speaker's irony and direct moralizing is enough to neutralize the enlargement/empowering that the author has lavished on his target here.

Thus what I have argued is that Juvenal's style, especially his humour, must not necessarily be regarded as a means to 'cover a host of sins',[161] but can be read *against* the apparent ideological

---

[161] Ibid.

message of the satire. The idea is that the humour, palatable in this 'supreme manipulator of the Latin language',[162] not only *seems to* soften the aggression and alter the message, but actually *does* alter the message. The images brought in for the splendour of Juvenal's art may prove less pliable for his ideology than he would have liked, their liveliness may drag along more ambivalence than he bargained for. It is not impossible to read the episode of Tullia's and Maura's pissing on the altar of Chastity and laugh *with* them rather than at them, and *at* the ridiculous husband who splashes through their puddles in the morning (6.306–13), though the historical Juvenal would hardly have appreciated such a reading.

It should be agreed that J. 6 is a misogynous satire on balance, but its texture is not homogeneous and should not be reduced to homogeneity. It is full of purple patches which are not wholly supportive of the main idea, and even contains patches that are contrary to it. It is a garishly coloured thing, alive with the energy of the struggle between the poet and the women, and although the outcome is in favour of the author, we feel that he has somewhere cheated us in the text, dazzled us and exchanged one colour for another—for otherwise he could not have been sure of his victory.

While the model of 'speaker—target—willing/resisting reader' is unique to Gold's analysis of J. 6, other points important to her reading had already appeared in Richlin's study of Roman sexual humour, notably the view of the (reverse) stereotype of lustful women as humiliating to women in itself. This is a view that these readings share with Juvenal's persona, who no doubt *means* the caricatures to be humiliating to women, but I have argued that they may also be read against the persona's explicit wish. More particularly, it seems that Richlin's powerful model of the Roman satirist as a Priapus who rapes the targets of his satires can be somewhat modified in application to Juvenal's sixth satire. In this connection it should be mentioned that Richlin does not make a difference between the persona and the (implied) author, and that she sees no gap between the outlooks of the satirist and his speaker in the satires. She occasionally acknowledges sudden turns and ambivalences in the speaker's view. Mostly, however, she sees the behaviour

---

[162] In the formulation of Mason, 'Is Juvenal a Classic?', 176.

and world-view of the speaker as a direct manifestation of the Priapic satirist's world-view.

So, for instance, in the central tableau of J. 6, the Bona Dea episode (301–51), less is made of the women's licence than could have been done. The women meet for the festival of the goddess Bona Dea, traditionally celebrated by women in strict isolation from men (in fact from all male creatures), and under sexual abstention. The historical anecdote about how Clodius had entered the celebrations dressed as a female musician, in order to seduce Caesar's wife, had been a scandal loud enough to be well remembered in Juvenal's time, and it is used in the present episode. The satirist begins by stating directly that the 'secrets' of the good goddess, or Bona Dea, are well known by now, and immediately proceeds to a description of the orgy, which begins by an exciting dance. In three lines we learn the secret: the supposedly chaste festival is a Bacchanal, and the god worshipped therein is—Priapus:

> nota *bonae* secreta *deae*, cum tibia lumbos
> incitat et cornu pariter vinoque feruntur
> attonitae crinemque rotant ululantque *Priapi*
> *maenades.* (6.314-17)

The secret rites of the Good Goddess are no secret: when the flute fires the loins and the frenzied women, Priapus' maenads, are carried away by horn and wine alike, tossing their hair and howling.

In Juvenal's satire, these matrons have replaced the silent, chaste cult of a *good* female deity with howling, head-banging orgies in honour of a 'bad' male deity. With their violent behaviour, no wonder the secret is out. This position of sexually licentious women as Priapus' friends and protégés is very much in line with other such relations in Priapic literature, unaccounted for in Richlin's model. In the *Priapea*, a first-century AD collection of poems dedicated to Priapus, poems 4, 10, 19, and especially 27, all deal with less than virtuous women who hope either to seduce Priapus, or to get his help for professional success in attracting men. In Petronius' *Satyrica*, Priapus' priestess Quartilla enacts an orgy in the god's honour, complete with wine, aphrodisiacs and sex of different kinds;[163] Quartilla's retinue consists

---

[163] Elsewhere I have analysed this inverted episode and its literary implications (Plaza, *Laughter and Derision*, 73–83, 212–15).

of women and *cinaedi*, in themselves most un-Priapic characters, who seem to be accepted by the god thanks to their excessive sexual appetites. Priapus, usually full of aggressive contempt for women, appears to make an exception for sexually insatiable women and/or professional prostitutes, who may even hope for the god's protection. The exception has a certain logic: such women would be least vulnerable to rape as a means of attack and humiliation, they share Priapus' interest in 'immoral', and often violent, orgies, and—in symbolic terms—they also share his aspect of transgression and festive licence. Nevertheless, it is a surprising, inverted alliance that is struck between the macho god and the women that, in real life, were placed at the very bottom of the social hierarchy. The humorous potential of this surprise and inversion is exploited in the *Priapea*, in the Quartilla and Oenothea episodes in the *Satyrica* (*Sat.* 16-26.6; 134-138.4), and in Juvenalian passage quoted above. In Juvenal, the Priapic women are presented in a particularly disquieting manner, for they are both married Roman matrons, supposed to be celebrating the rites of the Bona Dea, and at the same time ('really') nymphomaniacs, allied to Priapus. As matrons, they should be shamed, stained, and violated ('raped', in Richlin's terminology) by being associated with Priapus, but as 'whores', they actively seek the association with the same god, and are protected by him. In Juvenal's scene, the matrons-whores worship Priapus, and are called his maenads, which, it seems to me, makes the application of Richlin's model of the satirist as Priapus raping his objects problematic in the passage. Rather, the women are cast in the role of the rapist: disrespectful, fierce, and sexually insatiable. It seems clear that the persona begins the scene with the intention to denigrate the women. Unlike the narrator of the *Satyrica*, he is careful not to grant the women a voice of their own to express their point of view 'from within'. Still, his strategy to describe them as energetic Priapic maenads is a dangerous one, slipping out of his hands as the women become more powerful than is convenient if the ultimate goal is to squash them. The satirist saves his face formally in that the women are criticized in their role as matrons, but in drawing a picture of matrons that run amok and line up with Priapus he is too obviously letting slip what he really fears. If Roman wives and mothers gang up for orgies when they are supposed to worship chastity, then who will be the fool? The objects of Juvenal's derision grow so mighty as to attract even the god of sexual superiority humour, Priapus, to their side—and thus, by implication, casting men in the role of the butt of their sexual, violent hilarity.

When the women reveal their actual nature ('omnia fient | ad verum' ('everything is for real'), 324–5; 'tum femina simplex' ('then woman appears in her pure form'), 327), which consists of unbridled libido, they give a command for the men to enter, in mock-religious language, 'iam fas est, admitte viros' ('the time is right, let in the men!'), 329. There follows a quickly degrading cascade of possible lovers: the *adulter*, if he is not available, then the youth, the slave, the hired *aquarius* ('water-carrier'), and finally, should there be no human men around, a donkey (329–34). As has been noted,[164] the next step is to present a detached penis, and in the imagery this is achieved with the focus on the male organ of the false lady musician, Clodius:

> quae psaltria penem
> maiorem quam sunt duo Caesaris Anticatones
> illuc, testiculi sibi conscius unde fugit mus,
> intulerit ...   (6.337–40)

what harp-girl it was that carried a penis larger than both scrolls of Caesar's *Anticato* to the place from which a male mouse flees, conscious of the testimony of his testicles ...

The point is apparently that the heated women will copulate with anyone or anything. Several scholars have claimed that the inclusion of the donkey is a variant of the misogynous commonplace of comparing women to animals.[165] Yet the details of the imagery suggest that it is not the women who are likened to animals, but the men. Any male will do for these women, even a donkey, and so *the men* are exchangeable with animals. The somewhat later image of the male mouse fleeing from the Bona Dea rites, because conscious of his testicles, confirms the impression of exchangeability. Parallels from other literature, in fact, bring out this pattern: in *Pr.* 52.9

---

[164] Henderson, 'Satire Writes Woman'.

[165] A misogynous motif popular at least since Semonides, who treated it in an iambic poem in the 7th cent. BC . See Richlin, *Garden*, 206, and Gold ('Humor in J. 6', 109), who strangely claims that copulation with animals is 'an even closer tie' than being likened to them.

Priapus threatens to rape a man with the help of some asses, which puts the asses in the same role as Priapus himself; in Apuleius' *Metamorphoses* it is the phenomenon of a man in an ass's shape that is explored throughout, including the episode of 10.19–23, where a lady falls in love with Lucius the ass.[166] It is also important to note that the picture is not one of rape of the women, neither with the men nor with the ass. Rather, it is the women who crave the sex, actively moving to get it, even in the case of the donkey: 'inposito clunem summittat asello' ('she'll put her buttocks under a donkey'), 334. The picture in Juvenal of course implies that the women's lust is excessive, but it also places the men in an even less flattering role, that of the impersonal object of the women's lust. This is a complete inversion of the code of sexual roles, and if anyone is playing the role of Priapus here, it is the women, who sexually attack anything that moves.

The passage is humorous because it shows an impossible, frenziedly abnormal scene, and yet, once again, Juvenal steps very close to the real fears of patriarchy. In the Roman patriarchal system, men upheld their sexual superiority by binding women, and especially *matronae*, to chastity and the home, but fantasies of female resurrection and revenge kept haunting them, not least in their literature.[167] It is unconvincing to present a reading of J. 6 which makes a sharp separation between the male implied author and the male persona on the one hand, and the men presented as ridiculous exchangeable objects on the other hand.[168] If 'Juvenal' would step closer to the women's grotto, he too would be dragged in for copulation, for we are not informed of any fundamental difference between the persona and the men that are depicted in such a humiliating role in vv.329–34—at least not as regards the first categories (an adulterer, a youth). If, however, the persona stays on the fringe of the orgy, looking on, this position again has uncanny connotations: those of mythical Pentheus spying on an exclusively female bacchanal (e.g. in Euripides' *Bacchae*), before being discovered and torn to pieces by the

---

[166] Richlin, *Garden*, 206 n. 68.

[167] Almost all the articles collected in S. J. Joshel and S. Murnaghan (eds.), *Women and Slaves in Greco-Roman Culture*, discuss such hauntings by women and slaves, from different angles.

[168] Richlin, *Garden*, 202–7.

women. Juvenal's Bona Dea episode may be a male fantasy,[169] but it is a dangerous fantasy, more akin to a male nightmare than to a pornographic joke. It is not sufficient to say that 'the power relationship is reaffirmed',[170] for although the persona has had this effect in mind, he has perhaps empowered the women too much in making them not only sexually assault the dumb men, but also show, through their behaviour, the exchangeability of men and animals and dildos.

Before the concluding moralistic exclamation (6.342–51), the pictorial part of the passage closes with the contrasting images of Clodius' enormous penis entering the sacred rites and of the little male mouse piously fleeing from the same rites. The picture of the ball-conscious mouse again points to the parallel between men and male animals in the episode, but other effects are also involved. Apart from the moralistic surface sense there is comic relief in the scurrying rodent after the monumental fresco of the Priapic orgy of high-born matrons. Furthermore, as has been noted by Mason, there is also a technical brilliance in the contrast between the line endings of vv. 338–9, the first long and sonorous ('Caesaris Anticatones'), the second anticlimactically chopped off and comical ('conscius unde fugit mus').[171] In the first line the words are majestically long—and the length of the signifying words mirrors the length of the signified. The second line recalls Horace's 'ridiculus mus' ('ridiculous mouse', *Ars* 139; perhaps also the episode of the mice in *Satire* 2.6) and mimics the minuteness of the mouse's balls.[172] Mason further claims that the raising of the humour to the level of literary wit is achieved 'at the cost of blowing away all serious thought that might have been gathering in the preceding lines'. After his acute observations about the passage in question, this conclusion seems too limited. It is true that the lines are very carefully chiselled, and that this, together with the comic anticlimax of the mouse creates a distancing, 'cool' effect after the red-hot description of the women. If 'Juvenal' is so detached here—the reasoning goes—then he cannot have meant much when

---

[169] Thus perceived in Richlin, *Garden*; Gold, 'Humor in J. 6'; Henderson, *Writing down Rome*; and Mason, 'Is Juvenal a Classic?'. Mason, however, speaks of detachment on the part of the author, achieved with the help of cynicism and 'male humour' (p. 151).

[170] Gold, 'Humor in J. 6', 109.   [171] Mason, 'Is Juvenal a Classic?', 152.

[172] Ibid., cf. also Courtney, *Commentary on Juvenal*, ad loc.

he was screaming some verses ago; but this swaying between detachment and frenzy is only a seeming impossibility, and is in fact typical of Roman satire and part of its paradoxical essence.[173] The satirist must appear as a heated moralist, but the pretence should not be too complete, there should be art as well as feeling, and the reader may well occasionally be reminded of the rhetorical skill and cool head of the author.

In Juvenal the two poles of moral indignation and rhetorical detachment are particularly extreme, and it is only the careful, almost rhythmical placement of the contrasting passages within his satires that save the mixture from appearing mad and maddening. A detached, ironical comment will often be placed at the end of an especially indignant scene, cooling the sizzling metal into artistic form, rendering the sense more complex. When regarded closely, these vacillations actually do appear mad and maddening, but at the normal distance created in a straight reading of the satire they are not noticed for themselves, but serve to give Juvenal's text that high-tension quality which is its trademark. Still, this does not mean that such sobering, often comical passages drain their greater context of 'serious' meaning (if by 'serious' we mean 'signifying, not nonsensical'). On the contrary, they strengthen certain undercurrents which have already vaguely featured in the preceding episode by bringing them to an extreme conclusion. The construction of the text seems to trip farcically and fall over itself, but in the end only stresses a tension and a movement that was there all along, and continues rocking violently without falling or disintegrating. So, in the lines about Clodius and the mouse, there is a hurried movement in (monstrously big lust enters the Bona Dea celebration) and out (modestly small piety flees the same). The size of Clodius' member and the grand connotations of *Caesaris Anticatones* serve the same inflation and empowering of the satirical target which we have observed throughout. The small mouse, on the other hand, parallels the position of the satirical persona, crowded by vice and fleeing from it. He is much less powerful than his vicious enemies in terms of physique, but superior

---

[173] Kernan, *Cankered Muse*, 1–7, 14–30, esp. 30: 'Every satirist is something of a Jekyll and Hyde'; cf. also H. C. Fredricksmeyer, 'An Observation on the Programmatic Satires of Juvenal, Horace and Persius,' *Latomus* 49 (1990), 792–800.

in his moral make-up—note that the mouse independently *decides* to flee, because he is *conscious* of his virility ('testiculi sibi conscius').[174]

Yet there is also another shade of meaning, present already in the preceding bacchanal—that of male anxiety. Since Mason stamps the Bona Dea episode as the outcome of 'adolescent male humour', by which he seems to mean obscene humour, he is not interested in any particulars of the humour, until he reaches the lines of *Anticatones* and mice. When closer attention is paid to the humour in the bacchanal, however, it may be observed that it holds a doubleness between the dismissal of the misbehaving women and the comic triumph of these women, though with the stress put on the dismissal. In the concluding images, the triumphant member of vicious Clodius goes in to the women, while the mouse with its tiny balls (even phrased in the singular) goes out from their rites. This is presumably in accordance with what the lusty women just described would have wished. The chaste mouse, like the chaste satirical persona, can only deal with these women by fleeing. They are right in fleeing, for the example of Pentheus shows what may happen to an unsympathetic intruder into women's bacchanals. Unfortunately, the persona's and the mouse's behaviour suits the villainous women perfectly: the moralists stay out and do not disturb.

Then again, the Horatian allusion inherent in the words 'unde fugit mus' ('the place from which a mouse flees') ties Juvenal's mouse to the passage of Horace's *Ars Poetica* which treats anticlimaxes ('parturient montes, nascetur ridiculus mus' ('the mountains will give birth, a ridiculous mouse will be born'), *Ars* 139). Juvenal's contrast between Clodius' enormous member and the small mouse exactly repeats Horace's contrast between the mountainous expectations and the resulting mouse. Juvenal's mouse is also placed in the same (unusual and clumsy) final position in the line as Horace's, stressing the animal's short, quick body. The overarching intention of Juvenal's text here is to set off huge and strong vice against weak virtue, but the humour of anticlimax is also drawn in, detaching the language from emotion. The doubleness between the dismissal/

---

[174] Parallel to Horace's fleeing country mouse in *S.* 2.6.113–17, and the dinner guests fleeing from the tasteless dinner of Nasidienus at the close of *S.* 2.8 (vv. 93–5). As I have suggested for Horace's 2.8 (above, § 'Satire's metaphor: the spectacle of a falling curtain'), so here, too, fleeing is not an altogether convincing punishment.

comic triumph of the empowered target is repeated with the emphasis upset. Clodius, though criticized, resembles a mimic hero, while his virtuous little opponent is a funny mouse that is also in danger of appearing as a *ridiculus mus*. Thus, far from annihilating the thoughts in the scene of the bacchanal, these verses hook on to those thoughts, underline their complexity and point to their ambiguity. The special satirical twist makes the reader laugh and accept the paradoxical message without even noticing the paradox.

It remains to look closer at the part of the Bona Dea episode which describes the desecration of the image of Chastity. The passage, which immediately precedes the bacchanal, states the anarchic behaviour of women in even stronger terms, and runs as follows:

> i nunc et dubita qua sorbeat aera sanna
> Maura, Pudicitiae veterem cum praeterit aram,
> Tullia quid dicat, notae collactea Maurae.
> noctibus hic ponunt lecticas, micturiunt hic
> effigiemque deae longis siphonibus implent
> inque vices equitant ac Luna teste moventur,
> inde domos abeunt: tu calcas luce reversa
> coniugis urinam magnos visurus amicos.   (6.306–13)

Now you needn't wonder with what grimace Maura sniffs the air as she passes the ancient altar of Chastity, or what Tullia, Maura's foster-sister, says to her. At night they set down their litters here; they piss here, wetting the goddess' image all over with long jets. They take turns to ride each other while the Moon looks down on their movements, then they go home. When daylight returns you splash through your wife's urine on your way to visit your great friends.

The goddess Chastity had been described as fleeing the earth together with her sister Justice (Astraea) at 6.19–20, in connection with the full-scale entrance of adultery into history in the Silver age, when Jove grew up. Here Chastity is present as an old memory, with a decrepit altar passed with contempt by the women of the modern age. Not content with mere grimacing, the women climb down from their litters (the contemptuous *lecticae* again!) and piss on her sanctuary with long squirts—as if they were men, as Richlin correctly observes.[175]

---

[175] Richlin, *Garden*, 206.

Two implications of this scene deserve particular attention, one connected to Rome, the big city at the heart of Juvenal's satire, the other connected to the narrative workings of the satire itself.

The first implication entails a concretization of the cosmic development of the Four Ages (at the beginning of the sixth satire) to the reality of the Urbs. This ties in neatly with the observations made above on the contempt for Concordia, and other good old deities, in the first satire. The citizens had begun to neglect the gods representing the traditional Roman values, which was bad enough, but 'Juvenal' is perhaps most upset by the tangible evidence of that neglect in the profile of the city: the contamination of Concord's temple by a noisy bird, and a foreign bird at that. What Concordia means as an emblem for the stable hierarchy between the social classes, this Pudicitia means for the hierarchy between the sexes. *Pudicitia* is a virtue demanded primarily of women,[176] and among these, of high-born women. Chastity would keep them in their subdued role in a patriarchal society, prohibit them the sexual licence granted to men, and ensure the legitimacy of aristocrat children. In this case too, there is tangible staining of the concrete altar of Chastity, the city's architectural manifestation of its once-treasured value. In the climactic passage in the sixth satire, the altar is desecrated by precisely the group which Chastity was supposed to subdue. The women, at least one of whom, Tullia, seems to be a high-class matron, complete their subversive rebellion by (1) pissing like men, and (2) having sex with each other, taking turns to be on top.[177] This is not only the elimination of men, but the active usurpation of their roles, and the turning of these roles against the emblems of patriarchal power: Pudicitia's altar, decorous heterosexual coitus. The universe of Juvenal's satires is the Roman empire, and for most of the satires simply the city of Rome—so whatever is wrong with the world sets a visible stamp on the capital. The sanctuaries of Concordia and Pudicitia are stained,

---

[176] T. Reekmans, 'Juvenal's Views on Social Change', *AncSoc* 2 (1971), 127, 133, 137. In this connection, cf. also the discussion Juvenal's use of the notion *pudor* as a general standard of excellence for both sexes in U. Knoche, 'Juvenals Mass-stäbe der Gesellschaftskritik,' in D. Korzeniewski (ed.), *Die römische Satire*. (Darmstadt: Wissenschaftliche Buchgesellschaft, 1970), 507–9.

[177] Richlin (*Garden*, 206) comments that this is the 'ultimate removal of man', but does not draw any further conclusions from this fact.

the streets are swarmed with the litters of the undeserving rich, the decent man walking is run down by all kinds of morally offensive aggressors, and it is only a matter of time before a temple to Pecunia will be raised. In fact, as a significant passage in the third satire proclaims, the whole city is very near collapse, only held up desperate by lies:

> nos *urbem* colimus tenui tibicine fultam
> *magna parte sui*; nam sic labentibus obstat
> vilicus et, veteris rimae cum texit hiatum,
> securos pendente iubet dormire ruina.   (3.193–6)

We live in a city supported, to a large extent, on nothing by a thin column—this is how the landlord hinders the houses from falling. When he's covered up the surface gap of an old crack in the wall, he tells us to sleep easy, while ruin is poised all around.

The image, which is a symbol for all of Juvenal's complaints, is important not only for its claim that things in Rome have gone terribly, fatally wrong, but also for the suggestion of *the way* in which they have gone wrong. The building of Rome has become unstable, it is slipping out of place and falling apart. What the Romans are fooled into believing is only a crack (*rima*) will actually lead to ruin (*ruina*) while they are submerged in falsely carefree sleep (*securos dormire*). The threat to Rome's structure is the resurrection of groups that should, ideally, be firmly subdued: foreigners, freedmen, the plebs, women. Once we grasp the centrality of the Urbs in Juvenal's work, and especially of the city's buildings—implying, ultimately, the monumental building of Rome itself—the importance of the scene at Chastity's altar becomes clear. Just as the temple of Concordia was contaminated in a significant way, so is the altar of Pudicitia. In the case of the former, the 'right' and harmonious placement of the social ranks (concordia ordinum) was at stake, and the stork, a low-born and foreign bird, moved in to a holy and elevated place—the roof of the temple. In the case of the latter, the *chastity* of *women* is at stake, and Tullia and Maura contaminate the sanctuary by demonstrating their *lust* (copulation) and their *refusal to play the woman's role* (their manly pissing, their deliberate exchange of passive/active roles in sex). The shocking behaviour of the women is not even noticed by those who will ultimately suffer from it. The husband, already humiliated by having to fawn on his mighty friends through early morning visits, does not know that he is even more cruelly humiliated by slipping on his wife's urine. This is not all: the fact that a real altar in the actual city of Rome is stained makes the insult more universal. Not only a particular husband, but all men in the city, as the 'tu' in the address to the husband underlines, are contaminated; even the city itself is contaminated by the nightly misbehaviour. The earlier scene of the empress Messalina's lurid nightly adventures in a brothel (6.115–35) likewise had the effect not simply of staining her husband the emperor, but of staining the whole of Rome, through the metonymy of staining its leader and his bed. Rome is falling apart, and with it—the world, for to Juvenal, Rome *is* the world.

On the scene of contemporary social life, women's resurrection was hardly a reality, only a latent threat that had perhaps become somewhat more palpable than it had been in Augustan time, when Horace's Priapus had easily scared off the witches from the Esquiline (*S.* 1.8).[178] Yet it is a poet's task to make the factually marginal, but symbolically central, the main concern of his work, and this is what Juvenal does. In Juvenal's satire, the sanctuaries of Concordia and Pudicitia, the values that had ensured the immobility of the lower social ranks and women respectively, are desecrated—a terrifying sign. The immobility of the subdued human mass that formed the base of the Roman empire was crucial for the stability of the empire monument, and Juvenal's satire is full of anxiety about the horrible possibility that this base had begun to shift. Juvenal's work is bursting with movement. Money and fortune move people randomly up and down, the Greeks move in to the city centre, the Egyptians move their jaws in cannibalism, and the lusty women make ungodly movements under the moon ('Luna teste moventur', 6.311). Humour thrives on this movement, but the ideology of Juvenal's writings is all against it. The base of the empire monument is moving, there is a crack in what should ideally be a stable and dumb foundation, and the elite males

---

[178] Richlin (ibid.) notes that the moonlit desecration of Chastity's altar (J. 6.306–13) is clearly an allusion to Horace's *Satire* 1.8, where there are also two females behaving sacrilegiously under the moon.

who, like Juvenal, inhabit the upper storeys, are haunted by visions of the heavy, ruinous fall.[179]

The second implication of the desecration scene in the sixth satire is that the women in it take on a role parallel to that usually played by the satirical persona himself. As Richlin has reasonably claimed, urination occasionally functions as a metaphor for satire both in Persius and in Juvenal,[180] so that to urinate on something is to lower it, to degrade it through satirical derision. In both authors, the objects concretely pissed upon are monuments to characteristically empowered satire targets: inflated poetry in Persius; absurdly presumptuous foreigners in Juvenal. Thus, much in line with the pattern which I have traced throughout this chapter, the satirical persona steps up to a grand and pretentious but really hollow object, and though he himself is modestly weak, directs his squirts against the inflated object, mimicking the direction of his contemptuous, degrading laughter. Now the scene where Maura and Tullia urinate on Chastity's altar adheres to this pattern with curious exactness.[181] The women step up to the ancient sanctuary of a goddess, a hallowed place that demands respect. Yet this goddess, Chastity, is one whom they do not consider worthy of worship, one that they do not, as it were, believe in. From their comparatively low position as human beings, and females at that (i.e. particularly expected to honour the

---

[179] Just as Umbricius is afraid of the fall of Roman houses in *S.* 3.193–6. Fruelund Jensen ('Juvenal's Umbricius', 193) suggests that in this passage, Juvenal is 'depicting a *social* process in physical terms', though he sees this process differently than I do—as the elimination of the lower middle classes rather than as a dangerous shift in the disfranchised foundation of society. Cf. the observation of Holt Parker in an essay on slaves and women in Roman *exemplum* literature: 'The masters-husbands-authors demonstrate an awareness of the discordant elements and potential fissures which have always existed in their society's fundamental institutions' (H. Parker, 'Loyal Slaves and Loyal Wives: the Crisis of the Outsider-within and Roman *Exemplum* Literature,' in S. R. Joshel and S. Murnaghan (eds.), *Women and Slaves in Greco-Roman Culture*, 153).

[180] Persius 1.113–14 'pingue duos anguis: "pueri, sacer est locus, extra | meiite." ' ('paint two snakes: boys, the place is sacred, piss outside'); Juvenal 1.129–31, 'inter quas ausus habere | nescioquis titulos Aegyptius atque Arabarches, | cuius ad effigiem non tantum meiere fas est' ('among which some Egyptian Arabarches has dared to set up his image, with his titles listed. Right it would be to piss on his statue, and not only piss, too'); Richlin, *Garden*, 187, 200, 206–7.

[181] Richlin (*Garden*, 206) parenthetically notes the similarity, but does not discuss it further.

deity in question), they dare to mock her with fearless abandon. Instead of kissing the hand as a sign of respect, Maura sniffs the air with a grimace, an expression not far from grinning with contemptuous laughter, just as the word *sanna* means 'grin'. Tullia, in turn, says something that Juvenal will not repeat ('dubita . . . Tullia quid dicat' ('you don't need to doubt what Tullia says')). At this point, the ladies have their litters put down, and urinate on the altar, filling the statue of the goddess with those long, manly squirts. It is symbolically significant that the women climb down from their height on the litters before attacking the effigy, so that their attack, like a satirist's, does not emanate from above. It is likewise significant that the word used for the target of their urine is the same that was used for the target of the persona's urination in the first satire, *effigiem* ('statue'), 6.310; 1.131. The target of their 'satirical' mockery is Chastity, as well as the husband who slips on their urine in the morning, again someone normally mightier, whom they manage to taunt literally from under his feet. The main aim of this 'satire' in the wrong direction is full inversion, so complete as to grant the object the power to mock the persona and his class (moralistic men), if only for a moment. The traditional power hierarchy is soon restored by direct criticism of women, moralistic exclamations, caricature and so on. Yet this short scene, where the object is allowed to play satirist, also connects to a larger pattern in the sixth satire: the consistent depiction of women as extremely powerful creatures who ultimately decide over the life and death of men. As has been noted above, the whole of J. 6 passes from madness to madness and death induced by women, and the Bona Dea episode in the exact centre may well be described as a general rape of men by women. They are Priapus' maenads (6.316–17), and for a short spell, even pseudo-satirists.

What I would like to conclude from this is that the model of the satirist-as-Priapus, raping the objects of his attack, is not applicable to the sixth satire. In this case Juvenal goes so far in his wish to invert the world and empower his objects, that he grants them, as it were, the role of the aggressive Priapus, and in the middle of his poem even the role of the satirist. All of this is done to laugh them down all the more fiercely from the position he has hoisted them up to, and he is ultimately out to humiliate them, there is no doubt about that. However, since this empowering is so exaggerated, and since the women rule, hilariously, for most of the monumental poem, it seems that the satirist has lost control of the balance, and let the women run amok more than was optimal for his moral message. Although the massive misbehaviour of the women is what makes this satire so impressive, it displays too much of the substantial patriarchal fear that the women's power might turn out to be not fake, metaphorical power granted by the satirist for the sharpening of his derision, but real power, leading to Rome's real ruin.

In conclusion of this discussion on women in Juvenal it should be pointed out that the possible 'reading against the grain', which I have tried to demonstrate above, is not meant as a mere formalistic exercise, to show what can be done in principle; rather, it has the very concrete aim of highlighting what *is actually there* in the text, although followed by explicit denials in the voice of the persona's moralistic comments. My claim is that the women's temporary rule and gross transgression, which is the source of most of the humour in the sixth satire, cannot simply be undone by expressed dismissal of it wedged in every now and then in the much duller moralist's voice. All in all, the ideological message is a misogynous one, but because of its cavalcade of colourful, hilarious images it is less misogynous than the persona would like it to be. Instead of saying 'beware of women, for they are bad', it amounts to saying 'beware of women, for they are powerful, and we men don't like that'. The long humorous scenes where the speaker seems to be carried away by the current of the action, and fails to include chastizing comments or adjectives after every move, may be bad for the moral criticism, yet they are very good for the esthetical quality. But there is more: the sparkling, funny form, the bright images are not only an esthetical ornament—they also smuggle their meaning into the poem. The overwhelming presence of triumphing transgressive women will not be erased by a lesser amount of commentary, which is also less imaginative than the scenes of transgression. The meaning will be balanced, the triumph of transgression will be contradicted, and even conquered. Yet it cannot be entirely annihilated, for satire is made of language, and this triumph of transgression has been expressed in language. What has been said cannot be unsaid. Juvenal's satire, like Roman satire in general, performs its mission of humour largely by drawing energy from the powers released by inversion and transgression, but the moral mission demands that these powers be stuffed back into their cage at the end. This is a basic paradox of the genre.[182] A woman in Juvenal's satire says 'clames licet et mare caelo | confundas' ('you can scream, and confound heaven and earth'), 6.283–4. This statement will not be undone by the persona's protests, when he screams, and confounds heaven and earth in his fight against these words.[183] The woman's statement *is still there*, and this makes all the difference in the world.

'Juvenal' attacking cinaedi . . .

Something must now be said about the theme of homosexuality in Juvenal, which is partly akin to his treatment of women. The one category of sexual orientation which can reasonably be called 'homosexuality' in the Roman world, adult passive male homosexuality,[184] is made the object of two rather different satires, 2 and 9. These two poems may well be discussed together, so that their common key motifs and different solutions of form may be compared and contrasted. Like the complaints about women in the sixth satire, the complaints about pathics are first and foremost oriented towards their transgression of established social rules and hierarchies, which are conceived of as natural rules. In both the second and the ninth satire an important role is also performed by the additional motifs of money and fortune, as opposed to the aristocratic hierarchy based on birth, and of promiscuity, as opposed to chastity. Both poems also make use of what I have termed 'secondary personae',[185] the less than respectable first-person speakers Laronia (in J. 2) and Naevolus (in

---

[182] Cf. above, § 'The paradoxes of satire, as mapped by Alvin Kernan'.

[183] Thus I disagree with the opinion of Gold, 'Humor in J. 6' and Henderson, *Writing down Rome*, that the woman's claim 'homo sum' *merely* functions as a derisive insult against females in the context of J. 6. It is instructive to compare almost the same utterance spoken by one of the freedmen at Petronius' *Cena Trimalchionis*: 'Homo inter homines sum' ('I'm a man among men'), *Sat.* 57.5. As I have argued elsewhere (Plaza, *Laughter and Derision*, 131–42), the freedman's claim is partly ridiculous, partly proved to be *true* by the context.

[184] See Richlin's article of 1993, 'Not Before Homosexuality: the Materiality of the *Cinaedus* and the Roman Law against Love between Men', *Journal of the History of Sexuality*, 3 (1993), 523–73, where the issue of Roman homosexuality is polemically and fruitfully explored.

[185] See Introduction § 'A note on author and persona'.

J. 9). In a somewhat simplified form it can be said that the difference lies in the space and importance granted the transgression vs. the stable order: in the second satire, the transgression is strictly limited and expressly denigrated, whereas in the ninth, the transgression rules the progress of the poem as a whole, and is only indirectly attacked.

The second satire first poses as an attack on hypocrisy, more specifically the hypocrisy of the men who play macho Stoic moralists, but really are pathics. Then Laronia, a woman, is introduced to denounce the effeminates with the classical rhetorical device of 'they are even worse than X', with X meaning women, and an additional twist in the fact that Laronia-the-speaker belongs to this category. Laronia is, in Henderson's happy formulation, 'the satirist in drag', but she is no more than this. She is in fact only a paper mask through which the main persona's patriarchal views are spoken.[186] Her lines are, however, less declamatory than the rest of the poem. In accordance with her smile as she begins speaking ('ita subridens' ('smiling, she said the following'), 2.38), she uses more irony than is used in the other parts. Laronia reveals the posing moralists for what they are: the third Cato before her wears a very nice perfume all over his hairy neck, she would like to know where it can be bought (40–2). The object of the mockery is characteristically hoisted by the ironic likening of him to the Catos, and the image of him falling from heaven ('e caelo cecidit Cato' ('a Cato fallen from heaven'), 40) mimics his downfall when he is derided. When attacked, Laronia further tells the reader, the effeminates will close their ranks, for their solidarity is great, 'magna inter molles concordia' ('there is great concord among the pansies'), 47. Here is *Concordia* again, the civic virtue and pride of the Roman people, dragged in the dirt along with military glory, as the despicable *molles* turn these solemn concepts inside out. Once Laronia is finished with the pathics, they have no other alternative but to run away, for she has spoken nothing but the truth: 'fugerunt trepidi vera ac manifesta canentem | Stoicidae; quid enim falsi Laronia?' ('trembling, the sons of the Stoa fled from the prophetess of manifest truth—for what had Laronia said that was untrue?'), 64–5. Her revelations constitute the bridge between the

[186] Henderson, *Writing down Rome*, 196.

attack on hypocrisy, and the attack on open outrage (i.e. pathic behaviour) which in the second part of the satire turns out to be even worse in the eyes of the satirist. Open outrage consists primarily of dressing in sexy, or frankly female, clothes, and of men marrying men, where the text relies heavily on the joke of using *nubere* with a male subject (2.134–5). The military metaphor is exploited in the description of how emperor Otho went to war with his mirror and face mask (99–109). Similar military associations turn up again in the Underworld scene describing the shock of the warlike Romans of old, when they witness the arrival of a modern pathic—their degenerate descendant (149–58). At the end of the satire the diagnosis is pronounced: all this immorality is due to the fact that although the empire is geographically expanding, it is rotting from within, at the very heart, its capital. Unmanly behaviour and sexual perversity, presumably originally alien to Rome,[187] have become so rooted in the city that they are now exported. First the proverbially perverted Eastern barbarians arrive as prisoners and hostages, and soon find Roman lovers, learning from these to be men of the world, though not *viri*: 'aspice quid faciant commercia: venerat obses, | hic fiunt homines' ('look what commerce does: he had come as a hostage, but here they become men of the world'), 166–7. A longer sejour in the Urbs will make the barbarians drop their attributes such as trousers and knives, and in the final joke of the satire, they will bring back the Roman habit even to Artaxata: 'sic praetextatos referunt Artaxata mores' ('thus they bring back to Artaxata the morals of our youngsters'), 170. As Henderson notes, there is sound-play to reflect the paradox of sin-being-transported-in-the-wrong-direction, in that ' "Artaxata" is both a palindromous response to refer*unt* and the echo and "mirror-image" of *praetextatos*'.[188] 'Commercia', that familiar villain of exchange of wares for money, is revealed to lie at the bottom of all this immorality—just look what it does, *aspice quid faciant commercia*.

Throughout the satire, the reader is explicitly told what to think and what to laugh at. Close to the beginning, where the main joke is

---

[187] As Juvenal himself has it in the *locus de saeculo* 6.294–300.

[188] Henderson, *Writing down Rome*, 315 n. 91; cf. Courtney, *Commentary on Juvenal*, 150 (on 2.170): 'of course moralists, and particularly Juvenal, usually speak of foreigners corrupting Rome ... so what we have here is something of a paradox.'

the contrast between the rough and hairy outside and the soft and effeminate essence, we are told about the doctor who laughs as he cuts away the philosopher-pathic's piles:

> hispida membra quidem et durae per bracchia saetae
> promittunt atrocem animum, sed podice levi
> caeduntur tumidae medico ridente mariscae   (2.11–13)

shaggy limbs and the bristling hair on your arms suggest a fierce spirit, but from your smooth ass the surgeon cuts away swelling piles, laughing.

No doubt an image of the satirist as the surgeon of society, laughing and wielding his scalpel. Somewhat later the reader hears about normality's right to laugh at the abnormal, 'loripedem rectus derideat, Aethiopem albus' ('let the straight-limbed laugh at the cripple, the white man at the Ethiopian'), 23,[189] followed by a row of examples of villains accusing others of the very villainy they are themselves guilty of (24–35). At this point Laronia, smiling contemptuously, takes over. The scenes in between the comments are not allowed to grow particularly long or lively, and the pathics do not get to speak other than to splutter hypocritical moralistic commonplaces. A small inverted celebration of the Bona Dea rites, with men only (86–92), consists in dressing as women while not allowing real women to enter, and is but a tame rehearsal of what is to come in the sixth satire. Unlike the case in J. 6, where the deity to be worshipped was inverted, the pathics' Bona Dea celebration in J. 2 only constitutes an inversion of the worshippers, while the ritual in itself remains basically intact. This is very much in line with the modest transgression characteristic of J. 2 in general, where the main vice remains cross-dressing. Unlike Maura and Tullia in the sixth satire, who could, if only momentarily, overthrow the male order altogether by having sex with each other and dismissing Chastity, the pathics of the second satire keep bumping into the sarcastic limits put up by the satirist, the limit of their bodies, of 'Nature'.[190] Once they are married, they will not be able to please their 'husbands' with the means of children—the only meaning of a Roman marriage—

---

[189] On this sudden acknowledgement of relativity, see Ch. 3, § 'Juvenal: of monsters great and small—describing a grotesque world'.

[190] This is well discussed in Henderson, *Writing down Rome*, 196–7.

and it is just as well that Nature has granted the mind no power over the body, for they will thus, mercifully, die sterile (137–40). The pathics are monsters who can produce no offspring, neuters that are *neither men nor women*. Because of this, they cannot change the normal, i.e. patriarchal, order of things, and this normal order is expressly authorized to laugh at their 'abnormality'.

... and one cinaedus talking back

In the ninth satire, the disturbance is much deeper. The entire satire consists of the male prostitute Naevolus' professional complaints of not getting his due payment, and of having grown too old for this kind of trade anyway. Traditionally read as a moral critique of both the main character Naevolus and his patron-cum-customer Virro, this poem has been seen as essentially a restatement of J. 2, cast in dialogue form. In such readings, the other party of the dialogue, 'Juvenal', is equated with the author, and what he says is therefore taken as ironic, and as mockery of Naevolus' immorality.[191] Some recent readings, however, have pointed to inconsistencies in such a 'moralistic' interpretation, and suggested other solutions. Mason began, drastically, by seeing the poem as devoid of moral coherence. Richlin, in accordance with her model of Priapus as satirist, claimed that 'the satirist in effect rapes Rome with Naevolus as his agent', although to her, this does not exclude Naevolus simultaneously being sneered at by the author.[192] Henderson gives a short sketch rather than a developed analysis, but his keen observations come closest to explaining the intricacy of the ninth satire:

This voice is the satirist's supreme creation and challenge. Naevolus is the only one who deserves to share a whole poem in dialogue with J. Faced with Naevolus the 'Superstud', *Egito* meets his match, the Man with (too much of) everything ... For here is a Male who has taken as seriously as can be that 'healthy' simplicity of a 'Penetrate-All' male sexuality. *Naevolus* ... is its logical conclusion, Priapus-as-*homo*.[193]

---

[191] e.g. Highet, *Juvenal the Satirist*, 117–18; Fredericks in Ramage, Sigsbee, and Fredericks, *Roman Satirists*, 154–5.

[192] Mason, 'Is Juvenal a Classic?', 107; Richlin, *Garden*, 202

[193] Henderson, *Writing down Rome*, 200; original emphases.

This picture must be developed further, for it is indeed remarkable that the Juvenalian persona's only true dialogue partner is male bisexual prostitute.

Just as in the second satire, so in the ninth Naevolus' and his customers' immorality is shown to be based on commerce, more exactly the replacement of the noble, friendship-like relationship between patron and client by commerce, i.e. trade of sex and money. The structure of this satire, however, is tighter than that of J. 2, and instead of having to wait until the end for the revelation of the source of Rome's misery, the reader is plunged into the context of violence (9.2), obscenity (3–4), and monetary affairs (6–8) from the very beginning, if only through the images used to describe the nowadays so despondent Naevolus. At vv. 22–6 all curiosity about his line of business is satisfied ('fanum... | notior Aufidio moechus celebrare solebas, | quoque taces, ipsos etiam inclinare maritos' ('an adulterer more notorious than Aufidius, you used to frequently visit the temple..., and what you don't mention, you used to make their husbands bend over too')), and from then on the comic shock-value of the poem lies in his matter-of-fact narration of sexual and ma-terialistic outrages. *Commercia*, the dealing in sexual services for monetary retribution is the very engine of the poem, for Naevolus, the secondary persona who gets to speak his mind, lives by his loins, 'pascitur inguine venter' ('the belly is fed by the loins'), 136. Thus Naevolus is a personage who feeds off the two things which in Juvenal's satires constitute major threats to the aristocratic, stable world-order: sex and money. These are, outrageously, the rules by which all of depraved Rome lives today, and so, 'Juvenal' comfort-ingly says, Naevolus will never have to fear unemployment as long as the Seven Hills are extant:

> ne trepida, numquam pathicus tibi derit amicus
> stantibus et salvis his collibus; undique ad illos
> convenient et carpentis et navibus omnes
> qui digito scalpunt uno caput. altera maior
> spes superest, tu tantum erucis inprime dentem.   (130–4)

Have no fear: as long as these hills stand firm, you'll never lack a pathic friend. Those who scratch their head with one finger flock to these hills by coach and ship from every corner of the world. There is another (and greater) hope for you, just crunch your rocket.

Yet sex and money are fleeting and unstable principles, ready to destroy not only the traditional order they oppose, but also the easy riders who momentarily seem to be the winners of their commerce. Consequently—and characteristically—Naevolus believes in Fortune, that non-deity who will be taunted in the next satire, J. 10. His creeds are comically put together in his cynical, lowering utterance that fate rules men along with their genitals:

> fata regunt homines, fatum est et partibus illis
> quas sinus abscondit. nam si tibi sidera cessant,
> nil faciet longi mensura incognita nervi,
> quamvis te nudum spumanti Virro labello
> viderit et blandae adsidue densaeque tabellae
> sollicitent, αὐτὸς γὰρ ἐφέλεκται ἄνδρα κίναιδος (32–7)[194]

Fate rules men, and the parts covered by clothes have their fate as well. For if the stars turn away from you, the unheard of length of your member won't help you, even if Virro drools when he looks at you naked and bothers you with a continuous stream of love-letters, *since a man is attracted by the very sight of—a pansy*.

With κίναιδος put into the parodic quotation of Homer (*Od.* 16.294; 19.13) instead of σίδηρος ('iron', and hence: 'weapon'), we reach the ninth satire's pithy counterpart of the thoroughgoing martial metaphor in the second satire, for Naevolus 'substitutes for the *naked weapons* at the end of the line the surprise-word *pathics*'.[195] The comic substitution is still more intricate: the Latin translation of σίδηρος is *ferrum*, the (iron) sword, a metaphor for the penis. No wonder Naevolus exerts such an attraction on all men—he is both a *cinaedus* and an iron tool. In J. 6, where women's love of gladiators was discussed, it was ambiguously said that 'ferrum est quod amant' ('what they love is the sword/ penis'), 6.112. Naevolus is thus a curious pathic, and the most ambivalent character Juvenal ever allows to enter his text.[196] He is ambivalent in the simple sexual

---

[194] The punchline is well discussed in Martyn, 'Juvenal's Wit', 236.
[195] Mason, 'Is Juvenal a Classic?', 103.
[196] The only comparable personages, the heterosexual and lustful pathics in the O-fragment (O1–26) and vv. 366–78 in J. 6, are characteristically silent targets of

sense active/passive, homo-/heterosexual, but also, interestingly, in his position of near-authority in the satire. In sharp contrast to meek Laronia, who advocated the same patriarchal views as her lord 'Juvenal',[197] Naevolus speaks the very opposite of what the satirist believes in. Much more is reversed here than the superficial and essentially innocuous feature of dress. Nevertheless, Naevolus the secondary persona is granted the privilege of speaking in the first person, a narrative position which immediately carries a great deal of authority with it.[198] The reader's reflex is to sympathize with the first-person speaker, especially in satire (where it is normally the privilege of the greatest authority, the satirical persona himself), and the speaker will have to disqualify himself heavily before he loses the sympathy of the reader. It may be argued that Naevolus does disqualify himself enough by his profession, his materialistic interests, and his shamelessness about both of these—and yet there are also arguments in his favour, strengthened by his narrative privilege.

First, he occupies the position of the little man oppressed by the rich and depraved patron, who happens to wear the same name as the terrible host in J. 5, Virro. There can be little doubt that Virro is ultimately worse than Naevolus: he is driven completely by effeminate lust, greed, and hypocrisy, while Naevolus is after all earning his living, no matter how disgracefully. Naevolus may be stained by the key objects of Juvenal's scorn (sex and money), but Virro is even more stained, for his involvement with these is more wilful and unnecessary, summarized in the deflating, alliterative mock-*sententia* 'computat et cevet' ('he counts his money and waves his butt'), 40, put in Naevolus' mouth. The relationship between Virro and his

derision, never allowed to 'talk back' like Naevolus. The odd figure of the *cinaedus-adulterer* (though silent) is also found in Mart. 10.40. Cf. the brief discussion of this character in Anderson, *Essays*, 384.

[197] In addition to being the satirist in drag, Laronia can also be seen as representing that realistic group of compliant women of which I have spoken above.

[198] Cf. the happy formulation of Booth on a literary consciousness central to its story (= a 'reflector'): 'He wins our confidence simply by being the reflector, because in life the only mind we know as we know [his] is our own'. Since this reflector is in fact unreliable, Booth comments that 'to read the story properly we must combat our natural tendency to agree with the reflector' (*Fiction*, 352). Such a combat is also involved in reading Naevolus. The issue of the reliability of the central speaker will be further discussed in Ch. 2, § 'The question of trust in Juvenal's speaker'.

client is an extreme one, but it is still the logical conclusion of the degeneration of the patron-client relationship by the intrusion of commerce, a degeneration deplored from the first satire on. There, the motif was introduced with the image of the poor noblemen waiting in queue for their *sportula* (1.95–126), and the speaker had sympathy for the penniless clients, close to the poor pushed-around persona himself in their undeserved humiliation. In J. 5, the poor client enduring the humiliating dinner given by his patron was criticized for his lack of dignity. In J. 7, the impoverished intellectuals, scorned by their patrons, were again pitied. Naevolus' demands (to be treated with more respect and generosity by the patron whom he loyally serves, 9.48–69, 137–47) are degrading to him because of the nature of his service, but such claims also have positive precedents in Juvenal, and their negativity is therefore ever so slightly destabilized.

Secondly, as has already been intimated, Naevolus is sexually both passive and active, a 'superstud' presenting himself as a *cinaedus*, a satisfaction both for men and for women. While the pathics of the second satire were exposed as neither men nor women, Naevolus is both, just as he is both subject and object of the satire at the narratological level. This connects interestingly with the issue of the grotesque in Juvenal. In a crucial essay on Bakhtin's notion of carnival and the negative grotesque in Roman satire, Paul Allen Miller has argued that the grotesque bodies in satire are icons of sterility, and that such an understanding can also be traced in Bakhtin himself, who distinguishes between negative, satirical grotesque and the affirmative, regenerating grotesque of carnivalesque literature.[199] While I agree with Miller's general argument and most of his examples, some reservations must be stated about his discussion of Naevolus, in the description of whom there is vivid grotesque:

> an facile et pronum est agere intra viscera penem
> legitimum atque illic hesternae occurrere cenae?
> servus erit minus ille miser qui foderit agrum
> quam dominum.   (9.43–6)

[199] Miller, 'Grotesque in Roman Satire'. While Miller's description of Bakhtin's line between satire and carnival is correct, the matter is made difficult by the fact that Bakhtin's view of satire changes. Sometimes he excludes satire from the realm of carnival laughter, dismissingly calling it 'criticism' or 'rhetoric' not laughter, but occasionally he includes Roman satire, or parts of it, in the same category of carnivalized literature.

Do you think it's nice and easy to drive a fair-sized cock into your guts and encounter last night's dinner? The slave ploughing his master's field is less miserable than the one that ploughs the master himself.

Here, Miller claims, the lower bodily stratum leads to nothing: food does not produce new life, only excrement; the excrement represents no source of fertility, only an obstacle to joyless sex; the agricultural metaphor of ploughing does not look forward to harvest. According to Miller, the act is sterile both literally, in that it cannot produce offspring, and metaphorically, in that it brings neither monetary nor emotional rewards.[200] This analysis makes Juvenal's text, for once, somewhat more negative than it is. The claim about metaphorical sterility is not exactly true, for Virro is rewarded with pleasure, while Naevolus is rewarded with 5,000 sesterces (v. 41), although he sees himself as absurdly underpaid. Even the literal sterility, so stressed in J. 2, receives a curious twist in this poem. At the exact centre of the satire we learn that Naevolus ploughed not only the master, but the mistress as well, at the explicit request of the former (9.71–8). If he would not have served Virro in this way, Virro's wife would have remained a virgin (an image of sterility), or divorced him. Now the marriage is saved from wreckage, and children have been born, allowing the master to boast of fatherhood and decorate the doors with garlands. Absurdly enough, grotesque Naevolus has brought fertility into the house. In this case, the ambivalence of transgression is not deadly, but paradoxically life-giving. Unlike the pathics of J. 2, who in their mule-like monstrosity brought sterility to their marriages, Naevolus the two-legged ass (9.92) brings offspring to the sterile marriage of others. The question is of course which of these is morally worse: the end of the line of perversion, or the proliferation of it. Yet the second variety is surely the more lively, for although its grotesque is fertile in a horrid way, it still brings something of its revivifying energy, and frantic, unstopped movement, and so makes the satire potent.

Finally, the most remarkable feature about Naevolus is that he is not only a critic of morals (i.e. Virro's unjust treatment of him), but also a joker, and a poet. He knows his Homer and the Latin poets well enough to include unobtrusive and witty parodies of them in his

---

[200] Miller, 'Grotesque in Roman Satire', 262.

speech. He also knows how to be witty in an obscene, but hilarious style, and it seems impossible to make a stylistic differentiation between his and lines and those of 'Juvenal' in this poem. He is also depicted as a humorist in 'Juvenal''s opening harangue to him:

> certe modico contentus agebas
> vernam equitem, conviva ioco mordente facetus
> et salibus vehemens intra pomeria natis.   (9.9–11)

surely you used to be content with little, playing the clownish squire, a witty dinner-guest with your mordant jokes and sharp town-bred humour.

This description of Naevolus as a *scurra* at dinner parties, full of native wit, sounds curiously positive in a satire, and cannot be taken as ironic, since Naevolus' utterances amply prove that it is true. Furthermore, this description is oddly reminiscent of Horace, even at the word level. Naevolus is said to be 'modico contentus', and Horace uses the word *contentus* abundantly in his satires, both of his persona and of people with whom he sympathizes.[201] A parallel that should be particularly emphasized is Horace's famous passage about the rare, ideal man who steps out of life as a satisfied dinner guest: 'qui... exacto *contentus* tempore vita | cedat, *uti conviva* satur' ('who when his time was up would leave life contentedly, as a dinner guest that has had his fill'), 1.1.117–19; for in this case there is also the further similarity of a dinner guest, *conviva*, just as Naevolus is said to be a *conviva*. Horace speaks of himself being equipped with the joke, *iocus*; and praises Lucilius for being *facetus*; in a well-known passage of the *Epistles* he refers to his satires as 'Bioneis sermonibus et *sale nigro*' ('conversations in the style of Bion, and black humour'), *Ep.* 2.2.60; cf. *S.* 2.4.74, a phrase very close to 'salibus vehemens' (Juv. 9.11). While Juvenal's Naevolus is characterized by his native wit, 'salibus vehemens intra pomeria natis', in Horace's *S.* 1.7, one of the humour contestants is similarly armed with native Italian mockery ('expressa arbusto convicia', 'Italum acetum' ('"abuse pressed from the vinyard", "Italian vinegar"'), vv. 29, 32), while the other is described as a violent salty stream ('salsus multusque fluens', v. 28). Finally, even the word combination 'vernam equitem' is not inno-

---

[201] *S.* 1.4.108; 1.6.96; '*contentus paucis* lectoribus' ('content with but few readers') 1.10.74; '*contentus parvo*' ('content with little') 2.2.110, ironically in 1.3.16.

cent, for Horace himself had reached the status of an *eques*, while being born in the home of a slave, albeit a former one, and so could be associated with a *verna*, a home-born slave. The antithetical combination of *verna* and *eques* alludes to Horace's own insistence on his comet-like social career, from a near-slave to an aristocrat. This social career had begun with his satires, and in them his display of wit—just as *verna* has the additional meaning of 'a witty person'. All of this, I submit, comes very close to making Naevolus a satirist, and even alludes to the Roman satirist *par excellence* at this time, Horace. In the fourth satire, Juvenal had chosen a *cinaedus* writing satire as an example of terrific impudence, when a character had been called even more shameless than this: 'inprobior saturam scribente cinaedo' ('more impudent than a pathic writing satire'), 4.106. Naevolus is almost an impersonation of that adynaton, *saturam scribens cinaedus*. The witty male prostitute may be dismissed in the end, but first he puts up a fight worthy of a fellow satirist—he is indeed Juvenal's 'supreme creation and challenge', for in Naevolus, Juvenal encountered his underground self.

2

Humour Directed at the Persona

All the Roman verse satirists use humour directed at their own persona, although this is potentially a disruptive strategy, since it can ultimately undermine what the persona says, i.e. the entire message of the satire. When carefully employed, on the other hand, self-directed humour can strengthen the authority of the persona and help to win the audience's sympathy. Various kinds of humour are used against the persona in Roman satire, running the gamut from making him an ironic quasi-author to revealing him as a laughable quasi-object. There are however also distinct limits to the forms this humour may take. This chapter will explore the subtle regulations of persona-oriented humour, as well as the functions this humour performs in its regulated forms.

An important distinction that must be noted is that between 'self-humour' entirely on the part of the persona (he is shown to mock himself) and humour directed at the persona from beyond his horizon, by the implied author (the implied author mocks the persona). The first kind will tend to present the persona as being in full control of himself and his presentation, and so strengthen his authority, the latter kind will present him as overlooking ridiculous faults in himself, as being vulnerable to derision from outside, and so it will undercut his authority. Intimately connected to this distinction is another one, that between mild mockery, which gravitates towards implicit praise of the persona, and harsh mockery, which gravitates towards correction of the persona. Not surprisingly, the mild variety, often in the form of self-irony, is by far the most common in Roman satire, and especially so in Horace, where it can be said to dominate the profile of the persona. This form of self-mockery is innocuous to the message of the satire. It is also consonant with the tendency to lower the persona for his laughing attacks on outside targets, which, as we have seen above, are often heightened, so as to maximize the distance between attacker and attacked. Harsh mockery of the persona has been argued to take place in Juvenal,[1] and this argument will be discussed below. Here it will suffice to say that such mockery would need to be shown to the reader by blatantly abnormal and reprehensible behaviour on the persona's part, or contradictions in his character and statements, and that something of the kind is indeed discernible not only in Juvenal, but also in Horace.

While lowering and belittling mockery of the speaker is common, the raising of the persona for subsequent degradation (as is done with objects) is extremely rare, although I will analyse a couple of passages where this might be seen. Characteristically, in these places moral and discursive authority becomes vague, and the reader feels the ground beneath him giving way—the persona is too strongly undercut by this violent kind of humour.

It is my contention that the generic constraints of satire never allow the persona to lose his authority altogether, as an 'unreliable narrator' might do in the novel, or a dramatic character on stage— the persona after all shares the author's name and profession as satirist, and this investment is too substantial to give up. The persona may, however, break in two, as happens in Persius' third satire, or he may share the floor with another speaker, even awarding his interlocutor the greater role. In the latter case I call the original persona a 'subdued persona', and the interlocutor a 'secondary persona'.[2] Both subdued personae and secondary ones are occasionally made targets of humour. The primary persona, the one who shares the name of the author, is at his weakest when he plays the role of a *subdued persona*, since it then becomes possible to mock him through the mouth and eyes of the interlocutor. This is a rare possibility to see the persona from the outside, not from the lofty level of the implied author, but from aside, as one person sees another. The secondary persona can be

---

[1] Anderson, *Essays*, 293–361; Winkler, *Persona*; Braund, *Beyond Anger*. See below, § 'Juvenal: to laugh with him or at him?'.

[2] See above, §§ 'A note on author and persona', and 'Horace: lowered subject'.

made to expose himself to shame by his role even more, since he has all the discursive properties of an I-speaker, but none of the impeding pride invested in the primary persona. The secondary persona thus offers a transitional stage between subject and object.

As for the function of persona-directed humour, I will argue the following theses. Reasonably kind mockery of the persona, including all self-mockery and self-irony on his part, as well as external exposure of mild weaknesses in him, are used to create a character that is fair and straightforward, just as Kernan discovered the persona must be in satire in order to prove his moral points to the audience.[3] This forms part of one of Kernan's paradoxes, that of the persona as 'the artless artist', who despite clever rhetorical manipulations lays claims to 'blunt, straightforward, and unskilled honesty'.[4] Humour helps to cover the paradox, as the persona may pretend to reveal his roughness by mistake with an embarrassed laugh, or have it revealed in the mockery of others. Physical shortcomings, low or rural origins, and lack of manners will all belong to this group of humour triggers. This image helps create confidence for the speaker, since an unpolished man seems less likely to scheme and lie, especially if he is 'simple' enough to expose his unpolished nature to laughter. At the same time, it places the persona in a 'low' position handy for satirical attack on an object from below. Such an attack will use a much more vehement kind of humour against the object, but this is not immediately obvious, and self-irony intermingled with derision of targets is often read as fairness on the part of the speaker—he not only attacks others, but sees faults in himself as well.

Moreover, the tendency to ascribe wisdom to self-ironic people is strong: a person who is able to laugh at himself is felt to be in complete control of himself and of discourse, since he alone is both subject and object in the discursive game of humour. This enables the satirist to get away with a weak or trite argument in the shade of self-irony, or almost no argument at all, as in Horace's S. 1.5.

Antiquity had a specific icon of the ironic man, Socrates. The understanding of irony had developed with the image of the great philosopher, and the initially suspect concept had been shaped into a more positive form by his combination of self-belittling and

---

[3] Kernan, *Cankered Muse*, 1–7, 14–30.   [4] Ibid., 4.

mockery.[5] The role of Socrates, ugly on the outside but brilliant underneath, was gladly taken up by the Roman satirists, especially Horace, in their self-directed humour.

While all these positive associations can be claimed for the tactic of self-mockery, the same tactic can effectively be used to cover things too. It directs the reader's gaze to a certain blemish that the satirist is not afraid to reveal in his persona, for instance his uncouth manner, and thereby stops the reader from searching for faults elsewhere. While a perfect, non-comic speaker deriding others might perhaps provoke the line of the imaginary interrupter in Horace, 1.3.19–20, 'don't you have any faults?', the admission of some funny drawback prevents the discovery of other faults, and also invites sympathy for one who has such forgivable faults and is able to laugh at them.[6]

In cases where the mockery is strong, and directed at the persona not by himself but by the (implied) author, the effect is that the author need not take responsibility for what the persona says. This is used to soften moral outrage and naïvety and ungentlemanly expressions. It may, theoretically, be used to demolish the whole message mouthed by the persona and to deride that message, but I doubt that this happens in extant Roman satire. In a few cases the consequences of persona-oriented mockery are nevertheless considerable, undermining the moral/ intellectual authority of the persona so much that the reader is put at risk, momentarily not knowing where to place his sympathies. There, perhaps the satirists get more from humour than

---

[5] See Sack, *Ironie*, 8–11, 14–15; Pavlovskis, 'Aristotle, Horace, and the Ironic Man'.

[6] There is also an invitation to friendship addressed to the reader, since someone who can show us his laughable side—and is a good sport by being the first to laugh at himself—resembles the close friend with whom we share jokes, and even laugh at one another. It is interesting to compare this with what the anthropologists call 'joking relationships'. In one of the earliest, and still very authoritative, articles on the phenomenon, A. R. Radcliffe-Brown defines a *joking relationship* as 'a relation between two persons in which one is by custom permitted, and in some instances required, to tease or make fun of the other, who in turn is required to take no offence' ('On Joking Relationships,' *Africa* 13 (1940), 195). The satirist invites us, his readers, to a close, teasing friendship not unlike a joking relationship. Radcliffe-Brown further observes that joking relationships often express a social connection comprising both friendliness and antagonism. This, too, is relevant to the 'relationship' suggested by the satirist, for while he wishes to be our friend, he also wants to present himself as an aggressive, even dangerous joker.

they bargained for, and come too close to revealing that moral zeal is not in fact their primary concern.

This must now be shown, but before I turn to discuss persona-oriented humour in the individual satirists, I would like to include a few comments on mockery directed at the Muses, who may reasonably be claimed to be part of the persona, or at least very closely allied with him.

THE MUSES OF SATIRE: WALKING, SITTING, AND ABSENT

Horace

In his most persona-centred *sermo*, S. 2.6, Horace famously invokes 'the walking Muse' of satire, placing the invocation between a prayer to Mercury and another to Janus. A somewhat longer quotation is in order:

> ... si quod adest gratum iuvat, hac prece te oro:
> pingue pecus domino facias et cetera praeter
> ingenium utque soles, custos mihi maximus adsis.
>   Ergo ubi me in montis et in arcem ex urbe removi,
> quid prius illustrem satiris Musaque pedestri?
> nec mala me ambitio perdit nec plumbeus Auster
> autumnusque gravis, Libitinae quaestus acerbae.
> Matutine pater, seu 'Iane' libentius audis,
> unde homines operum primos vitaeque labores
> instituunt (sic dis placitum), tu carminis esto
> principium. Romae sponsorem me rapis: 'eia!
> ne prior officio quisquam respondeat, urge.' (2.6.13–24)

... if I am content and happy with what I have, I direct the following prayer to you: make my cattle fat, and everything else too, except my brain, and remain, as you have always been, my main protector.

Now that I've withdrawn from the city into my castle in the mountains, what should I first praise in my satires with my walking Muse? I'm not overcome by foul ambition, nor by the leaden sirocco and the difficult autumn, that source of income for cruel Libitina. Father of the Dawn, or

'Janus' if you prefer to be thus called, you from whom men begin the labours of their daily life (so the gods have willed it)—be the beginning of my song. You rush me off to Rome as guarantor: 'Come on! Hurry up so that no one answers the call before you!'

Here we are particularly interested in Janus and the Muse, the two deities that are directly involved with Horace's present project of writing satire, and thus most closely parallel to the satirist himself.

After the mention of the Muse, to which I shall return presently, there follows a jocular appeal to Janus, the god of the new year and generally of beginnings and entrance doors. This apostrophe has not been taken as seriously as the prayer to Mercury for material security. Commentators are usually content to discuss whether *Matutinus pater* was an established name for the god, and to point out that the passage uses formulaic features of prayer, such as the alternative name and the use of *tu* and *esto*.[7] Yet there is a special significance in this invocation of Janus instead of Jove (the god from whom poetry traditionally took its beginning).[8] The satirist is pointing out the ambivalent nature of his genre, stressing that it is both true poetry and yet different. The god Janus, master of thresholds and passages between different compartments of life, seems an apt emblem for this kind of liminal poetry. Like Janus, satire faces in two opposite ways, and is never caught off guard. In connection with this last feature we may compare a later appearance of Janus, in Persius' satire:

O Iane, a tergo quem nulla ciconia pinsit,
nec manus auriculas imitari mobilis albas
nec linguae quantum sitiat canis Apula tantae.   (1.58–60)

O Janus, whom no stork has pinched from behind, at whose back no hands move nimbly to imitate white ears, and no tongues hang out, long as that of a thirsty dog in Apulia.

---

[7] Kießling and Heinze, *Satiren*, ad loc.; Fraenkel, *Horace*, 139–40, with the dismissive formulation 'We need not trouble about the jocular apostrophe to *Matutinus pater*' (p. 140); Coffey, *Roman Satire*, 87: 'By contrast ('with the prayer to Mercury)' the address to Janus is an ornate stylistic flourish with a measure of parody to lower the tone'; F. Muecke, *Horace: Satires II*, ad loc.; for prayer formulas see E. Norden, *Agnostos Theos: Untersuchungen zur Formengeschichte religiöser Rede* (Leipzig: Teubner, 1913), 144–6.

[8] Cf. Virg. *Ecl.* 3.60, and Hor. *C.* 1.12.13 with the comment in R. G. M. Nisbet and M. Hubbard, *A Commentary on Horace: Odes. Book I* (Oxford: Oxford University Press, 1970). See further F. Muecke, *Horace: Satires II*, to Horace's *S.* 2.6.22–3.

Persius addresses Janus as the opposite of incompetent poetry-wielders among the Roman nobles, who can buy false but not true praise for their literary products. As Bramble has noted, the derisive animal gestures made with the hands behind the back of the reciter indicate poor quality in literature.[9] The sense is that unlike Janus, the high-born poetasters are not able to preserve themselves from the secret scorn of those who praise them to their face. In the next two verses these poets are admonished to face the jeering grimace at their back door—so far they have managed to live in blindness to what is going on behind their back, 'quos vivere fas est | occipiti caeco' ('who must live without eyes in the back of your head'), 1.61–2. What then is represented by Janus, who is not to be fooled in this manner? I believe it is again the genre of satire. It is easy to see satire in the scornful grimace at the back of the nobles, or even in the gestures made with the hands, seemingly parallel to the 'dog letter' sounding at the thresholds of the rich (1.109–10). But in fact the images are not parallel: the angry snarl of the satirist-as-dog is open (it is dangerous to himself precisely because it is heard by the master of the house), while the mocking fingers and grimaces in the Janus-passage are hidden. Consequently, 'Persius' is not content to join the secret scorn, but invites the inept poets to learn the truth about themselves. 'Persius' is a true critic, who wants to draw backside criticism into the open, and who wants men to see both what is in front of them and what is behind them, as he himself presumably does. His own understanding of literature has not degenerated into the kind of snobbishness which does not deign to look back; his moral and literary standards are unrelenting but he has not lost touch with his unrefined provenance as a *semipaganus* ('half-peasant')—in this the satirist is like Janus, alertly facing both ways.

To return to Horace, and the apostrophe to Janus in *S.* 2.6, we must note another, more concrete function which the double-faced god performs in this passage: he provides the link between the poetry that Horace is writing (*carminis* 'song') and the unpoetic, realistic,

---

[9] Bramble (*Persius and the Programmatic Satire*, 115–16) quotes Callimachus' second *Iambus*, where almost all the animals in Persius (dog, ass, and in the *Prologue*, parrot) are employed as vehicles of literary criticism. Bramble also suggests that the passage in Persius is inspired by Horace's sentiment about hired critics in *Ars* 433, 'derisor vero plus laudatore movetur'.

hectic subject matter of the satirist's day at Rome. The word *principium* is ingeniously placed between the startling and unique use of the lofty word *carmen* for the *sermones*,[10] and the concrete sketch of 'Horace' s day:

> tu carminis esto
> *principium*. Romae sponsorem me rapis: 'eia!'   (2.6.22–3)

of my song you shall be *the beginning*. You rush me off to Rome as guarantor: 'Come on!'

Principium also provides a graphical border between the two levels of high poetry and busy reality: it is a run-over line from the passage dealing with poetry and at the same time the stressed first word[11] of the first verse describing the urban day. Janus, the god of beginnings and borders, performs his task supremely, securing for Horace's satire both a poetic nature (*carmen*) and a responsible, down-to-earth topic (*Romae sponsorem me rapis*).[12] Surely the formulation 'operum primos vitaeque labores' in the preceding verse (21), in addition to the surface sense 'the beginnings of *single tasks* and *life as a whole*', also has the same doubling reference to the labours of poetry (*opus*) and life (*vita*).[13]

The third deity in the passage, the briefly mentioned Muse (v. 17), is most obviously relevant for Horace's poetic enterprise. Nevertheless, she is not always recognized as a deity at all here, since the structure of the sentence requires 'Musa pedestri' to refer to the writing over which she presides. There is no question about the lexical primacy of the meaning 'writing, style', but the meaning 'goddess of inspiration' is surely alluded to as well, since the passage

---

[10] Described by Fraenkel as a 'momentary elevating of the present poem to a higher level, the level of... lyric,' (Fraenkel, *Horace*, 140).

[11] Note also that it is marked by trithemimeres.

[12] Furthermore, the first satire of Book 1 had featured a man reluctantly being dragged to Rome to stand bail (*S*. 1.1.11–12)—there may be an allusion to that *literary* beginning here as well.

[13] *Pace* Kießling and Heinze, *Satiren*, ad loc.: 'Das *carmen* ist nun freilich kein *labor*, aber die überraschende Wendung klärt sich sofort auf: es schildert zunächst die *labores* des Stadtlebens.' In fact, Horace repeatedly uses *labor* of the poet's literary work: 'piger scribendi ferre laborem' *S*. 1.4.12; 'si non offenderet unum | quemque poetarum limae labor et mora' *Ars* 290–1; 'cum lamentamur non apparere labores | nostros' *Ep*. 2.1.224–5.

is formed as an invocation, and since the frame of two other deities foregrounds the Muse's animate self.

The doubleness which we have observed in the addresses to Mercury and Janus is also present in the appeal to the Muse, in the most cogent and amusing form among the three invocations. In the question 'quid prius illustrem satiris Musaque pedestri?' ('what should I first praise in my satires with my walking Muse?') the genre in which Horace is speaking is called *satira*, as if an exact denomination were necessary in the poet's invocation of his Muse. The words *Musa pedestris* may in fact be seen as a synonymous expression to *satira*, poetically doubling the notion of this genre and explaining it through naming its constitutive parts: poetry (*Musa*) and prosaic style and subject matter (*pedestris*).

It has not escaped Horatians that the passage contains a number of poetic clichés, such as the retirement into the mountains to write poetry (v. 16), the hymnic tag asking what to begin with, 'quid prius', and the verb *illustrare*, carrying connotations of praise and beautification.[14] The phrase *Musa pedestris* itself has been seen to correspond to other descriptions of the low style in Horace: 'sermones...repentis per humum' ('discourses crawling on the ground'); 'sermone pedestri' ('foot-going discourse'); 'humili sermone' ('lowly discourse'); beyond the Latin this kind of expression harks back to Callimachus' πεζὸς λόγος ('foot-going language').[15] The discussion has been taken further by Freudenburg, who has stressed another relevant intertext, Dionysius of Halicarnassus' *On Word Arrangement* 26. There Dionysius had spoken of a kind of poetry which consciously sought to resemble the (prose) language of relaxed conversation, in his words 'foot-going diction', τὴν πεζὴν λέξιν. As Freudenburg observes, Horace's *sermones repentes per humum* and *Musa pedestris* are virtually literal translations of the Greek expression, thus placing satire in the same department as prose.[16] The paradoxical nature of 'the walking Muse' is cogently summarized by the same scholar:

---

[14] Kießling and Heinze, *Satiren*, 301, for *in montis* and *illustrare*; Fraenkel, *Horace*, 140, compares 'quid prius' to beginnings of hymns such as Pindar fr.89a.

[15] *Ep.* 2.1.250–1; *Ars* 95 (referring to comedy), 229; Call. *Aet.* 4, fr. 112.9 Pf.

[16] Freudenburg, *Walking Muse*, 180–3.

Musa Pedestris is an oxymoron: muses do not walk, they fly. The idea of poetic prose is equally incongruous, for to make poetry of prose is to destroy all that made it prosaic, the unregulated, free-flowing character that differentiates prose from poetry. Their mixture, then, is odd and impossible, yet this is exactly what Horace proposes to write in his *Satires*, a genre that always prided itself in oxymorons: the 'unified diversity' implied by the *farrago* and *satura lanx*, the 'seriocomic' (τὸ σπουδαιογέλοιον), 'prosimetry,' in the case of Menippean satire, and so on.[17]

Freudenburg refers to the muses' customary way of travel as flying, Kießling and Heinze say that the Muse ought to ride the way poetry does (while prose walks), Radermacher more specifically maintains that the Muse ought to ride Pegasus.[18] Whatever she should do, she should not walk on the ground. While agreeing with the widespread interpretation that the Muse's walking refers to the prosaic style of satire, I would like to draw attention to yet another aspect of this image, and then generally to the funniness of the phrase.

   The neglected aspect of the Muse's walk can be called its topography. The fact that the goddess' movement has been concretized, literally brought down to earth, allows us to ask a specific question: *where* does she walk? And I believe that a very concrete answer is suggested in the text: through the streets of Rome. When first addressing the Muse, 'Horace' states that he has retired from the city to a castle in the mountains ('me in montis et in arcem ex urbe removi')—a move typical of high poetry, but strange for satire, the most urban of genres. Ofellus, the speaker of 2.2, had stayed away from the city to good effect, but he was, after all, not the satiric persona himself, and the exact satiric impact of his lesson is in fact far from clear. At the beginning of 2.3 we saw 'Horace' withdrawn to the countryside from the turmoil of the Saturnalia in Rome—only to be struck with terrific writer's block (2.3.1–16), which yields the bulk of 2.3 to the voice of the interlocutor Damasippus. There, in 2.3, the problem was likewise that of writing satires, but the satirist was stuck: 'nil dignum sermone canas' ('you sing nothing worthy of discourse/ satire'), v. 4. In 2.6, 'Horace' has prepared himself for the combination of high poetic song (*carmen*; cf. *canas* in 2.3.4) and prosy satire (*satirae, Musa pedestris*, cf. *sermone* in 2.3.4), but wisely begins by

[17] Freudenburg, *Walking Muse*, 183–4.
[18] Kießling and Heinze, *Satiren*, ad loc.; Radermacher, *Weinen und Lachen*, 144.

turning to inspiring deities for help. He asks to what topic he should first direct his Muse, then appeals to Janus that this god, the father of mornings and opener of doors, should assign a propitious beginning to his poem. Janus resolutely rushes the satirist back to Rome so that the *sermo/ carmen* may take its beginning in the metropolis. So much for retirement into the mountains for inspiration. It is true that the movement in v. 23 is *within* Rome rather than *to* Rome ('Romae'), but if one looks carefully, a movement back to the city from the mountainous countryside has to be understood between verse 16 and verse 23. In 23 the word *principium* at the onset of the verse is immediately followed by *Romae*, for the beginning of satire can be nowhere else, as the Muse and Janus well know.[19] The Muse itches to walk on the ground, Janus rushes 'Horace' through the city centre. In the description of 'Horace''s urban morning verbs for walking, and otherwise moving along the ground, enliven the narration. After *rapis* of Janus' first movement, sweeping the satirist off with him, we learn that it is necessary for 'Horace' to walk on his civil duties through whatever weather, 'ire necesse est' ('I have to go'), he has to physically fight his way through the crowd, 'luctandum in turba'. The slow pedestrians shoved aside by him protest that he is urging his way with angry feet, 'iratis pedibus', an expression which plays on the meaning of *pedes* as metrical feet, of angry rushing (metrical) feet as the typical mode of satire, and of the direct reminiscence of 'Musa *pedestri*'. If not before, here we clearly perceive that the Muse of satire is running along with her poet on the streets of the *urbs*. Finally, as 'Horace' reaches the Esquiline, other people's problems, hundreds of them, are said to jump over his head and around his sides, 'aliena negotia centum | per caput et circa saliunt latus'.[20] In Rome everything is down to earth, and 'Horace', his friends, and his enemies all move along the ground, however quickly. This is the realistic, workaday, human, and urban subject matter of satire, a genre low in style as well as in content. Moreover, the setting of satire is specifically Roman rather than Greek, the city is not any metropolis but Rome, significantly named at the beginning as the locus of further

---

[19] It may be noted that Horace as a young man, a satirist to be in 1.6, was brought by his father along the same route: 'sed puerum est ausus Romam portare' (1.6.76). On this 'autobiographical' fact, cf. Gowers, 'Fragments of Autobiography', 66.

[20] vv. 23, 26, 28, 30, 33–4. Cf. Anderson, *Essays*, 30.

development: 'principium. Romae...'. This morning, the satirist has not come to Rome alone, but accompanied by the Roman godhead Janus, and the vaguely Greek Muse, who has however been endowed with walking feet for this mission. When first invoking the Muse, 'Horace' was in the mountains, a lofty, nationless setting reminiscent of the Muses' home on Mount Helicon. Yet on the advice of Janus he leaves the mountains behind and walks down to concrete Rome, bringing the Muse with him. She is the very equivalent of his satires (as we saw in v. 17), and his satires must begin in the specific, named capital, *Romae*. The Muse of satire, being a good walker, swiftly comes down from the vague mountain peaks and energetically enters the streets of Horace's city, rubbing shoulders (and feet) with the busy townsfolk, viewing Rome from a realistic, no-more-than-human angle—for she is not now flying, abstractly looking down on humankind—but still a goddess, guaranteeing the satirist's status as an inspired poet. As Horace led the Muse into the city by foot, new territory was covered by poetry: the dirty, noisy streets of Rome, where Muses had previously feared to tread. The Muse of satire stayed in Rome until Juvenal's voice fell silent, and was later to reappear in other big, busy cities, and true to her character, urgently push her way through their crowds *iratis pedibus*, with angry feet.

The oxymoron of the walking Muse at Rome is made possible through being funny.[21] It is humour that holds together the two ambitions of the satirist: to walk the streets and know real life at first hand, and yet to write inspired poetry. The *Musa pedestris* is an embodiment of what Kernan named first among the paradoxes of satire, the paradox of the unpoetic poet, or 'artless artist'. It will not do to iron this out by calculating the exact percentage of low and high style in Roman satire—though such a ratio is of course there to be calculated, it will not explain the paradoxical, elusive nature of satire. We must follow Kernan in his realization that the paradoxes of satire are conscious teasers, incongruities upon which the genre is precariously founded, rifts bridged by humour. Humour invites the reader to accept the rifts easily, and helps to keep him in a good mood once he begins to suspect that he has been fooled.

---

[21] Though generally commentators are not so keen on pointing this out. Kießling and Heinze, *Satiren*, ad loc., say that the expression is 'halb scherzhaft', by which they seem to mean that the image also has a serious significance.

The humour bridging this important paradox is of a mild kind, the kind most often used against the satiric persona himself. The Muse after all is almost the same entity as the poet-persona, and the image of the walking Muse is satire's self-humour. The goddess is lowered, but only to a point, for her original height and dignity are not revealed to have been false, as was the procedure with humour directed against the objects of satire. It is significant that the lowering part of the combination, the walk, is not in itself ugly or morally corrupt—it is only low (and so laughable) in comparison with the Muse's divine highness. Walking also brings positive connotations of poor but honest people, and even trails a whiff of ancient *simplicitas*, which so far from being despicable, was exceptionally moral to Roman minds. Moreover, walking the streets in this simple fashion has the obvious positive effect of being able to speak the honest truth, a trait in which satire took particular pride. Thus a closer investigation reveals that the speaker has not really degraded the Muse, since both elements of the paradox are in fact positive, only in different ways: one small and humble, the other grand and glorious. This is not the laughter of superiority; the speaker has simply distanced himself just enough from the Muse to make her funny, though in a sympathetic way. Instead of triumphant superiority, as was often the case with the object, the speaker's amusement conveys control: he is not a malicious person but a detached ironic man in full command of his artistic means. He can afford to lower his own Muse—how rich and generous he must be! The fact that the lower level to which she is brought down is not very bad is forgotten behind the humour. Through his humour, the artist has managed to make his reader believe in *both* the contradictory parts of the paradox—satire is both inspired poetry and rough, honest conversation; the speaker is both the ironic man who can afford to laugh at his Muse and the simple fellow who walks by foot—and so the Muse has begun her satiric promenade.

Persius

Persius will have nothing to do with the Muses.[22] He tells his readers as much in the very first lines of his *Prologue*, which falls naturally

---

[22] Ovid had likewise stated that he was not inspired by the Muses in *Ars Amatoria* (1.27–8), 'nec mihi sunt visae Clio Cliusque sorores | servanti pecudes vallibus, Ascra,

into two halves. The first seven verses renounce, and make fun of, the Muses' mountain and Pegasus, and end by a glimpse of 'Persius' himself, carrying his poetry to the rites of bards. The following seven verses (8–14) show the beginning of his proper satirist's craft: he brutally reveals what underlies the poets' grandiose and foggy phrases—the belly. The claims of contemporary would-be poets are comically degraded and made concrete by being tied to the needs of the belly, the real source of their imitative, unoriginal poetry. Once there is a sparkle of a coin, then you will hear the crow poets and magpie poetesses sing the nectar of Pegasus, says Persius, thus ending where he had begun.[23] For our focus on the Muses and the satirist's representation of himself as a poet, the first half of the *Prologue* is of particular interest:

> Nec fonte labra prolui caballino
> nec in bicipiti somniasse Parnasso
> memini, ut repente sic poeta prodirem.
> Heliconidasque pallidamque Pirenen
> illis remitto quorum imagines lambunt
> hederae sequaces; ipse semipaganus
> ad sacra vatum carmen adfero nostrum.   (*Prol.* 1–7)

I never washed my lips in the nag's fountain, nor do I remember dreaming on two-peakedarnassus. I leave Helicon's Muses and pale Pirene to those whose busts are licked by clinging ivy. Myself, I bring my song to the bardic rites as a half-peasant.

Beginning head-on with the Muses' spring on mount Helicon, a metaphor for poetic inspiration, 'Persius' declares two things: first, that he has no part in such inspiration, and secondly, that it is not worth partaking in. The first is said *planis verbis*, the second expressed in the disrespectfully derisive choice of words and images. The spring of the Muses was created when Pegasus struck the earth with his hoof, hence it was called Hippocrene (literally 'the horse's

---

tuis' (Clio and her sisters did not appear to me when I was herding my flock in the valleys of Ascra), but he had stopped short of mocking the Muses and their milieu in this apology. Rather, he moves on to the goddess he *will* invoke for her truthful and useful advice, Venus.

[23] As noted in G. Lee and W. Barr (eds.), *The Satires of Persius* (Liverpool: Francis Cairns, 1987), 66.

spring'), here rendered, in a translational pun, as 'fonte ... caballino', 'the nag's fountain'. The transformation of winged Pegasus into a Latin workhorse, with associations of walking on the ground with a heavy load,[24] is a drastic remake of Horace's walking Muse: Persius not only drags the image of inspiration even further down to earth, but he even says that he has not drunk from this source. Nor does he remember dreaming a prophetic dream which would suddenly make him a poet—unlike, it is implied, the row of poets from Hesiod, through Callimachus, and to Ennius and other Roman poets, who had all claimed such dreams for themselves.[25] The maids of Helicon, i.e. the Muses, and 'pale Pirene' the satirist will leave to poets past and present who like to parade their busts in public. 'Pale Pirene' is constructed of a combination of the inspiring place with the pale faces of modern literati thus inspired,[26] but over this meaning lies the direct emotional effect of the resulting image, that of the very place of heavenly creativity paling away with old age, repetition, and misuse. Even the Muses themselves are only indirectly named with the parodically clumsy word 'Helicon*idas*que', connected to the following 'pall*idam*que' by a jingoist near-rhyme, and end up, in the phrase of one commentator, as 'rather tired girls'.[27]

In sharp contrast to these bloodless maidens 'Persius' is a vigorous half-rustic, having his source, as it were, in himself, as he stomps out *ipse* at the middle of v. 6. As readers have noticed, there is considerable pride in the next verse, particularly in its choice of the word *carmen* and in the end-line emphasis on *nostrum*.[28] This is again satire's paradox of the artless artist which we saw in Horace above: *carmen* is used (as it was only once used of the satires by Horace, *S.* 2.6.22), 'Persius' 's contribution is a song described as *nostrum*,

---

[24] For the flavour of the vulgarism 'caballus', cf. V. Väänänen, *Introduction au latin vulgaire* (1963; 2nd, rev. edn., Paris: Klincksieck, 1967), 80.

[25] Hesiod *Theog.* 22–34, Callimachus *Anth.Pal.* 7.42, Ennius *Ann.* 1.2–11 Sk. See comment in Lee and Barr, *Satires of Persius*, 64.

[26] See Lee and Barr, *Satires of Persius*, 64–5, and Reckford, 'Studies in Persius', 502, where it is further noted that Persius sneers at the fact that their 'creative powers are idiotically judged by their appearance'. Cf. Whitehead, 'Etruscan Humor', 19.

[27] Reckford, 'Studies in Persius', 502.

[28] Reckford ibid; D. Hooley, *The Knotted Thong. Structures of Mimesis in Persius* (Ann Arbor: University of Michigan Press, 1997), 236–7; Freudenburg, *Satires of Rome*, 146–8; Kißel, *Persius*, 85–9.

personal and specifically Roman,[29] perhaps even Etruscan, and yet he is only a *semipaganus*, not a real poet. The adjective *semipaganus* is intriguing. It seems to refer to the village community (*pagus*) of the poets, where the satirist is not a full member, but it may also be taken as meaning 'half-rustic', thus stressing the fresh outsider energy that 'Persius' is bringing to the literary scene of his contemporaries.[30] The first significance makes him half-way-in, the second half-way-out, and as he is by necessity both, the word *semi-paganus* emerges as an excellent pun on the borderline status of the satirist in the realm of poetry.

In the same passage we also learn that there is after all such a thing as 'sacra vatum' ('bardic rites'), and that 'Persius' is willing to take part in these. This may provoke us to reconsider the first half of the *Prologue* as a unit, and when we do so a remarkable feature emerges. It becomes visible that, in a way, Persius does begin his poetry at Hippocrene, by saying that he does not begin it thence—a satirist's tale of inspiration indeed! He introduces mount Parnassus by saying that he *has no memory* of dreaming there (could he have forgotten? he did, after all, somehow become half a poet), and he nods to the Muses by pushing them aside, 'illis remitto quorum imagines lambunt | hederae sequaces' ('I leave them to those whose busts are licked by clinging ivy'). Even in the second part of the *Prologue*, which is generally not concerned with the dwelling-place of the Muses but with the more earth-bound conditions of contemporary

---

[29] *Romanitas* is stressed by Dessen (*Iunctura Callidus Acri*, 18–19), who relevantly compares Persius' 'nostrum' to the same word in Quintilian's description of satire, 'Satura quidem tota nostra est' (*Inst.* 10.1.93; the comparison was first made in H. Küster, *De A. Persii Flacci elocutione quaestiones*, i–iii (Löbau, 1894–7), ii. 13), where it obviously refers to the Romanness of the genre. One should however be careful to take this argument too far, for Persius does not generally show contempt of things Greek, and actually praises Greek philosophy. Unlike Juvenal, and (to a lesser degree) Horace, he does not make fun of the Greeks, and the apology here is better taken as renouncing high poetry as such rather than Greek high poetry in particular. Persius' 'nostrum' cannot be reduced to the meaning 'Roman': it is also a pointer to the specificity of satire and this poet's unique tone of voice.

[30] The former interpretation is espoused in V. Ferraro, 'Semipaganus—semivillanus—semipoeta', *Maia* 22 (1970), 139–46, and Lee and Barr, *Satires of Persius*, 65; the second in Dessen, *Iunctura Callidus Acri*, 19. Reckford, 'Studies in Persius', 502, and Whitehead, 'Etruscan Humor', 20 and 32 n. 24, recognize the expression as ambivalent, comprising both interpretations.

poetasters, Pegasus turns up in a last twisted reference, 'cantare credas Pegaseium nectar' ('you'd think that they were singing Pegasus' nectar') in v. 14, which has correctly been seen to be comically condensed to the point of becoming revolting.[31] This is an image of the poetasters' misuse of poetry for their greedy, materialistic ends.

In a bold and original article ('Etruscan Humor') Jane Whitehead has attempted to place Persius' apology within what she reads as a tradition of Etruscan humour. Looking primarily at Etruscan art, she traces as specific humorous devices a tendency to parody epic themes, and a tendency to 'borrow visual forms from Greek art, remove them from their meaningful context, and lampoon them'.[32] As Whitehead correctly notes, both these devices can be paralleled in the Tuscan satirist's *Prologue*, with the latter device corresponding to Persius' radical linguistic usage, his famous *iunctura acris* ('bold combination'). The outsider's mockery at pompous and sterile elements in canonical literature may of course be explained by the poet's origin from Volaterrae in Etruria, and the word *semipaganus* seems to strengthen such an interpretation. Yet Whitehead's reading overlooks other aspects of the poet's position. It should be remembered that outsidership was an essential trait of the genre: a satirist should write about the city from the point of view of a surprised stranger, perhaps a rustic with unspoiled morals.[33] The Roman satirists, all situated in the capital, variously try to achieve this marginal position for their personae: so Horace had stressed his liminal origins at *S*. 2.1.34, 'Lucanus aut Apulus anceps' ('in between being a Lucan and an Apulian'), and Juvenal was later to hint that he only felt truly relaxed in his native Aquinum, letting his friend Umbricius say: 'quotiens te | Roma tuo refici properantem reddet Aquino' ('as often as Rome allows you to return to your native Aquinum, where you run for recreation'), 3.318–19. Again, the two humorous techniques which Whitehead singles out as Etruscan (both extreme forms of *ostranenie*, defamiliarization, the device of making the familiar strange) are not exclusive to the humour of ancient Etruria. They are

---

[31] Whitehead, 'Etruscan Humor', 19. Reckford ('Studies in Persius', 503) on the other hand, oddly takes this image as an expression of Persius' true longing for poetry.

[32] Whitehead, 'Etruscan Humor', 21.

[33] Cf. Kernan, *Cankered Muse*, 17–18.

common traits of humour in general, and as regards the connection
to epic, this is typical of satire in particular. However, the two
explanations of Persius' humour in this passage—Whitehead's ethnic
and my generic—may well be combined. Since the marginal genre of
satire can be seen to stand in the same relation to epic as the
peripheral Etruscan culture stands to the cultural centre at Graecizing Rome, it makes good sense to add that Persius' satirical 'strange-
ness' is clad in specifically Etruscan dress.

In Horace's day, it was strange and funny enough to introduce the
Muse to the streets of Rome; in Persius' day—after the Augustan
age—Rome was old territory for the Muses, and further degradation
was required in introducing the non-canonical genre of satire.ersius
responds to the challenge by mentioning the traditional metaphors
of poetic inspiration only to dismiss them, and placing his persona
half outside the realm of urban culture by calling him *semipaganus*.
As in Horace's case, the lowering term (*semipaganus*) is not altogether negative, allowing the self-directed joke to remain soft
rather than strictly pejorative. Even as regards Pegasus, the degradation making him into a workhorse must have been a realistic and
warm image for the rustic-at-heart Romans, though it was also funny
through its incongruity.[34] The *Prologue* begins and ends with Pegasus, and thus, although Persius may denounce the stale metaphors of
poetry, he has in fact made his way into the body of his writing with
the help of that old nag.[35]

[34] The difference becomes clear when we compare this degradation with the much
more aggressive one of the contemporary poets as subhuman crows and magpies
ridiculously attempting to express the song of heavenly nectar, inspired at lofty
Hippocrene; or the inspiration for their poetry being not the Muses' mountain
but—the belly. Persius' fellow poets are, unlike the Muses and Pegasus, true objects
of his satire, and are more roughly derided, cf. the discussion above, under 'Persius:
swollen objects'.

[35] It is true that the Muse is invoked in another passage in Persius, 5.21–5, there in
her Roman guise *Camena*. At the beginning of *Sat.* 5 the satirist has again dismissed
the Helicon, leaving it to big mouths to 'collect fog' there (5.7), but then he says that
his devotion to Cornutus still has to be described with the traditional attributes of
grand poetry, including the Muse's adhortation ('hortante Camena', 5.21). This
passage however can hardly be called humorous, and it is close to overstepping the
boundaries of the genre in its sincerity; thus it will not be further discussed here.

Juvenal

Juvenal does not dismiss the Muses like Persius, but he goes further than the other verse satirists in that he comes close to insulting them. As with Horace, his mention of the goddesses comes well into his opus, in his fourth satire. This poem is a mock-epic account of how a giant turbot is taken by its catcher to Domitian, whereupon the emperor summons his cabinet for discussion about further procedure, since the fish is too big for any available dish. After much flattery from the ministers, it is finally decided that a special dish should be fabricated for the monster, and that potters should forthwith always accompany the emperor on his campaigns. The satirist ends with a serious exclamation that it would have been a wonderful thing if Domitian had always stuck to dealing with such nonsense, instead of bringing about the ruin of many brilliant and worthy men. Digression is also what opens the satire, as an introduction (4.1–33) tells of the fornication and generally depraved life-style of the Egyptian Crispinus, 'Juvenal''s enemy from *Satire* 1.26. The portrait-sketch is rounded off with the story of how Crispinus bought an overly large mullet all for himself, so that the fish motif provides the common denominator between the courtier and the emperor, thus bridging the two parts of the poem. As Courtney notes in his commentary, the thematic arrangement is chiastic, moving over 'crimes of C., follies of C., follies of D., crimes of D.'.[36] It must further be stressed that the subject matter is both ridiculous and important. The fish affairs are mockingly hyperbolic, and incongruously yoke together the low and belly-bound image of food with big money and big politics. The framing crimes of the two villains, on the other hand, are serious enough, amounting to the destruction of a Vestal virgin in the case of Crispinus, to destruction of the whole world in the case of Domitian.[37] Seen from such a perspective, the fish may well grow into grotesque symbols of the monstrous vices of the two men, so that an impression of attacking big and ugly monsters is created, and linearly

---

[36] Courtney, *Commentary on Juvenal*, 196.

[37] A. Luisi, *Il Rombo e la Vestale. Giovenale, Satira IV* (Bari: Edipuglia, 1998), has developed the interpretative pattern further, in arguing that the big turbot is symbolically equivalent to the *Vestalis maxima*.

increased as the satire progresses.[38] Crispinus' fish of six pounds passes over into the beast served to Domitian, about which it is hinted that it is as big as the world, just as Domitian is lacerating the whole world.[39]

The Muses are mentioned exactly at the conjunction between the two stories, where the introductory, minor story of Crispinus passes over into the major story of Domitian and his Council of the Turbot. The speaker has just smashed down Crispinus from his new height as a courtier by reminding us of his past, when he was selling second-class fishes, fellow citizens from the same province as he. At this point the satirist dives into the mode of mock epic by addressing the Muses:

> incipe, Calliope. licet et considere: non est
> cantandum, res vera agitur. narrate, puellae
> Pierides, prosit mihi vos dixisse puellas.   (4.34–6)

Begin, Calliope. And do sit down—you don't have to sing, this is a true story. Tell the tale, Pierian virgins, and may it bring me luck to have called you virgins.

The goddess mentioned by name is appropriately enough the Muse of epic, Calliope. Normally, she would stand up for the task,[40] but

---

[38] For the related idea that especially the latter fish is an emblem of satire, whose subjects have grown so big and grotesque in Juvenal's time that no container (of literary form) will hold them, see the elegant analysis in Gowers, *Loaded Table*.

[39] The winning suggestion that a special dish should be designed is phrased 'testa alta paretur | quae *tenui muro spatiosum* colligat *orbem*' ('Let's make a deep dish which will encircle the turbot's *sizeable rounded bulk* with its *thin walls*)', 4.131–2, and while the immediate meaning is of course that the circumference of the dish should be surrounded by a finely worked brim, the choice of vocabulary (the words emphasized in the quotation) creates associations to the earth, or perhaps to the Roman empire, surrounded by a half-geographical, half-symbolical wall. (For the argument that the casserole represents the Roman empire, see Hardie, 'Domitian', 137–8, who further uses the observation, in my view less convincingly, for his larger thesis that J. 4 is of Hadrianic date.) The *spatiosus orbis* of the dish no doubt ties in with the joint introduction of Domitian's world-wide power and of the enormous fish: 'cum iam semianimum laceraret Flavius *orbem* | ultimus et calvo serviret Roma Neroni, | incidit Hadriaci *spatium* admirabile rhombi' ('When the last of the Flavians was tearing to pieces the half-dead *round of the earth* and Rome was slaving under a bald Nero, an Adriatic turbot of wondrous *size* happened (to be caught))', 4.37–9.

[40] As examples of this, Courtney (*Commentary on Juvenal*, 196) cites parallels from Ovid, *Met.* 5.338–9, and Lucian, *Icaromenippus* 27.

'Juvenal' tells her to do the very opposite. It is significant that the verb is 'to sit down' ('*con*sidere') rather than 'continue sitting', and that the Muse is thus supposed to *move* in the opposite direction from the expected. With symbolic exactness, the Muse of heroic poetry is invited for the parodic task of mock-heroic writing, but moves downward on the scale of genres rather than upwards. If we see her, as we should, as parallel to the poet (who is the subject of the satire), we may also note that she is placed beneath the objects of the satire, preparing for the pattern of mockery issued from below.[41] The reason given for the admonition to sit down is that what is to be performed is no poetic fiction, but pure fact, 'res vera agitur'. Court-ney is right to compare this intention to 'haec ita vera' ('This is the authentic truth') which Seneca had stated at the opening of his fantastic Menippean satire *Apocolocyntosis* (1.1), and to Lucian's *True History*, a later comic tale of a journey to the moon, and to comment that the latter example shows how we are to understand such protestations of truthfulness, including Juvenal's.[42] Yet apart from their phantasmagoria, another aspect of these examples is equally important: their humour. All three works are comic, all in a broad sense 'satirical', and all protest that they will speak about real life, unlike high literature, which does not. Once the insistence on truthfulness is seen in this light, we may add the programme claimed by Ovid at the beginning of his *Ars Amatoria* (1.30), 'vera canam' ('I will sing the truth'), significantly after his dismissal of the Muses (*Ars* 1.27–8), Horace's formula 'ridentem dicere verum' ('tell the truth while laughing'), *S.* 1.1.24, and Martial 10.4. 'Verum' then emerges as a tongue-in-cheek signal not of truth in the meaning realism, but of a comic truth, devoid of the beautification of high literature, and even of the bowdlerization of decorum—the truth which underlies the surface of things. In consistence with this, 'Juvenal' asks the Muses to translate their song into speech, using 'narrate', a word more reminiscent of prose than of poetry.

Finally, the boldest move in the Juvenalian passage is his address to the Muses as 'puellae' ('girls', *or* 'virgins', *or* 'maidens'), and the subsequent comment that he hopes it will be to his advantage to

---

[41] For the pattern of mockery from below, see Ch. 1.
[42] Courtney, *Commentary on Juvenal*, 197–8.

have called them so. The Muses had been called 'puellae' before (e.g. Prop. 3.3.33), so the disrespect here lies in the hint that this epithet is somehow more than they deserve. The scholiast seems to take this as an indication that Juvenal simply does not find the Muses particularly praiseworthy, and laconically glosses 'Ad laudem vestram suffici<a>t vos puellas nominatas' ('Calling you "girls" should be praise enough').[43] Mayor comments that this is a specific jeer about their not being virgins, and several translators seem to take it thus.[44] Yet judging by the word used, it is most probably a reference to age, and an intimation that the Muses are no longer so attractive. So far from being reserved for virgins, 'puella' is the standard word for the sexually attractive and experienced mistress in Latin erotic poetry. The question of who can still be called a *puella* is decided by looks, charms, and young age, as comic poems clearly show (e.g. *Priap.* 57). But a lack of these qualities can easily be overcome, so these nasty poems tell us, if the 'girl' has something else to recommend her, such as money: 'si nummos tamen haec habet, puella est' ("But if she has money, she is a girl"), *Priap.* 57.8. A similar twist is present in our passage: the flattering function of 'puellae' implies that the Muses are the opposite of the primary connotations of this word, i.e. that they are old and worn rather than young and attractive.[45] Nevertheless Juvenal, wishing to write in the mock-epic mood, needs their help, and so is willing to flatter them, pedantically (and comically) pointing out his flattery. The joke takes up the request that the Muses sit down, for it is appropriate that ladies past their first youth should be asked to take a seat. Most importantly, it subtly symbolizes Juvenal's satire, both in this poem and outside it: the Muses are not dismissed but invited to participate in his poetry, to sit down and speak in satire's prosaic voice (*narrate*). By joking about Calliope he engages her for his own project and transforms her into the subject speaking

[43] Wessner, *Scholia in Juvenalem*, 55.

[44] Mayor, *Juvenal, with Commentary*, i, *ad loc.*: 'Amid the general profligacy, and when many poets speak of Orpheus as son of Calliope, and of other Muses as mothers, it is no slight compliment to call you *virgins*.' Cf. the translation of Peter Green 1974, 106: 'And I hope that calling you "virgins" will work to my advantage'; the translation of Niall Rudd 1999, 26: 'may I win some credit for calling you maidens.'

[45] In hinting at their age Juvenal also picks up the comment of Persius, where the Muses had been bundled together with 'pale Pirene' and dismissed as irrelevant for the satirist (Pers. *Prol.* 4–6).

in satire. The satiric Calliope retains epic's great ambitions to speak of the whole world, but is tempered by humour to a purely human position and tone.[46] Juvenal's joke at the Muses' expense is harsher than in both Horace and Persius, but it is still one which allows the Muses to stay on the scene in a fairly acceptable pose, parallel to the pose of the satirist himself. The Muses have in fact performed the opposite movement from that of Juvenal's objects: rather than being hoisted and hurled down from that artificial height, they have been moderately lowered at the outset, so as to assist 'Juvenal' in his low-against-high attack on Domitian.

HORACE: PROFITABLE SELF-IRONY

From a generic point of view it is good for a satirical persona to be simple, including not being well-bred, rich, and beautiful, and Horace exploits his potential for such simplicity admirably. His low birth, his less than handsome appearance, and (initially) his outsider status could not be completely hidden. They were real drawbacks for an official career even as a poet. An imperfect physical appearance was probably more of a drawback than we sense today, given antiquity's great appreciation of corporeal beauty and ready willingness to laugh at misshapenness. Thus, instead of trying to create a persona devoid of these defects—which would have been a hazardous, perhaps even a hopeless, undertaking—Horace put them to use in his satire. This was a genre where, with some moulding, they could prove an asset. The faults are flashed in a brief mention, preferably seasoned by a

[46] I would thus not agree that this is nothing but 'a poor joke', as Courtney says (*Commentary on Juvenal, ad loc.*). Witke's interpretation (*Latin Satire*, 80), that the Muses 'are annihilated' by the joke, is unconvincing at the other end of the scale: the Muses are teased about their age, but their most important quality, that of poetic inspiration is not really challenged—on the contrary, the satirist wishes to make use of it for his poem. Like jokes which the satiric persona includes about himself, this joke laughs about secondary aspects of the Muses and does not humiliate them or 'reveal' them; such harsh treatment is reserved for the objects of satire. Contrast the comments of Luisi (*Il Rombo e la Vestale*, 110–12), who takes the invocation altogether seriously, interpreting it as a poet's classical gesture when embarking on a major topic.

smile, and then 'forgiven': sometimes because they are insignificant, but often by means of rhetorical strategies such as humorous association, contrast, or oxymoron.

A lowly character for a low genre

So, close to the beginning of 1.3, the persona imagines a protest from his interlocutor: 'Nunc dicat aliquis mihi "quid tu? | nullane habes vitia?" immo alia et fortasse—minora' ('Now someone might say to me: "What about you? Don't you have any faults?" Yes, I do, but they are different and perhaps—smaller') vv. 19–20. 'Minora' strikes a comic note παρὰ προσδκίαν, but the admission has been made: 'Horace' does have some minor faults. Here, we want to know, first, how he will deal with this confession, and secondly, what these faults are. The answer to the second of these questions is suspended for some time in Horace (if an answer can be said to be given at all), and we may suspend it in the present discussion as well.

The first point, that of how the admission is treated in its context, is more concrete. Immediately after the statement about himself 'Horace' gives the example of Maenius, a Lucilian character,[47] who generously forgives his own faults (vv. 21–4). To Maenius an interlocutor says 'heus tu ... ignoras te an ut ignotum dare nobis | verba putas?' ('Hey you, ... don't you notice what you yourself are like, or do you think you can fool *us* into not noticing?'), thus a harsher reproach than that made to 'Horace' just before. He is also clearly censured in v. 24, which rounds off the passage: 'stultus et improbus hic mos est dignusque notari' ('this is silly and immoral behaviour, which deserves censure')—a line where the humour is gone and there is no place for ambiguity. 'Horace' may have momentarily exposed himself, but here he has definitely regained the true satirist's moral authority, complete with the censor's right to brand other people, *notare*.[48] Some critics notice the parallelism between the persona's behaviour and Maenius' and wonder about the implications. They

---

[47] Fr.1203–4 (M); probably a contemporary of Lucilius. Cf. Kießling and Heinze, *Satiren*; Brown, *Horace: Satires I*, to Hor. *S.* 1.4.21.

[48] Cf. the phrase 'multa cum libertate *notabant*' ('they branded them freely)' about the writers of Old Comedy at 1.4.5 (with Lucilius as their follower in this), and

speak uneasily of 'irony', including self-irony, but insist that 'Horace' is better, and that his faults are somehow small,[49] at least smaller than the other man's. But how are we to know if we only have the sinner's word about the seriousness of the sin? It is true that 'Horace' speaks of his mediocre sins again further on (1.4.129–31 and 1.6.65–6) and that those passages seem more serious, yet this does not alter the fact that his and Maenius' behaviour here amount to the same thing, that of forgiving one's own faults while picking on others. The difference lies in the words, for although both descriptions are humorous, they are so in different ways. While 'Horace' begins by admitting (*immo*) and thus shows himself as simple and unable to lie effectively, Maenius begins by redundant repetition of words for himself: *egomet—mi* ('I myself—me'), thus displaying his egotism and self-love. While 'Horace' is self-consciously uncertain about the slightly minor status of his faults (*fortasse—minora*), Maenius self-assuredly blurts out *ignosco* ('forgive'), creating a word-play that is not at all in his favour (as his 'excuse' picks up the preceding *ignoras* and *ignotum*). While the joke in 'Horace''s case depends on the unexpectedness of 'minora', a word which is positive in this context and which moreover connects to the satirist's device of making himself small before attacking the great, the joke in Maenius' case depends on the brazen cynicism of 'ignosco', a negative word in this situation. Most importantly, 'Horace' speaks first: what is meant to be perceived as his disarming honesty in admitting that he has faults not simply drowns in the onset of the traditional satirical criticism directed

---

'vitiorum quaeque notando' ('by branding all kinds of vices)' at 1.4.106 about Horace's own practice as instilled in him by his father. For the association of satire with censorship, cf. Fraenkel, *Horace*, 126, and LaFleur, 'The Law of Satire', 1795; *contra* Heldmann, who unconvincingly insists that the satirist's *notare vitia* is completely different from the censor's *notare homines* (K. Heldmann, 'Die Wesensbestimmung der Horazischen Satire durch die Komödie,' *AA* 33 (1987) 135). Outside the *Sermones*, one may compare Horace's use of the 'poet-as-censor' metaphor in *Ep.* 2.2.109–19, where, however, the question is one of aesthetics rather than morals. For good comments on the *Epistles* passage, as well as on other uses of metaphor in Horace, see D. Innes, 'Metaphor, Simile, and Allegory as Ornaments of Style,' in G. R. Boys-Stones (ed.), *Metaphor, Allegory, and the Classical Tradition* (Oxford: Oxford University Press, 2003); this passage is discussed on p. 25.

[49] Sack, *Ironie*, 43–4; Brown, *Horace: Satires I*, ad loc. Oesterlen (*Humor bei Horaz*, 20–1) strangely believes that Horace is not speaking about his own persona here, but rather parodying those who always claim to be better than others.

against Maenius, but has the curious effect of seeming to *be con-trasted* with it, although it is in reality parallel. The two jokes come in immediate succession, but where the joke about the object is really at the object's expense and made above his head, the joke about the persona is made by the persona himself and is not at his expense: in substituting the positive *minora* for an expected negative,[50] he manages to look better, not worse. The sins are parallel, but the jokes are not, they are opposite. The effect of Maenius' insistence on forgiveness for himself is that the readers condemn him, and forgive 'Horace' instead. A number of small moves have been performed, all of them profitable for the persona. He confessed to a weakness, displaying honesty. Since there was humour in the statement, he showed himself as skilful and confident enough to laugh at himself. Then he moved on to attack Maenius with satirical wit, and in doing so took back his satirist's position as a moral authority of the highest order (the censor with the right to brand). What he had played down in his own confession he heavily stressed in Maenius', making Maenius look like a caricature of the persona rather than his twin; in consequence, he took for himself the good effects of confession, and smeared off the bad effects on his target. Most amusingly, 'Horace' has us admire him while he is actually performing that of which he is accusing his target—attacking others while forgiving himself. Instead of laughing, we could appropriately face 'Horace' with the interlocutor's words to Maenius: 'ignotum dare nobis | verba putas?' ('Do you think you are unknown to us and can fool us?').

The device of this passage is one which I see as typical of Roman satire: the satirist cheats and fools us, but he occasionally allows us to glimpse that we are being cheated, with the effect of transforming lies into art, and giving us the sensation of participating in a game—the game of satire—on his side.

Turning to the second point—what faults 'Horace' has actually agreed to having—we note that the first examples appear in two passages later on in the same satire, 1.3.21–34 and 63–6. These faults turn out to be sloppy dress and impolite behaviour. In the case of the first of these passages, there has been some disagreement as to

---

[50] Sack, *Ironie*, 43, thinks that the expected ending is 'maiora'.

whether it really describes 'Horace',[51] and so a summary of the arguments in favour of this identification is in order. The passage reads as follows:

> iracundior est paulo, minus aptus acutis
> naribus horum hominum; rideri possit eo quod
> rusticius tonso toga diffluit et male laxus
> in pede calceus haeret: at est bonus, ut melior vir
> non alius quisquam, at tibi amicus, at ingenium ingens
> inculto latet hoc sub corpore.   (1.3.29–34)

He has a bit of a temper, and he isn't quite the right thing for the fine noses of these people. You could laugh at him for his countrified haircut and sloppy toga, and for that loose sandal which barely clings to his foot—but he is a good man, none better, and he is your friend, and there's a great talent hiding beneath that uncouth exterior.

First, this passage is closely parallel with that in 1.3.63–66, which is explicitly about 'Horace' ('simplicior... qualem me... | obtulerim tibi' ('a bit simple... the way I presented myself to you')). Secondly, the features of the man described here fit the bumpkinlike quality that Horace claims for his persona elsewhere, notably in *Ep.* 1.1.94–7: 'Si curatus inaequali tonsore capillos | occurri, rides; si forte subucula pexae | trita subest tunicae vel si toga dissidet impar, | rides' ('If you meet me when I've had my hair done by an uneven barber, you laugh; if I have a threadbare shirt beneath my brand-new tunic, or if my toga is lop-sided, you laugh').[52] The notion of a person small and insignificant on the outside but great on the inside, not least through his talent, is one which Horace repeatedly applies to his persona. He does so in comparing himself to an excellent body

---

[51] Kießling and Heinze, *Satiren*, ad loc., and Sack (*Ironie*, 44) exclude the possibility of the sketch describing Horace with the curious argument that Horace would never praise himself so highly as is done in 'ingenium ingens'—but we must remember that this was the man who would write *C.* 3.30, *Exegi monumentum aere perennius*, and the *Carmen saeculare*! Oesterlen, *Humor bei Horaz*, 21, believes that the sketch is abstract, though some of its traits may have been inspired by Horace. Brown, *Horace: Satires I*, ad loc., and Freudenburg, *Walking Muse*, 29, take the sketch as a self-portrait.

[52] Discussed in Freudenburg, *Walking Muse*, 28–32, where it is also pointed out that the image in *Satire* 1.3 draws on Theophrastus' *agroikos* (*Char.* 4.1–5), as well as on the comic stage. Cf. the observation of Fraenkel (1957, 87 n.7) that the explicit portrait of Horace in vv. 63–6 draws on *Char.* 12.2.

covered with moles on the surface (1.6.65–7), in speaking through the guise of Priapus, the god in the form of a log, in 1.8, or in likening himself to a tired donkey in 1.9, where he is actually shown to be a member of Maecenas' inner circle and a poet protected by Apollo.[53] This leads up to the third argument, which is that the features of this portrait fit not only 'Horace', but also his *genre*. The genre of satire sets itself up to be aggressive (*iracundior*), unpleasant for people with sensitive perception (*minus aptus acutis naribus horum hominum*), and using a linguistic form that is sloppy (cf. vv. 31–2), including being harsh and unpoetic in its treatment of metrical feet (*male laxus in pede calceus haeret*).[54] Satire's point of view for its critique of the vices of the metropolis should be that of an outsider, it can very well be the view of an innocent and unsophisticated country-dweller (*rusticius*). It occasionally invites laughter, though in the end it may be unwise to laugh (*rideri possit*). In essence, however, satire is morally upright ('bonus, ut melior vir non alius quisquam'), it serves the interests of good citizens (*tibi amicus*), and it may, particularly in Horace's variant, harbour great poetic talent underneath its rough exterior ('ingenium ingens inculto latet hoc sub corpore'). Thus I would conclude that this caricature depicts 'Horace' in a particular role, that of the persona as a satirist, or more drastically put, the man as his style.

The tactics of ironic self-description may reasonably be discussed together for the sketch of the ill-dressed bumpkin and the later passage at 1.3.63–6, which as we have said, is similar to the pseudo-anonymous sketch. In the passage at vv. 63–6 Horace includes simplicity like his own as the last example of easily forgivable imperfections in one's friends:

> simplicior quis est qualem me saepe libenter
> obtulerim tibi, Maecenas, ut forte legentem
> aut tacitum impellat quovis sermone molestus:

---

[53] On the image of the excellent body covered with moles (*S.* 1.6.65–7), see Anderson, *Essays*, 123. Anderson well points out that Horace's word choice, '*egregio* corpore' ('on an *outstanding* body)', has an allegorical relevance to his self-presentation as an inspired poet *above the common crowd*.
The examples of *S.* 1.8 and 1.9 will be discussed in further detail below.

[54] Freudenburg (*Walking Muse*, 31) correctly quotes Horace's judgement of Plautus in *Ep.* 2.1.170–4 as a more explicit counterpart.

'communi sensu plane caret' inquimus. eheu,
quam temere in nosmet legem sancimus iniquam!   (1.3.63–7)

A fellow is a bit simple—the way I often behaved when I happily presented myself to you, Maecenas—so that he may interrupt a man reading, or quietly thinking, with some discourse or other, a nuisance. 'He has no sense,' we say. Oh, how rashly we endorse a law that will work against ourselves!

Here, 'Horace' is the noisy nuisance, interrupting the leisurely silent Maecenas with his unrefined conversation. Even more clearly than in the former passage, this is an image of satire as much as of the satiric persona. *Sermo* is the commonest term for the genre in Horace's satires and the word used for them in the title (*Sermones*), while *simplicior* may stand as a summary of all the 'negative' qualities of the bumpkin above; *molestus*, again, is reminiscent of the sedulous attacks of satire.[55]

Yet the unpleasant and would-be ridiculous qualities of the persona, and by implication of the satiric genre, in both passages are not as harshly derided as they may seem to be at first sight.[56] To begin with the second passage, just quoted, we must note that a pleasant image of the indulgent Maecenas is imbedded in the critical terms (*simplicior* and *molestus*), and we may safely assume that he stands as an example of the generous friend who will not take offence at such trifles, otherwise 'Horace' would not have been able to happily interrupt him again and again (*saepe libenter*). At the end of the passage, the simple fellow who behaves like 'Horace' is chided with the phrase 'communi sensu plane caret', which in the mouth of Horace, never one for idealizing the common people, is more likely to be praise than blame—consider his flattery of Maecenas at 1.6.17–18: 'quid oportet | vos facere *a vulgo longe longeque remotos?*' ('what should you do, who are *so far removed from the crowd?*'). Then, the finishing line about too quick, unfair judgement (1.3.67) expresses clear condemnation, and the momentarily ridiculed persona is reinstated in his venerable position. The text then continues

[55] Cf. the discussion in Gowers, 'Fragments of Autobiography', 73.

[56] Pavlovskis takes this passage as ironic, consistent with Aristotle's notion of the ironic man as 'a dissembler, the slippery fellow who conceals his intelligence' (Pavlovskis, 'Aristotle, Horace, and the Ironic Man', 29).

with a repetition of the statement that everyone has faults and that he is best, whose faults are not so great, and balanced by assets (68–71). Thus the criticism against 'Horace' is not very heavy, softened as it is by Maecenas' unswayed friendship and by the hint that the satirist is only a nuisance in the eyes of the mob; the criticism of 'Horace''s critics, on the other hand, is rather substantial. In the earlier passage (29–34) we may observe that the suggestion to laugh at the Horatian personage, *rideri possit*, is cautiously voiced in the subjunctive mode, even before it is countered by the three counter-arguments (*at...a-t...at*). The adjectives describing the man's drawbacks are put in the comparative, the nominal equivalent of the subjunctive (*iracundior, minus aptus, rusticius*). It is as if the linguistic forms themselves were unwilling to admit any ridiculousness about this man. Although the speaker dares to include five small faults in his persona,[57] the positive traits are so impressive as to outweigh them easily. Thus in both passages the ridicule of the persona is undermined from within: by the language, then by Maecenas' friendship, resisting the laughter directed at 'Horace'.

Even more importantly, the humour directed at the persona is overridden by the massive praise of him, and chastisement of his critics. The positive assessment of him is placed last, rhetorically functioning as the heavier argument, and in combination with the humorous criticism of the persona makes use of the dichotomy between outer appearance and inner essence. The dichotomy is used in opposite ways in self-ridicule and in ridicule of the object. In the analyses of object-oriented humour we have repeatedly seen that a smooth appearance (often lofty or grand in social or historical terms) is revealed, or pseudo-revealed, as covering a rotten inside. This is a treasured device for the satirists when they are attacking their objects, it goes well with their official aim to censure society, and it is sometimes paradigmatically worded as the ideal procedure of satire.[58] When it comes to ridicule of the persona, the opposite

---

[57] Brown, *Horace: Satires I*, ad loc., counts three, probably taking 'rusticius tonso toga diffluit et male laxus | in pede calceus haeret' as describing one negative trait of clumsy appearance. It is however significant that the persona can 'afford' to add more negative than postive traits.

[58] e.g. in Horace 2.1.64–5 and Persius 4, esp. vv. 43–5 and 52. Cf. the formulation of Reckford in an article on Persius: 'the basic Socratic contrast between appearance

criticism, i.e. criticism of the outside appearance, is often jokingly served (especially in Horace), which with the same equation, but in the other direction, suggests that the inside is excellent. In the first of the two examples discussed here this suggestion is even spelled out explicitly: the ill-dressed country bumpkin is the best of men, a true friend, a genius. The mild mockery of the persona in these two passages is overshadowed by friendly indulgence, fully in accordance with the satire's Epicurean thesis that one should forgive minor faults. The forgiveness of 'Horace''s laughable faults and the insistence on his true excellence are repeated in the emphatic final lines: 'et mihi dulces | ignoscent, si quid peccaro stultus, amici | inque vicem illorum patiar delicta libenter | privatusque magis vivam te rege beatus' ('and my kind friends will forgive me if, foolishly, I make some mistake. I, in turn, will gladly tolerate their transgressions, and as a commoner I will live happier than you as King'), 139–42.

Thus the persona has been shown as having some faults, which makes him more human, but these are minor to start with and completely dismissed in the sum total of the poem. In fact, the hypocritical forgiveness of one's own sins, which had been mentioned at 19–20 and smeared off on Maenius, is continued on a grand scale throughout the satire. Humour is used to cover this, and to foreshadow other faults than those which, if discovered in his persona, could jeopardize the satire. As Kernan has taught us, the satirical persona pretends to be blunt and unsophisticated while really employing highly accomplished rhetoric in his well-plotted poetry.[59] This paradox is important to hide if the game of satire is to work well. If Horace's persona would say that one of his negative traits is cunning sophistry, this would be closer to the truth, and much more fatal for the satirical enterprise. The satirist is very far from undermining the satire by laughing at the satiric persona, for he shapes 'Horace' in the form of the ideal satirist, rusticity and bluntness and all. Even the 'admission' of a small number of ridiculous faults is likely to be read as proof of simplicity (he gives himself away and inadvertently exposes himself to mockery), while it is really

and reality, the contrast which above all others is dear to the satirist's heart' (Reckford, 'Studies in Persius', 498).

[59] Kernan, *Cankered Muse*.

a most sophisticated move. The indulgent 'forgiveness' effectively hides that what is being forgiven is the very opposite of what would need to be, and by association grants the persona forgiveness for all his other faults as well. It is thus difficult to agree with Freudenburg's contention that 'Horace' 'invites laughter ... at himself as an inept moralizer'.[60] Rather, the kindly laughter invited at his rusticity serves to make the reader perceive him as an innocent country cousin—a most convincing moralizer.

Mild self-humour

Poverty ... in things not worth having

Even more than a ruffled appearance, the motifs of low birth and poverty are constantly used so as to activate their transferred meaning, that of lacking some abstract quality. Since the things 'Horace' lacks are negative—he is too lowly for ambition and vainglory, too poor for an abundance of bad verses—what begins as self-ridicule metamorphoses into self-praise within the same structure.

To look at the motif of poverty first, we note that this turns up in 1.1.78–9, describing the satirist's attitude towards the worries of the rich man:

>   horum
> semper ego optarim pauperrimus esse bonorum.

I would wish to be always extremely poor in these goods.

He even *wishes* to be 'poor' on such rich man's cares, and this expression should be kept in mind when we next encounter the motif, in 1.4.17–18. Here, the connection between 'richness' in words (logorrhoea) and literal richness is graphically enacted. Horace passes from speaking of Lucilius and his prolific and indiscriminate writing (vv. 6–13), through Crispinus' worse ditto (13–16), including his challenge to 'Horace' to see who can write more in a limited time, then adds his own answer (that he is too poor in talent and quantity to compete with one who spits out verses like an untiring pair of

---

[60] Freudenburg, *Walking Muse*, 32.

bellows, 17–21). He goes on to the further explanation that he cannot openly recite his vice-deriding satire, since many people would feel offended, having much on their conscience (21–5). The first example of such sins as the public might be harbouring is greed, *avaritia*, which thus concludes the movement from Lucilius' exaggerated richness of production to monetary affluence (and the wish to keep or increase it). Both are now definitely negative qualities worthy of satiric censure. The lines that seem to ridicule the persona for his scarcity, while adding a streak of self-irony,[61] still emerge as basically working in his favour. They also work as a defence of his genre, the honed-down, lean variety of satire:

> di bene fecerunt inopis me quodque pusilli
> finxerunt animi, raro et perpauca loquentis   (1.4.17–18)

the gods were right to give me a poor little mind, which speaks very seldom and then says next to nothing

The startling phrase 'di bene fecerunt' and the colloquial forms 'pusilli animi' and 'perpauca',[62] point us towards the real meaning behind the apparently self-conscious admission about the smallness of the satirist's talent and output—in reality, this paucity is his very strength. There is a nod here towards minimalistic Callimachean aesthetics, as well as a hint at the figure of the small yet bold satirist, barking up the castles of the rich and mighty.[63] It is in this vein that we should take the comparison between 'Horace' and Lucilius in 1.10.48: 'inventore minor' ('not as great as the inventor'); and in 2.1, a programme poem generally filled with pride and self-assertion. When Horace says:

---

[61] Discussed in Sack, *Ironie*, 50–1, who strangely suggests that the device in these verses is to be termed 'understatement'.

[62] Sack, *Ironie*, 51.

[63] Cf. also the image of the muddy stream in *S.* 1.1.55–60, certainly an allusion to the Callimachean image of the clear fount, symbolizing minimalistic but pure ideal of Alexandrian aesthetics (Call. *Hymn to Apollo* 108). For the influence of Callimachean aesthetics on Horace's Sermones, see H. Herter, 'Zu ersten Satire des Horaz,' *RhM* 94 (1951), 29; K.Freudenburg, 'Horace's Satiric Program and the Language of Contemporary Theory in Satires 2.1,' *AJP* 111 (1990), 199–201, and id., *Walking Muse*, 185–235; Coffta, *The Influence of Callimachean Aesthetics*. The device of mockery from below is discussed throughout Ch. 1 above.

> ... quidquid sum ego, quamvis
> infra Lucili censum ingeniumque ...   (2.1.74–5)

...whatever I am, even though I am below Lucilius in income and in talent...

and then goes on to boast about his solid strength against Envy's teeth (75–9), then the tongue-in-cheek admission of smallness is seen to be nothing but a glide between real and transferred poverty. Being poorer than his predecessor in money, *censum*, poses 'Horace' in a better situation for uttering satire, for he is free from the rich man's cares (as we saw in 1.1). Being poorer in talent, *ingenium*, means (as we saw in 1.4, likewise in comparison with Lucilius) that he is less prone to writing a rich amount of insufficiently polished verses. His poverty makes him immune to the insult of being likened to a muddy river (said of Lucilius at 1.4.11–12, 1.10.50–1) or a futile pair of goat-skin bellows (said of Crispinus at 1.4.20–1). What had seemed a self-ironic confession is revealed as hiding a boast inside.

Finally, the accusation that Damasippus hurls against 'Horace', that he writes rarely and in small quantity (2.3.1–16), falls flat when we consider its context. The speaker, Damasippus, is a garrulous loser who has changed his profession from merchant to philosopher, and, being bankrupted in his own business has made a habit of interfering with the business of others (18–20). This ex-dealer in bric-a-brac is himself not in the least affected by poverty in words, and once he gets to speak, carries on, with very few cues from the main persona, for about 325 lines, making 2.3 the longest poem in Horace's two books of satires. The pseudo-Stoic sermon he delivers is surely meant to sound at least partly silly—his flood of words is another example of the muddy river, which Horace's persona is in fact glad not to emulate. And most importantly, the whole exchange takes place during the Saturnalia (5), the Roman feast of laughter *par excellence*, when everything is turned upside-down and the rules of reality are out of joint. Thus in a humorous key, the persona is chided for what we have learnt is his strength (the unwillingness to write μέγα κακόν—the 'great ill' constituted, for the Callimacheans, by a thick book), while the laughable Damasippus, an enthusiast of this wordy mode, is given the microphone for the long air time that he requires, and allowed to play the teacher to 'Horace''s pupil. In letting an outside commentator speak of the persona's poverty in words, Horace proves to us that his persona has been truthful when insisting on this before. When Damasippus misunderstands the virtue as a failure the satirist achieves two things not otherwise easily attainable: Saturnalian merriment (ah, the joy of laughing at the main preacher!) and the after-effect when the laughter, stuck in the reader's throat, teaches him that we should not hurry to laugh at people who may look risible, but who are really worthier than most. Once again, humour has allowed the satirist to have it both ways: to allow us to laugh at him, and to suggest righteousness and wisdom behind the ridiculous appearance.

Low birth ... for barking from below

The motif of low birth, another quality metonymically connected to smallness, finds its fullest expression in 1.6, a poem revolving around the success story of how 'Horace' became Maecenas' friend and protégé. His birth from a freedman father, in a formula reminiscent of the Cynic Bion,[64] *libertino patre natus* ('born of a freedman father'), echoes through the satire,[65] and is gradually transformed from a potential cause for mockery into the satirist's pride and glory. Horace reinvents his life narrative by *reinterpreting* the crucial fact of his birth from a freedman. On the one hand (he says), it means less than some people would have it, for it does not affect his innate nobility, on the other hand it means more, for it is something that stays with the satirist even after he has come to live with the great. At the outset of the satire, it is suggested that only Maecenas is above laughing at the persona's birth; most people do ('nec ... ut plerique solent, naso suspendis adunco | ignoto aut, ut me, libertino patre natos', ('unlike most people, you don't turn up your aquiline nose at people with unknown or (like myself) with freedmen fathers'), 3–6). This is the by now familiar Horatian device of having us laugh at something that is really worth our respect, only to turn the tables and expose the laugher as the truly ridiculous one. Soon we are told that

---

[64] D. L. *Vita Bionis* 4.46: 'ἐμοῦ ὁ πατὴρ μὲν ἦν ἀπελεύθερος', with commentary in Kindstrand, *Bion*, 6–7. On the connection to Horace's *libertino patre natus*, see Fiske, *Lucilius and Horace*, 316; Freudenburg, *Walking Muse*, 5, 205.

[65] vv.6, 21, 45–6, 58, 64; cf. also 7–8, 29, 36, 91.

'Horace' would indeed deserve censure if he were trying to climb above his station, but he is not:

> censorque moveret
> Appius, ingenuo si non essem patre natus—
> vel merito, quoniam in propria non pelle quiessem   (1.6.20–2)

Appius the censor would have expunged me from the list because my father wasn't freeborn—and he would have been right, since I wouldn't have rested quietly in my own skin.

Line 22 surprises the reader by replacing the expected protest and defence by a sudden admission that Appius would have been right in expelling 'Horace' if he had wanted to enter the senate—the reader laughs, seemingly at the speaker. Yet in fact the ridicule is directed at what the speaker does not do, at an imaginary non-Horace, the road not taken. The persona has parried the mockery at the last moment. The real 'Horace' is free from the demands of Glory, the ties of senatorship which prevent free walking, the extreme scrutiny that follows with a high position, the burden of responsibility. Those who perform the social climbing the persona has claimed not to perform attain names and march through the text: Barrus, the son of Syrius Dama or Dionysius, Novius—and the ridicule is smeared off on them. Then the speaker suddenly 'returns' to himself as if to something totally different:

> Nunc ad me redeo libertino patre natum,
> quem rodunt omnes libertino patre natum,
> nunc quia sim tibi, Maecenas, convictor, at olim
> quod mihi pareret legio Romana tribuno.   (45–8)

Now I return to myself—born of a freedman father, at whom everyone takes a bite, since, though I'm born of a freedman father, I'm now your close friend, Maecenas, while before I used to be tribune over a Roman legion.

The point of derision has here been shifted from the low-born man to his attackers, who are satirized with the metaphor *rodunt* (*literally* 'gnaw at'), making them both invidiously beastly and petty like rats. The ringing repetition of their sneer 'libertino patre natum' (45–6) serves to ridicule themselves instead. On the other hand, what is truly great is that his noble friend has recognized 'Horace' for his inner excellence, ignoring his lack of a splendid father (62–4). Immediately afterwards the humorous tone creeps back into the narrative, and the contrast between essence and surface is burlesquely likened to a beautiful body covered with moles (66–7). But this is not to say that the persona's freedman father is left standing as one of 'Horace''s moles, just another obstacle to overcome on his way.[66] For the father now enters the narrative in a new role. He is now the very cause of the persona's pure heart and excellence as a friend, i.e. exactly the qualities for which Maecenas (according to this satire) recognized him. While the father could not be *pater praeclarus* ('a father of splendid lineage'), he turns out to have been the source of *vita et pectus purum* ('a pure life and a pure heart');[67] and the drawback has been moulded into an asset. Interestingly, he is emphatically called poor ('macro pauper agello' ('a poor man with a scraggy patch of land'), 71).[68] The manner is much the same as that used when the persona was calling himself poor, i.e. poor in vain ambition and the worries of the rich. 'Horace''s family is poor and lowly in comparison with the laughable 'greatness' of the brawny centurions' sons at the local school:

> noluit in Flavi ludum me mittere, magni
> quo pueri magnis e centurionibus orti (72–3)

he didn't want to send me to Flavius' school, where the great sons of great centurions used to go

With the heavily ironic phrase 'magni … pueri magnis e centurionibus orti',[69] high birth has passed into the same negative knot of symbols as richness and greatness before. 'Horace', on the other hand, is raised in poverty but extreme honesty, as becomes a satirist, and indeed trained in the techniques of Roman satire by his ever more noble father, who teaches him to live well by censuring the bad examples of named others (as we learnt from 1.4.105–29).[70] He

---

[66] *Pace* Gowers, 'Fragments of Autobiography', 72.   [67] v. 64.

[68] This can hardly have been literally true; see Freudenburg, *Walking Muse*, 5.

[69] Discussed by Sack (*Ironie*, 66), who draws attention to the ironic contrast between the boys' 'greatness' and the poverty glimpsed in their going to shool unaccompanied, and the low fee.

[70] For the father as a proto-satirist, complete with the catchword 'satis est' (1.4.116), see Oliensis, *Rhetoric of Authority*, 25; Gowers, 'Fragments of Autobiography', 71.

would not wish for aristocratic parents, for they would have been 'a hateful burden', *onus molestum,* to him (1.6.99). In a comic move, high birth is once again shown as an impediment to freedom, above all freedom of speech, the *libertas* so essential to his genre. The rest of the poem tells us how he uses this freedom: 'haec est | vita solutorum misera ambitione gravique', ('this is the life of people who are free from heavy, wretched ambition'), 128–9. Very close to letting the reader laugh at the persona for his low birth, Horace has redirected the laughter at social climbers, while insisting that he himself is not one of them. Rather, he has been lifted up into Maecenas' company, as if not by his own will. In addition, this happened not *in spite of,* but *because of* his father, as this ancestor was himself poor but honest like a good satirist, and so raised his son into an egregious satirist. 'Horace' would not have liked to be high-born, he likes being low-born, unnoticed, and poor, for this allows him the freedom to move lightly, watch sharply, and speak unabashedly, as a satiric persona should. The odium that befell him because of his new status has been left behind as if it did not exist. By means of poetic and humorous manipulation, the root of *liberty* (*libertas*) in the '*liber*tinus pater' has begun to sound proud, paradoxically suggesting that the freedman father has prepared Horace for satiric *libertas* better than a freeborn father ever could.[71] As Horace indeed says in the satire's closing two lines—with a softening laugh:

> his me consolor victurum suavius ac si
> quaestor avus pater atque meus patruusque fuisset.   (1.6.130–1)

I comfort myself with this, and I will live a sweeter life than I would have lived if my grandfather, my father, and my uncle had all been quaestors.

Laziness ... in Maecenas' shade

Occasionally less clearly defined weaknesses appear and fall into a funny picture of the persona as a physically weak and slow, and yet excessively corporeal man. This man, who may be glimpsed in 1.5 and

---

[71] Cf. Pavlovskis' discussion ('Aristotle, Horace, and the Ironic Man', 32) of how the word *liberius* in *S.* 1.4 is used to designate Horace's essential nobility, his inner adherence to the humour characteristic of a freeborn man.

2.6, is passive, unable to perform highly even in his preferred material areas of food, sex, and comfort, and decidedly uninterested in more refined and active pursuits, such as politics. His exaggerated laziness makes the notoriously delicate Maecenas look strenuous and active in comparison. This aspect of 'Horace' is more ephemeral than his role as the talented freedman's son or the poet 'poor' in words, but it is tangent to these roles, sharing with them a carelessness about surface appearance and performance. This role serves as a comic hyper-Epicurean foil to Maecenas, shading him off as a great man of politics and vicariously carrying any ridiculousness that might otherwise have stained him. It works as an ironically materialistic interpretation of the good life, endearing through its self-consciousness. It is also a transition to 'Horace'-as-Socrates, satyric on the outside and divine on the inside.

Satires 1.5 and 2.6 contain relatively little target-oriented humour and thus do not fulfil the genre's nominal promise to attack vice, both are centred on the friendship with Maecenas, and both could be labelled 'On Life'—in the cameo form of a symbolic journey in 1.5, more literally in 2.6. In both these satires 'Horace' is shown following Maecenas as a devoted but not all too clever companion. Throughout 1.5 it remains somewhat unclear why the great patron brought along the whole entourage of literary friends on his diplomatic mission, and what Horace's role was on this trip. As readers have noticed,[72] the persona is at pains not to let the reader know what the important political situation was all about, deliberately turning a blind eye (in the homely image of anointing his eyes with black unguent) at the point where the purpose of the journey is for once teasingly adumbrated:

> huc venturus erat Maecenas optimus atque
> Cocceius, missi magnis de rebus uterque
> legati, aversos soliti componere amicos.

---

[72] Oliensis, *Rhetoric of Authority*, 28; Reckford, K. 'Only a Wet Dream? Hope and Scepticism in Horace, Satire 1.5,' *AJP* 120 (1999), 525; Gowers, 'Fragments of Autobiography', 60; and 'Blind Eyes and Cut Throats', 152. In the last of these passages it is ingeniously observed that by thus anointing his eyes 'Horace' turns himself into 'a minor, mundane version of Homer the blind epic poet'. For satire, and Hor. *S.* 1.5 in particular, as a mundane version of epic, see discussion below, Ch.3, under the section 'The sprinkles of non-aligned humour'.

hic oculis ego nigra meis collyria lippus
illinere; (27–31)

My great friend Maecenas, together with Cocceius, had come here—they were both sent on an important mission, as they were used to making peace between estranged friends. Here I anointed my bleary eyes with black unguent.

'Horace''s organs of perception are generally poor in both the satires under discussion: his eyes are bleary (1.5.30, 49) and his ears are leaky ('rimosa ... aure', 2.6.46). His whole figure gravitates towards what Bakhtin termed the lower bodily stratum, suggesting, in Emily Gowers' memorable formulation, 'a grotesque, porous body, focused on the lower regions, the 'obscene groin' (*obscenum inguen*) or the stomach (*supinum ventrem*) of a man with typhoid or lying on his back after a wet dream, by contrast with the 'uplifted head' (*sublimi vertice*) of the *Odes*.[73] Accordingly, Maecenas does not trust this man with any information about his civic business (2.6.53, 57), but shares with him the relaxation of small talk and watching shows (2.6.42–9). 'Horace' is here a hyperbolic, self-consciously comic Epicurean—concentrated on bodily pleasures and markedly unofficial friendship (not only with Maecenas, cf. 1.5.40; 2.6.65–76). To the burlesque Epicureans that have been spotted in the persona as he appears in satires 1.1–1.3, or again in the figure of Catius in 2.4,[74] I would thus like to add 'Horace' as a faithful but uninitiated companion to Maecenas in 1.5 and 2.6.

When the Epicurean *telos* of pleasure is here materialistically interpreted the effect is comic degradation. However, inserted meta-commentary[75] makes us understand that the persona, though

[73] Gowers, 'Fragments of Autobiography', 61. The Horatian quotations are from *S.* 1.8.5, 1.5.85, and *C.* 1.1.36.

[74] Turpin, 'The Epicurean Parasite'; C. J. Classen, 'Horace—a Cook?' *CQ* 28 (1978), 333–48.

[75] Such as the ending of 1.5, the explicitly joking conflation of food and philosophy at 2.6.63–4, or indeed the philosophical mice at the end of 2.6. The last verse of 1.5 is 'Brundisium longae finis chartaeque viaeque est' ('Brundisium is the end of this long tale ('lit.: 'paper')' and journey)', v.104. At 2.6.63–4 the menu includes beans, referred to as 'Pythagoras' relatives', pretending to take literally his thesis of the essential connectedness of all living things: 'o quando faba Pythagorae cognata simulque | uncta satis pingui ponetur holuscula lardo?' ('O when will we be served a bean, that relative of Pythagoras, and with it some vegetables well oiled with fat bacon?)'. In the story of the mice which ends 2.6, the city mouse is an obvious Epicurean, a comic move which I discuss in Ch. 3 § 'Epicurean secondary personae: fat-headed Ofellus, silly Catius, and a mouse'.

playing the fool, is in fact consciously plotting the comedy. This, in turn, suggests control on his part, his mastery of the poetic and philosophical discourse. Philosophy is caricatured with full knowledge of its rules, the persona is in reality wise enough to afford to cast himself in the role of the pleasure-seeking, unintellectual fool, and all of this is contained in the well-managed frame of comic, satiric poetry. *Satire* 1.5 is kept wholly within the Epicurean mode, enacting behind the humour a kind of philosophical life, free from the worries of official life, dominated by friendship and pleasure. Still, the picture is softened by the irony at 'Horace''s expense as he is unable effectively to enjoy the physical pleasures he values (frustrated eating at 7–9; frustrated sex at 82–5). Yet as the poem rounds off with the obvious reference to Epicurus' thesis that the gods do not care about human life, and with the joke against those who, unaware of this truth, believe in miracles (97–103), we may remember that the Epicureans thought mockery and laughter a valid method to refute wrong beliefs and propagate their own teachings.[76] In the end, the humour of 1.5, including its mild mockery of the persona, may be seen as part of its philosophical agenda: the harmonious, unambitious life, guarded from all excesses, and internally balanced, by *risusque iocosque* ('laughter and jokes') (98).

This kind of humour is exceedingly static, as is indeed the brand of wisdom it expresses. Since this is plainly a problem in a genre like satire, dependent on movement and challenge, there is not all that much of it even in Horace, the most static one of the Roman satirists. In 1.5, this philosophically smiling self-belittlement is matched by a wealth of humour spreading in all directions, sometimes rough and cheeky, as in the dozens contest between the two clowns (1.5.51–70). In 2.6, the smug Epicurean physicality and love of comfort which 'Horace' expresses in his own voice through the first part of the satire is ultimately smeared off onto the town mouse in the tale with which the satire ends. The mouse, having uttered a truly hedonistic speech (90–7), brings his friend the country mouse to his rich parasitic board, and the dinner there abruptly ends with the terrifying

---

[76] Cf. Epicurus, *Sent.Vat.* 41: 'γελᾶν ἅμα δεῖ καὶ φιλοσοφεῖν'; see further Reimar - Müller, 'Demokrit—der 'lachende Philosoph',' in S. Jäkel and A. Timonen (eds.), *Laughter down the Centuries*, i (Turku: Annales Universitatis Turkuensis, 1994), 44–5; Kragelund, 'Epicurus, Priapus, and Petronius'.

entrance of Molossian hounds. Here the humour belittling the unsuccessful Epicurean erupts from the balanced circularity kept in 1.5,
and looking much more aggressive and dynamic, runs off along with
the scurrying mice in an edgier, more satiric direction.[77]

Wearing the satyric mask of Socrates

The belittling self-presentation we have traced in 1.5 and 2.6, which
shows a man ultimately only wiser through his laughable outward
humility, flirts with the image of Socrates as an ironic man. Socrates
was the foremost example of an ironist in antiquity. It has even been
suggested that the notion of irony was gradually shaped into a more
positive form through his person, firmly associated with it from the
notion's very birth.[78] In Aristophanes and Plato an ironic man is one
who dissimulates in the direction of excessive simplicity, and only in
Aristotle does irony begin to hold a positive potential: at its best, it
can be used out of modesty by a superior man.[79] By the time of
Horatian satire, Socrates' brand of irony was being seen as entirely
positive. Socrates' stylized figure had entered Roman satire to stay,
and we can safely assume that Horace was familiar with it.[80] Several
critics have been willing to trace the persona-as-Socrates throughout
Horace's satires, but they have generally been too generous in grant-
ing the satirist the philosopher's wisdom upon spotting Socrates'
outer form in various passages.[81] What I am arguing is rather that
Horace employs the outward shape of Socratic irony as a device to
win his readers' sympathy, and indeed to make them expect, and look
for, deep wisdom in his satire, without necessarily expressing
that wisdom. Instead, he serves brilliant poetry, and mimetic repre-

---

[77] For this aspect of non-aligned humour in 1.5 and 2.6, see Ch. 3 §§ 'The
sprinkles of non-aligned humour (1.5)' and 'Epicurean secondary personae: fat-
headed Ofellus, silly Catius, and a mouse (2.2; 2.4; 2.6)'.

[78] In Plato, *Apol.* 38a; *Gorg.* 489e; Ar. *Clouds* 449; *Birds* 1211. Cf. Pavlovskis,
'Aristotle, Horace, and the Ironic Man'.

[79] Arist. *Nichomachean Ethics* 4.8.1124B. Theophrastus' description of the ironic
man in *Characters* 1, however, seems to be a step back to the purely negative
understanding. See further Pavlovskis, 'Aristotle, Horace, and the Ironic Man', 24–6.

[80] Lucilius fr. 709 M; Persius *S.* 4.1–2; Juvenal 7.205–6, 14.320. Horace is reading
Plato in *S.* 2.3.11, and mentions the moral wisdom of *Socraticae chartae* in *Ars* 310.

[81] Anderson, 'Roman Socrates'; Sack, *Ironie*; Pavlovskis, 'Aristotle, Horace, and the
Ironic Man'.

sentation of life's complexity, both of which are actually built into the surface. The real interest in his use of Socrates' figure lies not in the wisdom beneath the humble exterior, but in the exterior image itself. An example can be seen in the image of Priapus, a secondary persona donned by Horace in 1.8. Consider, first, the famous description of Socrates given by Alcibiades in the *Symposium*, where the philosopher is likened to the wooden figures of Silenus, containing gold statuettes of gods:

φημὶ γὰρ δὴ ὁμοιότατον αὐτὸν εἶναι τοῖς σιληνοῖς τούτοις τοῖς ἐν τοῖς
ἑρμογλυφείοις καθημένοις, οὕς τινας ἐργάζονται οἱ δημιουργοὶ σύριγγας
ἢ αὐλοὺς ἔχοντας, οἳ διχάδε διοιχθέντες φαίνονται ἔνδοθεν ἀγάλματα
ἔχοντες θεῶν. καὶ φημὶ αὖ ἐοικέναι αὐτὸν τῷ σατύρῳ τῷ Μαρσύᾳ.   (*Symp.*
215a–b)[82]

'I claim that Socrates is just like those Silenuses that stand in the workshops of artisans, carved to hold pipes and flutes, but when you open them in the middle, you find that they contain images of gods. I also claim that he resembles the satyr Marsyas.

Now consider the opening of Horace's eighth satire in Book 1:

> Olim truncus eram ficulnus, inutile lignum,
> cum faber, incertus scamnum faceretne Priapum,
> maluit esse deum. deus inde ego, furum aviumque
> maxima formido;   (1.8.1–4)

Once I was a trunk of a fig-tree, a useless piece of wood, when a carpenter, hesitating whether to make a bench or a Priapus, preferred me to be a god. A god I am since then, a great terror for birds and thieves.

As with Socrates, there is a carpenter present, making a figure of wood. The essence, likewise, is unexpectedly divine, for what began, in the first verse, as a useless piece of wood, *inutile lignum*, metamorphoses into a god in verse 3, proudly echoed *deum; deus*, with *deus inde* ('a god since then') in the exact middle further stressed by caesurae framing it. There is another similarity in the nature of the humble surface (silenus/satyr in one case, Priapus in the other). In both cases they are super-human creatures, but not quite respectable

---

[82] Cf. also *Symp.* 221e, where the same is said about Socrates' discourses: that they are at first sight ridiculous and lowly with their talk of asses and cobblers, but that they contain wisdom underneath, just like the outside of the mocking satyr.

as gods; more importantly, all are lusty, wine-loving, excessively corporeal, and rather ugly. All three are connected with both Venus and Bacchus, and all are usually represented with enormous erected phalluses. For Socrates, just as for 'the Roman Socrates' of Horace the satirist, such a being stands as the very opposite of what is hidden inside—the great soul, the great intellect, the great talent. The divine inside is abstract, connected to the domain of the head, while the outside is man's beastly nature, connected to the bodily lower stratum with its greediness in sex, wine, and food. The humble outside ironically hides the glorious inside. There is belittlement, but it is not meant to hide the greatness altogether. In both cases, the two sides combine to make up a well-balanced, exceptional individual. Yet here we also reach a crucial difference, for while the Greek philosopher is likened to two entities, one ugly containing another brilliant, the Roman satirist is both at once, two-in-one in Priapus, who is both a wooden scarecrow and a god. Horace has chosen his image with great care, for it both claims a kinship with Socrates and subtly changes the figure: there is still ironic self-belittlement and essential confidence, but unlike philosophy, which clad wisdom in motley, satiric poetry is both at once, its divinity lies in its laughable surface. The excellence of a poem such as 1.8 inheres in its images and poetic form, and breaking Priapus in two will only leave us with a cloven Priapus— and a laugh, as in fact happens at the end (1.8.46–50). Horace has made the move of likening his persona to Socrates, but led the reader right back to the surface again.

Likewise, whereas the form of Socrates' speech is in the *Symposium* said to resemble the skin of the satyr, and the donkeys in his utterances are said to be figures that hide important topics (*Symp.* 221), Horace's satires feature donkeys and mules as such (1.1.90–1; 1.5.13; 1.6.104–6; 1.9.20–1). In 1.6 'Horace' rides a donkey, and in 1.9 he is actually likened to one, and it performs the same function as Priapus in 1.8: it is the lowly, homely, corporeal creature contrasted with the divine talent of the persona. Yet just as the comic god of 1.8, so the tired ass of 1.9 is not a shell for a divine kernel, but is that divine creature in itself. The ear-drooping donkey, with a pun on Horace's name *Flaccus*, flap-eared, is saved, at the end of the Sacred Road, by none other than Apollo—thus forming the perfect image for a genre that finds its excellence not *despite* its ironically admitted smallness and ridiculousness, but *through* these very qualities.

No answer to accusations of lust

What we have looked at so far have all been faults that were not really faults at all, but modest and elegant pointers to virtues: simplicity, wisdom, a Socratic image. The question remains whether the persona has any true faults besides, and I believe that this must be answered in the affirmative.

One unexpected vice the persona is occasionally accused of is lust. While 'Horace' never explicitly owns up to this fault, the repeated accusations of his most satiric interlocutors, Damasippus and Davus, should not be entirely dismissed.[83] In both cases the persona leaves his accusers without a proper answer. When Damasippus, going through 'Horace''s faults, reaches 'mille puellarum, puerorum mille furores' ('your craze after a thousand girls, a thousand boys'), 2.3.325, 'Horace' ends the conversation by somewhat cheatingly turning the tables on his mocker: 'o maior, tandem parcas, insane, minori!' ('O you, who are the greater madman, do spare a minor one!'), 326. The laughter is turned against the other man, but the accusation remains basically unanswered. When his slave Davus accuses 'Horace' of being enslaved by lust, as he sneaks away in disguise to his mistress at night (2.7.53–71), or as he is goaded by sexual obsession (92–4), the persona only answers a feeble 'non sum moechus' ('I'm not an adulterer'), 72. This does not counter the bulk of the accusation, namely that 'Horace' is a slave under his own passions. Rather, the satirist's way out from this impasse is playing the Epicurean to his Stoic aggressors. Davus' argument that his master is only abstaining from adultery because of fear (2.7.72–7) is a shameful charge for a Stoic, but not for an Epicurean, to whom fear of subsequent suffering is an acceptable reason for checking his behaviour. The 'misera formido', *wretched fear*, imputed by Davus has in fact been used as a respectable (Epicurean) argument against

---

[83] Pointed out in A. Önnerfors, *Vaterporträts in der römischen Poesie, unter besonderer Berücksichtigung von Horaz, Statius und Ausonius* (Stockholm: Paul Åströms Förlag, 1974), 135–6.

seducing other men's wives throughout 'Horace''s reasoning in satire 1.2. Damasippus' allegation is likewise countered only by accusing him of being the greater madman of the two dialogue partners, presumably because he is a preaching Stoic.

All in all, this is a continuation of the persona's assumed role of the slightly ridiculous Epicurean, yet in two respects his control of Epicurean wisdom is nearing its limits here. First, unlike the other satires where this role is played out, such as 1.5 and 2.6, the persona's voice is not the only one, indeed not the main one, describing him now. His interlocutors Davus and Damasippus, the secondary personae of their respective satires, are made to describe him from outside, and from a compassionless Stoic viewpoint at that. Especially given 'Horace's' feeble defence, this kind of humour against the persona is less likely be read as mastery of the comic discourse than self-ridicule mouthed by himself. For a moment, his antagonists are allowed to get the better of the persona. True, both 2.3 and 2.7 take place during the Saturnalia, and so what is uttered in them is, as it were, an upside-down version of reality, or at least this can be claimed to defend the persona's honour. But as I repeat throughout this study, the first and most important reality of literature is its verbal level, including both the arrangement of the words and their meaning. Inferences from inherent contrasts or from context may contradict the verbal meaning, but they can never wipe it out altogether. Just as a joke is never without a message, so what is said during the Saturnalia has still been said. Secondly, sexual obsession has no place in a truly Epicurean life-style either. It is odd that the persona should repeatedly expose himself to accusations of sexual excess which he does not deny, when this fault is condemned by his chosen philosophy. In this he comes through as a caricature of an Epicurean rather than as a true, serious Epicurean—even more of the ridiculous 'Epicurean parasite' than in satires 1.1–1.3, where this mask of Horace's was spotted by Turpin.[84] This brings us to a possible answer to why the persona should so imperil his character: caricature is funnier than serious preaching, and so the Epicurean is made the more comic, even if the laughter is to be at his expense. Satiric humour craves excess, not least physical excess such as lust,

---

[84] Turpin, 'The Epicurean Parasite'.

gluttony, and love of comfort, which philosophy, including Epicureanism, forbids. All these physical vices—lust, gluttony, and love of comfort—are among the incriminations hurled against 'Horace' by his interlocutors. The satirist chooses to sacrifice the demands of philosophy to the demands of the genre, and to give up the respectability of his persona in order to save the funniness of his writing. Strong self-humour sets off the Stoics as unattractive bores, and underlines merry excess. The fact that both Davus and Damasippus also include *writing poetry* among their accusations of excesses (2.3.321–2; 2.7.117) subtly points to the literary motivation behind these excesses. In order to leave his back free, Horace has set these caricatures in a Saturnalian context. Yet the comic picture of the exaggerated Epicurean, salutary though it is for the humour of satire, brings us to the most problematic fault of Horace's persona—his excessive dependence on Maecenas.

Harsh self-humour: the mocker mocked

In the two Saturnalian satires, and by hints in 2.6, 'Horace's' dependence on Maecenas is uncomfortably highlighted. In 2.3, Damasippus says that in trying to emulate everything the great Maecenas does, small 'Horace' is like the frog who tried to inflate herself so as to mimic the size of a calf, and again that the poet is trying to look richer than he is. In 2.6, pedestrians in the street grunt that the persona sweeps away everything in his way as he rushes to Maecenas', though somewhat further on it turns out that the beloved patron never trusts him with anything of importance. Later, in the fable about the two mice there is clear derision of the parasitic life of the Epicureanish city mouse, as he is shown to live fabulously but always in fear of being chased off by the lord of the rich table, or by his dogs. Finally, in 2.7, which ironically takes up the persona's hesitation between city and country as well as the image of him as a caricaturesque Epicurean, Davus charges his master with running head over heels at Maecenas' smallest command, even when he is humiliatingly invited with short notice. Further on Davus concludes that 'Horace' is so enslaved by (among other things) this dependence that he is like a wooden puppet dancing under the movement of another man's strings.[85] The accusation of dependence on Maecenas in this last example has been elegantly analysed by Michael André Bernstein ('*O totiens servus*...'). Bernstein's main thesis is that the accusation of dependence is wiped away by association with the insubstantial accusation of adultery in the same poem. Still, even that analysis admits that rather than leaving the persona's moral appearance entirely clean, the inverted accusations in the complex Saturnalian situation have the effect of staining both accuser and accused.[86] It may be said that the imputation that 'Horace' is Maecenas' own 'parasite' is partly motivated by the same literary considerations as we have discussed above—an Epicurean parasite is funnier than an independent, ataraxia-enjoying Epicurean. The imputation may further have the extra-textual aim of flattering Maecenas in presenting him as so powerful. Yet as Seeck has pointed out in his excellent study on Maecenas as a reader of Horace, likening your patron to a big calf need not be a compliment.[87] Nor is it completely safe to show the satiric persona too much from the outside, as his aggressive and far from infallible profile is not likely to make the audience love him.[88] While the humour at the expense of the marionette-like persona reaches its liveliest, most truly dialogic apogee in these passages, Horace is sailing very close to the wind in giving away so much of his alter ego's unsympathetic weaknesses. In the Davus-satire this dangerous practice goes so far as to actually make the reader wonder whether we are meant to look with the persona (the norm in satire) or with his antagonist. Before leaving Horace for this chapter, we must take a closer look at this extreme case of persona-directed humour.

Satire 2.7, where 'Horace's' slave Davus is made to satirize his master for being enslaved by his desires, is a poem saturated with

---

[85] *S.* 2.3.312–20, 323–4; *S.* 2.6.27–31, 40–6, 57, 90–117; *S.* 2.7.33–5, 81–2. F. Boll ('Die Anordnung im zweiten Buch von Horaz' Satiren,' *Hermes*, 48 (1913), 144–5) stressed the continuation of the country/city theme from 2.6 to 2.7 in his article on the arrangement of Book 2 of the *Sermones*.

[86] M. A. Bernstein, '*O totiens Servus*: Saturnalia and Servitude in Augustan Rome,' *Critical Inquiry* 13 (1987), 450–74.

[87] G. A. Seeck, 'Über das Satirische in Horaz' Satiren *oder*: Horaz und seine Leser, z.B. Maecenas,' *Gymnasium* 98 (1991), 547.

[88] As the (later) failure of theatrical satire as a literary form has shown, Ramage, Sigsbee, and Fredericks, *Roman Satirists*, 177.

incongruities. It is in fact this proliferation of incongruities which makes it difficult ultimately to pin down the meaning of this satire. As Frances Muecke has correctly pointed out, when 'we protest against Davus that our Horace is not like that, we are put in the position of defending the satiric victim in general against doctrinaire moralizing'.[89] Why then should Horace so strangely, and hazardously, place his own persona in the position of a satiric target? This question can be answered at several levels. One answer is that given by Bernstein, that Horace wants to point out the price paid for loyalty to the emperor.[90] Another answer is offered by Oliensis, who argues that Horace recycles his old satires from Book 1, including their speaking subject, as objects of the satires in Book 2.[91] What I would like to propose here is a purely textual, genre-intrinsic answer: this poem problematizes satire, satirizes it as it were, presents the mocker mocked.

The difference from 2.3, another inverted poem where the satiric microphone is given to the persona's opponent (Damasippus), is that 2.7 is much more compact. Davus utters a lively *sermo* in the proper colloquial style, instead of abstract examples he constantly attacks 'Horace' in person, and by being a slave accusing his master of enslavement he embodies the main theme of the satire. Unlike Damasippus, Davus has a firm platform as a satirist. He effortlessly dons the role of the small but freespoken critic barking up the thrones of his masters. We have seen how attractive, indeed necessary, this role is for the Roman satirist, and we have observed how 'Horace' has ensured it for himself by stressing his smallness, poverty, insignificance, low birth, and how he has used metaphors (e.g. of himself as the lowly donkey) for the same purpose. Smallness, poverty, insignificance, and low birth come naturally to Davus, and he derides those with power over him more than 'Horace' ever did. Even concretely, it may be recalled that a servile origin was part and parcel of the image of several renowned proto-satirists: Bion of Borysthenes was the son of a freedman, Menippus had been a slave, and according to tradition, Diogenes the Cynic had also belonged to a master for

---

[89] F. Muecke, *Horace: Satires II*, 213.
[90] Bernstein, 'Saturnalia and Servitude', 473.
[91] Oliensis, *Rhetoric of Authority*.

some time. Furthermore, Davus has all the cleverness of the *servus callidus* of New Comedy, but comically chooses to use this against his master rather than for his comfort.[92] While Damasippus had only learnt argumentation from his Stoic teacher, Davus has studied satiric technique from master 'Horace' himself, as he says in the very first line: 'iamdudum ausculto' ('I have been listening for a long time').

Besides the validity of satirizing from below Davus also claims for himself the time-honoured part of the *liber amicus*,[93] which is again verbally underlined in the text—he calls himself '*amicum | mancipium domino*' ('the slave who is a friend of his master') and his master allows him to speak on the grounds of '*libertate* Decembri' ('December freedom', i.e. the freedom granted by the Saturnalia, vv. 2–3, 4). This Saturnalian freedom is also the free speech of satire, *parrhesia*, or *libertas* in Latin. The threat to Davus' authority as a satirist is that he displays the negative qualities that slaves were stereotypically believed to possess: he is lazy, greedy, and only kept in check by fear of punishment. Yet as will be seen further on in my argument, since the whole poem is about satirizing 'the satirist' and his inconsistencies, these weaknesses in Davus-as-satirist are not a demolition of his speech, but just another turn of the screw in this self-referential text.

The object of Davus' derision is, I posit, not any individual moral flaw in 'Horace', but his flaws *qua* satirist, and so ultimately, Davus derides satire as such.[94] As Kernan has shown, satire as a genre rests on a number of paradoxes about its persona.[95] It is these paradoxes, plus the additional paradox of the supposedly free-spoken but really unfree Roman satirist, that are probed in this Horatian satire. According to Anderson's paraphrase of Kernan, we meet the

[92] Note that 'Horace' calls him *pessimus*, when the 'best' quality of the crafty slave of comedy was exactly being *malus* (sly and cynically clever rather than 'bad' in a straightforward sense); see Rei, 'Villains, Wives, and Slaves in Plautus', 94.

[93] Noted in F. Muecke, *Horace: Satires II*, 212.

[94] I thus agree with H. B. Evans ('Horace, Satires 2.7: Saturnalia and Satire,' *CJ* 73 (1977–8), 311–12) that 2.7 is a satire on satire, although our readings of it only have this in common.

[95] See above, § 'The paradoxes of satire, as mapped by Alvin Kernan'. Anderson's paraphrase of Kernan's model, in more detail, will also be found there (Kernan, *Cankered Muse*; Anderson, *Essays*).

following paradoxes in the satiric persona: (1) the artless artist, (2) the untruthful announcer of truth, (3, 4) the immoral moralizer, and (5) the unreasonable reasoner. In addition there is the problem of the practitioner of free speech who is himself in various ways unfree. Throughout his mocking attacks, Davus exposes the inconsistencies of the satiric persona.

The inconsistency of the satirist as an artless artist, perhaps the most dangerous of all satire's inconsistencies since it is directly involved with its essence as poetry, is only very briefly, though significantly, touched upon in the reported utterance of the parasite Mulvius: 'verbisque decoris | obvolvas vitium' ('you wrap up your faults in pretty words'). So far from being what the satirist sets himself up to be, a good man speaking his moral lessons in blunt and artless language, 'Horace' is charged with being the very opposite, an immoral man hiding his character behind exquisite verbal art.

'Horace' is charged with not being truthful when he praises the mores of olden times, while he would actually not wish to find himself in that time, and when he congratulates himself on his simple, lonely meal at home while he actually wishes for nothing more than Maecenas' invitation (22–4; 29–35). If Davus' imputation of luxurious dining and fear of loneliness be true (105–15), then by implication, it may be concluded that the persona has not been truthful when elsewhere (in other satires) praising simple living and boasting of his expert use of solitary *otium*.

Davus accuses the persona of being an immoral moralizer when the lazy and greedy Mulvius is quoted complaining that 'Horace' attacks others while he is no better himself:

> 'etenim fateor me' dixerit ille
> 'duci ventre levem, nasum nidore supinor,
> imbecillus, iners, si quid vis, adde popino:
> tu, cum sis quod ego et fortassis nequior, ultro
> insectere velut melior verbisque decoris
> obvolvas vitium?'   (37–42)

'Well, I admit,' he would say, 'that I'm a flimsy character, led by his belly, my nose twitches when catching a smell... I'm weak, lazy, even a drunkard if you like, but you, who are no better than I and perhaps worse, you attack me as if you were better, and wrap up your faults in pretty words!'

'Horace's' irrationality is derided in all the vices he is accused of—dependence on Maecenas, lust, greed and gourmandizing in food, excessive fancy for pictorial art, inability to deal with mental monsters—but also, hilariously, in his panicky and aggressive reactions to Davus' utterances in the dramatic frame of the satire. Close to the beginning of Davus' performance 'Horace' calls his words *putida* ('rotten') and the slave himself *furcifer* and *pessime* ('crook, scum') (21, 22). This in spite of the facts that it is the Saturnalia and that he has himself given his slave permission to speak. Somewhat further on he is apparently making angry faces and starting, for Davus protests against this anger with 'aufer | me vultu terrere; manum stomachumque teneto' ('Stop making scary faces at me, hold back your fists and your temper'), 43–4, and the satire farcically ends with 'Horace''s hysterical threats, apparently his only means to silence his slave:

> 'unde mihi lapidem?' 'quorsum est opus?' 'unde sagittas?'
> 'aut insanit homo aut versus facit.' 'ocius hinc te
> ni rapis, accedes opera agro nona Sabino.'   (116–18)

'Where can I get a stone?'—'What for?'—'Where can I get some arrows?'—'The man is either mad or composing verse.'—'If you don't clear off at once, I'll make you the ninth drudge on my Sabine farm!'

Finally, the last, extra ambiguity of the enslaved practitioner of parrhesia permeates the whole poem, but is particularly spelled out in the passages where Davus challenges 'Horace' with being no freer than he is: 'o totiens servus!' ('You're a thousand times a slave!'), 70; 'tune mihi dominus' ('And you should be my master!'), 75;

> '... tibi quid sum ego? nempe
> tu, mihi qui imperitas, alii servis miser atque
> duceris ut nervis alienis mobile lignum.'   (80–2)

'... what am I to do? Don't you who give me orders, miserably serve another man, and twinge as a wooden puppet when the master's hand pulls the strings?'

Thus Davus satirizes the satirist, but then again it is all 'only' humour, spoken during the Saturnalia, by a comic speaker, making use of hilarious inversion. The question is whether the incongruities beneath the humour bear close scrutiny.

For humour at large, the general question of whether humorous incongruities bear scrutiny has been variously answered by different scholars. So Daniel D. Perlmutter, speaking for all kinds of humour, has proposed the thesis that some jokes are demolished if their constitutive incongruities are too closely analysed. A comic analogy yoking together distant contexts, for instance, may in fact turn out to be valid, which, it is argued, will dissolve the incongruity and kill the joke.[96] At the other extreme, Purdie has submitted that it is essential to examine the incongruities involved in what is funny, in order for the reader/ hearer not to lie to himself about what he is laughing at. Since getting a joke and enjoying it is pleasurable in itself, the audience may be tempted not to look too closely at e.g. a prejudiced stereotype at the bottom of the funniness. Yet the assumptions behind a joke are in fact, Purdie argues, crucial to the cognitive message smuggled in through all kinds of humour. For instance, she demonstrates how British jokes about Irishmen build on the pattern that Irishmen are silly but constantly try to be clever, while many jokes about women build on the assumption that women should be silent but like to talk excessively. Substituting Irish*women* for the Irishmen in a joke of the former category does not work: there is surplus information and the audience is confused as to what kind of incongruity to expect.[97] In studying the field of Roman humour, Richlin and Henderson express positions similar to Purdie's.[98] This second position seems to me much more persuasive, since it is easy to think of various classes of jokes which require certain assumptions in order for their incongruities to work in the expected way. Humour about oneself rarely proceeds from the assumption that 'I am stupid', and hardly ever from the view that 'I should be silent but tend to speak too much'. Actually, even the examples proposed by Perlmutter for his contrary position may be explained within Purdie's framework. Perlmutter's example about the too exact analogy is a joke about a nineteenth-century rabbi. The rabbi compares the newly invented telephone to a very long dog with its head in Minsk and its tail in Pinsk—when you pull its tail in Pinsk, it

---

[96] D. Perlmutter, 'On Incongruities and Logical Inconsistencies in Humor: The Delicate Balance,' *Humor* 15/2 (2002), 155–68.

[97] Purdie, *Comedy*, 133–4.

[98] Richlin, *Garden*; Henderson, *Writing down Rome*, not least in the chapters on Roman satire, chs. 7–10, 173–273.

barks in Minsk.[99] From Purdie's position it may be argued that far from causing the joke to fall apart, the actual validity of the speaker's comparison celebrates the entertaining cleverness of the rabbi. This creates the pleasant, warm impression of the joke, which is essentially friendly towards its main personage. It is not a joke likely to be used by a fanatical anti-Semite. Nor could one create a misogynist joke by replacing the rabbi by a 'Blonde bimbo'. Rather than being potentially disruptive, the cognitive value of the incongruity turns out to be pertinent to the joke's effect.

For persona-oriented humour in Roman satire, I have argued that in Horace's case the incongruities tend to play on the pattern 'frail body—great mind', thus celebrating rather than denigrating the persona. Less often, his self-humour uses the pattern of the persona as 'physically excessive like his genre'. To return to the Davus-poem, we may answer that the incongruities causing its humour are the incongruities typical of satire as a genre, and of its persona as a writer of satire. On closer examination, we must admit that Davus is right in the gist of his argument: 'Horace' is not a free and good man. But then in his role as satirist he could not be otherwise; he must exhibit the inconsistencies demanded by the genre. The wise man praised by Stoic Davus, who would be whole and self-sufficient, 'in se ipso totus, teres atque rotundus' ('whole in himself, smooth and round'), 86, could never write efficient satire. In this *sapiens*, there can be no movement, no excess, everything slips off his polished surface (87–8), and nothing can possibly provoke him into the stuff of satire— aggression and laughter. Nor is Davus himself, a satirist for the duration of this poem, anything like his Stoic sage—he is just as unfree, morally hypocritical, and unreasonably excessive as the generically encoded satirist must be. The cognitive value of the humour in this satire is to expose satire's paradoxes—a risky enterprise, barely carried off under the shelter of the comic.

The probing of satire's exigencies is slammed shut when 'Horace' declares an end to the Saturnalian licence, and Davus-as-satirist is returned to his subjection as a slave. If we think closely, this uncannily hints that a satirist is never really free. Here, playing the satirist, a slave has demonstrated it on his own example. And yet this is not the

---

[99] Perlmutter, 'Logical Inconsistencies in Humor', 163.

whole truth, for his Saturnalian humour and satire has reached our ears, he has, albeit as a joke, been given a voice. This is the true double-bind of satire: its humour makes it ambivalent, both said and 'unsaid' (with the move 'just joking'), both free in its permission to speak and unfree in the limits of its speech. Davus' harangue stays as a hook in the reader's guts, and whenever we come back to this poem, we are left to wonder whether it is for real.

PERSIUS' SPLITTING SELF

After Horace, the fully *self-controlled* self-irony by the persona retreats from Roman satire, to turn up in other genres, such as the epigram and the novel.[100] The persona-directed humour in Persius and Juvenal is no longer designed and uttered primarily by the persona himself, but fired at him by the implied author through the combination of what the persona says and does, or through the voices of other actors in the satires. This is directly connected to a larger change in the satiric persona after Horace: the role of 'autobiographical' information gradually dwindles, and when we reach the stage of Juvenal it is difficult to glimpse even a rudimentary outward view of his persona. As has been indicated above, the humour directed at the I-figure from the outside is almost automatically rougher than self-mockery in his own voice, which tends rather to strengthen his authority by suggesting that he masters the humorous discourse. This could clearly be seen in Horace's example. Whereas 'Horace' himself joked about his unsophisticated appearance, his lowly origins, and how these contrasted with his extraordinary inner qualities, Damasippus and Davus, deriding him from the outside, could make much edgier remarks, especially about his dependence on Maecenas. It was shown that mockery of the persona emanating from the outside was potentially subversive to his authority and consequently to everything he said. An extreme version is to turn the persona into

---

[100] The continuity of the persona's behaviour from Horace's satiric poetry (*Sermones* and *Epistulae*) to Martial's epigrams is subtly discussed in a forthcoming article by Elena Merli, 'Identität und Ironie: Martial innerhalb der Tradition der römischen Satire'.

the actual target, but in extant Roman satire there are no such openly inverted treatments of the persona as object. Instead, a delicate balance is upheld between three elements: the traditional derision of others *voiced by* the persona, self-mockery *by* him, and the potentially disruptive derision *of* him from outside. In Horace's Davus-satire this balancing act is cautiously played out under the shelter of the Saturnalia, while in Juvenal the teasing possibility that the persona is being derided becomes a real problem. Persius does not in general make much fun of his earnestly Stoic persona. There is, however, a notable exception: Persius' third satire. In this poem, the shift from self-mockery (dominant in Horace) to mockery coming from outside (dominant in Juvenal) is, significantly, enacted in the splitting of the persona's self.

Who is speaking in P. 3?

There has been much controversy over the number and nature of speakers in Persius' *Satire* 3. Some readers see two actors, some three, and the actors recognized are not the same ones.[101] In an article of 1913, A. E. Housman radically suggested that 'Persius holds parley with himself', only allowing for an intervention of a comrade in vv. 5–6.[102] Housman saw the opening of the satire as spoken by the whole satirist, with the verbs in the first person plural,[103] followed by a dialogue between his higher self and his lower self. The higher self rebukes the backsliding self in the second person, speaking of himself

---

[101] See the convenient summary in Gowers, 'Persius and the Decoction of Nero', 142 n. 107 (on 149).

[102] Housman, 'Persius', 17–18; citation from 18. To strengthen his thesis about Persius talking to himself, Housman pointed out that the interests and the education of the speaker in P. 3 are strongly reminiscent of the poet as we know him from the *vita*; to this Reckford ('Studies in Persius', 495) has added that the lines on the speaker's schooling also suggest the Stoic training of the persona ('Persius') in 5 and the secondary persona at the centre of 4 ('Alcibiades–Persius').

In addition to his sound arguments for this thesis, Housman also expresses the odd opinion that the speaker situation in P. 3 can readily be understood from a comparison with Horace's *S*. 2.3. Yet as Kißel (*Persius*, 368) rightly observes, the comparison is infelicitous, since Horace's satire—indeed parallel to P. 3 in some respects—is an unquestionable *dialogue* between 'Horace' and Damasippus.

[103] 'stertimus', 'findor', 'querimur', 'venimus' (vv. 3, 9, 12, 16).

in the first person singular; at length the lower nature finds a voice and answers with a brief complaint about his conditions.[104] Housman's solution, which is both sensible and much in line with Persius' repeated admonitions to begin moral improvement within oneself, has been substantially strengthened by an analysis by Gowers in her 'Persius and The Decoction of Nero', where she points out that the split in the persona takes place within the poem, beginning with *findor* (9, literally 'I am split in two').[105] She notes that the satirist's tools of the trade, his writing materials, include a twin-tone note-book, 'bicolor membrana' (10), and multiplying pens—either three pens or one pen mentioned with three different words ('harundo', 'calamo', 'fistula'; 11, 12, 14). Most importantly, when he tries to write, the ink of his pen drips with doubling drops: 'dilutas querimur geminet quod fistula guttas' (14). This last trait of the doubled writing, in turn, corresponds to they Pythagorean letter Y, standing for the two paths of life, which turns up later in the poem (56–7). Just so the whole satire revolves around the bifurcating roads of life, with Persius' higher self treading the narrow path of virtue and trying to persuade the lower self to abandon the path of dissolution where, in his neglect, he has found himself. To Housman's and Gowers' arguments I would like to add that the structure of the poem also mimics the dissolution of one personality. The satire begins with a close-up on a man drunkenly asleep, but already with something unwieldy about him, underlined by the word *indomitum* ('untamed') of the wine on his breath. It is midday, with bright light and insufferable heat, and as soon as he realizes this, he explodes with irrational anger and moves with crazed inefficiency. Then there follows the dialogue, and towards the end the narrative further divides into two sketches of irrational men driven to utmost depravation—a centurion with disdain of philosophy and a gourmand dying in the bath. After this, the threads of the narration are tied together again, and the focus narrows to a picture of the 'lower self', mad as Orestes. In his irrational madness, his eyes shine and his blood boils, recalling the sick heat of the Dog-star at the opening of the satire:

---

[104] To the back-slider: 'poscis', 'recusas', 'succinis', 'effluis', 'tibi' (18, 20); of himself: 'ego', 'novi' (30); the lower self answers 'studeam' (19).

[105] Gowers, 'Persius and the Decoction of Nero', 142–3.

> *siccas insana canicula* messes
> iam dudum *coquit* et patula pecus omne sub ulmo est.   (5–6)

the *mad Dog-star* is *baking* the *dry* crops and all the cattle are hiding under the spreading elm.

> nunc *face* supposita *fervescit* sanguis et ira
> *scintillant* oculi, dicisque facisque quod ipse
> *non sani esse hominis non sanus* iuret *Orestes*.   (116–18)

now when your blood, ignited by some *torch*, begins to *boil*, and your eyes *spark* with anger, and you say and do things that *mad Orestes* himself would swear to be *the deeds of a madman*.

'Scintillant', which is reminiscent of fire and so connected to the imagery of burning, primarily means 'sparkle', and therefore also recalls light imagery. It may thus also be compared with the sharp light at the beginning, described as if it were painfully entering sensitive eyes rather than a window: 'iam *clarum mane* fenestras | intrat et angustas *extendit lumine* rimas' ('the bright morning is already entering the windows and extending the thin cracks with its light'), 1–2.[106] The satire ends where it began.

Those who argue against the thesis that 'Persius' is speaking with part of his own self employ the logic of reality, not of literature. They concentrate on two aspects. First, they claim, someone who delivers such a reasonable, concrete speech as the mentor does here must be a living person (even if fictional). Second, the dialogue partners are too different to be parts of the same mind.

Yet against the demand for realism it must be noted that Persius is particularly free in his moulding of interlocutors, even to the point of admitting his first interlocutor's papery fictionality with the words 'quem ex adverso dicere feci' ('you, whom I have made answer my arguments'), 1.44.[107] For the third satire, the effect of drawing the reader into the discourse through a certain vagueness about the interlocutor has been forcefully stressed by Cynthia Dessen. She

---

[106] Cf. the observation of Squillante Saccone ('Techniche dell'ironia e del comico', 22) that the frantic burning of the Dog-star is comically paralleled by the lower self's scurrying back and forth as he finally realizes how late it is (3.7–8).

[107] Cf. 'Persius''s address to an heir as yet unknown—or perhaps wholly imaginary: 'at tu, meus heres | quisquis eris, paulum a turba seductior audi' (6.41–2).

rightly points out that the dramatic *in medias res* opening, in combination with the inclusive verb forms (*stertimus* ('we're snoring'),
querimur ('we complain'), *venimus* ('we come')) interrupted by
an address to the audience in the second person singular (*credas*
('you would think')), achieves 'a deliberate ambiguity' between the
narrator's remarks to us and the remarks addressed to the back-
sliding youngster.[108] This in turn encourages us readers to identify
with the startled youth, and almost voluntarily step into a position
where we will be criticized together with him. Such a reading is
convincing, but it need not exclude the possibility of the speakers
still being different parts of one person's psyche, as it seems to do
for Dessen. Nor is the rejection of a biographical approach to Roman
satire (a rejection adhered to by Dessen and by the present study) any
reason not to see P.3 as 'Persius' conversation with himself—quite the
contrary. This is connected to the second aspect that Housman's
opponents focus upon: the contrast between the two main speakers
in the poem. If we attempt to view the text as a realistic biographical
account, then indeed the conclusion must be that one and the same
person who behaves with uncontrolled fury, and then with
analytical detachment in immediate succession, shows 'schizophrene
Züge', as one commentator puts it.[109] If instead we regard the dialogue partners as emphatically fictional creations—as in fact the
author has hinted that they are, by making *both* of them resemble
himself in obvious formal traits,[110] and by building that ambiguity of
address noted by Dessen —then it makes perfect sense that they
should be different. They are then widely diverse, even opposed,
principles within one soul, and they fight out the drama of the
innate contradictions in man on the example of 'Persius'. In
addition, the schizophrenic switching between hot passion and cool
detachment tantalizingly recalls the split mission of the genre, and
the poem can so be seen to stage the integral inconsistencies of

---

[108] Dessen, *Iunctura Callidus Acri*, 48–50, quotation from 49.
[109] Kißel, *Persius*, 369.
[110] For the details of correspondence between the persona(e) of P.3 and Persius
the author as described in the *vita*, see Housman, 'Persius', 17.

satire.[111] Once the thesis of a split 'Persius' is accepted, it may form the basis for a closer investigation of how the satirist mocks his disintegrating persona here.

Mild humour against 'the higher self'

The kindest and most controlled mockery not surprisingly befalls the 'higher self', who himself admits that he, too, was once a young dog, more interested in play than study:

> saepe oculos, memini, tangebam parvus olivo,
> grandia si nollem morituri verba Catonis
> discere non sano multum laudanda magistro,
> quae pater adductis sudans audiret amicis.
> iure; etenim id summum, quod dexter senio ferret,
> scire erat in voto, damnosa canicula quantum
> raderet, angustae collo non fallier orcae,
> neu quis callidior buxum torquere flagello.   (44–51)

I remember that when I was a boy, I would often smear my eyes with olive oil if I didn't want to learn dying Cato's grand speech in order to be praised by my teacher, and listened to by my father, who would bring his friends and sit there, sweating. I was right! My greatest wish was to learn how much the happy six-throw would bring me, how much the ruinous 'doggy' would lose me, I wished to hit the narrow neck of the jar with my throw, and not to be outdone in cleverly whipping the wooden top.

This is as close as we get with Persius to Horatian self-irony: like 'Horace' in the satires, this fellow *describes himself* as having been small, *parvus*, in comparison with his mad teacher, his father sweating with ambition, and above all, with Stoic Cato's great words, 'grandia . . . verba'. He did not want their greatness, he wanted excellence in various games. The skills required for the games—intuition and cunning—could easily have been used as a metaphor for the skills of writing satire, but this is not done; rather, this part of Persius

---

[111] Cf. Housman's argument that the lines 10–22 are an imitation of Horace's *S.* 2.3.1–16, which he calls 'satire on the satirist's self' (Housman, 'Persius', 18). See also Gowers' ('Persius and the Decoction of Nero', 142) comment on 'the "split" decorum of hotch-potch satire'.

later abandoned games altogether in favour of philosophy. This speaker is different from 'Horace' in one respect, namely that far from accepting his father's education, he tries to cheat himself out of it by playing ill. Persius' persona (both his higher and lower self), born in a wealthy aristocratic family, has no need of working his way up by means of education and common sense. Served with Stoic philosophy from the outset, he can afford to try and escape it during a period, presumably a short one. Thus his smallness here is only smallness in the literal sense of size and age, it holds no suggestions of poverty, low social status, or, importantly, of implied superiority over people who are 'great' in that they are exceedingly ambitious and presumptuous in their morals, or richly verbose in their writings. From the outlook of Persius' satire, Cato's famous last words are truly great, this is not the hollow greatness which is satirically set up in order to be put down. On the contrary, it is the little boy who changes his size and leaves his smallness behind. Since his puniness has no deeper significance, it is fitting that it should be a passing state— quite unsatirically, this somewhat ironical scene will presently change *for the better*, not for the worse. 'Persius''s higher self is basically serious; his self-irony goes no further than to pointing out that he was once a child. His charade in smearing his eyes with oil in order to look ill may recall Horace's satiric persona with his repeated wriggling with the truth, with his *lippitudo* and eye-ointment (*S.* 1.5.30–1, 49), but it is only a superficial resemblance. Persius' speaker soon outgrows this unworthy behaviour, while 'Horace' always remains small and never drops the comic potential of the frail, low-born body incongruously wrapping his powerful talent.

Harsh humour against 'the lower self'

Considerably bolder mockery is directed against Persius' lower self, the back-sliding, crapulous student. He is derided both by the higher self playing his mentor and by the narrative describing his behaviour. It all begins with an ass, just as the whole of Persius' satiric opus began with ass' ears in the first satire.

> nemon? turgescit vitrea bilis:
> findor, ut Arcadiae pecuaria rudere credas. (8–9)

Is nobody there? My glass-green bile is swelling: I burst with the sound of all Arcadia's asses braying.

The splitting, just as Horace–Priapus's comic splitting at the end of his satire 1.8 (where the same verb is present in a compound, cf. 'dif*fissa* nate' ('with split buttocks'), Hor. *S.*1.8.47—'*findor*' ('I'm splitting')P. 3.9), gives off a loud sound, in Persius' case likened to the braying of hoards of Arcadian asses. These asses are a far cry from the ones with which Horace associated his persona.[112] Horace's donkeys are lowly, humble, and warmly comic animals, unsophisti-cated and low-born in comparison with the noble horse—just as 'Horace' is in comparison with the Roman aristocracy—but per-forming their work adequately enough, i.e. carrying people and goods on their backs, drawing carts and rafts, but refusing to learn performance at the Circus.[113] Persius' donkeys are comic in another, harsher way: to judge from both P.1 and the passage under discussion here, they symbolize stupidity and a lack of understanding; in P.1 there is probably the additional suggestion of garrulity,[114] here in the third satire there is an emphasis on noisiness. Asses' ears, paid particular attention by both the *Flacci*, are used by Horace to express his persona's moods in *S.* 1.9. His ears, compared to a donkey's, droop dejectedly as he loses a momentary hope of getting rid of the bore, and when the bore is dragged off to court 'Horace' triumph-antly serves as witness, happily offering his no longer drooping ear, a gesture which recalls the sad donkey's ears earlier in the poem. In Persius, the ass's ears that everybody in Rome is said to have (P. 1) signify a particular kind of stupidity, namely the inability to under-stand literature, and through the first satire's equation 'literary style = moral appearance', also inability to live morally. In addition, the allusion to King Midas brings connotations of tyranny and abuse of power. It is worth noting that the comic image of the ears is applied to the *object* of Persius' satire, being perhaps too harsh to apply to the

---

[112] See above, § 'Wearing the satyric mask of Socrates'.

[113] Horace, *S.* 1.1.90–1; 1.5.13; 1.6.104–6; 1.9.20–21.

[114] Traditionally associated with the donkey in antiquity; see Bramble, *Persius and the Programmatic Satire*, 27, and above, Ch. 1, § 'Inflating the bodies of men and poems (P. 1)'.

speaking *subject* as was done in Horace.[115] The association with Midas blots out the connotations of peaceful country life which were important for Horace's conception of satiric donkeys. In the passage in P.3, the simile with the asses is made more derisive by their being specifically the asses of Arcadia, the idyllic landscape evoked just before in the pseudo-bucolic lines of the comrade, 'siccas insana canicula messes | iam dudum coquit et patula pecus omne sub ulmo est' ('the mad Dog-star is burning the dry crops, and all the cattle are hiding under the spreading elm'), 5–6. There is comic hyperbole in the noise being compared to not one, but many braying asses.[116] Following Housman, we will read this derision as targeting the whole of 'Persius', at the very point where he is breaking up, which well suits the arrangement of the third satire as a whole. After this moment of fission, derision is concentrated on the lower self. He is mocked with accusations of softness, lack of self-control, and dissolution, with the last of these doubling, in a more outrageous degree, the fate that befell 'the whole man' at the beginning of the satire. In the discourses of antiquity, the qualities of softness and moistness tend to carry connotations of effeminacy, and this insulting suggestion, though not explicitly voiced, is certainly present here to give an extra edge to the humour.

The sarcasm in the lines which the higher self hurls against the lower self is made explicit as he is likened to another animal, the soft dove, and to a pampered royal baby, the comparison complete with effective sound-play in parodic 'motherese':[117]

> a, cur non potius teneroque columbo
> et similis regum pueris pappare minutum
> poscis et iratus mammae lallare recusas? (16–18)

ah, why don't you rather behave fully like a dove's chick or a baby prince, asking to have your din-din pre-chewed, and flying into a tantrum when nanny tells you it's bed-time?

---

[115] It is conceivable that the group attacked in P. 1, unworthy people at Rome, are meant to include 'Persius', but even if this is so, it is only an unspoken hint, and the main entity explicitly furnished with ass' ears is still the object of the satire.

[116] Both these points are noted in Kißel, *Persius*, ad loc.

[117] Pointed out by Squillante Saccone ('Techniche dell'ironia e del comico', 22), who however does not comment on vv. 20–1.

This explicitness of the mockery is even spelled out, meta-literally: '*tibi luditur.* effluis amens. | *contemnere*' ('You are *made a fool of.* You're oozing out of shape, you idiot. *You'll be despised*'), 20–1. The beginning of a new round of jeering, based on the metaphor of soft, wet potter's clay, is interwoven with these comments: 'effluis amens'. The man is leaking; he is in fact a comic opposite of the Stoic ideal of the self-contained, self-sufficient sage whose tight surface nothing can penetrate. In modern terms, this fits excellently with Bakhtin's notion of the grotesque body, a notion that emphasizes the body's apertures and protrusions, i.e. its points of contact with the outside world.[118] Persius' vessel is not only penetrable, it seems to be falling apart of itself, even before it is touched: 'viridi non cocta fidelia limo' ('a pot of green clay, not yet cooked'), 22; 'udum et molle lutum es' ('you're soft, wet clay'), 23; 'fingendus sine fine rota' ('you'll be endlessly shaped and reshaped on the potter's wheel'), 24.[119] Later on this disintegration, indicative of a lack of philosophical self-control,[120] is clad in the images of a mechanism come loose: 'stertis adhuc laxumque caput conpage soluta | oscitat hersternum dissutis undique malis' ('you are still snoring, and your lolling head with the slipping hinge of your mouth is yawning wide, to show yesterday's intake, between loose cheeks'), 58–9. Bergson, whose main thesis about the comic was that we laugh at living things when they appear mechanical, would have relished this example. Finally, Persius' lower nature is described as mad, in grotesque terms on the verge of passing from the humorous into the horrific. As soon as he sees a coin or a girl's smile, his heart gives a jump; he cannot eat simple food since his tender mouth hides a nasty ulcer; and the narrative ends with the portrait of him as crazier than Orestes (109–18). Again, there is dissolution, this time literal: heart leaping, mouth rotting, blood boiling. It is interesting to note that the simple peasant food which was an emblem of the good life in Horace's satire[121] and possibly in

---

[118] Bakhtin, *Rabelais*, 18–36, esp. 26–7.

[119] Squillante Saccone ('Techniche dell'ironia e del comico', 22–3) considers this passage of the metaphorical joking (vv. 22–4) 'più raffinato'.

[120] Dessen, *Iunctura Callidus Acri*, 53.

[121] See H. J. Mette, ' "Genus tenue" und "mensa tenuis" bei Horaz,' *Mus. Helv.* 18 (1961), 136–9; repr. in H. Oppermann *Wege zu Horaz* (ed.), (Darmstadt: Wissenschaftlige Buchgesellschaft, 1972).

Lucilius, has become inedible in Persius. Neither donkeys nor vegetables are what they used to be in Roman satire.

As has been noted, the two inset vignettes in this satire, one of a
centurion who scorns philosophy (77–87), the other of a man dying
in the bath upon overeating (88–106), have threads tying them to the
main discourse with the lower self. They may be read as hyperbolic
doubles of the lower self, as horror stories of what he might become if
he continues on the road of vice.[122] Both the centurion and the dying
man are proper satirical objects, and the typical pattern of the latter's
story has been discussed above as an example of object-oriented
humour.[123] As regards the description of the centurion, a comment
is required on the intriguing picture of laughter in the 'wrong'
direction, emanating from the centurion's plebeian admirers in response to his joke at the expense of philosophers. The military,
introduced as one of the 'gens hircosa centurionum' ('the goat-like
fraternity of centurions'), 77, has explained that he cares nothing for
anything beyond what he knows, especially not for the supposed
wisdom of philosophers who walk around staring into the ground,
talking to themselves or 'chewing rabid silence', and 'meditating over
the dreams of a sick man'. In his picture of philosophy the centurion
mangles up his facts badly. Is this something worth paling away
about, he then asks rhetorically, or to skip one's lunch for? At this
point his audience laughs violently:

> his populus ridet, multumque torosa iuventus
> ingeminat tremulos naso crispante cachinnos.   (86–7)

The crowd laughs at this, and the brawny youths guffaw over and over again,
cringing their nostrils.

Explicit laughter in Roman satire is most often an emblem of the act
of satirizing (with full authority, with the derision issued in the right
direction), and so it deserves to be taken seriously. Even in this case it
has been suggested that as readers, we are not only meant to laugh *at*
the centurion, but *with* him as well.[124]

---

[122] Dessen, *Iunctura Callidus Acri*, 56–7.
[123] In Ch. 1 § ' "Podgy exploding" and other horror humour (P. 3)'.
[124] See Ch. 1 n. 97.

This is problematic, for while the centurion does win a point through helping the philosophers to some of philosophic Persius' own medicine, I do not see how we could laugh with him without fatally undermining the rest of the satire. As Dessen has noticed, the centurion says that lovers of philosophy 'ponder the dreams of a sick man, grow pale over their studies, and stop eating, yet the man who ignores Stoicism turns pale, becomes sick, and eventually dies after a heavy meal'.[125] The 'torosa iuventus' laughing at the centurion's parody is muscular and anti-intellectual, which is bad in satire in general and Persius in particular, and in addition certainly to be contrasted with the good young students of philosophy, 'detonsa iuventus' ('youths with shaved heads'), 54. The main theme of P.3 as a whole is that one should listen to philosophy, particularly Stoicism, lest one end up as the very bad cases—dead man, or stupid centurion. The *varicosi centuriones* that likewise laugh at philosophers at the end of P.5 (5.189–91) seem even more unreliable. Unlike other examples in literature, where a respectable standpoint is actually being challenged by its opponent (as e.g. in Horace's Davus-satire 2.7), the centurion and his friends have no traits to recommend them. Nor is there any obvious truth in their opinion, while, conversely, the side of the higher self has no dubious traits that would render him more challengeable. Such recommendation of the opponent(s) is required if ambivalence between the persona's view and the opposite view is to arise. Rather than seeing ambivalence in this passage of P.3, I would opt for the solution that it is meant like Horace's 'rideri possit' ('you could laugh at him') about the bumpkin resembling 'Horace' (*S.* 1.3.30–4). You could laugh, the satirist says, but you should not really. The energy from this suspended laughter can then be turned against those at whom he wants you to laugh. Only here the connection is less smooth than in Horace, where a slight laugh at the bumpkin would not destroy anything, since the contents of that joke were harmless anyway. In Persius' third satire, by contrast, laughing with the centurion would confuse the message in a way which does not seem meaningful. Better to resist, but perhaps the military's rough sketch of the madly murmuring sages is too funny for this Stoic satire's good.

---

[125] Dessen, *Iunctura Callidus Acri*, 56.

Returning to the main topic of this discussion, the mockery directed at the split persona, we must now ask how far such humour is allowed to go. Is the main metaphoric pattern of deriding satirical objects, i.e. the pattern of raising/ inflating the target and then tearing it down/ punctuating it, ever used of the persona, albeit his lower self? Yes, in two passages. The more apparent one of these is found at 27–31:

> an deceat pulmonem rumpere ventis
> stemmate quod Tusco ramum millesime ducis
> censoremque tuum vel quod trabeate salutas?
> ad populum phaleras! ego te intus et in cute novi.
> non pudet ad morem discincti vivere Nattae.   (3.27–31)

Do you find it nice to burst your lungs with pride over counting your birth as the umpteenth branch of a Tuscan family-tree, and greeting your censor in a festive toga? Save these trappings for the crowd! I know you on the inside and in your bare skin. You're not ashamed to live like sloppy Natta.

The worse part of Persius is accused of taking undue pride in his fine family and ensuing high status. His lungs are *inflated* to the point of bursting,[126] his Etruscan family tree hyperbolically grows to have a thousand branches, he can greet his censor (here possibly referring to the emperor)[127] in purple dress. There is a lofty position, and most typical of Persius, inflation: of the lungs, the family tree, the man's pride. The higher self punctures him in line 30: the purple dress, the high birth are equated with trappings worn by soldiers at best, otherwise by horses. 'I know you on the inside and in your bare skin'—the speaker has penetrated the victim's inside, so the balloon has been popped. Underneath the precious *trabea* he knows the plain skin and the shameless willingness to live like Natta. Of course if they are the same person, he would know.

The other instance is less clear: this is the bursting of the persona in 8–9, *findor.* He has been swelling with anger, *turgescit vitrea bilis,* and then he explodes, and from then on the derision begins for real. This passage differs from the normal pattern in that the swelling is not a metaphor for false greatness, nor for wealth, and yet the images

---

[126] Cf. the same metaphor, used of a satiric object at P. 1.14.
[127] Lee and Barr, *Satires of Persius,* ad loc.

are so reminiscent of the derision pattern that this place cannot be overlooked. This image is also crucial to the arrangement of the satire as a whole.

As has already been mentioned above, this satire ends with a scene that is both metaphorically and verbally reminiscent of the beginning. In its own structure the poem does not remain shattered or dissolved, but collects its threads and creates a solid, whole frame— through images of fire and madness. In this the satire forms a circle, but in another sense it progresses linearly and ends with a situation different from the one at the outset. This is with the persona, who is not stitched back together again, but rather completes the separation. After the fatal *findor* the derision directed against the persona, or rather against his lower part, increased in force. The derisive images insisted that the lower self would dissolve still further. At 44–51 the higher self made an attempt at reconciliation with his slightly ironical childhood reminiscence, but no reunion followed, and at 56–7 the lower nature seems to have taken the wrong path at the philosophical crossroad and gone downhill. The mockery of him continued and the prophesized dissolution set in: his image glided into others which looked like caricatures of him, but which really represented what he could become if he did not turn back. These caricatures, while retaining a certain likeness to him, were satirical objects proper, without the brakes that set in when the object of mockery happens to be the persona. There were the examples of the rich attorney, the impudent goat-like centurion, and finally the fat sinner who exploded in the bath.[128] After the grotesque death scene, the lower self is shown as a mere madman whom even mad Orestes could laugh at. The multiplying images have been zoomed back onto a single man, Persius' lower self, but now he has lost his sense, and his selfhood with it, becoming a proper object. 'Persius' has carved away his lower self, and after this transitional satire, where both the lower and the higher self were present, there will not be much snickering at the authority of Persius' persona. Yet in P.3, which has one persona too many, both are nervously derided from various levels. There is self-irony in the higher self's tale about himself as a disobedient boy, there is derision of the lower self by the higher, most

---

[128] Attorney at 3.73–6; centurion at 3.77–87; fat man dying in the bath 88–106.

clearly in lines of direct address, and there is mockery of the lower nature by a narrative voice which may be read as a third voice, but better as an 'objective', narrative mode in the repertoire of the higher self.

All in all the mockery of the lower self is harsher than the self-humour which could be observed in Horace's satire, while the higher self's childhood story, in turn, was more harmless than much of Horace's self-irony, and hardly qualified as mockery at all. Persius' persona is indeed falling apart: the lower self gravitates towards the object, whereas the higher self, gravitating towards the implied author, sheds most of his outward shape and becomes almost immune to derision. There are crumbs of persona-directed humour in other satires of Persius, but P.3 seems by far the most interesting for this aspect, since it dramatically represents the transition from persona-controlled self-irony to a constellation where the persona becomes a helpless object of the author's derision.

JUVENAL: TO LAUGH WITH HIM OR AT HIM?

Persius' persona was first and foremost a student of philosophy, but Juvenal's persona, like Horace's, is first, last, and always a poet, a creator of satires. This leads to a few patches of Horatian artist's coquetry. Much more importantly, this formulates the general nature of Juvenal's persona-oriented humour, which, I will argue, is wholly focused on the paradoxes of satire. Horace was almost too harmonious for the genre of satire, Juvenal stands at the other extreme. Juvenal's satire is tougher and rougher than his Augustan predecessor's, his feelings stronger, his moralism more desperate, his sensationalism more glowing, and his writing feverishly pulsates with the premonition of the impending death awaiting Roman satire together with the culture it has been feeding on. For these reasons he is willing to lay bare the tensions of his genre in a hysterical manner unthinkable in Horace. It is as if he were a dying illusionist, feeling the closeness of the end, and wishing to shout out the mechanisms behind all his tricks to his admirers, before his last curtain. He does not give away all of his tricks, but what he does is enough to both dazzle and confound his audience.

Horatian coquetry

To begin with the milder, almost Horace-styled self-mockery, we note that in the first satire the persona 'admits' that he too has studied rhetoric, and so has no less a right to write than all the other poets swarming Rome, especially seeing that due to this proliferation of *literati* the paper will be destroyed anyway:

> et nos ergo manum ferulae subduximus, et nos
> consilium dedimus Sullae, privatus ut altum
> dormiret. stulta est clementia, cum tot ubique
> vatibus occurras, periturae parcere chartae.   (1.15–18)

Well, I too have snatched my hand from under the cane; I too have given Sulla the advice to retire and sleep the sound sleep of commoners. It is only stupid to show clemency—towards the paper that will perish anyway, with so many poets everywhere.

Here is the satirist's typical superficially self-belittling but actually proud introduction, an impression confirmed by the following lines, which loftily present his great predecessor, Lucilius, as an epic hero steering his horses down the path that he too is intent on following (19–21). Further on in the same poem 'Juvenal' says that although Nature has not granted him a poetic talent, he will still write with the help of his *indignatio*,[129] even if his verses come out no better than the poetaster Cluvienus':

> si natura negat, facit indignatio versum
> qualemcumque potest, quales ego vel Cluvienus.   (1.79–80)

If nature refuses, then indignation will make verses, of whatever quality it can—like mine, or like Cluvienus'.

Whereupon he proceeds to voice, in the grand style, the most ambitious claim made in extant Roman satire, namely that all that has happened to mankind since its creation will be the material for his book (81–6).[130] As it was with Horace's persona, 'Juvenal''s smallness

---

[129] Courtney (*Commentary on Juvenal, ad loc.*) fairly comments: 'since the modesty is clearly mock-modesty... Juvenal must intend to convey that he has both'; he well compares Horace's *S.* 1.10.88, 'haec, sint qualiacumque' ('this, whatever it's worth)'.

[130] For the meaning of 'nostri farrago libelli' in v. 86, see J. Powell, 'The *Farrago* of Juvenal 1.86 Reconsidered,' in Michael Whitby, P. Hardie, and Mary Whitby *Homo Viator: Classical Essays for John Bramble.* (Bristol: Bristol Classical Press, 1987).

and 'poverty' (this time in natural talent) only underline the excellence he wishes to parade.

In J. 7 the satirist even recommends certain groups to stop writing unless the situation changes (24–30, 171–5; cf. 48–9), which would seem comparable to Horace's manoeuvre in *S.* 2.1.5–7, but the question is whether 'Juvenal' includes himself in any of the categories of intellectuals in the seventh satire, even by implication. The more traditional approach to satire, coloured by biographical criticism, would say yes. So Highet, for instance, believes it is 'pretty clear that Juvenal himself had suffered', and so does Courtney, adducing the more objective argument that the first person plural in vv. 48–9 indicates the satirist's unity with the poets described.[131] Some theoretically sophisticated works, such as Braund's thorough discussion of the seventh satire, or Hardie's article of 1990, still see the Juvenalian persona as one of the intellectuals in this poem, though they make a clear distinction between 'Juvenal' the persona and Juvenal the author. These readings also allow for more complexity in the satirist's sympathies, recognizing refined patterns of humour and irony.[132]

I would proceed from the insights of Braund and Hardie about double-edged humour, and read J. 7 as a fusion of two aims: self-irony and object-oriented humour (against the intellectuals). Juvenal complains about the hard times for contemporary intellectuals including himself. He uses persona-oriented humour in pointing out the poverty of the writing profession, and in suggesting that unless one looks to the Emperor for patronage it is better to give up writing altogether. Bowing in hopeful respect to the Caesar makes sense only if one bows one's own head, and the potential irony in 'Juvenal''s address is not strong enough to obliterate the flattery, though it is enough to render it less embarrassing. The self-irony is kept light and almost transparent, so as not to tie 'Juvenal' too firmly to his contemporaries in the realm of letters. At the same time, Juvenal denigrates his colleagues and smears them with the suspicion that they deserve no better conditions than they get. This aspect of the satire entails harsh, object-oriented humour, with the fellow intellectuals as the object. Among other things, the intellectuals repeatedly

---

[131] Highet, *Juvenal the Satirist*, 108; Courtney, *Commentary on Juvenal*, 349–50.
[132] Braund, *Beyond Anger*, 24–68; Hardie, 'The Condition of Letters', 192.

come in for the lowering technique:[133] their lofty poems bump
against their low ceiling, their glorious trophies are exiled to the
stairs, and their specialist knowledge is wasted on a roomful of
masturbating pupils (27–9; 117–18; 229–41). Even truly elevated
worthies such as Horace, Virgil, and Quintilian come under the
satirist's fire (62, 69–71, 186–94, cf. also 226–7), which creates a
kind of virtual *onomasti kōmōdein*. Claiming that these two aims
are mutually exclusive is perhaps going too far, but they certainly sit
uncomfortably together, and the effect of the seventh satire, including its humour, depends on their dissonance.

The most Horatian of all Juvenal's satires is probably J. 11, an
invitation to 'Juvenal''s friend Persicus to join him for a quiet dinner
while the populace is overheated by the Megalesian games.[134] Kenneth
Weisinger has argued that this satire is permeated by moral ambiguity,
and that it contains as much irony over the satiric persona and his
friend as derision of Rome's corrupt mores. It is surely true that this
poem contains more ironic self-description than Juvenal's other satires, but the question is how far this self-irony really moderates the
moralistic argument. With Horace we only saw the problem of reliability come up in the Davus-satire; elsewhere the persona's smallness,
poverty, low birth, or uncouth manner did not disqualify him—within
the universe of the satires—for the task of passing moral judgement.

Looking closer at Juvenal's argument in the eleventh satire, we
observe that he opens the poem by setting up a contrast between rich
Atticus, who can properly afford to dine in luxury, and Rutilus, who
cannot, having already wasted all his money so that he must turn
himself in as a gladiator. The common crowd will always laugh
violently, Juvenal says, at the incongruity of the down-and-out gourmand, here designated by the famous example of Apicius:

> quid enim maiore cachinno
> excipitur volgi quam pauper Apicius? ...   (11.2–3)

For what is greeted with a greater guffaw by the crowd than a penniless
Apicius?

---

[133] Which I have traced in Ch. 1.

[134] As regards the charming J. 11, I would dare to disagree with the verdict of
Anderson ('Rustic Urbanity: Roman Satirists in and out of Rome,' *Thalia* 5 (1982),
33) that there is no 'rustic urbanity' in any Roman satirist except Horace.

The irony does not necessarily mean that he is not in some sense joining in the guffaw of the people. For Persius, I have argued that he sometimes dismisses the folksy laughter at his beloved philosophy, but it is not the same with Juvenal, who allows a broader range of laughable things around him. Even when ridicule is directed at items that rather deserve pity, such as the poor man in the capital or Shame fleeing Rome (3.147–53; 11.55), Juvenal is not altogether opposed to such cynical laughter. It must be remembered that he elsewhere expresses contempt for poor and weak people (esp. clients) who allow themselves to be humiliated. It is also the case that while philosophy is an absolute good to Persius, humiliated and derided poverty is not so to Juvenal. Rather, poverty in Juvenal is the other side of Roman degeneracy, which has led to no one now playing their proper roles, neither the mighty nor the dependent. If one wanted to name the Juvenalian equivalent to Persius' Stoic philosophy, i.e. the utopian opposite to the objects of his satire, this would probably be a Rome where the aristocratic hierarchy functioned, and where every Roman would play their proper role within that hierarchy without attempting movement. If any personage in Juvenal's satires dared to laugh at such an order, his laugh would presumably be dismissed as unacceptable, but no such laugh can be found in Juvenal. In Horace the good life was a real possibility, in Persius it was a utopian alternative to be fought for on the individual plane, and in Juvenal it is not even described anymore—except perhaps, in an ironical manner, in the eleventh satire.[135] Before laying out the more or less 'right way' of his own frugal dinner, however, the satiric poet begins by what is wrong, and presents laughter at the oxymoron 'pauper/ Apicius'.[136]

Next, the appearance of the classical motto *gnōthi seauton* ('know thyself'), and its ironic application to one's monetary strength, need

---

[135] Braund, *Beyond Anger*, 186–7 on the Horatian quality of this poem, including the presence of *holera* on the menu.

[136] Rochefort ('Laughter as a Satirical Device', 114–15) takes the people's laughter as endorsed by Juvenal; K. Weisinger ('Irony and Moderation in Juvenal XI,' *CSCA* 5 (1972), 228–9) on the other hand, seems to suggest that the laughter greeting the *pauper Apicius*, but not the rich *and* lavishly eating Atticus, introduces a kind of moral relativism which is then ironically negotiated throughout the poem.

not be meant to disqualify this precept (27–43).[137] *Gnōthi seauton* should be applied to everything in life, the satirist says, even to the acquisition of fish. The laughable incongruity in combining the philosophical principle with money is more likely to invalidate the money than the philosophy in this case. This is the only example of self-knowledge that is directly monetary, in an obviously comic way. All the other examples pertain to one's status of birth, nobility, and inborn talent—all things which Juvenal by implication seems to value.

The best basis for Weisinger's argument about moral ambiguity in J. 11 are two instances of self-commentary by the I-speaker. The first self-comment is when 'Juvenal' jokingly describes himself as Evander in the role of a host (60–3); the second when he boasts that his slave is so modest as to be used only to small thefts (142–4). When reading the first of these passages, where the persona promises to be an Evander to his guest, whereas the guest will come as 'the son of Tiryns [i.e. Hercules], or that smaller guest, who also touched heaven with his blood', one is tempted to agree with Weisinger's verdict that the hyperbole belies the moderation of the allegedly simple host.[138] At first sight, the mock-epic periphrasis of Hercules and Aeneas, the following chiastic reference to their apotheosis, and the allusion to Virgil, all seem to suggest that the exaggerated contrast between the present-day urban host and his mythic precursor at the dawn of Rome is meant to deride 'Juvenal' and his invited Persicus. Mockery is present to a certain extent, but it is important to note that this is not the device of raising an unworthy personage by comparing him to a heroic character and smashing him down against seamy reality, as is done e.g. in comparing the contemporary pathics to the Catos of old in J. 2 (2.40). If one looks closer at the intertext, *Aeneid* 8.359–65, it becomes evident that the heroic character of Evander is parallel to the role 'Juvenal' claims for himself, that of the modest host, in his combination of a lowly home with noble generosity. Both in Virgil and in Juvenal, the characters involved will show their true excellence by partaking in the poor dinner; their simple surface covers an inner greatness. In addition, the two texts share the fine stroke of a rustic meal in the heart of the capital, allowing the respective authors to

---

[137] As Weisinger argues ('Irony and Moderation', 230).   [138] Ibid.

combine the moral purity of the countryside with the glory of Rome. This is achieved by the prehistoric setting in Virgil, and by a satirist's import of rustic goods and manners into his urban *pied-à-terre* in Juvenal. Mark also that *pauper Evander* is not like *pauper Apicius* a contradiction in terms, but an image of the Horatian combination 'modest surface-inner excellence' which Juvenal's persona is here fashioning for himself. Under the humorous exaggeration, the resemblance between Evander and 'Juvenal' holds good. Like the joke about the rabbi's clever comparison of the telephone to a long dog, discussed above,[139] so this joke is really a compliment to the persona, softened by the humour so as not to sound presumptuous, but far from undone by it. This is not the satirist's disintegrating laugh, but a joke one can afford to make about oneself, Horace-style, certain of strengthening one's authority rather than losing it.[140] Closer consideration suggests a similar line of reading for the passage about the rustic slave-boy, 'tirunculus ac rudis omni | tempore et exiguae furtis imbutus ofellae' ('he's just a beginner, a rookie in everything, knowing how to steal only a small crumb'), 11.143–4. He is in fact the heir to Horace's forgivable small-time crook of a slave in *S.* 1.3.80–3:

> si quis eum servum patinam qui tollere iussus
> semesos piscis tepidumque ligurrierit ius
> in cruce suffigat, Labieno insanior inter
> sanos dicatur.

If some master crucified the slave who had licked at the half-eaten fish or lukewarm sauce on a dish he had been ordered to take away, sane people would consider him more insane than Labienus.

'Juvenal' the modest host of *Satire* 11, playing a Horatian role which involves knowing the right measure in everything, is not insane enough to confuse a small forgivable theft with the arrogant stealing of other slaves at Rome, 'nec frustum capreae subducere nec latus Afrae | novit avis noster' ('my boy has not learnt to steal the piece of a goat-steak or the wing of a peacock'), 142–3. He knows that slaves

---

[139] pp. 219–20.

[140] Courtney's (*Commentary on Juvenal, ad loc.*) classically low-key comment 'The grandeur with the humorous periphrasis is mildly ironical; Juvenal is poking fun at himself' turns out to be more accurate than the more exciting interpretation of authorial aporia.

will be slaves, and so (according to the preconceived truth of his times) will always steal; nobody is wholly without faults, but as Horace said, 'optimus ille est qui minimis urgetur' ('he who is weighed down by the smallest faults is the best man'), *S.* 1.3.68–9. By admitting, as if inadvertently, the naïve filching of his inexperienced slave, 'Juvenal' makes him even more endearing in his human, boyish imperfection. At the same time, the satirist shelters the boy, and by extension himself, from other accusations.

The satire closes with a final burst of Horatian flavour, complete with self-irony. Let the youths run along to the Circus to make their bets and sit close to the girls, says 'Juvenal', while we sunbathe our wrinkled old skin in the spring sun:

> nostra bibat vernum contracta cuticula solem
> effugiatque togam.   (J. 11.203–4)

our old wrinkled skin will imbibe the spring sun and be free from the toga.

Never before did Juvenal's persona have a skin, nor flesh, body, limbs—he was all perception and expression: eyes, ears, and tongue. Yet when one wishes to poke fun at oneself, to look at oneself with irony, one will have to look at one's skin, the membrane which separates the inner man from the outer, the outwards gaze from the gaze directed at oneself. Horace the satirist had done this when commenting on his persona's small, round self with bleary eyes but well-tended skin in the *Sermones* and the *Epistles*, notably in the famous invitation to Tibullus to come and see him (Hor. *Ep.* 1.4.15–16):[141]

> me pinguem et nitidum bene curata cute vises
> cum ridere voles, Epicuri de grege porcum.

when you want a laugh, come and see me: I'm a fat and smooth pig from Epicurus' herd, with well-groomed skin.

Juvenal never becomes quite as explicitly clownish in his persona-directed mockery: it is no coincidence that the well-groomed Epicurean skin (*bene curata cutis*) has here turned into the wrinkled, shrunk skin (*contracta cuticula*) of a slightly ridiculous *laudator temporis acti*. The persona of Roman satire has grown older, thinner,

---

[141] Cf. also 'Horace''s self-portrait in *S.* 1.5.

and much more bitter. And yet in the eleventh satire, where Juvenal wants to laugh in the vein of Horace, he pays an ostensible visit to his great satiric predecessor.

The question of trust in Juvenal's speaker

The biggest question about Juvenal's persona-oriented humour, however, is whether the blatantly prejudiced and extremist persona of many of his satires (esp. the earlier ones, satires 1–6) should be read as undermined or endorsed by the author. The former view, that Juvenal is really much more humane and reasonable than his angry persona, is currently the more popular, and it is fundamental to the most original and sophisticated analyses of Juvenal's persona in the last decades. Contemporary opponents of this view tend to express a general dislike of modern literary theory, to protest against what they perceive as a political standpoint behind the distrust in 'Juvenal''s reactionary opinions, and to advocate a return to taking 'Juvenal' straightforwardly at his word.[142] Yet what needs to be done is a critical examination of the suspicious view of Juvenal's persona on its own premises, to answer whether it holds in itself, if one accepts the kind of critical approach involved.

The case of Umbricius (J. 3)

The best points of the scholars who distrust the persona are scored on the material of J. 3, where for the greater part of the poem the primary persona gives up the floor to his old friend Umbricius, about to leave Rome for ever, since it has, according to him, become

---

[142] Important studies arguing for the separation of Juvenal the author and his persona are Anderson, *Essays* (esp. 'The Programs of Juvenal's Later Books', orig. 1962; and 'Anger in Juvenal and Seneca', orig; 1964) and id., 'Juvenal Satire 15: Cannibals and Culture,' in A. J. Boyle (ed.), *The Imperial Muse. To Juvenal through Ovid* (Berwick, Victoria: Aureal Publications, 1988); Winkler, *Persona*; Fruelund Jensen, 'Juvenal's Umbricius'; Braund, *Beyond Anger*; and ead., *Roman Satire*; A. Hardie, 'Juvenal, the Phaedrus, and the Truth about Rome,' *CQ* 48 (1998), 234–51. *Contra* K. McCabe, 'Was Juvenal a Structuralist? A Look at Anachronisms in Literary Criticism,' *G&R* 33 (1986), 78–84; P. M. W. Tennant, 'Biting Off More Than One Can Chew: A Recent Trend in the Interpretation of Juvenal's 15th Satire,' *Akroterion* 40 (1995), 120–34.

unliveable for a decent Roman. After the satirist has described the setting at the city gate where he is saying goodbye to his friend, he has Umbricius begin a ranting speech that goes on and on, for the rest of the satire. There are convincing, and above all many, hints that Umbricius-the-secondary-persona is not meant to sound altogether reliable and heroic.

The old friend admits formal blunders such as forgetting that he is only speaking to one person and bombastically addressing the citizens of Rome when complaining about foreigners:

> non possum ferre, Quirites,
> Graecam urbem.   (3.60–1)

O Romans, I cannot bear this Greek city!

Another apparent mistake is that, just having said that Rome is by now a city completely taken in by the Greeks, *Graeca urbs*, he corrects himself in the same line, pointing out that compared to other Orientals, the Greeks are only a minor part of the foreign invasion: 'quamvis quota portio faecis Achaei?' ('though what part of the dregs are actually Greeks?'), 61.[143] A subtle point is the irony inherent in the clash between Umbricius' violent xenophobia and the placement of the dialogue at Porta Capena, next to Aqua Marcia, an aqueduct important to Rome's water supply. As a background to the speaker's earnest rage the setting hints that Rome has not been self-sufficient for some time, and that its greatness is not least due to its ability to absorb the influx from other lands.[144]

---

[143] Witke, *Latin Satire*, 234 (though in general Witke favours a positive view of Umbricius); Fruelund Jensen, 'Juvenal's Umbricius', 189, with further references.

[144] Hardie, 'Juvenal and the Truth about Rome', 250. The argument is strengthened by a quotation of Frontinus' *De Aquis Urbis Romae* 1.4–5 (a work completed under Trajan): 'for 441 years, the Romans were satisfied with the use of such waters (*aquarum*) as they drew from wells or from springs (*fontibus*). Esteem for springs still exists and is observed with reverence. They are believed to bring healing to the sick, as for example the springs of the Camenae . . . Now, however, there flow into the city the Appian aqueduct, the Old Anio, the Marcia . . .' (Hardie's trans.). The critic comments that this passage helps to show 'that the waters dripping from Juvenal's ancient ("substitit ad *veteres* arcus madidamque Capenam", 3.11)' Aqua Marcia is imported and alien, in contrast to the indigenous supplies of the Roman *fontes*. Modern landscaping in a sacral environment, involving the importation of non-indigenous substances, is thus nothing new at Rome.' Cf. Courtney, *Commentary on Juvenal*, ad loc.

Furthermore, Umbricius' whole hysterical attitude to his social situation seems less than respectable, and his insistence that he himself is the paragon of virtue is at times suspect. Conspicuously missing from Umbricius' account is what in other satires (notably 1, 5, and 9) is presented as the worst part of Roman decadence: patrons at once self-indulgent and stingy—*luxuriae sordes* ('the filthy meanness of luxury'). Instead, he blames the patrons for preferring other clients, especially Greeks, to him personally and to men like him. The Greek competitors are preferred because they know how to do all sorts of things, and although their tricks are almost all dishonest, the reader begins to wonder what it is that Umbricius can do. He bitterly points out that the vicious circle of poverty prohibits him from becoming a successful legacy-hunter: 'quis pauper scribitur heres?' ('what poor man is named as an heir?'), 161—implying that if he could, he would happily play this role, branded as an object of derision by Roman satire in general and even Juvenal himself elsewhere.[145] Even Umbricius' exclamation 'quid Romae faciam? mentiri nescio' ('What should I do at Rome? I don't know how to lie'), 41, though meant by the speaker as the righteous lament of wounded virtue, begins to ring literally true. Once this angle of perception is opened, several grimly generalizing accusations by this Aventine-born *echt*-Roman appear as bursts of self-pity and at bottom as rationalizations of his painful experiences of being ousted by other groups.[146] When he is, most interestingly, given the line saying that poverty makes people like him look ridiculous (152–3), we must honestly ask whether he is not right. The image of which the line is part describes the laughable appearance of the poor man:

> quid quod materiam praebet causasque iocorum
> omnibus hic idem, si foeda et scissa lacerna,
> si toga sordidula est et rupta calceus alter
> pelle patet, vel si consuto volnere crassum
> atque recens linum ostendit non una cicatrix?
> nil habet infelix paupertas durius in se
> quam quod ridiculos homines facit. (147–53)

---

[145] Legacy-hunting is the target of satire at Juvenal 1.37–41, 55–7; 9.87–90; 12.93–130. For Umbricius' readiness to engage in *captatio*, if only the Greeks would not outwit him in the area, see Fruelund Jensen, 'Juvenal's Umbricius', 191–2; Braund, *Roman Satire*, 44–5.

[146] Fruelund Jensen, 'Juvenal's Umbricius', 190.

What about his also serving as everybody's laughing-stock and offering material for their jokes if his cloak is dirty and torn, if his toga is a little stained and one of his shoes gapes open with the leather split, or if coarse new thread indicates scars after more than one wound, sewn together? Wretched poverty holds nothing harsher than the fact that it makes people ridiculous.

Though formally this passage can be compared to Horace's description of the honest man in bad clothes, at whom one could laugh but should not ('rideri possit', *S.* 1.3.30–2),[147] Juvenal has twisted the idea considerably. In Umbricius' speech, unlike 'Horace''s, the ridiculous appearance is not balanced by the immediate description of inner excellence, such as moral purity and artistic talent. In fact Umbricius' questionable virtue combined with his pathetic bombast make us doubt that this latter-day poor man has any such contrasting inner features. In Horace, the outer shabbiness was used to make the inner glory shine the brighter, but Umbricius himself seems to value appearances above everything else. There is not only his insistence that looking ridiculous is the worst effect of poverty ('nil ... durius'), but also his later statement that he is part of the common fault of *ambitiosa paupertas* ('ambitious poverty'), 180–3,[148] and his admittance that in Rome one is ashamed of eating from terracotta plates though elsewhere one need not be (168–70). Umbricius does not exert Horatian self-irony: he is allowed to hang himself by his own rope.[149] In addition to these arguments, 'Juvenal's' friend has been convincingly undermined by analyses which have discovered similarities between him and the more obviously vitiated comrades Trebius (the parasitic client in J. 5) and Naevolus (the prostitute client in J. 9).[150] Even the very fact that he is called a friend, *amicus*, has been used against him, since *amicitia* can be shown to have sinister connotations of treachery and ill will throughout Juvenal's Book 1.[151]

---

[147] Discussed above, § 'A lowly character for a low genre'.

[148] i.e. trying to appear better-off than one is.

[149] Fruelund Jensen, 'Juvenal's Umbricius', 194–5; *contra* de Saint-Denis, 'L'Humour de Juvénal', who believes that Umbricius is self-ironic.

[150] F. Bellandi, 'Naevolus cliens,' *Maia* 26 (1974), 279–99; LaFleur, 'Amicitia and Juvenal's First Book', 163–4.

[151] LaFleur, 'Amicitia and Juvenal's First Book'.

In connection with 'Juvenal' himself the critical readings begin to tread less firm ground. Umbricius is teasingly both like and unlike 'Juvenal'. An obvious difference between them is that Umbricius leaves Rome while 'Juvenal' stays on, though he says he would prefer even the rocky island Prochyta to Roman down-town.[152] Another difference, which has gone unnoticed, though it seems important enough, is that the satirist has a profession that is tied to the big city, explicitly commented upon at the close of the satire (318–22), while his talkative friend can do nothing at Rome. In this last contrast we can be fairly certain that the author prefers the satirist's craft over no craft at all, and we can tentatively draw the conclusion that this implies a preference for Rome over leaving Rome. Yet at the beginning of the poem, 'Juvenal' has said that he would have preferred to leave, and has poignantly foreshadowed some of Umbricius' main arguments in his summary of the city's dangers:

> incendia, lapsus
> tectorum assiduos ac mille pericula saevae
> urbis et Augusto recitantes mense poetas?   (7–9)

continuous fires, collapsing roofs, and a thousand other dangers of the savage city—and poets reciting in August?

Of course we want to believe the satirist at least, if we cannot believe his friend, but the humour makes it all very difficult. The anticlimax of poets reciting in August as the very worst of the capital's disasters seems to disqualify the whole statement, but before we decide on such a disqualification, we may remember that the whole of Juvenal's satiric opus begins with the humorous and angry complaint about the never-ending recitals that shatter marble and columns at Rome: *assiduo lectore* ('readers reciting continuously'), 1.13 (cf. *assiduos* in the quotation above). In the introduction to J. 3, the lines just quoted are followed by the poet's partly lyric complaint about the destruction of Egeria's mythical valley, very much in line with Umbricius' sentiments. It has been ingeniously suggested that the fact of 'Juvenal's' prefiguring of his old friend's arguments means that he has heard it all before—but it may also mean that he is of the same opinion, only is able to express himself more wittily and

---

[152] Fruelund Jensen, 'Juvenal's Umbricius', 196; Braund, *Beyond Anger*, 14–15.

succinctly.[153] The very humour of the primary persona's frame to Umbricius' speech makes the frame inconclusive.[154]

For the reasons just recounted it may be assumed that Umbricius is an unreliable speaker; there are enough suggestive traits in the text to undercut even the natural inclination to trust a first-person speaker in satire. However, the fact that Umbricius is not to be equated with the subject, does not mean that he is an object—he can be something in between. It should be kept in mind that the objects of his attacks are the targets of Juvenal's satire to a higher degree than he himself is, not least because the aggressive satirical technique of 'mockery from below' is repeatedly used against them, but not against Umbricius. While there are features in the satire which undercut the authority of the speaker, there are none that would rehabilitate his victims, such as Greeks, foreigners in general, the rich who take advantage of and despise the poor, or the hooligans in the capital. Although the decline of Rome, or if one prefers, the decline of mankind, could be analysed differently from the way Umbricius does it, no such alternative analysis is suggested by the text. It has been observed that the satire indirectly mentions the inflow of the Aqua Marcia into the city, and by implication Rome's dependence on foreign influences.[155] Yet this fine observation is no proof that 'Juvenal' approves of such influences, though he is perhaps more resigned to them than his companion. There are three degrees of derision here: (1) the targets of Umbricius' speech (Greeks, the rich, hooligans), wholly derided by both speaker and author; (2) Umbricius himself, the secondary persona subtly mocked by the author by mistakes and self-contradictions that he is allowed to make; and (3) 'Juvenal', the primary persona, whose authority is less questioned than Umbricius', given the subtle differences between

[153] The arguments that the August recitals form a subversive anti-climax, and that the poet has heard Umbricius' litanies before, are given by Fruelund Jensen ('Juvenal's Umbricius', 196); the counter-arguments are mine.

[154] See D. S. Wiesen ('Juvenal and the Intellectuals,' *Hermes* 101 (1973), 482), who succinctly comments that the 'counterpoint of two opposite and conflicting themes, one of which questions the validity of the other, is an essential but little noticed characteristic of Juvenalian satire'; LaFleur ('Amicitia and Juvenal's First Book', 164 n. 17), who for J. 3 notes that 'the satire cuts in two directions'; Fredericks, 'Irony of Overstatement', 184–5; Courtney, *Commentary on Juvenal*, 349–50.

[155] Hardie, 'Juvenal and the Truth about Rome'; mentioned above, n. 144.

them. It seems to me that the gap between the secondary and the primary personae, including the primary persona's essential advantage of being a satirist by profession (which places him close to the author in the reader's mind), allows the author to save the credibility of 'Juvenal' almost intact. The facts that Umbricius' targets are left as targets within the impact of the satire as a whole, and that to a certain degree they coincide with what 'Juvenal' satirizes elsewhere (foreigners, the rich), suggest that Umbricius is partly right, just as he is partly wrong. When 'Juvenal' in his introduction both supports his friend's position and distances himself from it, he is presumably doing what the Roman satirists so often do—both having his cake and eating it. 'Juvenal' is careful not to identify with the most ridiculous aspects of the secondary persona (idling, leaving Rome in an irrational reaction), but willing to endorse his view of Rome's decline, and to grant him a loud voice by reporting his 300-line speech *verbatim*. I would say that the 'both-same-and-different' ratio between the primary and the secondary personae enables the author to present an amusing caricature of 'Juvenal', as indeed he was to do with even greater virtuosity in Naevolus in *Satire* 9. Umbricius, whose name has been seen to be connected to 'shadow', *umbra*,[156] is the satirist's exaggerated shade, grown into a parody of him, and therefore allowed to leave the scene (= Rome) after a final tirade. This is a move which leaves 'Juvenal' all but unsmeared by the hysterical content of J. 3, since it has all been voiced merely by a too coarse *alter ego* in the process of being shed.

The case of 'Juvenal'

The next question is whether, and if yes, to what extent, 'Juvenal' shares Umbricius' problems of credibility in other satires. Here the arguments of the distrusting school are vaguer and often work by implication and generalization. The starting-signal for this view of Juvenal's persona was Anderson's erudite and eloquent article 'Anger

---

[156] A. L. Motto and J. R. Clark, '*Per iter tenebricosum*: The Mythos of Juvenal 3,' *TAPA* 96 (1965), 275–6.

in Juvenal and Seneca', which originally appeared in 1964.[157] This essay consistently applied Kernan's theory of the complex satirical persona to Juvenal, and then went on to discover two different personae in his opus: 'the angry satirist' of *Satires* 1–6, driven by *indignatio*, and 'the Democritean satirist' best visible from *Satire* 10 and onwards, driven by *laughter*, and even a yearning for *tranquillitas* ('peace of mind'). According to Anderson, the emergence of a 'laughing satirist' in the later books implicitly made this latter persona 'the severest critic of the indignation exhibited in the earlier poems'.[158] Anderson's arguments were concentrated around two points: (1) that *indignatio* and the semantically akin *ira* were made the objects of the laughing persona's derision, especially in J. 10 and J. 13;[159] and (2) that anger was generally perceived as deplorable by the Roman mind. The latter point was strengthened by examples from other works that are almost contemporary to Juvenal, especially Seneca's *De Ira* and *De Tranquillitate Animi*. These ideas have since been developed both by himself in subsequent articles, and by other scholars, notably by Braund, Romano, and Martin Winkler.[160] Some new arguments appear—such as the dismissal of anger by other ancient genres such as tragedy and comedy, the discovery of some technical contradictions in e.g. *Satires* 1 and 15 (though these are not as persuasive as Umbricius' self-contradictions), and the general feeling that the position of the persona is too extreme to be straightforwardly acceptable.[161]

[157] Unless one counts the essay of Mason in 1963 (Mason, 'Is Juvenal a Classic?'), where it was argued that Juvenal, like Martial, had little interest in moral arguments and teaching, engaging rather in lascivious *ad hoc* wit. This discussion, however, was not as theoretically worked out as Anderson's, and has not given a new direction to the study of Juvenal, though it should be said that despite its sweeping and unconvincing main thesis, Mason's article contains a number of excellent observations about Juvenalian passages.

[158] p. 295; I quote by the reprint of 'Anger in Juvenal and Seneca' in Anderson, *Essays*, 293–361.

[159] In J. 10 it is said that one should pray for a calm mind which 'nesciat irasci' (he does not know anger), v. 360; J. 13 is in its entirety a mock-*consolatio* to Calvinus, an angry friend who has been unable to collect an insubstantial debt.

[160] In Anderson's '*Lascivia* vs. *ira*: Martial and Juvenal', orig. 1970 (repr. Anderson, *Essays*, 362–95) and id., 'Cannibals and Culture'; Braund, *Beyond Anger*, and *Roman Satire*; A. C. Romano, *Irony in Juvenal* (Hildesheim: Olms, 1979); Winkler, *Persona*.

[161] For contradictions in J. 1, see Braund, *Roman Satire*, 41–3; in J. 15, see Anderson, 'Cannibals and Culture'.

The argument from a comparison with the treatment of anger and *indignatio* in other genres can be questioned precisely because of the difference in genre. It is, for instance, not at all certain that Juvenal the satirist would share the world-view of a Stoic philosopher like Seneca. Philosophy wanted to teach by clear reasoning, explaining the way to the good life, free from worries and excessive emotion, while satire claimed to teach by showing the unacceptable and (sometimes implicitly) denouncing it with vehemence and wrath.[162] As we have seen even in Juvenal's calmer predecessors Horace and Persius, vehemence and emotion was part and parcel of the genre, and 'Horace' was occasionally frenzied and 'Persius' quite angry, though explicitly a Stoic. Even Anderson admits that rhetoricians allowed angered oratory in particular cases, and that Juvenal's early, angry satires are especially effective in their rhetoric.[163] The comparison with a genre such as comedy is more intriguing, since the simultaneously attractive and denounced nature of angry comic personages may indeed be exploited in Juvenal, but more on this presently. The argument from contradictions in the persona's speech is not strong enough, as there are not so many examples. The conclusion that 'Juvenal' is unreliable because he is too extreme or prejudiced can be disarmed as too subjective and in danger of being anachronistic.

The argument from a difference in Juvenal's own tone in the earlier and later books has, with good reason, remained the heaviest one. Yet even this argument has its problems.

First, even the satires where the persona's reasonable attitude is best seen, J. 10 and J. 13, are in themselves ironic and ambiguous. *Satire* 10, for example, closes the famous passage on what to pray for, including the advice to become impenetrable to anger and possessed of a *tranquilla vita* ('tranquil life'), with the sarcastic comment that if sense would reign, people would realize that divine Fortune is only an illusion:

---

[162] Cf. McCabe, 'Anachronisms in Literary Criticism', 81.
[163] In 'Juvenal and Quintilian' (orig. 1961, repr. in Anderson, *Essays*), 422–8. For Juvenal's use of rhetoric, the classical study is J. DeDecker, *Juvenalis Declamans. Étude sur la rhétorique déclamatoire dans les Satires de Juvénal* (Gent: Librairie scientifique van Goethem & Cie, 1913).

orandum est ut sit mens sana in corpore sano.
fortem posce animum mortis terrore carentem,
qui spatium vitae extremum inter munera ponat
naturae, qui ferre queat quoscumque dolores,
nesciat irasci, cupiat nihil et potiores
Herculis aerumnas credat saevosque labores
et venere et cenis et pluma Sardanapalli.
monstro quod ipse tibi possis dare; semita certe
tranquillae per virtutem patet unica vitae.
nullum numen habes, si sit prudentia: nos te,
nos facimus, Fortuna, deam caeloque locamus.   (10.356–65)

You should pray for a healthy mind in a healthy body. Ask for a valiant spirit free from the fear of death, which counts a long life as a gift of nature, which is able to suffer any kind of pain, and which does not know anger. Such a spirit desires nothing and reckons the hardships and grim labours of Hercules as better than the loves, banquets, and plumes of Sardanapallus. I am showing you what you can give to yourself: the only path to a tranquil life is surely through virtue.

You have no divinity, Fortune, if people could only have the sense to see that! It is we, we ourselves, who make you a goddess and place you in heaven.

As has been pointed out, the last two verses take up the figure of Democritus, who gave Fortune the finger (10.52–3), and give a more nihilistic twist to Democritean laughter. If the irony of these lines is fully taken into account, the philosophical content of the poem, including the advice to abstain from anger, is potentially demolished. What emerges on such a reading is a 'distrustful and scornful attitude towards *any* positive and comforting ideals'.[164] Similarly, J. 13 contains derision not only of Calvinus' *ira* ('anger'), but also of the contemporary scene, where his expectations of honesty are absurd. The contrasting image of the Golden Age (13.38–59), when even slightly disrespectful acts were severely punished, must not be too hastily dismissed as ridiculous. The immediately following passage describes how an honest man in contemporary Rome would be as surprising as a prodigy (13.60–70). It is highly questionable whether

---

[164] D. Fishelov, 'The Vanity of the Reader's Wishes: Reading Juvenal's Satire 10,' *AJP* 111 (1990), 370–82, quotation from 382.

this passage can be read as the satirist's *norm*.[165] If it is not his norm, the satire must be mockery of Roman decadence as well as Calvinus' anger, and the overall thrust of the poem becomes complex—it criticizes not only anger but the situation that arouses this anger as well.

Secondly, even if one wishes to stress the difference between the persona's attitude in the first and last books respectively, what is to prove that the later, calmer persona is all right, and the earlier, angry persona is all wrong? Why should the later persona be the standard by which the earlier one should be corrected? The persona may, after all, be changed from book to book in order to simulate the development of a real human mind, and in order to show the satiric topics from different angles. A feature of Juvenal's opus which would suggest such a structure is the apparent reversal to an angry speaker in J. 15 and 16, complete with a condemnation of all mankind and the pitiless diagnosis that men have nowadays grown so smallishly despicable that whenever a god looks at them, he laughs with hate: 'ergo deus, quicumque aspexit, ridet et odit' ('so whenever a god sees them he laughs, and feels hatred'), 15.71.[166] In this connection, I fully agree with Braund that rather than simply coming full circle, in Book 5 Juvenal delivers the condemnation of mankind 'from a higher plane of aloofness'. However, I wonder if this spiral development does not complicate the issue of anger more than simply including 'the anger of Book I as one of man's faults.'[167] It is difficult, to my mind, to see anger as unproblematically included as one of man's faults in J. 15, where both the anger of the cannibalistic Egyptians and that of the satiric persona describing them are at their red-hot greatest. Instead it seems that the author is playing with the conventions of satire by letting the angry persona meet the angry object in a kind of meta-literary cannibalism.

---

[165] I thus find it difficult to agree with the reading in Anderson, *Essays*, 282, which seems to suggest that the persona is cynically reconciled with the picture he paints in vv. 68–9.

[166] Cf. the fierce comments in Richlin, *Garden*, 208–9.

[167] Braund, *Beyond Anger*, 198. As Braund also observes, and as we have seen in the discussion of Horace above, the Augustan satirist also reused the material of his first book from a higher outlook in his second book.

Thirdly, the persona should not be made *the object* of the satires in order to save the apparent objects. It is tempting enough for a modern reader to take the persona as an angry extremist 'with the addition of misogyny to his homophobia, chauvinism, and other bigotries'[168] and to proceed to the conclusion that this persona is the real target of Juvenal's satire while what he is saying is, by implication, disqualified. Thus above the head of the prejudiced bigot *'Juvenal' the persona* the modern reader may be able to save *Juvenal the talented poet* as a man armed with 'liberal didacticism' for the purpose of guiding his reader to become a *vir bonus* by refuting the example of the untrustworthy persona.[169] With some regret, I would say that such a reading is not warranted by our text, where the primary persona is not so violently and unambiguously undermined as to become *the target*, nor the objects of the satires rehabilitated enough to cease being objects. In the latter half of the twentieth century, feminist and other ideologically oriented critics have laid bare, and stressed, the violent nature of Juvenal's derision of certain parts of society—such as freedmen, foreigners, pathics, women—and we should recognize these critics' discovery.[170] The awareness that what the persona attacks as immoral or ugly is in fact often what is threatening to his own position as an elite Roman male was made possible precisely by the perception of the persona as an entity with contours, placed and defined as to social status, sex, and ideology. A reading that tries to present Juvenal the author as a liberal teacher simply has to skip (or dismiss) too much of the text, and risks leading us back to an uncritical reading where the just, wise, and divinely transparent satirist slips back in, albeit at another level.

Finally, the attempt to explain the inconsistency between irrational anger and moral didacticism with the gap between an earlier and a later persona, or between the persona and the author, is ultimately an attempt *to solve* the paradoxes which Kernan has shown to be intrinsic to satire.[171] His observations that the satiric persona claims to be

---

[168] Braund, *Roman Satire*, 47.   [169] Winkler, *Persona*, 227–8.

[170] Richlin, *Garden*; Henderson, 'Satire Writes Woman' and id., *Writing down Rome*; Gold, 'Humor in J. 6'; Miller, 'Grotesque in Roman Satire'; and Walters, 'Making a Spectacle'.

[171] Kernan, *Cankered Muse*, 1–7, 14–30; cf. Ch. 1 § 'The paradoxes of satire, as mapped by Alvin Kernan'. In fact, it is precisely from these paradoxes that Anderson

rational while adopting the most irrational attitudes, that while proclaiming the truth of what he says he is distorting his facts, and that while claiming to loathe vice he is often an eager sensationalist, all lack a solution in Kernan's scheme. Criticizing such solutions from the camp of biographical criticism, he writes:

Every major writer of satire has been praised by some critics for his fearless determination to tell the truth about his world and damned by others for a twisted, unstable, prurient liar whose works no careful father should allow his children to open.[172]

In its extension, the argument proposed by Anderson and others is solving 'Kernan's paradox' by praising Juvenal the author 'for his fearless determination to tell the truth' and damning the persona 'for a twisted, unstable, prurient liar', whom every careful reader should see through. It seems to me that given the presence of multiple outlooks in Juvenal's satirical work, such a solution is in the end impossible. Juvenal requires hard work of his audience 'by inviting us simultaneously to accept and reject the speaker's views'.[173]

From this examination it may tentatively be concluded that while Juvenal's persona is occasionally ridiculed, his authority is not altogether destroyed, certainly not to the degree of making him the victim of the satires. More than the other satirists, Juvenal lays bare the paradoxes of the satiric genre and plays with them, provoking the reader to enter into dialogue with him. The gaps between the poles of the paradoxes are bridged by humour, which is notoriously unreliable and often multiplies meaning rather than pinpointing it. Humour cuts both ways, and the comedy-style funny, angry persona may not only lose, but also *gain* sympathy for being irrational.[174] He

begins his big discussion of *ira* ('Anger in Juvenal and Seneca'), and yet in the end he tries to get away from them.

[172] Kernan, *Cankered Muse*, 4.

[173] These are the words of Braund, *Roman Satire*, 47–8, though her own reading perhaps gravitates more towards rejection.

[174] Cf. the modern example of the sitcom hero Archie Bunker in the television series 'All in the Family': while devised by his creators as a vehicle for satirizing bigotry, the quintessential, all-American bigot Archie, constantly quarrelling with his liberal son-in-law, won the sympathy of more viewers than had been expected. A humour-impact study by Surlin 1973, where subjects who had watched the series were asked to rate the degree to which they liked and agreed with the dogmatic father-in-law, showed that even the viewers who disagreed with his views tended to like the

is, after all, the first-person speaker, and thus closest to the reader's mind—perhaps he can even allow us to vent our prejudices without taking the responsibility for it, since the speaker is also laughable. Although I would say that the overwhelming evidence is in favour of reading the persona's views as endorsed by the author, they are still undercut, especially in the satires which feature secondary personae such as Umbricius or Naevolus.

As has been suggested above, in J. 9 Juvenal even staged a dialogue between his primary persona and a kind of monster-satirist in the form of Naevolus.[175] This humorous subversion of his own prejudices allowed the satirist to have it both ways, perhaps too much so for the ideological position he wished to convey. Yet while his last satires are problematic *qua* satires as their moral message is destabilized, their spin on ridicule, like the spin in Horace's Davus-satire, points beyond them to other genres, such as the novel, where the laughter at all the world would be taken up and richly developed.

---

bigot (S. H. Surlin, 'The Evaluation of Dogmatic Television Characters by Dogmatic Viewers: "Is Archie Bunker a Credible Source?" ' (Paper presented at the *International Communication Association*'s Annual Convention, Montreal, 1973); cf. the discussion in C. P. Wilson, *Jokes: Form, Content, Use and Function* (London: Academic Press, 1979), 197–8.) What has happened to Juvenal in modern times seems to be the inverse of this case: liberal readers, liking the impression of the satire but disliking its prejudiced hero, are trying to save at least the poet through the gap that humour creates between the author and his bigoted character.

[175] See Ch. 1 § '. . . and one *cinaedus* talking back'.

3

Non-Aligned Humour

THE CONCEPT OF NON-ALIGNED HUMOUR IN SATIRE

The fact that the satirists' jokes are sometimes beside the mark, contributing nothing to the derision of the object, has been a recurring cause of embarrassment in satire scholarship. I call humour of this kind 'non-aligned' because, unlike the kinds of humour discussed in the preceding chapters, it is not tied either to the object (butt) or the subject (persona) of the satire where it occurs. It is a feature which has been regarded as a sign of the satiric genre's immaturity in antiquity, and it has also led to the curious labelling of individual poems as 'unsatirical satires'[1] or even to assertions of occasional artistic failures on the part of the satirists. Some satire theorists, however, have insisted on the integral role of such 'non-aligned' humour in a genre whose essence (as the etymology of its name, *satura*, indicates) is to serve a generous portion of mixed offerings.[2] This second line of reasoning seems much more satisfactory, since it is intrinsically improbable that poets of the stature of Horace or Juvenal should repeatedly include a meaningless and genre-flawing element in their satires. While some qualified readers thus acknowledge the place of non-aligned humour in Roman satire,

---

[1] Cf. e.g. J. Brummack, 'Zu Begriff und Theorie der Satire', *Deutsche Vierteljahrs-chrift für Literaturwissenschaft und Geistesgeschichte* 45 (1971), 276; *contra* C. J. Classen, 'Eine unsatirische Satire des Horaz? Zu Hor. Sat. I.5', *Gymnasium* 80 (1973), 235–50; the problem is discussed in Heldmann, 'Wesensbestimmung der Horazischen Satire', 124–5.

[2] Oesterlen, *Humor bei Horaz*, Mason 1963; Henderson, 'Satire Writes Woman' and id., *Writing down Rome*.

they do not explain it as having any particular *meaning*, and its *function* is vaguely seen as giving Roman satire its specific character, or as entertainment, as mere 'show'.

As it is the contention of the present work that a joke is never devoid of meaning, we must bore deeper into these peripheral jokes and ironies, so as to give them a fuller explanation. Moreover, the 'unsatirical' satires of Horace, such as 1.5 and 2.4, strike many readers as brilliant pieces, and the colourful vignettes and metaphors in Juvenal are felt to heighten the lustre of his satire. The intuitive understanding of a first reading, then, seems to be in favour of the sprawling humour, not against it—and such an intuitive understanding is not to be underestimated when the poets under discussion are masters of rhetorical impression.

In this connection, Peter Thorpe's metaphor of satiric attack as 'a fire hose under full pressure which has just been let go of'[3] is very useful to think with. In Roman satire, the humour sometimes works exactly so, spraying everything in sight; but sometimes 'the hose' is more steadily held in hand, so that a central direction is clearly discernible for the stream, though many sprinkles still wet irrelevant spots, more or less distant from the target. Starting from this, I will investigate the individual satirists in order to give more detailed descriptions of how this particular aspect of their satire functions.

HORACE: OPTICAL GREY—THE BALANCE OF EXTREMES

So Horace generally builds his *aurea mediocritas* out of extremes, creating a balanced philosophy and poetics not by picking his way in the middle, but by invoking opposing extremist positions and playing them off against each other, having them fight and undercut each

---

[3] P. Thorpe, 'Thinking in Octagons: Further Reflections on Norms in Satire', *Satire Newsletter* 7 (1969–70), 91–9; repr. in B. Fabian (ed.), *SATURA. Ein Kompendium moderner Studien zur Satire* (Hildesheim: Olms, 1975), 415.

other.[4] While the ideological or aesthetic statement that results is a moderate one, often approaching the commonplace when summarized, the effect of his poetry is quite different, being both rich and dynamic. The same is true of Horace's use of humour in his satires: when summarized it is often said to amount to mild mockery of the satiric targets and mild self-irony. Yet on its way to that summary it permeates all the satires in a variety of ways, some of them violent.

Humour is what holds the incongruous parts together, the axis which allows the reader to accept Horace's satires as wholes despite their many paradoxes. To put it sharply, we might say that the only truly consistent ingredient in Horace's satires is humour—for while the ideological message suffers from being expressed in the inconsistent juxtaposition of extremes, the humour feeds on this very inconsistency. Humour is manifestly present in all the satires, not least in those that have sometimes been considered 'unsatirical'. The larger, overarching inconsistencies in Horace—his image of himself as an intrinsically noble freedman's son, as a great talent contained in a plain, frail body (sometimes likened to an animal such as a donkey or a pig), and his philosophical and poetical views which borrow from Epicurus, Aristotle, the Cynics, and the Stoics—all of these are bridged by humour.[5] Humour is what makes these impossible combinations appear real, and even, oddly enough, harmonious.

The clowns in Horace's satires, sharing with him the urge for self-expression, double up and confront one another: as in the humour contest of Sarmentus and Messius Cicirrus in 1.5, or in that between Rupilius Rex and Persius in 1.7, or even in the discussion between the

---

[4] Ter Vrugt-Lenz ('Horaz' "Sermones": Satire auf der Grenze zweier Welten', *ANRW* II.31.3 (1981), 1828) observes that the satires reflect Horace's own liminality as person and poet: between low and high social strata, between Republic and Empire, between different schools of philosophy. Similar views are developed in J. Moles, 'Cynicism in Horace's *Epistles* 1', *PLLS* 5 (1985), 33–60; Freudenburg, *Walking Muse*, and *Satires of Rome*; J. Christes and G. Fülle, 'Causa fuit pater his: Überlegungen zu Horaz, *Sat.* 1,6', in C. Klodt (ed.), *Satura Lanx. Festschrift für Werner A. Krenkel zum 70. Geburtstag* (Hildesheim: Olms, 1996).

[5] Here I step outside the limits of the *Sermones* in order to give a fuller picture of Horace's persona. For humour in his lyrical poetry, see H. Antony, *Humor in der Augusteischen Dichtung* (Hildesheim: Verlag Dr. H. A. Gerstenberg, 1976), and P. Connor, *Horace's Lyric Poetry: The Force of Humour* (Berwick, Victoria: Aureal, 1987).

town mouse and the country mouse in 2.6.[6] Both sides are partial, caricaturing images of the author himself, and in their battles the incongruities of his literary self are pictorially fought out, with humour both as their weapon and their result. In this connection, it is interesting to recall the reasoning of the Russian literary historian Dmitri Lichačëv, who in his study *Laughter as Worldview* (first published in 1973) claims that splitting into two parts, or doubling, is an inherent characteristic of all humour ('laughter' in his terminology):

> The essence of laughter is connected splitting to two parts. ... The world of laughter is itself the result of a humorous splitting of the real world; it can therefore, in turn, double up in all its directions. ... The forms of splitting in the world of laughter are richly varied. One of them is the appearance of humorous doubles. The two comic personages are essentially identical. They resemble each other, they do the same things, they suffer similar misfortunes. They are inseparable. They are, in essence, one character in two forms.[7]

It is this kind of 'one character in two forms' (of which Lichačëv furnishes many examples from old Russian literature and from folklore) that I believe can be seen in Horace's satires. There is occasionally a palpable folkloric quality to episodes in Horatian satire, most obviously in the case of the tale of the town mouse and

---

[6] For the humour-*agon* between the Sarmentus and Messius in 1.5, see Reckford, 'Hope and Scepticism', esp. 538–43. For the idea that both the town mouse and the country mouse are Horace, see Brink, *On Reading a Horatian Satire*, 9; D. West, 'Of Mice and Men: Horace, *Satires* 2.6.77–117', in A. J. Woodman and D. A. (eds.), *Quality and Pleasure in Latin Poetry* West (London: Cambridge University Press, 1974), 74–6, 78; F. Muecke, *Horace: Satires II*, 195; and K. Reckford, 'Horatius: The Man and the Hour', *AJP* 118 (1997), 590–1. West, in all simplicity, puts it well: 'The Town Mouse is Horace or, to be exact, one aspect of the *persona* Horace is presenting, and the Country Mouse is another.'

[7] D. S. Lichačëv, *Istoričeskaja poetika russkoj literatury. Smekh kak mirovozzrenie i drugie raboty* ('A Historical Poetics of Russian Literature. Laughter as Worldview and Other Works') (St. Petersburg: Aletheia, 2001), 369, 371, and 373 (I quote from a later edition of the work in a collection); my translation. As regards the terminology, Lichačëv claims to follow Bakhtin in his use of the notion 'laughter'. In the run of his study, however, he develops in another direction, and towards the end strays rather far from Bakhtin's understanding. Lichačëv's use of the word 'laughter' vacillates between (1) laughter as a physical act, (2) laughter in the Bakhtinian sense of 'laughter culture' (= 'the culture of folk humour'), and (3) humour. The last sense is the most thoroughgoing.

the country mouse (*S.* 2.6). Horace's comic doubles often accumulate the humour by turning on each other with almost mechanical, 'aping' similarity in their exchanges. The satire is in many places the sum of such comic combats, sometimes visual, more often in abstract form.

To explain the effect of sprawling, non-aligned humour in Horace's *Sermones*, one may borrow a term from art studies, 'optical grey'. In pictorial art, 'optical grey' refers to an effect achieved when several colours are combined into a surface which looks smooth and one-coloured, greyish, when regarded casually, but which conveys a special impression of vividness and depth. The effect can be achieved either by applying layers of different colours one over the other, or by painting small brush-strokes of different colours next to each other. The colours are thus not really blended, but optically blended, as it were, resulting in an effect which is at once both modest and intriguing; the opposite of garish, but interesting and lively to look at. This is, I submit, exactly like the effect of Horace's satire: the humour turned in opposite directions, the philosophical extremes, the extravagant characters raging from lovers caught *in flagrante delicto* to Stoic sages—all of these are paradoxically applied side by side rather than forced by reasoning into agreement, and the result is the optical grey of the balanced Middle Way. Yet all the extremes are still there,[8] the picture is far from the same as a simple representation of the Middle Way, painted with an avoidance of exaggeration.

The presence of Horace's extreme images and positions, though rarely remembered after a reading at normal speed (not the reading for analysis) leaves with the reader an impression of the fullness and richness of life. Simple and modest at first sight, these poems are deeply satisfying as vivid images drawn by a wise artist. This is not merely an aesthetic effect, for the lingering presence of the many peripheral excesses also means something: it makes the *aurea mediocritas* a choice of inclusion rather than exclusion, it suggests knowledge of the world, humanity, and acceptance of the different colours

---

[8] As Freudenburg (*Walking Muse*, 41–2) says: 'The satirist draws his illustrations from a comic world. It is a world of extremes only, as we see in the characters of Maltinus, Rufillus, and Gargonius ... who embody the principle "there is no mean" (*nil medium est*, [1.2.])28)'.

of life.[9] With incongruities and irony in abundance, there is also the teasing possibility that any given passage is not meant seriously. Such a possibility, even when it is not realized, still softens the message of what is said and precludes any kind of authoritarian confidence. The door is left ever so slightly open for relativity, which fits well with Horace's philosophy.[10]

The presence of extremes, even if in dismissed form, helps to negotiate the gap between his peaceful philosophy of moderation and the violence and abundance expected of satire. It is only by sculpturing his *satis* ('just enough') from repeated invocation of its opposites, the 'too little' and 'too much', that he can remain at least nominally faithful to this angry genre.[11] Thus it is incorrect to rephrase Horace's satires without humour and without their particular technique, trying to catch hold of 'the message', i.e. the ideological, political, or even poetical message—the paraphrase loses the magic of the Horatian text, just as if one were to replace optical grey by plain, flat grey. It may be observed that Horace's satires, the least straightforward among the extant Roman satires, are particularly ill-suited for paraphrases, and that summaries of them tend to make an impression fatally different from that made by the poems.

Whereas no one aspect of ideological (moral, critical) content can be shown to appear in all the satires, humour is present in every one of Horace's eighteen satires. As the humour makes sense of the narrative jerks, ties the incoherent parts together, adds small details which seem irrelevant but which serve to reveal intimate features of the artistic universe, and of course destabilizes seriousness, it actually *does change* the message through changing the form.

The sprinkles of non-aligned humour (1.5)

In a detailed discussion of Horace's non-aligned humour, particular attention must be paid to *Satire* 1.5, the whole of which can be said to

---

[9] Cf. Horace's own statement in 2.1.60, that he will write no matter what colour his life might take on: 'quisquis erit vitae, scribam, color.'

[10] For Horace's philosohical position between Epicureanism and the Peripathetic School, see ter Vrugt-Lenz 'Satire auf der Grenze zweier Welten', 1827–8.

[11] Cf. Freudenburg's ironic question 'since when is "enough" a "feast"?'—part of the title of a section—and the following discussion (Freudenburg, *Satires of Rome*, 44–51).

be a shower of non-aligned humour, which wets both the satires before it and those after. (The sprinkles of non-aligned humour in 1.1–1.4 look forward to the shower of 1.5, those in 1.6–1.10 recall it.) *Satire* 1.5 also shows an inner universe filled with sprawling humour. It relates an *Odyssey*-parodying journey undertaken by 'Horace' in the company of Maecenas,[12] the dedicatee of the book. The structure of the satire shows certain similarities to the larger structure of Book 1. For instance, just as *S.* 1.5 with its 'pointless' humour is placed at the middle of the whole book, so 1.5 itself contains a 'pointless' humour-*agon* at its centre (vv. 51–69 out of 104; day 7 out of the 15 days of the journey[13]). This humour-*agon* takes place when mid-way through their journey, Horace and his friends are entertained at the villa of a certain Cocceius. In this setting two clownish characters, Messius Cicirrus and the freedman Sarmentus, engage in a humorous battle of insults, somewhat like modern dozens. Each of them uses weaknesses in the other's physique or status for derision: so Sarmentus likens Messius to a wild horse etc. This kind of coarse humour obviously delights both the immediate audience and the narrator (who had also been part of that immediate audience).[14] This makes 1.5 important among Horace's satires, and it has reasonably been suggested that the journey in this poem is a metaphor for life, or that it is an image of Horace's writing.[15]

It must thus be noted that a satire which is in several respects central to the whole book is characterized by non-aligned humour, with a battle of humour at its own centre. This battle between the *scurrae* Sarmentus and Messius Cicirrus forms an image of the internal fight of the extremes within Horace's satires. These extremes are the doubled poles of the same clownish principle (for the two

---

[12] For parody of the *Odyssey*, see K. Sallmann, 'Die seltsame Reise nach Brundisium. Aufbau und Deutung der Horazsatire 1,5' in U. Reinhardt and K. Sallmann (eds.), *Musa Iocosa: Arbeiten uber Humor und Witz, Komik und Komödie der Antike* (Hildesheim: Olms, 1974), esp. 200–6.

[13] Fifteen days according to the calculations of Kießling and Heinze (*Satiren*, 90), which seem persuasive.

[14] See Rudd, *Satires of Horace*, 63–4, including his excellent comment that 'Clearly this boisterous humour appealed to something very deep in the Roman character, something which the imperial *gravitas* overlaid but never wholly effaced' (64).

[15] A metaphor for life in Sallmann, 'Die Reise nach Brundisium', 206; a metaphor for writing in E. Gowers, 'Horace, *Satires* 1.5: an Inconsequential Journey', *PCPS* 39 (1993), 48–66.

antagonists, like several other pairs in Horace, look much alike[16]), fighting each other with humour. It is as if the central placement was meant to draw the reader's attention to the symmetrical and dynamic construction of the image, 'pointless' at a superficial level, and make him search for meaning in the details.

In this satire, 'the dominant mood is laughter', as Gowers has well noted,[17] and the dominant theme is a careful presentation of 'Horace' himself, shaped exactly as the persona is meant to come across throughout the *Sermones*. He is a master of good taste and of laughter, clever and kind to his friends, keen of observation and free from superstition, though he has no luck with women (who are anyway unimportant), and is tied down by his frail physique. He has no interest in politics, but all the more interest in entertainment, preferably of a humorous kind. His talent is implied in the fact that Maecenas has brought him along, and in his friendship with Virgil. Horace's poetic talent is also foregrounded in the last line of the satire, which makes the written character of the account explicit. This is 'Horace' on his journey through life, a latter-day Ulysses who has exchanged the full sails of epic for the mules of satire, but who still has the ambition to speak of the most important questions, such as: how should one live one's life? The answer given here is: cultivate your friendships, live as an unnoticed private citizen ($\lambda\acute{\alpha}\theta\eta$ $\beta\iota\acute{\omega}\sigma\alpha\varsigma$ ('live hidden')), pass good judgement on what you see, laugh when you can, and if you write—keep your writing short, so that it does not outgrow life.[18]

---

[16] Persius and Rupilius Rex in 1.7; the two mice in 2.6, and to some extent 'Horace' and the pest in 1.9. On a larger scale, Canidia with her connection to *ars*, *carmina*, and can*ere* (in both the *Sermones* and the *Epodes*), may be seen as a hellish double of 'Horace'; see Oliensis, 'Canidia, Canicula, and Horace's *Epodes*'.

[17] Gowers, 'An Inconsequential Journey', 58. Cf. also Rudd's observation that this satire exhibits a 'delightful combination of Roman *urbanitas* with the humour of rustic Italy' (Rudd, *Satires of Horace*, 61).

[18] In the end it thus parts ways with the predecessor of this satire, Lucilius' long description of his journey to Sicily, the remains of which have come down to us in fragments 9–12 (M). For commentary on Lucilius' *Iter Siculum*, see Marx, *Lucilius*, ii. 46–71. For the relationship between the two satirical trips, see Reckford, 'Hope and Scepticism', esp. 528, with the felicitous observation that 'their journeys to Sicily and Brundisium would coincide as far as Capua and then diverge, a fine living metaphor for the creative and critical work of Horatian *aemulatio*'.

In Homer's epic, laughter was a quality of the gods,[19] in satire there are no gods, and laughter has become the privilege of the satirist. In this central satire on his life and his writing, Horace's laughter knows no boundaries—truly a hose let go of, it sprinkles his own persona, his occasional objects (vain or superstitious men), his friends, and the land he travels through, complete with boatmen, frogs, and mosquitoes.

Attempts have been made to see the whole of 1.5 as a satire on ambition. This would force 1.5 into the framework of object-oriented humour, more obviously associated with satire. Such a reading, however, lacks the proper textual basis. Moreover, it would primarily insult Maecenas, who is, on the contrary, described with respect and sympathy throughout 1.5.[20] My own view is rather that the object-oriented humour present in this text (against the vain Luscus 34–6; an excessively ambitious host 71–6; the superstitious inhabitants of Gnatia 97–100) has been reduced to the peripheral position usually occupied by non-aligned humour. In a kind of inversion, non-aligned humour has moved to the centre instead.

While it is difficult to see criticism, attack may perhaps be seen in the willingness to laugh at everyone and everything. In 1.5, humour ensures Horace's power over life and art, as when the major inconsistency of the satiric persona, the one between his mighty talent and his weak body, is bridged by humour. Now we can see more clearly that the fighting clowns in the middle of the satire are indeed shadows of Horace,[21] for they try to gain power over each other by means of humorous insults, in a parody of the ritual exchange of abuse of epic heroes about to engage in battle. When introducing the competition, 'Horace' invites the Muse to tell about the descent of

[19] Though men also laugh in Homer, their laughter is rare, and different from that of the gods—it is generally not the laughter of joy. See further Paul Friedländer 'Lachende Götter', *Die Antike* 10 (1934), 210–26; M. Colakis,'The Laughter of the Suitors in *Odyssey* 20', *CW* 79 (1986), 137–41; Jäkel, 'Laughter in the Iliad'; and C. Miralles, 'Laughter in the Odyssey', in S. Jäkel and A. Timonen (eds.), *Laughter down the Centuries*, i (Turku: Annales Universitatis Turkuensis, 1994).

[20] The satire as critical of ambition: Anderson, *Essays*, 20, 36; the objection about Maecenas: Brown, *Horace: Satires I*, 140.

[21] Reckford ('Hope and Scepticism') suggests that Sarmentus may be thus regarded, but it seems to me that the difference between Sarmentus and Cicirrus is too slight to justify the claim that only one of them is a shadow of Horace.

the two heroes. This is a move of comic degradation. Like Horace, they are both of lowly descent: one of them, Sarmentus, is a freedman, like Horace's father, the other an Oscan, thus belonging to a people whom the Romans considered particularly oafish. In his invocation to the Muse the persona asks who their fathers were, 'quo patre natus uterque' ('of what father each of them was born'), 53—recalling the paternal motif that recurs, primarily in connection with 'Horace' himself, in the satires which frame this one, 1.4 and 1.6.[22] Furthermore, both Messius and Sarmentus are physically ugly in easily ridiculed ways: the former is hairy with a scar on his face, the latter abnormally thin. Both use this outer appearance to taunt each other: Messius is likened to a wild horse (possibly also a joke on his name)[23] and to the Cyclops, Sarmentus has to hear jokes about how little food his mistress had to waste on him (again a joke on the name, *sarmentum* meaning 'twig'). Likewise, 'Horace' occasionally jokes about his big belly, and may even make use of his stature to liken himself to a pig.[24] Both clowns seem to accept the ridicule graciously, and Messius even plays along in impersonating the wild horse. Sarmentus is granted a Homeric reference in his mention of the Cyclops, though it is embedded in a mime of the same name. Finally Messius Cicirrus is accused of being his mistress' slave still, though he is formally free, an accusation which 'Horace' will have to hear about his own dependence on Maecenas in *S.* 2.7. Thus like Horace, the two *scurrae* arrive on the scene from less than perfect initial positions, but like Horace, they control their existence by humour, entertaining with success even the choosy audience comprising Virgil and Maecenas. Their mutual aggression, while leading nowhere, functions much like Horace's choice of satire as his first genre—it makes the scene dynamic and theatrical, and enacts man's struggle with himself and his conditions.

[22] Explicit references to fathers, parents, sons are given in 1.4.105 and in 1.6.7, 10, 21, 29, 36, 38, 41, 45–6, 64, 71, 89, 91, 131.

[23] See O. Skutsch, 'Messius Cicirrus', in J. H. Betts, J. T. Hooker, and J. R. Green (eds.), *Studies in honour of T. B. L. Webster* (Bristol: Bristol Classical Press, 1986).

[24] *Ep.* 1.4.15–16.

The life journey of 1.5, with its battle of wits in the middle, with its friendship, its occasional physical hardships, its peripheral women,[25] and above all its spreading, sprinkling, untamed humour, stops with a surprising ending. In the final line the reader is suddenly told that this was a *written* journey. An elegant zeugma equates the geographical way with the paper on which the literary journey has been made:

> Brundisium longae finis chartaeque viaeque est. (104)

Brundisium is the end of this long tale [lit. 'paper'] and journey.

The capping joke of the poem is thus meta-literal: pointing to its own limits, the written satire mocks those who had been carried away by its journey and its mimesis of life. At another level, it is a way of pointing to victory over the intertext, Lucilius' *Iter Siculum* (Book 3), which had been too long both in days and in verses. Finally, it is perhaps also an identification of Horace's life's path, *via*, with his writing, *charta*, significantly cast in the form of a joke.

The minor passages of non-aligned humour in the surrounding satires in Book 1 may be seen as squirts cascading out from the fountain in the self-describing 1.5.[26] In this central poem both mild and aggressive ridicule is found, but it is generally non-aligned. This is humour in pure form, which lets slip the secret that a target is secondary to Horace's satire. When the two comic entertainers exchange banter to the delight of Horace and his friends, with no winner in the potentially endless stream of ridicule, humour is revealed to be almost entirely independent of an object of criticism. The joking attacks are reversible, the faults of hairiness and skinniness inessential —it is the joke structure and the activity of humour that matters, a kind of *jouissance* where only the name has to be changed in order for the joke to shoot in another direction.[27]

---

[25] At vv. 15 and 82–5, one fifteen verses from the beginning, the other twenty verses from the end; significantly, both girls are explicitly *absent*: 'absentem ut cantat amicam', 15; 'mendacem stultissimus usque puellam | ad mediam noctem exspecto', 82–3.

[26] In what follows I will discuss a set of significant examples; it is not my aim to enumerate all the instances of non-aligned humour in Horace's satires.

[27] The satirist himself has famously formulated this principle at 1.1.69–70: 'quid rides? mutato nomine de te | fabula narratur'. On the exchangeability of targets and the importance of the 'joke mechanism' itself, cf. Purdie, *Comedy*, 45.

In the satires that precede 1.5 the squirts of non-aligned humour, small jokes turned in the other direction from the one which dominates the poem, are as yet unexplained in the text, appearing as question-marks in what should be the confident preaching of diatribe (1.1–1.3) or of literary programme (1.4). These jokes look forward to 1.5 in that they bar any moral/aesthetic fanaticism on the part of the speaker, and hint that he is more interested in making keen observations as he walks along than in presenting a consistent ideological argument.

Moralist or thief? (1.1)

So the first satire, immediately after presenting the solemn Lucretian image of the wise man as a guest at the table of life (1.1.117–19), ends with an unexpected joke about Crispinus the Stoic:

> Iam satis est. ne me Crispini scrinia lippi
> compilasse putes, verbum non amplius addam.   (1.120–1)

Enough now. I wouldn't want you to think that I have pillaged the note-books of sore-eyed Crispinus, so I won't add another word.

The joke stresses the brevity that Horace values so highly, and of course makes fun of Crispinus. 'Horace' will laugh at him several times more, in one instance (1.4.14) again for this Stoic poet's graphomania, as contrasted with 'Horace''s unwillingness to write a great amount of verses quickly.[28]

Lippus ('sore-eyed') is probably, in addition to being an insult making use of physical defect,[29] also an allusion to faulty judgement

---

[28] For the demand for brevity, cf. e.g. the programmatic 'est brevitate opus' at 1.10.9 and the abrupt ending of 1.5.104, cutting off the satire with an ironic complaint about its great length, 'longae finis chartaeque viaeque est'; *Ars* 25 and 335. The other passages where Crispinus is mocked are 1.3.139 and 2.7.45.

[29] For such invective, frequent in antiquity, see Garland, 'Mockery of the Deformed in Graeco-Roman Culture'. In Roman thought, physical characteristics were easily taken as signs of mental/ moral features, as witness several examples (and warnings) in Cicero's treatise on the comic in *De Or.* 2, notably the one at 2.266, where the speaker, Julius Caesar Strabo, retells how in fulfilment of his promise to describe 'what kind of man' his opponent was, he pointed to Marius' shield, suspended above the opposite shops, with its image of a distorted Gaul—and raised general laughter.

and inability to see clearly in matters of philosophy and poetics. Yet this adjective is also one that 'Horace' uses of himself (1.5.30), of his adressee (1.3.25), and of an audience that has heard the tale he is about to tell in 1.7 (v. 3), likewise with overtones of insufficient clear-sightedness.

More problematically, when considered more closely these last lines seem to imply that there is a kind of proximity between Horace's and Crispinus' *writings*, for otherwise there would be no danger of the listener's suspicion of stealth from Crispinus. Surely the mere fact of a lengthy poem would not be enough to suggest a particular poet. There is a hint that philosophical schools may be exchangeable in matters of basic morals.[30] A joke of this kind is an example of a sprinkle of non-aligned humour. After the serious and beautiful Lucretian simile of the dinner guest, which has made the reader interpret the satire as an Epicurean diatribe, there comes the suggestion that it might as well be stolen from the notebooks of a Stoic. The reader is doubtless meant to conclude that it has *not* been stolen, but in the admonition 'you mustn't think that' such a possibility is still literally stated.

In addition to the philosophical point there is also the playful irony which falls back on the persona.[31] The verb *compilasse* echoes *compilent* earlier in the same satire, in the description of the thieves and fleeing slaves who threaten to steal the rich man's fortune at any time of the day (76–9). The verbal echo invokes a comic picture of 'Horace' rummaging the cylinders of Crispinus' work-in-progress. The irony is underlined by the fact that the earlier scene of theft is placed entirely within the fictional universe of the satire, while the last lines lie partly outside this universe in that they speak of *the writing* of the satire, and so of creating that universe. Thus, if the implication is drawn all the way, it will be that 'Horace' shapes a morally pure self-image for the inside of his moralistic universe, but

[30] Herter ('Zu ersten Satire des Horaz') believes that the likeness lies in the style of the diatribe as such, which necessarily carries with it some monotony and generalization.

[31] Herter, 'Zu ersten Satire des Horaz', 18; followed by Sack (*Ironie*, 33) and Brown, *Horace: Satires I, ad loc.* Strict order would require this aspect of the joke to be treated in my second chapter, but it seems more reasonable to deviate from the rule and treat the different aspects of the same passage together, esp. since they tend to be intertwined.

that he actually, outside it, may be so corrupt as to steal stories from his opponents.[32]

In a softer manner, the shift from one narrative level to another can be said to be slightly comic in itself, for the reader has adapted his imagination to the universe of the story and suspended his disbelief, when he is suddenly shaken out of that universe by a reference to its making. Such narrative frames at the beginning and/or end of a poem, joking about the creation of the story within, are in fact typical of Horace, and I will return to this device below. In the case of 1.1, the disturbance caused by the joke is not strong enough to overthrow the Epicurean–commonsensical message of the poem. Nor does this joke make the poem truly ambivalent between Horace and Crispinus, between Epicurus and Stoa, between moralism and relativistic indifference. Yet it makes the satire end with a wink, a small question-mark whose exact meaning is not easily pinned down: it suggests the reversibility of humour, for the stream of ridicule that was previously directed at 'Horace''s opponents, now wets both Crispinus and 'Horace' at the same time, and both Stoic and Epicurean philosophy as well.

Long dresses and Catia's short one (1.2)

1.2 is a relatively consistent attack on the contrasting follies of chasing married matrons and of wasting one's fortune on low-class prostitutes, but there are nevertheless several points at which the humour involved turns in the 'wrong' direction. One example of humour in the wrong direction is found in a section on the regrettable tendency of matrons to hide their bodily disadvantages and underline their charms (80–103). This is a tendency they can freely indulge in with the help of their long skirts and generally abundant clothing and ornaments. The acquisition of a woman is compared to the buying of horses, where the buyer may also be tricked if the horse is covered (83–5), and contrasted with the laudable behaviour of

---

[32] This is of course fiction as well; no literary work can truly step outside itself, no matter how much it claims to do so. Another level of narrative is simply added: we are faced with a (fictional) 'Horace' who has written a satire where 'he himself' features as a character.

prostitutes, who show their wares openly (101–3). On a matron one can see nothing but her face, the rest being covered by her long dress. Then, embedded in this section (v. 95), comes a sudden counter-example of a provocative matron, Catia, who shows all. The immediately relevant part of the passage, after the comparison with the bying of horses, runs thus:

> ne corporis optima Lyncei
> contemplere oculis, Hypsaea caecior illa
> quae mala sunt spectes. 'o crus, o bracchia!' verum
> depugis, nasuta, brevi latere et pede longo est.
> matronae praeter faciem nil cernere possis,
> cetera, *ni Catia est*, demissa veste tegentis.
> si interdicta petes, vallo circumdata (nam te
> hoc facit insanum), multae tibi tum officient res;
> custodes, lectica, ciniflones, parasitae,
> ad talos stola demissa et circum addita palla,
> plurima quae invideant pure apparere tibi rem.
> altera, nil obstat: Cois tibi plane videre est
> ut nudam, ne crure malo, ne sit pede turpi;
> metiri possis oculo latus.   (1.2.90–103)

You mustn't examine the best parts of her body with the eyes of Lynceus, while turning a blinder eye than Hypsaea's on the bad bits. 'O what a leg! O what arms!' But she's derrièreless,[33] big-nosed, with a short waist and enormous feet. On a matron, you can't see anything except her face, since she covers the rest with her long dress—*unless it's Catia*. If you're after forbidden fruit, surrounded by a wall (and that is exactly what drives you crazy), then there'll be a lot of things in your way. There are her attendants, the litter, coiffeuses, hangers-on, a dress reaching to her ankles and a mantle on top of that—there's no end to the obstacles that grudge you a clear view of the thing itself. With the other one, nothing gets in the way. In her Coan silk you can see her virtually naked. You can check that she doesn't have bad legs or ugly feet; you can measure her waist with your eyes.

Unless of course it is Catia—'cetera, *ni Catia est*, demissa veste tegentis' (95). This side-swipe against Catia involves a real

---

[33] In 'derrièreless' I quote Richlin's ingenious translation (Richlin, *Garden*, 176) of what appears to be Horace's coinage from Greek πυγή ('backside') and the Latin prefix 'de-'; cf. Greek ἄπυγος.

contemporary person, of whom the scholiast recounts that she wore a short dress, and that she was also otherwise shameless.[34] The odd thing about this kick of ridicule is that it is turned in the opposite direction from the argument around it, even surrounding it in the same verse. The clause is emphatically placed between the trithemimeral and the penthemimeral caesura, and embellished by alliteration and an equal amount of syllables with '*cetera*': '*Catiast*'. The stressed, framed position and the alliteration suggest that the Catia-clause is important. Unlike the scholiast, Horace is not concerned with the shamelessness of matrons, nor indeed of any women, in this satire; his focus is on availability and comfort. The warning against affairs with matrons is founded on the discomforts such liasons bring upon the lover, not on moral indignation over the fact of *adulterium* or on any strict moral standards required of upper-class women. Exhibiting her body, Catia is in fact behaving in the same manner as the *togatae* ('professional prostitutes'), i.e. in the best manner possible according to the speaker. The overdressed ladies are flanked by references to honest call-girls (83–5; 101–3), just as the daring Catia is flanked by overdressed ladies (90/94–100, with Catia in 95[35]). There is a balanced symmetry, and this is also what enables the joke to work, for it is completely unexpected in its immediate context. The jibe against Catia, though not in line with the pragmatic attitude that holds most of the satire, is in line with a more widespread Roman opinion, namely that women should be honourable. In connecting to this background morality, the tiny

---

[34] Porphyrio: 'ob pulchritudinem crurum pudore neglecto alta veste utebatur. haec autem adeo vilis fuit ut in aede Veneris theatri Pomepiani adulterium cum Valerio Siculo colono tr. pl. obducto velo admiserit' ('Because of her beautiful legs she wore a short dress, neglecting all shame. She even lowered herself to committing adultery with the Sicilian Valerius, tribune of the people, behind a curtain in the temple of Venus at Pompey's theatre'), in W. Meyer (ed.), *Pomponii Porphyrionis Commentarii in Q. Horatium Flaccum*, rec. Gulielmus Meyer (Leipzig: Teubner, 1874), 196. The passage is quoted in Kießling and Heinze, *Satiren*, ad loc.
We may note that this is one of the few examples of *onomasti kōmōdein* in Horace's satire. On this trait of the passage, see Rudd, *Satires of Horace*, 132–59; LaFleur, 'The Law of Satire'. Fraenkel, *Horace*, 85–6, sees Horace's occasional strokes of personal invective, including this one, as nods to the genre's requirements, but otherwise 'for a moment's amusement, nothing more' (85)

[35] The passage on ladies begins at v. 90 if the warning not to overlook corporeal defects is taken as a reference to such ladies (as I think it should be), at 94 if one waits for the word 'matronae'.

inserted joke suggests that the attitudes of the rest of the satire are perhaps not the best possible, but rather those of a playboy trickster, at least formerly a seducer of other men's wives. The surface of the satire begins to oscillate with the suggestion that different outlooks are possible.

Laughing at the Epicurean ideal: doting fathers and misbehaving friends (1.3)

Satire 1.3 develops the Epicurean thought that one should forgive one's friends, and ridicules the Stoic maxim that all sins are equal. 'Horace' recounts some very drastic, but oddly comic, examples of faults to be forgiven. First, there is the list of faults that fathers forgive their sons, a kind of behaviour that is recommended in regard of one's friends (1.3.43–54). The list is entered upon by means of a reference to the commonplace that 'love is blind': lovers see the beloved's faults in a reconciliatory light or indeed see them as advantages, 'as Bambinus did with Hagna's polyp' (40). Similar arguments had been developed by Plato (*Resp.* 474d–e) and especially by Lucretius, an Epicurean like Horace, in a 'satiric' list of lovers' euphemisms (*De Rerum Natura* 4.1153–69). Horace is out to invert these catalogues.[36] In Horace's catalogue, it is only the one example of Bambinus and Hagna's polyp that is in line with the catalogues in the literary predecessors, as Brown observes in his commentary on *Sermones* Book 1. After this, the 'negative criticism is turned to positive advantage with the argument that, in friendship, such charitable indulgence is desirable (41–54)'.[37]

What is remarkable in Horace's rewriting is the inversion of humour. While Lucretius' passage uses straightforward satirical attack, exhibiting as ugly and ridiculous what he wishes the reader to dismiss, Horace exhibits as ugly and ridiculous what he wishes the reader to accept, even accept as a model of excellence.

[36] Kießling and Heinze, *Satiren*, *ad loc.*; Brown, *Horace: Satires I*, *ad loc.* For the satirical mode in Lucretius, see C. Murley, 'Lucretius and the History of Satire', *TAPA* 70 (1939), 380–95, who mentions our case on page 387.

[37] Brown, *Horace: Satires I*, ad loc.

Lucretius had given thirteen examples of physical drawbacks in women, each of which the lover would rephrase with an endearment. To strengthen his argument, Lucretius included laughing characters in his catalogue. These laughers laughed at the ugly women and their lovers, inviting the reader to laugh with them ('inrident' ('they laugh'), 1157; 'cachinnant' ('they guffaw'), 1176; 'omnis inquirere risus' ('they make all kinds of jokes'), 1189). Horace is not unwilling to laugh at women and silly lovers, but he has left this theme behind in the previous satire (1.2), and is speaking of a different love altogether in 1.3, the laudable love between friends. At the beginning of the passage under discussion, there are verbal reminiscences of Lucretius: 'amatorem caecum' ('blind lover') looking back to Lucretius' 'cupidine caeci' ('blind with desire'); 'turpia decipiunt' ('the ugly parts escape them') and 'vitia... | delectant' ('the defects delight them') recalling 'pravas *turpis*que videmus | esse in *deliciis*' ('we see that even deformed and ugly women are kept as sweethearts').[38] Soon, however, Horace's *amator* is superseded by *amicitia* and *amici* (41, 43), and loving fathers (43). The catalogue that follows gives only four examples of physical faults, afterwards gliding into admonitions to indulge the moral shortcomings of friends (again four examples, 49–53) and three instances of the converse, which allegedly happens in reality: the virtues of friends being treated as faults, 55–67. Thus where Lucretius had thirteen examples all shooting in the same direction, Horace has eleven, 4 + 4 + 3, with every group showing a different angle. The resulting text runs as follows (I indicate the different groups with numbers in the quotation):

> vellem in amicitia sic erraremus, et isti
> errori nomen Virtus posuisset honestum.
> ac pater ut gnati, sic nos debemus amici
> *Group I*
> si quod sit vitium non fastidire, (1) strabonem
> appellat paetum et (2) pullum, male parvus
> si cui filius est, ut abortivus fuit olim
> Sisyphus; (3) hunc varum distortis cruribus, (4) illum
> balbutit scaurum pravis fultum male talis.

---

[38] Hor. *S.* 1.3.38–9—Lucr. 4.1153; Hor. *S.* 1.3.38 and 1.3.38–9—Lucr. 4.1155–6.

Group II

(1) parcius hic vivit: frugi dicatur. (2) ineptus
et iactantior hic paulo est: concinnus amicis
postulat ut videatur. (3) at est truculentior atque
plus aequo liber; simplex fortisque habeatur.
(4) caldior est: acris inter numeratur.

                  opinor,

haec res et iungit iunctos et servat amicos.

Group III

at nos virtutes ipsas invertimus atque
sincerum furimus vas incrustare. (1) probus quis
nobiscum vivit, multum demissus homo: illi
tardo cognomen, pingui damus. (2) hic fugit omnis
insidias nullique malo latus obdit apertum
cum genus hoc inter vitae versemus ubi acris
invidia atque vigent ubi crimina: pro bene sano
ac non incauto fictum astutumque vocamus.
(3) simplicior quis et est qualem me saepe libenter
obtulerim tibi, Maecenas, ut forte legentem
aut tacitum impellat quovis sermone molestus:
'communi sensu plane caret' inquimus. eheu,
quam temere in nosmet legem sancimus iniquam!   (1.3.41–67)

I wish we would make this mistake in friendship, and that Virtue would have given this error an honourable name. As a father does with his son, so we should behave towards our friends: we should not be disgusted if there is some defect.

Group I. A father calls (1) the squint-eyed 'Stray-eye'; if he has (2) a miserably short son, like the dwarf Sisyphus, he calls him 'Chick'. This one (3) with deformed legs is called 'Bowie'; of that one, (4) who can hardly stand on his distorted feet, his father lisps that he is 'Thick-foot'.

Group II. (1) This man is rather close-fisted: let's call him 'thrifty'. (2) Another one is tactless and a bit of a braggart: he wants his friends to think him 'sociable'. If (3) someone comes close to being rude and is unreasonably outspoken, let's think of him as 'frank and fearless'. This one (4) is a little hot-headed: let's count him among 'keen' men.

I believe that this practice both forms friendships and preserves them.

GROUP III. But we even overturn the very virtues in our zeal to dirty a clean vessel. (1) A friend of ours is a decent, completely unassuming fellow: we give him the nickname 'Snail' or 'Fathead'. (2) This one avoids all kinds of intrigue and won't appear unshielded before an enemy—since in this life of ours, envy is sharp and slander never sleeps. Instead of calling him a fully sensible man, not rash, we call him 'false and calculating'. (3) A fellow is a bit simple—the way I often behaved when I happily presented myself to you, Maecenas—so that he may interrupt a man reading, or quietly thinking, with some discourse or other, a nuisance. 'He has no sense', we say. Oh, how rashly we endorse a law that will work against ourselves!

Lucretius had clear references to explicit laughter framing his list. Horace has one reference to explicit laughter (preceding his list). This reference is placed in a caricature of a man who has an uncouth appearance but excellent morals and talent: 'rideri possit' ('he could be derided'), v. 30. Horace says that one could laugh at this man's rustic exterior, but that one should not.[39]

If we look only at the moral message which 'Horace' spells out in this satire, we must conclude that we should not laugh at people who look bad but have inner merit. Thus the four middle examples are to be taken seriously as good advice. The three last examples are the only laughable ones, since they describe people's meanness and so constitute the legitimate object of this satire. On this reading, it is not clear what we should do with the humour of the first four examples—the sons in it are parallel to the rustic man above, and thus not to be laughed at, their fathers are the very paragon of virtue. On this reading, it seems that a straightforward list of examples like the last three would have served 'Horace's' moral message better than the solution he used.

Yet the funniness of the first four examples is hardly coincidental. They constitute the passage that most clearly connects to a literary commonplace, and to Lucretius' comic catalogue in particular. These examples use physical deformity, a direct and powerful source of humour to the Roman mind.[40] There is also an external joke pinned on: the euphemisms with which the loving fathers name their

---

[39] For this caricature, see Ch. 2 § 'A lowly character for a low genre'.
[40] This is the device used in the Lucretian list; cf. the insults of the clowns at the centre of *S.* 1.5.

deformed sons—*paetus, pullus, varus, scaurus*[41]—are all real cognomina used by outstanding Roman families.[42]

The reading I suggest acknowledges that Horace's satire contains humour in different directions, including that of laughing at the love-blinded fathers and their imperfect sons, with a side-swipe against influential Roman families. It seems to me that such ridicule of the fathers is present although it goes against the main message of the satire—to love one's friends and forgive their faults. The earlier phrase 'rideri possit' of the uncouth but worthy man, then, becomes a reminder of laughter rather than a warning against it. The quick move of humour direction from the first four examples in the list (ridicule of the fathers who see their sons as *better than they are*) to the last three (ridicule of people who see their friends as *worse than they are*) creates an inconsistency and something of a cognitive tumble. The effect is a sprawling exhibition of humour as a reversible device, wetting everything and leaving nobody dry; the effect is also to suggest a reality that is multiple and complex, where inconsistencies are not resolved. The sum message of the satire is clear, and yet the small humour contradictions render 1.3 a different poem than it would have been without them. It is more vivid, more balanced, even more comic, as the shifts in humour direction tend to become humorous in themselves. But the satire is also less firm in its moral message, for the invitation to laugh at the poem's moral 'heroes' hints, however slightly, that the poet is not completely serious in his praise of them, and this destabilizes the ideological structure. Lucretius' catalogue, paradoxically, reads as more serious moral satire than Horace's version in 1.3. Horace's satire gives up absolute ideological reliability for the invigorating delights of non-aligned humour.

Later on in the same satire Horace analogously insists on forgiving one's friends their misdemeanours, again with somewhat too funny examples:

[41] ('Squint-eyed'), ('dwarf'), ('bow-legged'), and ('swollen-ankled'). However, the words (and thus the cognomina) are kinder than their literal meaning, as I have tried to convey in my translation above, rendering them with 'Stray-eye', 'Chick', 'Bowie', and 'Thick-foot'.

[42] For the extra joke on cognomina, see Kießling and Heinze, *Satiren*, 53; Freudenburg, *Walking Muse*, 50.

comminxit lectum potus mensave catillum
Evandri manibus tritum deiecit; ob hanc rem,
aut positum ante mea quia pullum in parte catini
sustulit esuriens, minus hoc iucundus amicus
sit mihi?   (1.3.90–4)

What if he wet the couch when he was drunk? Or knocked down a plate, old enough to have been touched by Evander's hands, from the table? Or if he, when hungry, took a chicken from my side of the dish—would I like him any less as a friend for that?

These examples, though different in the amount of harm they would cause the host, have one thing in common in that they are all *physical* mishaps, bad table manners. They are all connected to the Bakhtinian material bodily lower stratum: hunger satisfied by grabbing a chicken, incontinence satisfied by wetting the couch, and unsteady movements, presumably due to drunkenness. In an interesting detail the unruly guest literally lowers the authority of king Evander, a legendary hero, when he throws down ('deiecit') the precious bowl that had been handled by the king's hands. The scene is a dinner party, a motif central to the genre of satire, and metonymically connected to its name, *satura*, the full plate.[43] The examples probably refer to one friend in different hypothetical situations, but since they share the same environment and are heaped upon each other, the impression is inevitably one of misbehaviour at the same party, perhaps by several guests. As the friend engages in this merry, lowering, carnivalesque acting at Horace's feast, he is in fact helping the satire along. The satirist gets to make his point that physical mishaps are easily overlooked while moral transgressions, such as breach of confidence, are not (94–5). At the same time the satirist adds some boisterous humour of excess, albeit in the wrong direction. Such farcical excess is useful for the genre (the feast of *satura*!), but not in line with the ideology of moderation which Horace ostensibly preaches. So he smuggles in the excessive images as examples, balancing them with the bare mention of worse vices, but in the process embarrasses readers who want to find a clearly logical connection between idea and image.

---

[43] For further references, see Ch. 1, n. 90.

Another trait of Horace's satire may be observed from the examples discussed here: unlike several other Roman authors, including Persius and Juvenal, Horace does not equate a person's appearance with his/her inner qualities (moral and intellectual), nor does he always equate manners with morals. In fact, one of the most important images in his satires is the clumsy, laughable creature with a heart of gold and a great, even divine talent. This is his favourite image for his own persona, as well as for other characters with whom he sympathizes, and he is well aware of the comic possibilities of this contradictory image.

Always as peaceful as he claims? (1.4)

In the following satire, the first of Horace's programme satires, there are several twists in the argument, but the last one, closing the poem, is definitely the most remarkable. It has long been recognized that the argument of 1.4 is an Aristotelian literary programme for comic writing, in this case satire. In his argument, Horace stresses two elements: that Roman satire does not employ aggressive, illiberal humour, and that it is not really poetry. Both elements pose problems.

The first rule, that satire should not include scurrilous humour that may hurt people, is contradicted by the emphatic opening reference to Old Comedy as the inspiration of Lucilius (1.4.1–6). The contradiction is strengthened by Horace's insistence on the branding, free-spoken humour within that inspiration ('multa cum libertate notabant. | hinc omnis pendet Lucilius' ('they branded them freely. It is this aspect that Lucilius is wholly dependent on')). Horace then distinguishes himself from Lucilius in claiming that his style is sparser and more carefully composed than his predecessor's (8–13). However, he never claims that there will be a difference in humour between them. In fact, he shows an interest in *libertas*, the free branding of those who deserve it with the brand of derision, for which he establishes a tradition from the Old Comedy to the *primus inventor* of Roman satire, and by implication to himself. Thus Horace ostensibly renounces 'bad', aggressive humour in favour of 'good', well-bred and moderate humour, in line with the prescription of

Aristotle. Yet Horace also associates himself, via Lucilius, with the humour of Old Comedy, which Aristotle renounced as vulgar and unworthy of a well-bred man.[44] Horace could not have missed Aristotle's dislike of the jests of Old Comedy, precisely when drawing on the philosopher's discussion of the comic.

The moral reasoning which Horace later on in the poem claims to have learnt from his father—to teach oneself how to live, and how *not* to live, from the examples of others—again seems closer to aggressive derision than to innocuous joking, 105–29. The same verb is used of the father's practice (*notando*, 106) as of the writers of Old Comedy (*notabant*, 5).

The second rule in Horace's programme, that satire is not poetry, intensely proclaimed in vv. 39–44, is problematized further on, in the example of high poetry (60–2). Taking a passage of Ennian epic as his example, Horace insists that even if it is taken apart, its limbs will speak of its status as poetry. In his study *The Walking Muse* (1993) Freudenburg has shown that the passage on high poetry mocks *one* notion of poetry, the Stoic notion, which said that noble poetry had to be composed of noble words. Freudenburg shows that this mockery rests on another understanding of poetry, that of the atomistic Epicureans. According to the Epicurean understanding, the key to poetry lay precisely in composition itself, i.e. in the combination of words and phrases. Horace, the supreme mosaic-maker, satirizes both the pathos of high genres and the organic definition of poetry held by the Stoics by his careful wording of the passage in question and the grim humour of the poet, not the poem, lying about in pieces ('disiecti membra poetae' ('the scattered limbs of a poet')).[45]

Thus the argument of 1.4 is far from straightforward even before the end. Before the final joke 'Horace' speaks of his own tendency to continue his father's reflections, by disputing with himself about concrete examples of right and wrong behaviour, occasionally

---

[44] In one of the very passages that Horace is presumably drawing upon: *Eth.-Nic.* 4.8. It is true that Cicero once lists Old Comedy together with New Comedy as examples of liberal humour (*Off.*1.104), though in another passage he criticizes Old Comedy for its scurrilous, defamatory attacks both on guilty and on innocent people, *Rep.* 4.10–11. But there is no reason to assume that Horace would be following Cicero over Aristotle.

[45] Freudenburg, *Walking Muse*, 145–50.

writing these down—presumably with the *Sermones* as result. He has previously told the interlocutor that he himself is not free from some minor faults (1.3.19–20). Now he points out the habit of writing down his moral discussions as one of these faults, and rounds off the satire with the following joke:

> ubi quid datur oti,
> illudo chartis. hoc est mediocribus illis
> ex vitiis unum; cui si *concedere* nolis,
> multa poetarum veniat manus, auxilio quae
> sit mihi (nam multo plures sumus), ac veluti te
> Iudaei cogemus in hanc *concedere* turbam.   (1.4.138–43)

when I have some free time, I play with writing. This is one of those medium-sized faults of mine—and if you're not prepared to stand it, a numerous company of poets will rally round to my assistance (for we outnumber the others by far) and like the Jews, we will force you to stand with our band.

The joke is multiple. There is the word-play on *concedere* (140 and 143): 'if you will not *make way* for it ... we'll force you to *make your way* into our throng.' There is the comic hyperbole that poets outnumber non-poets. Above all, there is the absurd threat of forcibly turning the interlocutor into a poet.[46] 'Horace' has previously said that he is not one of the poets, 'primum ego me illorum dederim quibus esse poetis | excerpam numero' ('First of all, I exclude myself from the number of people whom I grant the title "poet" '), vv. 39–40. Here a throng of poets rallies to his support, and from being helped by them, he glides into their midst as the verb is changed to the first person plural, *sumus*. The transferred use of *concedere* ('cui si concedere nolis') referring to forgiveness, and the conditional of v. 140 give way to military connotations (in the words *manus, auxilium, cogere,* and *concedere* in the concrete sense) and the future of 'cogemus', v. 143.

In addition to making the satirist a poet, the final jest is also rather aggressive, or at least threatening, and so both the elements of satire

---

[46] The problem is not solved by pointing out that Rome held large numbers of Jews and that these were known for their proselytizing zeal, as some commentators do. Cf. Brown, *Horace: Satires I*, ad loc., who adduces the parallels of Cicero, *Flac.* 67, and Matt. 23:15.

laid out in this poem—that it is not a poetic genre and that it spurns aggressive humour—are compromised by this joke.

Oesterlen has paid attention to this passage in his commentary on humorous places in Horace, *Komik und Humor bei Horaz* (1885–7). Here Oesterlen exclaims that even when Horace is trying to be serious, his humour sweeps him off into the most unrestrained prancing.[47] This is an artistic and somewhat imprecise way of pointing to something that is truly important. When 'Horace' is laying out the 'serious' part of his programme, restraining himself to the limits of Aristotelian propriety, he is cheating: he presents his satire as more innocent and more respectable than it is. It is presented as non-violent, well-bred, and modest in its aspirations (not aspiring to the status of poetry). Yet he also has an interest in making his satire into something more than this, and even to let slip, in his programme, that it is more, i.e. that it is poetry with aggressive humour.

An unruly joke at the border of the programmatic satire—thus almost outside 'the document'—is the perfect way to achieve this paradoxical end. In this manner Horace can have it both ways: the modest, innocent programme has been spelled out, and its negation is stated as well, in the form of an almost involuntary laugh. With this final laugh the satirist declares that he would like to be peaceful, but if you do not accept him, he also knows how to be violent.[48] Still, 'Horace' can escape full responsibility for the comic ending by disguising it as light-hearted. The joke will out in the end ... but it is 'only a joke'.

There follows 1.5, the journey together with Maecenas, and with fellow poets, such as Virgil and Varius: a poetic journey parodically connecting to the grand sailings of epic. Simultaneously, Horace is also challenging his predecessor in his own genre by attempting to write a better on-the-road satire than Lucilius had done. As I construe this satire, it is the depiction of an ideal life with poetry, friendship, and humour; it is 'Horace''s declaration of his chosen identity and his insistence on its dignity. With its non-aligned

[47] Oesterlen, *Humor bei Horaz*, 31: 'was kann der Eindruck ... anders sein, als daß Horaz, auch wo er ganz ernsthaft anfängt, oder ernst werden will, von dem Genius seiner Komik und seines Humors erfaßt und zu den ausgelassensten Sprüngen fortgerissen wird!'

[48] This pirouette is repeated in another programmatic satire, 2.1 (vv. 39–46).

humour, 1.5 takes up and supports the meaning of the final joke of the preceding piece: satire is poetry and its humour will not be tamed down into a polished instrument of moral education.

How to praise your two different fathers at once (1.6)

After such a comprehensive journey, it is time for a new, fresh start, which follows in the next satire, 1.6. This is also the first poem in the second half of the book as a whole, an apt place for an emphatic statement.[49] Thus there is another address to Maecenas, the dedicatee of the book, just as there was one at the opening of 1.1. The two addresses are, however, different. The first was simply a gesture to invite Maecenas as the satirist's prime listener, a gesture not entailing any description of the addressee's character or of the relationship between poet and patron; the second address introduces a discourse on the closeness between Maecenas and 'Horace'. It is as if the relationship between 'Horace' and his patron had developed over the span of the satires; while there were only two (rather timid) references to Maecenas up to 1.5,[50] after that road travelled down together the references to the patron become more frequent, more extended, and more openly affectionate, though often with a comic tinge.

A picture of the great patron is an important ingredient in 1.6, for one of its main themes is 'Horace''s odium-provoking friendship with Maecenas, another main theme being 'Horace''s low birth. These two points, which an unsympathetic public uses to accuse 'Horace', are accompanied by his arguments of defence, namely that his freedman father was an excellent person, and that his closeness with Maecenas is on the one hand well deserved, on the other hand not indicative of excessive social ambition. 1.6 is directed against ambition, but the satire is also the manifestation of the poet's new relationship with Maecenas, so close now as to invite the envy of Rome. To praise both noble Maecenas and his freedman

---

[49] Just as it is in Virgil's *Eclogues*, the elegant model of Alexandrian patterning in Roman literature. See Zetzel, 'The Structure of Ambiguity', 66–7.

[50] Apart from the address in 1.1 a sketch in 1.3.63–6, where 'Horace', interrupting Maecenas, exemplifies the somewhat unrefined character who is nevertheless lovable.

father, to reject ambition and to glory in his own admission to the great patron's circle—bringing these themes together was not easy. The satirist employs gliding and redefinition to solve the problem,[51] but he also resorts to comic juxtapposition.

While praising Maecenas, 'Horace' also mocks him, presumably just in the right measure for the mockery to look like the aristocratic bantering between equals.[52] So the degrading metaphor of 'naso suspendis adunco' ('turn your nose up', but literally 'weigh by hanging on your hooked nose'), v. 5, is certainly meant as a teasing hint at Maecenas' aquiline nose, although the phrase refers to what he does *not* do.[53] Again, the fact that the poem begins with praise of Maecenas because of his high birth, and ends with praise of the satirist, whose low-class life is said to be much more pleasant than high-class life, seems to contain a humorous nudge. There is even a verbal echo in the word *avus* ('grandfather'), which ties the two passages closer together (used in connection with 'Horace' at v. 3, in connection with Maecenas at v. 131).

In this satire, Horace jokingly plays out the ambivalence between two attitudes towards his social status. On the one hand, 'Horace' protests against people who believe that his low birth precludes a career (1–21). On the other hand, he insists that he himself is unwilling to rise above his original status (22–44). The first harsh clash between these two attitudes comes in v. 22. Before this verse (in vv. 15–21), the satirist derided those who only care about descent, and said that if he himself would have attempted social climbing, Appius the Censor would have expelled him. Here, he suddenly declares 'vel merito, quoniam non in propria pelle quiessem' ('and he would have been right, since I wouldn't have rested quietly in my

---

[51] Gliding with regard to his father's acceptability in Maecenas' eyes (although he was not a freeborn man); see Christes and Fülle, 'Causa fuit pater his', for a discussion of this twist. Redefinition in the careful differentiation between a political career and the closeness to Maecenas (esp. vv. 49–50).

[52] For the joking culture at Rome, see F. Graf, 'Cicero, Plautus and Roman Laughter', in J. Bremmer and J. Roodenburg (eds.), *A Cultural History of Humour* (Cambridge: Polity, 1997); and (better) Vogt-Spira, 'Das satirische Lachen der Römer'.

[53] The dive from the lofty style of the opening lines to the amost vulgar 'naso suspendis adunco' is noted in Kießling and Heinze, *Satiren*, ad loc.; for the suggestion that Maecenas' nose is particularly being meant see Bernardi Perini, 'Suspendere naso', 244–8, with references.

own skin'), 22. There is dramatic surprise after a beginning which teased the reader to believe that 'Horace' was going to claim his right to a social career.[54]

Near the centre of the satire, in the charming description of the poet's first encounter with Maecenas (52–62), the text suggests by its imagery that Maecenas' decision to take up 'Horace' into his circle is equivalent to a second birth:

> Vergilius, post hunc Varius dixere quid essem.
> ut veni coram, singultim pauca locutus
> (infans namque pudor prohibebat plura profari),
> non ego me claro natum patre, non ego circum
> me Satureiano vectari rura caballo,
> sed quod eram narro. respondes, ut tuus est mos,
> pauca. abeo; et revocas nono post mense iubesque
> esse in amicorum numero.   (1.6.55–62)

Virgil, and then Varius spoke to you about what I was. When I came before you, I spoke a few words, stammering—for my speechless shyness hindered me from saying any more. I didn't pretend that I was born of a distinguished father, nor that I rode around my country estates on a Tarentine nag. No, I told you what I was. You answered with a few words, as is your habit. I left. You called me back after nine months and bade me be one of your friends.

Thus on his first visit, arranged by Virgil and Varius, 'Horace' could only stammer a few words, impeded by his 'speechless' shyness ('*infans* namque pudor prohibebat plura profari'), and afterwards he had to wait nine months for Maecenas to become his second father, 'revocas *nono post mense* iubesque | esse in amicorum numero'.[55] Later, in *Epistle* 1.7.37–8, 'Horace' will claim that he has often piously called Maecenas 'father'.[56] Here, in *S.* 1.6,

---

[54] Brown, *Horace: Satires I*, 152. Cf. also my discussion above, in the section 'Horace: Profitable self-irony'

[55] Henderson (*Writing down Rome*, 184) notes the 'nine months' mental gestation', but does not discuss it further. Similarly C. Schlegel ('Horace and his Fathers: Satires 1.4 and 1.6', *AJP* 121 (2000), 110), who however adds the important observation that: '*Infans* describes both speechlessness and the state of infancy, the situation of the newborn is marked by its relation to language.' Of this newborn in particular— 'Horace' is being born anew *as a poet*.

[56] *Ep.* 1.7.37–8: 'saepe verecundum laudasti rexque *pater*que | audisti coram, nec verbo paucius absens' ('You often praised me for my modesty. You heard me calling you "patron" and "father" to your face; I called you nothing less when you were not present'); cf. Braund, *Roman Satire*, 26.

'Horace' emerges as a fully developed friend of Maecenas—which of course means that he is a poet—and he uses speech, now at his command, to praise his benefactor:

> Magnum hoc ego duco
> quod placui tibi, qui turpi secernis honestum,
> non patre praeclaro sed vita et pectore puro.   (1.6.62–4)

I consider it a great thing that I won the favour of a man like you, a man separating the honourable from the foul, and that I did so not by a splendid father, but by the purity of my life and heart.

He then praises his own *character* (avoiding the mention of *poetry*), exaggeratedly flauting his moral purity, even with the obviously ironic parenthesis 'ut me collaudem' ('to praise myself'), 70, and then explains that this is all due to his biological father's efforts. Yet earlier 'Horace' has expressly said that Maecenas was not interested in who your father was, as long as you were yourself freeborn: 'cum referre negas quali sit quisque parente | natus, dum ingenuus' ('When you say that it doesn't matter who a man's father was, as long as he himself is freeborn'), 7–8. After this, the glowing praise of his biological father rings slightly mocking towards Maecenas. Here is lavish praise of a person who would, according to explicit previous information, not please Maecenas. The biological father was (1) not a freeborn man, and he was (2) 'Horace's' *father*, exactly the category Maecenas did not care about.

There are further incongruities about the real father. Despite the satirist's earlier stance that one should 'rest quietly in one's own hide', his father is commended on giving 'Horace' the education of a senator's son (72–8) and making him look rich at school (78–80).

Finally, 'Horace' asserts that even if Nature would offer one a choice of new parents at a certain age, he would never want another, nobler father (93–9). But such a second, nobler father is exactly what he has acquired in Maecenas. He has recounted this acquisition in this very satire. The merry, non-aligned humour covers up the awkwardness.

Thus while the satirist had only one father in 1.4, before accompanying Maecenas on the journey of 1.5, he now has two. With the double gratitude comes double trouble, especially since the two fathers are, to say the least, very different. For the arrangement and presentation of this new picture of his family, Horace needs all his tricks of the trade, including humour jets in the seemingly wrong direction.

The muddy authority of Lucilius (1.10)

As regards 1.10, a programme satire, I would like to assert that its humorous incongruities are altogether in line with the non-aligned humour of the other programme satire of the first book, 1.4. In both cases the satirist claims two intense, contradictory positions for himself and his satire. In 1.4 he claims that he is no poet *and* that he is one; about his humour that it is not aggressive *and* that it is. In 1.10 he offers both high praise *and* fierce criticism of Lucilius as a satirist. In both cases he places the incompatible statements alongside one another within the same satire, and uses paradoxical humour to connect them.

At the opening of S. 1.10 Lucilius is attacked for the excessive quantity of his work and his negligence of form, as well as for the unnecessary affectation of mixing Greek and Latin. After having stated his own decision to write satire, 'Horace' suddenly declares that he is a lesser writer than the *inventor* of the genre, Lucilius, and that he would not dare to tear down the crown of honour from Lucilius' head.

> inventore minor: neque ego illi detrahere ausim
> haerentem capiti cum multa laude coronam.   (1.10.48–9)

though I'm below the inventor [of the genre]. I wouldn't presume to tear down the crown that clings so gloriously to his head.

The only good thing 'Horace' has said of Lucilius so far in 1.10 is that he rubbed down Rome with the salt of his wit (3–4). But then so did Laberius, and one could not praise his mimes as if they were beautiful poetry (5–6). In everything else Lucilius has only been carped upon, and rather sharply at that. The lines awarding him a place above 'Horace' are so sudden as to be almost comic, an effect that is strengthened by the words 'illi detrahere' ('snatch from him', lit. 'tear down from him'). These words conjure up an image of the squat Horace stretching out his arms to haul down the crown sticking to the head of a bust—even though he tells us that this is exactly what he dare *not* do. The unexpected praise is immediately followed by the next sharp turn, for now 'Horace' blurts out that he did, however, say that Lucilius flowed like a muddy stream, often carrying more unnecessary things than necessary:

> At dixi fluere hunc lutulentum, saepe ferentem
> plura quidem tollenda relinquendis.   (1.10.50–1)

But I did say that he flowed like a muddy stream, often carrying along more to be removed than retained.

The two statements are pressingly close, and a mean, derisive judgement will make the greater impact if placed side by side with a laudatory one. Given this, it is legitimate to wonder whether one of the things better lifted off Lucilius (*tollenda*) is not his crown. The satire then continues in the same jumping vein.

When summarized, these widely differing evaluations of Lucilius (which are layered upon each other throughout) result in the wrong picture. Commentators tend to say that although Horace expresses respect for Lucilius as a humorist and as the founder of satire, he claims that he himself is the better craftsman.[57] Something like this must no doubt be the answer to the question of what opinion on Lucilius Horace manifests in 1.10. But does this mean that such an answer is also the explanation of the meaning and effect of *Satire* 1.10? Absolutely not. The alternation of humour directed at Lucilius, at 'Horace', or at a third party (such as the jibe at Laberius or the comic simile about Arbuscula the mime-actress) does not amount to their mutual annihilation. Rather, the sprawling bursts of humour make up a delicate balance where the extremes *are still present* in the picture, though they are necessarily lost when the 'statement' of the satire is paraphrased.

My argument about both 1.4 and 1.10, the two programmatic satires in Book 1, is that humour enables Horace to keep both poles in a superficially unobtrusive manner, with a conveniently double effect. The theoretical sum of each satire will be a moderate statement. Still, the extremes are there to render the picture vivid,

---

[57] e.g. Rudd, 'Libertas and facetus'; Brown, *Horace: Satires I*, 182–3; Barbieri, 'Praeco-poeta'.

and to suggest the complex fullness of life, or as in the case of 1.4 and 1.10, the fullness of satire as a genre for the depiction of life. In addition, the lingering presence of the extreme position will justify the satirist should he wish to behave in accordance with any of these extremes elsewhere. He can, for instance, include some aggressive humour, for he did after all claim aggressive humour as his own, albeit in comic form. A joke is an excellent way of both saying and not saying a thing at the same time, a most useful device for a genre which constantly had to pose as bolder and more single-minded than it was.

In Book 2 non-aligned humour multiplies. This book is more ironic than the first, rerunning the material of the previous book in various polyvalent ways, raging from respectful allusion to derision.[58] Arguments double, turn back on themselves, mirror each other in not-quite accurate ways, often comically. The sprinkles of non-aligned humour that were only occasional occurrences in Book 1 are a palpable presence in Book 2, threatening to dissolve the satiric direction of several poems. One of the main devices to create this pervasive but fleeting humour is the use of dialogues—all satires here except 2.6 are cast in this form—much more real and vivid than the dialogic passages of the first book.

Horace experiments with the role of the satirical persona, often by leaving an interlocutor named 'Horace' but giving the bulk of the message to the other interlocutor, who becomes what I have called a 'secondary persona',[59] and gets to stand in as the satire's guarantor. It has been observed that these secondary personae are lower down on the social scale than Horace was by this time.[60] What is more is that their social/mental/moral status is often suspect, and they become *unreliable guarantors* for the message they speak. These constellations open up for humour in different directions, but are potentially disastrous for the message: if the speaker of a moral lesson is a fool and/or a crook, then his lesson may be (1) nonsense, (2) the opposite of a lesson, i.e. a bad example that turns out to be the real object of the satire, (3) a valid lesson nonetheless, or (4) any mixture

[58] See Oliensis, *Rhetoric of Authority*.
[59] In Ch. 1 § 'Horace: lowered subject'.
[60] Oliensis, 'Horace, Nasidienus', 95–6.

of these. To navigate between these possible meanings becomes one of the challenges involved in reading the looking-glass world of *Sermones* Book 2.

In order to avoid repetition, and to limit my discussion of non-aligned humour in the second book to a manageable amount of examples, I propose to highlight the narrative frames of the individual poems, i.e. their beginnings and/ or endings, and explore their consequences for the humour involved. The device of unreliable guarantors will be central to the discussion. Other passages than those in the frame will occasionally be brought in where this seems necessary.

Mock-consultations: peace-loving violence and an unreliable seer (2.1; 2.5)

The tone is set in the opening poem, 2.1, Horace's third and last programmatic satire, this time shaped as a consultation of the lawyer Trebatius about the writing of satire. To 'Horace''s complaints about negative reactions to this genre Trebatius offers the mixture of warnings and unacceptable advice—the usual interlocutor's lines in programmatic satires from Lucilius to Juvenal.[61] Dismissing all the interlocutor's arguments, 'Horace' insists on his satire in its present form, and comically escapes Trebatius' last warning, that there is a law against malicious incantations, *mala carmina*, with a pun and a reference to Augustus, whereupon Trebatius has to admit the triumph of the satirist's humour. The implications of this closing 'programmatic joke' have been discussed above,[62] here I would like to draw attention to the element of aggressive humour, familiar from the dispute about it in 1.4, and to the role of Trebatius. When accused of aggression in his satire this time (2.1.21), 'Horace' answers that he cannot do anything else, this is his nature (24–9), and then draws a picture of himself as a Venusian, living on the border of different territories and prepared to fight off either (37–9). Tongue in cheek he

---

[61] Cf. Shero, 'The Satirist's Apologia'; Kenney, 'The First Satire of Juvenal'; Griffith, 'Juvenal's First Satire and Lucilius'; and Introduction § 'Programmatic statements on humour in Roman satire'.

[62] Under 'Programmatic jokes—the hidden agenda of ambiguity'.

reassures his interlocutor and audience that although his pen may be compared to a sword for self-defence, he would prefer it to rust away, peaceful as he is (39–44). In the next line he adds that should someone attack him, they will cry (45–6).[63] This is the same mocking fusion of a declaration of peace with the warning of potential violence as we have already seen at the end of 1.4, only much louder here. This is the satirist's terror control, characteristically clad in laughter, as the ensuing examples of counter-attack show (47–56). Lucilius had been associated with the sharp derision of Old Comedy in 1.4, here this aspect of him is described with a strong metaphor when it is said that he used to flay his victims:

> primus in hunc operis componere carmina morem
> detrahere et pellem, nitidus qua quisque per ora
> cederet, introrsum turpis   (2.1.63–5)

He was the first to compose poetry of this kind, and to strip off the skin in which each went sleekly groomed in public, while inwardly foul.

Even in the last joke, seemingly conciliatory, 'Horace' uses the Cynic dog joke of himself (2.1.84–5), thus remaining a potentially angry canine.

Far from being proved false, the accusation of aggressive humour is all but confirmed in the Trebatius satire, and non-aligned humour is used to confuse the accusers. This teasing about whether he will use aggressive humour or not lies wholly with 'Horace'. The interlocutor's role is passive, and even somewhat naïve in that he is made to understand several lines too literally.[64] The consultation is thus a mock-consultation, where the consultant ('Horace') knows all the answers and the advisor (Trebatius) gives impossible suggestions. Trebatius' only really important contribution lies, I believe, in his

---

[63] Elliott (*The Power of Satire*, 124) points out that Horace's formulation is reminiscent of a fragment of Archilochus.

[64] Thus to 'Horace's' tongue-in-cheek complaint that he cannot sleep if he does not write satire (vv. 6–7) Trebatius answers with concrete advice about remedies of insomnia (7–9), and when 'Horace' declines to sing Augustus' praise in epic because of a lack of creative powers, surely saying, politely, that he does not want to write about Augustus' merits at all (12–15), Trebatius ingenuously suggests praising the ruler's justice and fortitude (16–17). LaFleur ('The Law of Satire', 1802 n. 31) and Anderson ('Roman Socrates', 31–2) consider Trebatius to be represented as somewhat silly, *contra* Kenney, 'The First Satire of Juvenal', 37.

final admission that 'Horace''s humour will carry the day, freeing him in a court as the accusation is dissolved in laughter. As an expert of law, the famous jurist is adduced as a guarantor of the satirist's humorous success, but also as an internal audience, providing the reader with a cue as to where to laugh.[65] The picture at the end suggests that 'Horace''s humour leads to the dissolution of the accusations against him. Book 2, then, begins with an inverted consultation, and an accusation of aggressive humour which comes close to being confirmed—but which is overridden by laughter. If read carefully, 2.1 already suggests that humour will be an independent authority.

The opening mock-consultation is matched by an even less serious consultation in 2.5, at the beginning of the second half of the book: the encounter between Ulysses and Teiresias in the underworld.[66] This dialogue has been discussed as an example of object-oriented humour above;[67] here we must stress its speakers' unreliability, an inversion of what is expected of a consultation in the underworld. In 2.1, the advice offered by Trebatius did not seem useful to the consultant, but the advice of Teiresias is much worse still: his prescriptions about how to fish for legacies are clearly so (morally) bad advice as to become the object of the satire. From a moral point of view his speech is unreliable. Generally, Teiresias is the most obviously unreliable guarantor in Book 2. Yet as regards his description of the conditions among the living—how people yearn for money, how they are blind to their faults, how all virtue has its price—his analysis must be regarded as correct. Since this description is comic, and Teiresias' speech thus reveals the moral corruption of the contemporary scene, he may properly be said to play the role of a satirist from this point of view. Furthermore, he is a *vates* ('both *poet* and *seer*') inspired by Apollo, and these are qualities that allude to Horace himself. The role of satirist-poet would require his speech to be reliable. There is at least one passage where Teiresias' general

---

[65] Cf. Horace's (later) famous dictum about the need for picturing the reaction one wants from one's audience: 'ut ridentibus arrident, ita flentibus afflent | humani vultus' (*Ars* 101–2).

[66] Boll, 'Anordnung im zweiten Buch', 143–4; Braund, *Roman Satire*, 23.

[67] See Ch. 1 § 'The satirical sequel to the epic conversation between Odysseus and Teiresias'.

reliability is crucial for the meaning, and this is the short, lofty-styled prophecy about Augustus' reign:

> Tempore quo iuvenis Parthis horrendus, ab alto
> demissum genus Aenea, tellure marique
> magnus erit ...   (2.5.62–4)

In a time when a young man, feared by the Parthians, of Aeneas' noble line, will be a great ruler over land and sea ...

If the speaker is reliable, Augustus is praised; if not, he is mocked. Even if we set aside the latter possibility as improbable, the shadow of mockery still lingers on to complicate the picture. But the implications of the questionable reliability of Teiresias as a caricature of the satirical persona and as a guarantor for the moral message are more far-reaching still: they make the whole genre suspect, undermining its very frame. In fact, the comic undercutting of satire's frame, i.e. the moral authority of its guarantors, is what haunts and enlivens most of the poems of this book. Teiresias says that through a gift of Apollo everything he says will either come true or not (59–60). The careful placement of this utterance points to the non-coincidental quality of this play with speech authority. In this way, paradoxically, Teiresias, the seer speaking from the middle of the book and from the realm of the dead, both traditional *loci* of authority, fulfils the expectations of an important utterance. He reveals a central characteristic about these satires when he points to the dubious reliability of its guarantors, and thus to their dubious reliability in general. The use of the comic here is programmatic—the satires in Book 2 are humorous not only despite their moral ambiguity, but also through it. Often they contain this kind of 'meta-humour', which jokes about the conventions of satire rather than deriding vitiated objects.

Epicurean secondary personae: fat-headed Ofellus, silly Catius, and a mouse (2.2; 2.4; 2.6)

Among the unreliable guarantors scattered throughout Book 2 there are several dubious Epicureans (2.2, 2.4, 2.6) and two fanatic Stoics (2.3, 2.7). The Epicurean to appear first, Ofellus, gets to speak the bulk of 2.2, a satire that is traditionally interpreted as 'serious' in its moral message. The satire is a sermon on the 'simple life', with most of its examples drawn from the area of food. While the style of the poem is not adapted to Ofellus' persona,[68] and while the admonition to live simply and even the prominence of *mensa tenuis*[69] are decidedly Horatian traits, it must nevertheless be noticed that Horace strongly distances himself from his speaker in the opening lines:

> (nec meus his sermo est, sed quae praecepit Ofellus
> rusticus, abnormis sapiens crassaque Minerva)   (2.2.2–3)

(these are not my own words, but the teachings of the farmer Ofellus, an irregular sage with a fat head)

The attributes describing Ofellus in this presentation are usually smoothed over as unusual rather than truly pejorative, but their negative connotations should not be disregarded, especially when they are accumulated as here. *Rusticus* ('rustic, of the country') is associated with roughness and boorishness, and is particularly suspect in the context of satire, an urban genre celebrating the quality of *urbanitas*. The fact that *rusticitas* is also associated with the healthy life of the countryside does not totally outweigh the negative ring of the word. *Abnormis* is difficult because found only here in classical Latin, but judging from analogous constructions seems to mean 'foreign to the norm', 'irregular'. When paired with *sapiens* it creates a comic effect, pointing both to the doubleness of the satire and to a certain ridiculousness in Ofellus.[70] The ridicule is particularly underlined by the final attribute, stressed by its position in the clause as well as in the verse: *crassa Minerva*. The expression *crassa Minerva* is found elsewhere in Latin literature, e.g. in *Priapea* 3.10. There are also analogous expressions such as *pingui Minerva* (Cic. *Lael.* 19; Colum. I praef. 35) and *crassiore Musa* (Quint. I.10.28). To judge from these uses, the function of the phrase must be a humorous transference of thought. The idea of a 'fat' (= silly, dull) intellect is transferred to the image of Minerva, the godhead in charge of the intellect—since Horace's speaker is a 'fathead', he is jokingly called a

---

[68] F. Muecke, *Horace: Satires II*, 114; cf. Kießling and Heinze, *Satiren*, 193.

[69] Mette, 'Genus tenue—mensa tenuis'.

[70] Thus I find it difficult to agree with F. Muecke's confident statement that the 'collocation of words is not meant as criticism of Ofellus' (*Horace: Satires II*, ad loc.).

man 'with a fat Minerva'.[71] In fact, in another satire Horace asks that the talent of his own persona not be made fat, *pingue*: 'pingue pecus domino facias et cetera praeter | ingenium' ('make my cattle fat, and everything else too, except my brain'), 2.6.14–15, thus clearly indicating that 'fat' as applied to an intellectual quality is negative in his universe. Read together, as it stands, a description amounting to 'rustic Ofellus, an irregular sage with a fat head' seems to undermine the wisdom of the speaker considerably, and suggest more than 'a Platonic distancing device'.[72] It must also be noted that 'Horace' says that this sage's words are not his *sermo*, playing on the double meaning of the word as both 'speech' and 'satire'. Ofellus should not unproblematically be taken as the mouthpiece of Horace.[73] The seriousness of this sermon still outweighs the humour undercutting it, but the satirist is no longer willing to speak his diatribes directly, as he was in Book 1. The destabilizing, non-aligned humour against the guarantor of this satire is not yet fatal to the overall meaning, but it is a step in the direction of more severe destabilizing, especially if seen in connection with the other Epicurean speakers in this book.

The second Epicurean guarantor, Catius, speaks in 2.4, a satire on the right arrangement of food, which is not usually taken seriously at face value. While the poem has even been construed as metaphorically speaking about the writing of satire, the common reading remains taking it as criticism of the triviality of Catius' 'wisdom', or more specifically of his trivial interpretation of Epicureanism.[74]

Like Ofellus, Catius does not explicitly call himself a follower of Epicurus, he only emerges as such from the contents of his reasoning. Other points of kinship between the two speakers should be noticed: Catius is also introduced as a kind of philosopher, and both Catius' and Ofellus' speech centres on food. Where Ofellus spoke of *tenuis victus* ('simple food', 2.2.53, 2.2.70) Catius speaks of *tenuis res, tenuis*

---

[71] So Kießling and Heinze, *Satiren*, ad loc.

[72] F. Muecke, *Horace: Satires II*, 114.   [73] Cf. Anderson, *Essays*, 44.

[74] For the idea that the food discussed in 2.4 stands for writing, see Gowers, *Loaded Table*; for 2.4 as a critique of Catius Rudd, *Satires of Horace*, 207–13 (Catius accused of pedantry, conceit, and second-hand knowledge); for Catius accused of a banal brand of Epicureanism, Coffey, *Roman Satire*, 85, Classen, 'Horace—a Cook?'.

ratio, and even *tenuis sermo* (2.4.9, 2.4.36, 2.4.9).[75] He thereby steps
closer to a parody of a satirist, as the simple life is translated via food
into the simple/ fine language that was the hallmark of Horace's
satire (*sermo*). In all these respects Catius is the continuation of
Ofellus' laughable qualities: he is even sillier, even more concerned
with the material matter of food, and at the same time even more
pretentious as to philosophy. Ofellus' introduction as a fat-headed
sage may be compared with the lines with which Catius introduces
himself:

> 'Non est mihi tempus aventi
> ponere signa novis praeceptis, qualia vincent
> Pythagoran Anytique reum doctumque Platona.'   (2.4.1–3)

I have no time, for I'm eager to write down this new teaching, which is of
such a quality that it will outdo Pythagoras and the man accused in Athens
and the learned Plato.

Catius is all loaded with new philosophical knowledge. The humour
suddenly explodes at v. 12, where it is at last revealed that the subject
of this superb philosophy is cooking. In this satire Horace has
thoroughly distanced himself from the speaker, and the mockery of
Catius is much more pronounced than was the mockery of Ofellus.
Catius as guarantor is not only ridiculed, but also said to be a
secondary expounder of his message. He is only retelling (perhaps
inaccurately) the words of a master. Catius refuses to disclose the
name of his master, which further undercuts the message of the
satire: 'celabitur auctor' ('the author will remain secret'), 11. Nobody
takes the responsibility for this poem's message, its *auctor* will remain
hidden, while the extant speaker is derided. Non-aligned humour is
beginning to deconstruct the moral message of Horace's satire.

The last Epicurean to be encountered in this book has shrunk in
importance to a mere caricature to be dismissed, and to the size of a
mouse: this is the urban mouse in the fable of the two mice, inset in
2.6 (vv. 79–117). Dismayed by the poverty of a meal he is treated to by
the rustic mouse, the urban mouse invites his country friend to the

---

[75] ('Refined things'), ('a refined manner'), and ('simple/ refined language'). In the
last expression, *tenuis sermo*, *tenuis* means both 'simple' and 'refined, elegant' (from
the sense of not being heavy, overloaded); *sermo* means 'speech' and 'conversation',
but is also the technical term for 'satire' and the title of Horace's work (*Sermones*).

house where he lives, in order to taste the good life. As has been noted, his short speech presents him as a perfect Epicurean, equipped with arguments on the shortness of life and the inevitability of death, and considerably reminiscent of Horace himself:[76]

> tandem urbanus ad hunc 'quid te iuvat' inquit, 'amice,
> praerupti nemoris patientem vivere dorso?
> vis tu homines urbemque feris praeponere silvis?
> carpe viam, mihi crede, comes. terrestria quando
> mortalis animas vivunt sortita neque ulla est
> aut magno aut parvo leti fuga—quo, bone, circa,
> dum licet, in rebus iucundis vive beatus,
> vive memor quam sis aevi brevis'   (2.6.90–7)

At last the town city mouse turned to him and said: 'Listen, my friend, why do you like to suffer through your life on a steep wooded ridge? Wouldn't you want to exchange the wild woods for life among human beings in the city? Come along with me—trust me! The creatures of the earth are fated to live with mortal souls, and neither large nor small can escape death. So live happily, my good man, and enjoy all pleasures while you may. But live without forgetting how short your life is.

His philosophy, attractive though it sounds, is proved untenable. The good life turns out to be too dangerous. The mice are scared away from the rich leftovers by the master's Molossian hounds—competing parasites, as Braund has acutely pointed out.[77]

The episode ends with the country mouse repudiating this kind of life and returning to its home in the woods. In the case of the town mouse, the Epicurean philosophy has slipped into the more vulgar ideal of 'sweet life' ('rebus iucundis vive beatus') rather than 'simple life'. Still, this minute Epicurean is surely meant to recall Horace's persona with his interest in friendship, his seductive speech, his invitation to a feast, and finally his parasitism at the rich man's table. The mouse's Epicurean outlook may be brought to shame here, but his finely sculpted personality lingers on as one of the two aspects of 'Horace', here comically represented by two rodents. This is clearly one of Horace's comic doubles, where what is essentially one

---

[76] So West, 'Of Mice and Men'.

[77] S. H. Braund (ed.), *Satire and Society in Ancient Rome* (Exeter: University of Exeter, 1989), 42.

character is split in two forms, who turn on each other in dialogue.[78] The humour involved has completely broken down the authority of Epicureanism, and seems more interested in exploring the inner complexities and incongruities of a personality.

Stoic secondary personae: Damasippus and Davus at the Saturnalia (2.3; 2.7)

The two Stoics, unlike the Epicureans, have no authority to start with, and only get to speak in the time of the Saturnalia (2.3.4–5; 2.7.4). In 2.3 this is the bankrupted merchant Damasippus, who explains his interest in morals with the remark that no longer having any business of his own, he interferes with that of others (2.3.19–20). In 2.7 the Stoic speaker is 'Horace''s slave Davus, who gets to utter the wisdom he has picked up from the janitor of Crispinus. In both poems 'Horace' is made the object of the satires—as should be in the inverted festival of the Saturnalia. In the first case the theme is the Stoic tenet that all men except the *sapiens* are mad, in the second case the tenet that all men except the *sapiens* are slaves. Both satires have been read invertedly, so that 'Horace''s is still taken to be the real mocker, while Damasippus and Davus (respectively) are seen as really being the objects of their satires.[79] However, the opposite interpretation has also been made, claiming that the Stoic speakers, though imperfect, are still made to stand in for the satirist and allowed to utter some valid points.[80] There is material for both interpretations in the text. Those who claim that the satires should be understood backwards can point to the disrespectable characters of the preachers, to Horace's mockery of Stoics in these satires and elsewhere, to the disturbing pattern of 'Horace' being made the object of their criticism, and to the abnormal state of the Saturnalia. Those of the other interpretation can say that some of the speakers' points are moderate and commonsensical rather than exclusively

---

[78] See above, the introduction to § 'Horace: optical grey—the balance of extremes'.

[79] Cf. Coffey, *Roman Satire*, 83–4, 88–9.

[80] Oesterlen, *Humor bei Horaz*, esp. 67–78, 90–6; M. J. McGann, 'The Three Worlds of Horace's Satires', in C. D. N. Costa *Horace* (ed.), (London and Boston: Routledge & Kegan Paul, 1973), 73–81.

Stoic, that some of these points are made by 'Horace' himself elsewhere, that the Saturnalia need not signal abnormality but may rather suggest the treasured free speech, *libertas*, of satire. It seems that the status of Damasippus and Davus as guarantors for their messages is mixed, featuring both authorizing and undercutting elements.

The employment of Saturnalia canonizes 'Horace''s position as a satirical persona by suggesting that it is so well established as the workaday norm that it will be inverted during the festival. At the same time, it borrows some of the festival's aura of merry freedom to the satires where it features. It is a clever device which, just like joking, allows the poet to say something and 'unsay' it in the same move. Screened by both Saturnalia and humour Horace may thus explore difficult inconsistencies in his persona, such as the sexual promiscuity of which both Stoics accuse him (2.3.325; 2.7.46, 53–67, 89–94),[81] and above all his dependence on Maecenas (2.3.307–20; 2.7.32–5, 75–6, 81–2, cf. vv.111–15).

The last point is brilliantly exploited in 2.7 in particular, where it can be integrated with Davus' status as a slave, as well as with his argument that all men are slaves.[82] The satirist's friendship with Maecenas is so well established in the second book as to allow some non-aligned humour to tease it,[83] whereas this kind of humour only helped to build it in the first book. Again, the Saturnalian teasing of this relationship both confirms its canonicity and vents its problem, the conflict between 'Horace''s alleged independence and his relationship with Maecenas.

In his excellent analysis of Saturnalia and servitude in 2.7, Bernstein has shown that Horace uses Davus' Saturnalian voice to

---

[81] 'Horace''s inconsistency as to sexual behaviour is discussed in Önnerfors, *Vaterporträts in der römischen Poesie*, 135–6. Cf. also G. Highet, ('Masks and Faces in Satire', *Hermes* 102 (1974), 321–37), who speaks of 'sharp contradictions and serious inconsistencies' filling the *Sermones*. Highet contrasts the preaching of 1.2 with Davus' accusation that Horace is an adulterer, but solves the problem by turning to Horace's biographical person and imputing a contradictory character to him

[82] Cf. my discussion of the Davus satire (in regard to Horatian self-irony) in Ch. 2 § 'Harsh self-humour: the mocker mocked'.

[83] See Seeck, 'Horaz und seine Leser', for a sensitive discussion of the pros and cons of having a powerful millionaire for one's best friend, including the problem of how to joke with/ about such a friend.

smuggle in the serious accusation of servility among easily repudi-
ated accusations of gluttony and fickleness. Horace is thus able to
vent and at least partially acknowledge his real 'anxiety about his
ascendancy into the inner circle of Rome's rulers',[84] and then use his
legitimate denial of the other points to get himself absolved from this
one as well, through 'innocence by association'. The satirist is also
protected by a refuge to irony guaranteed by the Saturnalian context.
Rather than strictly inverting the roles of Horace and his slave,
Bernstein sees this literary Saturnalia as spinning round all roles so
that the accusations of servitude and self-deception adhere to all
actors in the end.

What then, of satire as a form, and the slave-as-satirist over his
master? It seems to me that in the Davus satire, the wildly unfocused
humour suggests mockery of the genre as a whole. Satire is implied to
be the Saturnalia, a feast that will end and send the satirist back to his
slavery, with his comfort-prize of momentary derision. What he says
will not change the world. Yet there is also another aspect. Although
'Horace' allows Davus to speak at the beginning of the poem (2.7.1–
5) and stops his speech at the end of it, his closure is not altogether
convincing as the rightful return of the norm. Rather, unable to stand
the satirical accusations any longer, 'Horace' cries out that he will kill
Davus, or at least send him to the heavy work on the Sabine farm
(116–18). This mimic ending hints that Davus' verbal arrows have
found their mark, and that the mocked target of satire can do
nothing but stop Davus-as-satirist with threats of physical arrows.
This is the reaction 'Horace' himself boastingly complained about in
his programmatic poems, and it is a reaction that confirms the
validity and success of satire. By suggesting that his master is either
raving mad or writing poetry again—which for Davus may amount
to the same thing, and which is comically true in this case—Davus
gets the last witty word, while 'Horace' only gets the last word by
means of violence. This 'infinite regression of ironic mirrors'[85] makes
it very difficult to decide the resulting value of Davus' satire, for
humour moves in all directions. Here, near the end of Book 2, the
realm of Horace's humour seems to grow broader than the

---

[84] Bernstein, 'Saturnalia and Servitude', 464.
[85] F. Muecke, *Horace: Satires II*, 213.

realm of the moral critique; this is satire on the point of outgrowing itself.[86]

Canidia's last breath (2.8)

In the last poem, 2.8, Horace gives us more traditional satire again, with a clear butt in Nasidienus and humour directed at him. There are, however, small problematizing traits in the frame of this satire as well: the implication that 'Horace' was not invited to Nasidienus' dinner as his friends were (vv. 1–3),[87] and the ending, where the speaker Fundanius and his company take their revenge on the host by fleeing without eating anything, as if the witch Canidia had breathed all over the dishes (93–5). On the one hand, 'Horace' and his friends will have nothing to do with Nasidienus and Canidia, and so scorn them by fleeing from them, on the other hand, fleeing is a questionable victory. Canidia may be seen as frightening off 'Horace's' friends just like he, in the shape of Priapus, once frightened off her in *S.* 1.8. As he takes adieu of the feast of satire, the poet intimates, in a final destabilizing joke, that Canidia can have the last word, or rather the last breath, over this feast.

Before I pass on to Juvenal, something needs to be said about Persius. It is my contention that his satire does not contain non-aligned humour in an amount that would warrant discussion of it. Humour is ambivalent in itself, and this may make it possible to stretch certain humorous passages to embrace more than the immediate need of the satire's direction, but there is always a clearly discernible kernel in Persius' laughter. Usually this is the object, occasionally the persona of the satire. His humour is indeed 'satirical' in a straightforward way in that it is neatly arranged around the axis speaker–target, with heavy emphasis on the target. Attempts to find sudden turns in Persius' meaning, for instance the claim that the laughing centurions (in P. 5.189–91 and 3.86–7) are not only mocked by the author but also invite the reader to join their laughter at

---

[86] See Evans, 'Saturnalia and Satire', who takes this idea so far as to suggest that Horace ends his satire-writing with this genre-demolishing poem, and that 2.8 is not really a satire at all.

[87] See Ch. 2 § 'Satire's metaphor: the spectacle of a falling curtain'.

philosophers,[88] remain somewhat unconvincing. This Spartan arrangement of humour gives Persius the opportunity to be more ideologically concentrated than the other Roman satirists, with fewer literary features to muddle his philosophical message. He is the only one among the four to whom moral-philosophical improvement of society and mankind seems to be a primary concern, the only one who cannot risk having his semantic message undercut by unruly humour. Yet at the same time this neatness of structure places him at the border of the genre, and makes his work more two-dimensional, schematic, and closed where the satires of the others are lifelike, (seemingly) dishevelled, and open, pointing the way to the open genre *par excellence*, the novel. His lack of non-aligned humour makes him clearer and better at keeping his programmatic promises. The other Roman satirists' use of non-aligned humour makes them outgrow the narrow limits of explicit satirical programmes and step into another ambition. This is the epic ambition of describing the human condition in the world with everything in it—but, unlike epic, on a purely human level. Given the fantastic ambition, there always remained much to be done, the project seemed unfinished. In the realm of satire it may not be coincidental that Persius, in his finality, never became the fountainhead for later satirical writing, whereas both Horace and Juvenal were taken as models, for Horatian and Juvenalian satire respectively.[89]

All of these questions will be further discussed in connection with Juvenal and in the conclusion of this chapter. Here I would like to point to a particularly striking example of Persius' technique of satirical humour, namely a recurring move of narrowing and concentration of meaning in his allusions to Horace's satires. Generally, allusions tend to multiply meaning, and humorous allusions usually multiply humour, but in Persius it seems to be the other way around.

Persius repeatedly *reduces* the ambiguity when he alludes to Horace's ironic *Sermones*. One example is Persius' serious treatment of the Stoic tenet 'only the wise man is free' in P. 5, which is a poem based on Horace's slippery Davus satire, S. 2.7. Where Horace complicated his position by giving the sermon to the slave Davus—who

---

[88] Cf. Ch. 1 n. 97.   [89] See Weber, 'Comic Humour and Tragic Spirit'.

was neither free nor wise—Persius gives similar reasoning to his own persona, and so on.

Another small, but intriguing, instance of Persius' 'straightening' allusions is found at the end of his first satire. Setting out the programme for his kind of writing, Persius stresses laughter (humour) but dissociates it from the vulgar and provincial humour of those who gladly laugh at foreign things such as mathematics and philosophy, or at people's handicaps.[90] The last of the 'bad jokes' is when someone laughs as a saucy tart tweaks the beard of a Cynic sage:

> multum gaudere paratus
> *si cynico barbam petulans nonaria vellat.* (Pers. 1.132–3)

ready to be greatly amused if a cheeky call-girl pulls a Cynic philosopher's beard.')

As has been noticed,[91] this harks back to a passage in Horace's *Satire* 1.3, where this earlier poet had waged a diatribe attack on a Stoic, playing around with the Stoics' claim that 'the wise man is king' and placing his target 'the king' in the humiliating situation where boys pull his beard and he can only defend himself with a stick:

> *vellunt tibi barbam*
> lascivi pueri; quos tu nisi fuste coerces,
> urgeris turba circum te stante miserque
> rumperis et latras, magnorum maxime regum. (Hor. S. 1.3.133–6)

cheeky boys pull your beard, and if you do not keep them at bay with your stick, you'll be mobbed by the throng, and you'll miserably burst with angry barking, O greatest of Kings!

Commenting on Persius' technique of associative allusion in this instance, Rudd observes that there is 'a difference of intention

---

[90] The example of the latter is a one-eyed man, jeered at with the nickname 'One-Eye' (1.128). Hendrickson ('Horace 1.4', 140), who argues that the whole of Persius' humour programme is a rephrasal of Aristotle's doctrine of the liberal jest, points out that the example is reminiscent of Aristotle too, *Eth.Nic.* 3.5 (15): οὐδεὶς γὰρ ἂν ὀνειδίσειε τυφλῷ φύσει ('nobody would reproach a person blind from birth'). Cf. also Cicero *De Or.* 2.246.

[91] e.g. N. Rudd, 'Association of Ideas in Persius', in *Lines of Enquiry* (Cambridge: Cambridge University Press, 1976); Lee and Barr, *Satires of Persius*, 87.

between these two passages', since Horace is concerned to ridicule his philosopher (= the Stoic), whereas Persius is not interested in ridiculing his philosopher (= the Cynic). Rudd recognizes that Persius' real aim is to ridicule those who mock the Cynic, and he well notes that 'to make the impertinent behaviour more vulgar and less excusable he replaces the cheeky boys with an adult'.[92] Not only an adult instead of innocent children, but also a disreputable *woman* instead of *men* (albeit not fully grown). Yet there are also other significant features to the Stoic satirist's transformation of the scene. The allusion is highlighted by the fact that the verbal echo (*barbam vellere* + dative) occurs in verse 133, exactly the verse where Horace's beard-pulling took place (*S.* 1.3.133). Most interestingly for my perspective here, compared to the lines of his predecessor, Persius' version cuts off the possibility of joining in the jeering against the philosopher. Rudd does not exclude the possibility that Persius is incidentally letting his mockery sweep over the Cynic as well, but the text does not really allow for this. The philosopher's tormentor is given a negative attribute, *petulans*, and although this adjective is akin to Horace's *lascivi* (of the boys) through their common connotation of playfulness, *petulans* has none of the charm of *lascivus* while concentrating the tinge of naughtiness to the full colour of offensiveness. A person who is *lascivus* may well be a comic hero; not so one who is *petulans*; he is most likely to be an object of derision. Horace's Stoic was mocked outside the scene as well as within it, where he was being pressed by all and sundry: boys (in the plural), the persona, and a massive mob around him. He was ridiculous even in his distress. Persius' philosopher, on the contrary, seems to be a venerable man unfairly insulted by a single impertinent prostitute. Those who laugh at the scene are expressly scorned. In the surrounding context we find the same pattern, with all the targets being defended, all the laughers criticized. Thus, not only are the positions of hero and villain inverted from Horace's version and the sprinkling humour concentrated to a tight jet of ridicule against the tart. There is also explicit dismissal of those who enjoy such vulgar jokes as tweaking philosophers' beards, and who comes to mind if not Horace in the passage pointedly alluded to, where he was the one to laugh at exactly such a

---

[92] Rudd, 'Association of Ideas in Persius', 64.

scene! Borrowing the happy formulation of Reckford, we may say that Persius 'un-deconstructs' the (mock-)moralistic story he has here inhereted from Horace.[93] The Augustan satirist, laughing even at his friends who opened their hearts to him (as Persius has said earlier in the same satire, 1.116–18), was too keen on laughter for his stern young successor's taste, and so Persius underlines, at the end of his programmatic poem, that *his* satire will have none of this indiscriminate humour.

In Persius, there is no room for alternative humour, the ideology is clear and didactic. But what is won in moral/ideological message is lost in liveliness: his universe is a closed one, and since everything was already in its right place, his style of writing satire was not taken up by later generations of poets.

JUVENAL: OF MONSTERS GREAT AND SMALL—DESCRIBING A GROTESQUE WORLD

Juvenal's satires are swarmed with monsters, often shocking yet almost always comic at the same time. They span a broad spectrum from full-blown portraits to minute metaphors hidden within a turn of phrase; from actual omens explicitly designated as such to distressing images which are only slightly screwed out of the normal. These brutes have not gone unnoticed in Juvenalian criticism, particularly not the larger ones, such as the fiendish emperor Domitian in J. 4, and in the same satire, the grotesque fish which bursts the limits of all existing plates, those emblems of civilization.[94] It has been recognized that Juvenal paints his most hated targets as

[93] Reckford, 'Reading the Sick Body', 351. Reckford uses this expression in a discussion of another example of Persius' humour straightening: in the third satire's allusions to Horace's 2.3. In Horace, this is a poem where the Stoic Damasippus, who gets to develop the Stoic paradox that 'only the wise man is sane', is part-speaker, part-object. In P. 3 the same paradox is treated respectfully—as Reckford says, 'Persius un-deconstructs the Stoic sermon'.

[94] Discussed in LaFleur, 'Amicitia and Juvenal's First Book'; Anderson, 'Imagery in the Satires of Horace and Juvenal', (repr. in Anderson, *Essays*: 115–50); M. Winkler, 'Satire and the Grotesque in Juvenal, Archimboldo, and Goya', *AA* 37 (1991), 22–42; Gowers, *Loaded Table*; Luisi, *Il Rombo e la Vestale*.

monsters, thereby adding a touch of the literally inhuman and supernatural to his outraged vision, and adding depth to both his indignation and his humour.

Yet I would like to go further, and argue three more points. First, that there are many more monsters than have hitherto been seen (as well as minor anomalies which are not, strictly speaking, monsters, but which can nevertheless be counted as such on the basis of their deeper kinship with real monsters). These contribute to the apocalyptic 'feel' of Juvenal's work and indeed lie close to its satiric kernel in combining the abominable with the laughable. Second, that their humour potential leads the reader in different directions, not only to laughing at the target of the satire as a whole, but also to laughing at entities which are actually opposed to it, or which are unrelated to it—in other words, monster humour can be object-related, subject-related, or non-aligned. Third, that there are degrees among Juvenalian monsters, so that all kinds are (re)presented: bloodthirsty demons, naughty metaphoric monsterlings,[95] and even endearing giants. Together they add up to a universe which though generally dark, is not without its own variation and hierarchy.

With Juvenal, as in the Latin language, a *monstrum* is first and foremost defined by being a breach of accepted limits, by falling between two or more existing categories of living things. Often the mixture of two categories is obvious: a woman gives birth to a calf, a boy is born with a doubled body, fishes are found in the field. If dirt, the impure, according to Mary Douglas' anthropological definition, is 'matter out of place',[96] a monster could be called *a being out of place* (and in an extended sense it also includes natural phenomena out of place, such as raining stones). In fact monsters are often 'impure' in the cultural-religious sense, in their function as prodigies, and require purification rites to set the world straight again and avert the bad sign. The purification reassures the community that the monster was only a chance anomaly, and that it has not affected the flow of events, which still adheres to received categories. The primary function of monsters is to warn and threaten, but in being built on an

[95] By 'monsterlings', 'small monsters', or 'mini-monsters' I mean that they occupy a small place in the text, not that the creatures described are small (these are usually large).

[96] Douglas, *Purity and Danger*, 41, *et passim*.

inconsistency between incompatible entities, they easily become comic, and perhaps always carry a reminder of the closeness between the frightening and the ridiculous. We may also note that what may be threatening in real life automatically becomes less so when it is described in a literary work. Thus Horace at the opening of his *Ars Poetica* describes a grotesque mixture that could very well be called a monster as the very essence of the laughable:

> Humano capiti cervicem pictor equinam
> iungere si velit et varias inducere plumas
> undique collatis membris, ut turpiter atrum
> desinat in piscem mulier formosa superne,
> spectatum admissi risum teneatis, amici?   (*Ars* 1–5)

If a painter decided to place a human head on a horse's neck, and add many-coloured feathers to different limbs, collected from everywhere, so that the top of a beautiful woman would disgracefully end in a black fish, would you then, when allowed to admire this, be able to hold back your laughter, my friends?

According to several humour scholars, a perceived inconsistency which is threatening will give rise to fright, one that is not threatening (or not strongly so) will give rise to laughter.[97] It follows that a comic writer may exploit a tension-building, fearsome image as a preliminary which is then revealed as insubstantial in its threat and thus all the funnier, and vice versa for a writer of Gothic stories.[98] Both movements are crucial to Juvenal's art, whose satirical universe is built around the axis of horror and laughter.

On one side the word *monstrum* is related to the verb *moneo*, 'to warn, advise, remind', since its original sense appears to have been that of a prodigy, a warning sign from the gods or other supernatural powers. In this early sense, it warns human beings of gruesome events which lie in the future or which have already begun—so the grammarian Festus (second century AD) says 'monstrum dictum velut monestrum, quod moneat aliquid futurum' ('It is called

---

[97] Rothbart, M. K. 'Incongruity, Problem-solving and Laughter', in A. J. Chapman and H. C. Foot (eds.), *Humour and Laughter: Theory, Research, and Application*. (London: Wiley, 1976); Lewis, P. *Comic Effects. Interdisciplinary Approaches to Humor in Literature* (Albany, NY: StateUniversity of New York Press,1989).

[98] Lewis, *Comic Effects*.

"monstrum" as if "monestrum" (*warning*), because it warns us of something in the future').[99] This meaning is amply present in Juvenal's satires, both in its literal interpretation, synonymous with prodigy (2.121–3, 153–8; 4.97; 6.84; 13.62–70) and as an overtone in all his many instances of the word *monstrum*. On its other side the word *monstrum* leads to the verb *monstro*, 'to show, indicate' and even 'to teach', so that what warns is simultaneously a spectacle, a concentrated mimetic show of what is to come or of what is already all around us in a deeper, less immediately recognizable sense. It will easily be seen that this meaning is likewise present in Juvenal.[100] The *monstrum* becomes a perfect focal point between the central functions of his writing: to warn his audience that Rome has reached the last stage of depravity (1.149, cf. 15.30–2), and to exploit the shock-value of this depravity to put on a yet-unseen freak-show. Behind the respectable aim of moralizing against contemporary vice, this show will offer sensational thrills away from the strictures of normality, somewhat in the manner of our time's tabloids.

Since monsters are beings that burst traditional categories, they are found everywhere in Juvenal's world, which is characterized precisely by being out of joint, with traditional values and hierarchies breaking down everywhere. A woman who claims to be part of *man*kind with the phrase 'homo sum' ('I am a human being', 6.284) reaches outside the limits that define 'woman',[101] and is thus called a monster ('unde haec monstra tamen' ('Where do these monsters come from...?'), 6.286). The court dandy Crispinus whose only strenuous quality is lust and who inverts normal behaviour by seducing all women but the unmarried ones, is a monster (*monstrum*, 4.2). So is his master's

---

[99] Quoted by Paulus Diaconus, 138, 140 in Karl O. Müller's edn., Festus, *Sexti Pompei Festi De verborum significatione quae supersunt: cum Pauli epitome* (Leipzig: Weidmann, 1839); see Lewis and Short, s.v. Cf. Cic. *Div.* 1.42.93, 'quia ostendunt, portendunt, monstrant, praedicunt, ostenta, portenta, monstra, prodigia dicuntur' ('since they manifest, portend, show, and predict, they are called "manifestations" (*ostenta*), "portents" (*portenta*), "monsters"/"shows" (*monstra*), and "prodigies" (*prodigia*)').

[100] After writing this, I have found that the same point about Juvenalian monsters is made in S. H. Braund and W. Raschke, 'Satiric Grotesques in Public and Private: Juvenal, Dr. Frankenstein, Raymond Chandler, and *Absolutely Fabulous*', *G&R* 49 (2002), 79.

[101] Latin *homo*, like English *man*, means both 'human being' and 'man' as opposed to 'woman'.

giant fish in the same satire, a turbot exceeding the limits of private kitchens and royal plates (4.66, 72; *monstrum*, 45; *belua*, 121, 127). Pathics who play the philosopher with cropped hair are prodigies, and if not earlier, this will be discovered when they descend to their elders in Hades—the manly Romans of old will wish for an act of purification in hell when they see the deceased *cinaedus* (2.149–58). Yet even these *cinaedi* will have to stand back for the monstrosity of a man from the Gracchus family, hyperbolically called no less high-born than the emperor (2.148), ignobly acting as a gladiator at the games ('vicit et hoc monstrum tunicati fuscina Gracchi' ('still worse is the monstrous sight of a Gracchus with a gladiator's trident'), 2.143).[102] And of course cannibalism is monstrous (15.121, 172). In this light Juvenal's many oxymoronic images appear as shadows of monsters: *meretrix Augusta* ('the Queen-whore'); *magnae pallor amicitiae* ('the pallor induced by a great friendship'); *luxuriae sordes* ('the miserliness of luxury'); *praetextatus adulter* ('an adulterer in a school-boy uniform'); *serpentum maior concordia* ('greater concord among snakes'); etc. Note how the incongruity of the thing described is mimicked by the jarring contrast (semantic always, occasionally stylistic too) between the two poles of the compact oxymorons.

Juvenal's satires abound in monster-like expressions and images, for instance in animal pictures, where wild animals dominate over tame, and unpleasant over pleasant ones: we meet apes, elephants, snakes, various fishes, and even the domesticated beasts are represented by pigs and mice. This is not all. Remarkably, Juvenal manages to suggest that since his time is so bad, good men or good morals would be so much out of place in it as to look monstrous! In the thirteenth satire his persona says that a friend who would return his debts would be a sign calling for purification, and that any upright man would strike him as a prodigy (13.60–70). In the fifteenth satire, the Egyptians consider it an unholy crime, *nefas*, to eat leeks or slaughter a goat—while they eat human flesh (15.9–13). At the beginning of the sixth, the big hairy Golden Age woman, who unlike contemporary women was faithful and fertile, looks decidedly

---

[102] This is a standard move in Juvenal: to say that a thing is *still worse* than something notoriously horrible he has just described, as with Gracchus being more monstrous than the pathics here. This device is described as an effective rhetorical move in Quintilian, *Inst.* 6.2.21–3.

monstrous (6.1–10). As he plays off the two extremes of decadent reality and unbelievable fairy-tale against each other, he leaves some room for difference, and I will argue below that there are ways of telling a good monster from a bad one in Juvenal's universe. For now it will suffice to stress again that all these bogeys are potentially funny, balancing on the edge between the threatening and the merely ridiculous, between warning and showing and even showing off. This is what makes *monstrum* such a common vocable in the last satires of Rome.

In addition to the connected possibilities of threat and show a monster is also a rewarding image for a satirist because it coincides with the pattern of 'shooting from below', discussed above in my chapter on object-oriented humour (Ch. 1). Monsters are usually big, aggressive, and unintelligent, which gives the satirist excellent opportunities to play the fearless little fighter who challenges and overcomes a seemingly attacking enemy with the help of his sharp wit. Wit is shown as superior to brute force, prevailing in the name of justice and good morals—the cherished self-presentation of satire. Recognising this pattern, Frye says that in satire 'the *alazon* is ... a giant prodded by a cool and observant but almost invisible enemy into a blind, stampeding fury and then polished off at leisure'.[103] Exactly, and it is very handy if the giant is literally blind. The archetypal blind colossus, Polyphemus, had been described by Virgil in a haunting line, which carefully eliminated the comic potential, in favour of the horrific potential, by means of assonance, poetic vocabulary, and a solemn circumlocution for 'blind' (*A.* 3.658):

monstrum horrendum, informe, ingens, cui lumen ademptum[104]

a horrible, deformed, enormous monster, bereaved of light

---

[103] Frye, *Anatomy of Criticism,*, 228.

[104] Cf. also *A.* 4.181–2, 'monstrum horrendum, ingens, cui quot sunt corpore plumae | tot vigiles oculi subter' ('a horrible, enormous monster, with so many feathers on its body, and just as many eyes underneath'); after a similar beginning the monster turns out to have too many rather than too few eyes. For a brilliant selective discussion of how the line at *A.* 3.658 lived on in later poetry, see M. Riffaterre, *Semiotics of Poetry* (Bloomington: Indiana University Press, 1978), 23–5.

Juvenal reworks the image in his description of Domitian's informer Catullus, but as a satirist, he is interested in both the frightening and the ridiculous side (J4.115–16):

> grande et conspicuum nostro quoque tempore monstrum
> caecus adulator[105]

a great and conspicuous monster even for our time, a blind flatterer

The sombre spondaic rhythm of Virgil's line is exchanged for the more common alternating hexameter rhythm, the poetic circumlocution has been replaced by the simple word *caecus*. The key word *monstrum* has been moved from the first position in the line to the last one. This gives the typically satiric jerk of surprise at the end, where Virgil's first note, instead, set the awesome melody at the outset of the line. 'Caecus adulator', the prosaic explanation of why Catullus should be considered monstrous, is likewise delayed and then served as a lowering surprise after a line-break. The picture is still recognizable: *grande* is the less sublime synonym of *ingens*, *conspicuum* a disrespectful echo of *horrendum* without the element of holy fear. The incongruity is left, the awe is strongly diminished, and ridicule peeps out. Significantly, a distancing, ironic piece of information is added in Juvenal's version: 'nostro quoque tempore'. Apparently, there has been some inflation in monsters, the times have grown rougher, and what was a reasonably conspicuous brute for Homer or Virgil is not immediately one in Juvenal's contemporary tale; Catullus Messalinus however, stands the test. This business-minded comment about the increase in monstrosity is bound to sound comic in the mock-horrific context. Another shift is that 'the monster of our time' is a man, not a supernatural creature, and in fact all Juvenal's monsters will be human or animal (in these cases the animals usually stand in for humans anyway), since the universe of satire is a sober, purely human world.

A remarkable feature is the Silver Latin satirist's consciousness, even admission, of the relativity of what is strange, and what is funny. This is foreshadowed in his savage *sententia* 'loripedem rectus

---

[105] This passage in Juvenal is discussed in LaFleur, 'Amicitia and Juvenal's First Book', 170, and Garland, 'Mockery of the Deformed in Graeco-Roman Culture', 79–80, but none of them pays attention to the Virgilian parallel.

derideat, Aethiopem albus' ('let the straight man laugh at the crippled, a white man at the Ethiopian'), 2.23—where a meta-literary rule for laughter is laid down as if it could well be the other way around. A consciousness of relativity is carefully embroidered in a digression in the thirteenth satire:

> quis tumidum guttur miratur in Alpibus aut quis
> in Meroe crasso maiorem infante mamillam?
> caerula quis stupuit Germani lumina, flavam
> caesariem et madido torquentem cornua cirro?
> ad subitas Thracum volucres nubemque sonoram
> Pygmaius paruis currit bellator in armis,
> mox impar hosti raptusque per aera curuis
> unguibus a saeva fertur grue. *si videas hoc*
> *gentibus in nostris, risu quatiare; sed illic,*
> *quamquam eadem adsidue spectentur proelia, ridet*
> *nemo, ubi tota cohors pede non est altior uno.*   (13.162–73)[106]

Who would gape at a swelling throat in the Alps, or a breast larger than the fat baby sucking it in Egypt? Who would be startled by blue eyes in a German, by his yellow hair and greased curls twisted into the shape of horns? When the Thracian birds suddenly swoop down in a noisy cloud, the Pygmy warrior runs up against them in his minute armour, but he is immediately proved to be no match for his foe, and is carried through the air in the curved claws of the cruel crane. *If you saw this among our people, you would shake with laughter, but there, where the entire army is no taller than one foot, nobody laughs, although they see battles like this one all the time.*

In the last sentence, which I have put in italics, the author comes very close to giving away one of the dearest secret tricks of satire, viz. that it does not care about the truth as long as the incongruity makes the reader laugh. And yet paradoxically, he rounds off the dangerous revelation with the trick at work, trying to amuse us with the image 'tota cohors pede non est altior uno' ('the entire army is no taller than one foot').

Having sketched the main features of Juvenal's monsters in general, I will now move on to those monsters and monstrosities that are of special interest to this chapter—those whose ridiculousness is not

---

[106] Verse 166, which was deleted by Markland and Pinzger, whom Clausen follows in his edition, has been omitted in the quotation.

directly tied to either the object or to the subject of the satire, i.e. those characterized by non-aligned humour. The following discussion will look at three types of monsters:

1. More or less prodigious incongruities which are loosely connected to the satiric object but not strictly necessary for its attack.
2. Some less noticeable monsterlings which seem unrelated to the object and usually hide in throwaway metaphors and other minute images, weaving a mad texture as a background for the major monsters.
3. The monsters that seem, if anything, to go against the main drift of the satire, and to be set up in opposition to the satiric targets.

Monsters loosely connected to the object: elephants, whales, and vegetables (J. 10; 11; 12; 15)

One example of grotesque creatures playing a minor role on the side of the object is that of the elephants. These animals, always a distorted version of normal beasts to the Roman eye,[107] had connotations of exotic foreign lands, war (especially the Hannibalic war), luxury, and extravagant shows.[108] Threatening and immoral and spectacular all at once, they made an excellent object for moralizing discourse, and Juvenal mentions them in the three satires of his fourth book: satires 10, 11, and 12. Characteristically, these collateral monsters underline different sins in the three passages: vanity in J. 10.157–8, luxury in J. 11.120–8, and flattery in J. 12.102–14. All three arguments could stand without the elephants; nevertheless, Juvenal chisels their images with loving care. In J. 10, one-eyed Hannibal on his exotic mount is a sight truly worthy of being made into a picture—'o qualis facies et quali digna tabella, | cum Gaetula ducem portaret belua luscum!' ('O what a sight, worthy of a painting: the Gaetulian beast carrying the one-eyed prince!'), 10.157–8. A picture is of course exactly what the satirist makes for his audience.

---

[107] Cf. Varro's etymology for *bos Luca*, a Roman expression trying to make sense of the elephant: 'nostri, cum...in Lucanis Pyrrhi bello primum vidissent apud hostis elephantos, ...Lucam bovem appellasse' (*L.* 7.39).

[108] For the connection with Hannibal cf. Livy 22.2; see Mayor, *Juvenal, with Commentary*, ii. 122, for further references.

The prince of the enemy, *dux*, with the help of the elephant turns into that blind stampeding monster mentioned above, presented in a near-golden line with maximum clash between the stylish pace of the hero and his prodigious reality. Persius had said in his programme that the humour of calling a one-eyed man 'One-eye' was unsophisticated, but Juvenal is not above using this rough effect.[109] Thus the alien general is already half-blind or cyclopean, and the Gaetulian beast, *Gaetula belua*, adding to the whining u-assonance of the verse, finishes the huge and ridiculous caricature. The beast had been foreshadowed in v. 150, where the question of Hannibal's importance was opened with a camera-sweep over his native Africa, ending with the southern limit 'ad Aethiopum populos aliosque elephantos' ('facing towards the Ethiopians, and towards another kind of elephants'). From its home there, at the outskirts of the known world, the creature is now entering Italy, heading for Rome. At close view it looks bigger, a *belua* rather than the technical *elephantus*, and ripens the image for the satirist's dismissal of Hannibal, in 159–67. In J. 11 we hear about luxurious Romans who have no appetite unless they eat off ivory tables. The material for their furniture comes from tusks ('dentibus' ('lit. "teeth", 11.124'), with slightly disturbing connotations of rapacity) which the beast, again *belua*, has laid off in an Arabian wood once they became too heavy for its head. The decadent inhabitants of the capital are scorned for gaping at 'the mere refuse of a foreign monster', as Courtney puts it.[110] The twelfth satire speaks of the exceeding flattery of legacy hunters, who would gladly sacrifice an elephant in honour of their rich 'friends', if these animals were not a caesarean privilege. This passage is the most detailed picture of the elephants, making them out as emphatically foreign ('nec Latio aut usquam sub nostro sidere talis | belua concipitur' ('this beast is not born in Latium or anywhere under our sky'), 12.103–4) but royal cattle, *armentum*, kept in Italy only in an exclusive herd for the emperor's use.

The recurring references to elephants in Book 4 have caught the eye of Juvenalian scholars, and Braund has forwarded the excellent observation that the passages allude to Horace's *Epistle* 2.1.196,

---

[109] As is seen here and at 7.128. To 10.158 Mayor (*Juvenal, with Commentary*, ii, ad loc.) quotes the passage from Persius (1.128), but does not develop the point.

[110] Courtney, *Commentary on Juvenal*, to v.11.127.

where an elephant occurs in context parallel to the programmatic statement in Juvenal's *Satire* 10 (vv. 28–53). Like Juvenal, Horace said that if Democritus had lived to see Rome, he would have laughed (*Ep.* 2.1.194–8):

> si foret in terris, rideret Democritus, seu
> diversum confusa genus panthera camelo
> sive elephans albus vulgi converteret ora;
> spectaret populum ludis attentius ipsis,
> ut sibi praebentem nimio spectacula plura

If Democritus were still alive, he would laugh if the crowd would be enraptured by that mixture of a camel and a leopard, or by a white elephant; he would watch the people more closely than the games themselves, since the people would offer him incomparably much more of a show.

On Braund's reading, Juvenal is 'using the repeated elephant in Book IV to remind us of its Horatian context and thus of the Democritean character of his speaker'.[111]

To this insight a further comment may be added from our specific point of view here. Horace had already stressed the freakish aspect of the critters regarded by the people: a giraffe is presented as the conundrum of panther mixed with camel, the white elephant does not even need any further linguistic elaboration to challenge the giraffe as mutant and audience magnet. The two miscreations are relatives of Horace's grotesque mermaid at the beginning of the *Ars Poetica*, the one that would have made anyone laugh. Thus Democritus in his wisdom may be laughing at the people rather than at the spectacle, but we, Horace's audience, are invited to laugh at the fantastic animals as well—though, strictly speaking, this is not good for the argument, since it puts us on the same level as the foolish people, not as the philosopher.

Much the same thing happens to Juvenal's elephantine humour, in that it not only underlines the point it apparently serves, but digresses from it as well. We are made to laugh at the images themselves instead of focusing our gaze on the sin which they illustrate.[112] The laughable aspect of the elephant-monsters centrifuges the reader's

---

[111] Braund, *Beyond Anger*, 188–9; quotation from 189.

[112] To some extent the effect of multiplying meaning, not pinpointing it, is a feature of all metaphor, as William Empson taught us in *Seven Types of Ambiguity*

attention, spreading a shadow of the grotesque throughout the Roman empire, as well as through Book 4.

In all three passages the idea of unnecessarily, in fact immorally, importing the alien beasts into Rome is central. Yet of course the satires mimic exactly this import by introducing the monsters into the text. 'These do not belong here' the text says, while at the same time bringing them on, even focusing on their journey into the capital, with gusto. Of the treatment in *Satire* 11, for instance, it must be observed that whether Juvenal believed in the tales of elephants shedding their tusks or not,[113] the image of the *belua* purposefully laying down its over-heavy 'teeth' in the heart of the African forest is surely a joke, and a somewhat 'unsatirical' one at that. While the joke's purpose may easily be explained as deriding the mores back at Rome, the orderly hygiene of the monster in the wilderness also carries overtones of a universe out of bounds, out of its mind. If all three passages in *Satires* 10–12 are read in a row, we get the progress of the elephants from the margin into the centre of the empire: first there is Hannibal's introduction of the beast to Italy (J. 10), then its piecemeal immigration through ivory (J. 11), and finally its position as the exclusive pet of the Roman emperor (J. 12). These alien prodigies, unshapely compositions of disparate pieces rather than proper useful animals, burst the boundaries of the normal and mix categories that should be kept apart in a sane structure; transgressive in themselves, the elephants further transgress geographical boundaries as they enter Rome, while the narrative of the satire turns to the far corners of the world where they used to dwell. With the help of these mini-monsters the satirist warns and shows and puts on small shows—the marginal beasts become emblems of, and actors in, a world which falls apart, laughing.

In *Satire* 10 death-bringing riches are likened to the great whales of Britannia, in that an enormous fortune of this fatal kind is said to excel all other inheritances as much as the *ballaena Britannica* ('British whale') exceeds ordinary dolphins (10.13–14). Although all the

---

(London: Chatto & Windus, 1930), but I would dare to suggest that it is even more a feature of humorous metaphors, since humour also carries its own ambiguity with it.

[113] This was believed in antiquity; cf. Pliny, *NH* 8.7–8 and comment in Courtney, *Commentary on Juvenal*, 506.

wrong wishes people make in their prayers destroy them, Juvenal says, nothing kills as many as money does. The image of the whale thus crowns a two-staged intensification: first, wealth is the greatest source of destruction, and second, this is particularly true of great wealth, which towers high among normal patrimonies. Yet the picture of the Britannic behemoth is perhaps not the most persuasive to deride money, the surface aim of the passage. It is a monster, just as money is monstrous according to the satirist's thesis, so far so good, but then it is as if the image swam off into a direction of its own: it is humorous in the thrilling way of sailors' stories about unbelievable prodigies encountered at the limits of the known world. 'Rare in the Mediterranean',[114] rare also in Latin literature, the *ballaena* had earlier appeared metaphorically in a passage of Plautus' *Rudens*, 545–6 'quaenam ballaena meum voravit vidulum | aurum atque argentum ubi omne compactum fuit?' ('What whale has swallowed my purse, with all the gold and silver in it?'), a hilarious image resounding of the comic hero's greed and trickery, and also, as with the satirist, of money. Juvenal's whale is an escape from the familiar, an exhilarating excursion into the unknown and barely possible, and yet it is, significantly, placed within the empire. Horace had mentioned Britain's sea-monsters in an ode (*C.* 4.14.47–8), stressing how everything obeyed Augustus, even the wildest, remotest parts of the Roman dominion. In Juvenal's time, and in his chosen genre of satire, the beasts of the Roman realm are not obedient. On the contrary, the exaggerated, transgressive bulk of the whale is emphasized. The creature exceeds the limits of the normal, flashes its monstrosity, and suggests that far from being under control, the empire swarms with unruly prodigies—in the monetary habits of its subjects as well as in its zoology. Yet the monsters are not altogether depressing: they are the big fish drawing gasps of admiration and envy rather than disgust, least of all contempt. Once we also note that the other pole of the comparison, the dolphins, are if anything pleasant animals, associated with kindness and help, it may be seen that the image, although seemingly in line with the moral point being made, is not *completely* in line, but has its laughter spread wider than the one straight direction. A similar effect, only on a

---

[114] As Courtney, *Commentary on Juvenal*, comments ad loc.

larger scale, is achieved when J. 10 ends with a jest against believing in the gods about whose right and wrong address the whole preceding poem has spoken (vv. 365–6).

In the fifteenth satire even some monstrous vegetables turn up, as objects of worship among the man-eating Egyptians. At its opening the satire presents a series of animal-gods in Egypt (at least since Herodotus the classical land of inversion to the Greco-Roman mind), and expressly designates these as monsters: 'qualia demens | Aegyptos *portenta* colat?' ('what *portents* does mad Egypt worship?'), 15.1–2.[115] At the end of this list of monkeys, cats, and crocodiles, the satirist places leeks and onions:

> porrum et caepe nefas violare et frangere morsu
> (o sanctas gentes, quibus haec nascuntur in hortis
> numina!)   (15.9–11)

It is sacrilege to violate leeks and onions by crunching them with your teeth. O what a holy people, in whose gardens such divinities grow!

The combination 'porrum et caepe' was taken from a passage in Horace's *Epistles* ('seu porrum et caepe trucidas' ('if you kill leeks and onions'), *Ep.* 1.12.21), where it had figured in a joke on Pythagoreanism. Thus while the holy leeks do not seem to have been supported by either reality or general belief,[116] they do have an ancestry of literary humour. Juvenal, as often, rubs in the point: in a dark caricature of the Golden Age, the murderous Egyptians enjoy everyday encounters with the gods—gods that grow in their garden. Eating human flesh, however, is allowed, Juvenal harshly tells us at the end of the introducing passage, παρὰ προσδοκίαν. The shock is sharpened by the fact that the words are placed after a line-break, without any warning: 'carnibus humanis vesci licet' ('eating human flesh is allowed'), 13. There follows the grisly story of the event of cannibalism in Egypt, but at the very end of the poem the image of venerated vegetables returns:

> quid diceret ergo
> vel quo non fugeret, si nunc haec monstra videret
> Pythagoras, cunctis animalibus abstinuit qui

---

[115] Cf. also 6.526–41, another passage where Juvenal derides Egyptian religion.
[116] Courtney, *Commentary on Juvenal*, ad loc.

tamquam homine et ventri indulsit non omne legumen?   (15.171–4)

what would Pythagoras say, or where would he flee, if he were to see these enormities now, that man who abstained from all kinds of meat as though it were human, and even denied his belly certain vegetables?

Here the argument is presumably that Pythagoras' selective vegetarianism (due to his belief in the transmigration of souls, *metempsychosis*, which could place a human soul in an animal or even a plant of certain kinds) stands for piety and civilization, in maximum contrast to the Egyptians' barbarism. In lines 9–11 the point was that the Egyptians' religious abstention from vegetables contributed to their utter perversion, and was perfectly in line with their cannibalism, since in their inverted logic they did everything the opposite way from normal people. The passages need to be read in different directions in order to make sense, and the tension between them is made worse by the fact that Pythagoras' theory may have originated in Egypt.[117] The joke on leeks and onions is also complicated by the association with Pythagoreanism in the Horatian intertext to Juvenal's vv. 9–11.

These opposite applications of vegetarianism within the same satire have not escaped notice, but have been differently explained. So Anderson has interpreted the incongruity as an authorial hint at the persona's confusion and a warning against taking him at his word.[118] A more traditional approach is trying to soften and excuse the apparent inconsistency. For example, Courtney, though admitting that there is a difficulty, lays down that it is not so important as to destroy the main effect:

Juvenal's declamation is not concerned to arrive at a consistent moral evaluation of abstinence from meat and vegetables, but only with its application for the immediate effect of whipping up the reader's feelings in each context, even two opposite applications within the same satire. ...

---

[117] See Courtney, *Commentary on Juvenal*, 611–12.

[118] Anderson, 'Cannibals and Culture', 213–14 n. 20; R. McKim ('Philosophers and Cannibals: Juvenal's Fifteenth Satire', *Phoenix* 40 (1986), 58–71, 69–70) makes a similar interpretation, seeing an implicit joke on the part of the author who makes the persona commit the 'climactic blunder' of forgetting how he had used the image of vegetarianism at lines 9–11; *contra* see Tennant, 'The Interpretation of Juvenal's 15th satire', 132–4.

He is quite prepared to poke fun at the objects of his respect ... but it would be totally discordant with the tone of this poem to suppose that he ends with a purely destructive irony.[119]

P. M. W. Tennant, adopting a very similar position, speaks of 'the opportunism of Juvenal's satirical method', which causes the satirist to rely on the force of his humour 'to capitalize on its *immediate* context and the spontaneous audience response', even to the detriment of the wider logic. Tennant corrects Courtney's assumption that there cannot be any destructive irony at the end because it would be out of tune with the rest of the satire, saying instead that the end-joke *may* be thus interpreted by an 'objective, thoughtful and unprejudiced listener', but *should not*, since Juvenal's intended audience was not of this kind.

To my mind it seems utterly improbable that a poet like Juvenal would have overlooked, or noticing would not have cared about correcting (since his audience was too stupid anyway), an inconsistency in a relatively short poem. Anderson's opposite line of reading, which takes the combined vegetable references as completely overthrowing the authority of the main argument, seems overstated, and uncomfortably has to look away from the poem's obvious intention to disparage the Egyptians' cannibalism. I would suggest that a solution lies in developing Tennant's embryonic insight about readers of different competence. It is idle to deny that at a surface level, the contrast between eating human flesh and abstaining from vegetables is amusing and effective enough in its unambitious point, and so the reader interested in smug self-congratulation in comparison with barbarians (either limited to Roman Egypt or transferred to any other barbarians he would like to see derided) may laugh his fill. Yet underneath the easy surface there is a disturbing contradiction to be caught by the subtler reader, no less funny in its way, but far from straightforward in its implications. Pythagoras, the humane philosopher and moral flower of Graeco-Roman culture is shown to be laughable on the same plane as the Egyptians are when they worship

---

[119] Courtney, *Commentary on Juvenal*, 612; in the same passage Courtney also points out that Pythagoras had earlier been the object of Juvenal's joke at 3.229, where the image comprised a small garden 'unde epulum possis centum dare Pythagoreis'.

their onions, though not of course on a comparable scale. The main force of the joke remains in favour of the philosopher and against the outsiders, but the repercussions of the humour produced by the prodigious, as-if living vegetables turn in other directions as well. The monstrous greens suggest a mad world, where perverted moral positions are adopted by both centre and margin,[120] both the very best and the very worst. In a gesture not of 'purely destructive irony' but of *centrifugal* humour. In a Horatian move of jeopardizing what has gone before in the final joke, Juvenal adds a sting in the tail for the discerning reader without destroying the pleasure of the simpler part of the audience.[121]

Marginal monsterlings: Umbricius' lizard, Virgil's snakes, and the centaur's tail (J. 3; 7)

As I pass from the first group, that of small monsters which are in line with the general attack but not strictly indispensable to it, to the second group, that of diableries unrelated to either object or subject, a certain arbitrariness in my classification is exposed: in reality there is a continuum from *properly satirical* monsters (in the sense of being grotesquely immoral creatures, fit objects for satirical attack) to *less and less satirical* monsterlings. There is no sharp line between the groups, it is a gradual transition; yet it is hoped that even a grouping that is somewhat arbitrary on the fringes may be accepted for the sake of clarity.

Among the middle grotesques I would place Umbricius' lizard at 3.230–3, where he says that one should buy a little land outside of Rome, where it is cheaper, since even the smallest dominion is always

---

[120] Cf. J. 2.166–70, where it is described how the migration of corrupted *mores* has been inverted: instead of flowing into the centre, depravation is now moving out from Rome to the notoriously depraved provinces.

[121] Allowing this meaning to be expressed, however indirectly, may be a blunder at the level of the persona, but not at the level of the author, especially not if the latter is understood in the sense of the implied author (as is done in the present study). If the authorial level is thus seen as *intentio operis*, then every strain of meaning found in the text on a reasonable analysis is there to be explained, not brushed off as a result of negligence, since this 'human factor' in the author's persona is no longer under consideration at all.

something: 'est aliquid, quocumque loco, quocumque recessu, | unius sese dominum fecisse lacertae' ('it is something to become in whatever place, in whatever remote corner, the master of one lizard'). If we as readers are to believe that Umbricius' critique of Rome is valid, that his lamentation is in fact the bulk of the satirical message in this poem, then it is odd that we should be made to smile at what the speaker sets up as an ideal, the idyll of a life in the country. The mockery creeping in with the lizard is suggesting that the idyll is dominated by need and poor company.[122] Martial's poem 11.18, a complaint about the smallness and meanness of the villa given to the poet by a patron, is mentioned in the commentaries as a parallel,[123] but there is a vital difference: Martial's humour in saying that only one ant could feed off the land (11.18.6) strikes against the patron whose stinginess the whole epigram derides, whereas Juvenal's humour about ruling over no more than one lizard does not mock in the same direction as the satire as a whole, that is, the disagreeableness of the city. It is rather a smirk against the desolation and poverty of the country. Note also that Juvenal's one lizard is a condensed version of a whole line of solitary animals in Martial (cicada, ant, snake, worm, gnat, mole, mouse, swallow), awaiting its *dominus* in the wasteland at the edge of the known world. If we look close enough, we will see that the little piece of land in Umbricius' dreams, however humble, is connected to ownership and material greed, so hated by the satirist. At bottom, there is thus still a link to immorality, though it is now off the road and getting weaker and weaker.

Another instance of mockery whose relevance is not immediately perceived are the images of 'high poetry without money' in the seventh satire, which as a whole laments the bad conditions of contemporary intellectuals. Although Juvenal most certainly admired Virgil, he lets his persona air the opinion that Virgil would instantly have lost his genius if he had been bereft of his comfortable life:

---

[122] Cf. the other line in Juvenal where a lizard turns up (adduced in Mayor, *Juvenal, with Commentary*, i, to line 3.231): 'serpente ciconia pullos | nutrit et inventa per devia rura lacerta' (14.74–5). Again a desolate place with an unpleasant fauna. There is also an overpaid jockey named Lacerta at 7.114.

[123] Mayor, *Juvenal, with Commentary*, i; Courtney, *Commentary on Juvenal*, ad loc.

nam si Vergilio puer et tolerabile desset
hospitium, caderent omnes a crinibus hydri,
surda nihil gemeret grave bucina.   (7.69–71)

if Virgil wouldn't have had a slave-boy and tolerable lodgings, then all the snakes would have dropped from the Fury's hair, and the trumpet would have gone mute, giving off no sound.

The Fury is monstrous by essence, but when the snakes fall from her hair humour is added to horror, and she is transformed into the monster-shape favoured by satire: instead of the epic monster enthroned—a *monster decrowned*, at once frightful and funny. Moreover, dropping her snakes she becomes less divine, less magical—in fact she turns into a mere woman, albeit a very disagreeable one. In a swift movement laden with meta-literary consequences she passes from the epic to the satiric, through the link of the monstrous. Horace, we have been told in the same satire, never wrote his odes on an empty stomach: 'satur est cum dicit Horatius "euhoe" ' ('Horace's belly is full when he says his "evoe" '), 7.62. Interestingly, the 'euhoe' signifies lyric poetry in particular, so perhaps Juvenal did not regard the state of satiety as a prerequisite for Horace's satirical writing. Thus epic and lyric poetry, the high genres, seem to require that the poet is well fed when writing them. The question is whether satire, as a genre, does as well—or whether Juvenal in the seventh satire is actually showing that *satura* can be written by a poet who is not *satur* at all? In the metaphors, the monsters pass from epic to satire: as Virgil's character drops her snakes, Juvenal is there to pick them up. The war-trumpet, a signal of heroic poetry, turns mute, and the Fury passes from playing the *monstrum* connected to *moneo*, the supernatural creature who is an emblem of nearing catastrophes, to the role of *monstrum* as mere show, and a farcical show at that.

Compare the centaur Chiron, who appears later on in the same poem as an example of a good teacher properly appreciated by his pupil, an ideal contrasted with the present state of affairs, when good teachers are mistreated. Chiron's tail could perhaps be laughed at, but his pupil Achilles, in decorous respect for physical punishment, was above such laughter:

di maiorum umbris tenuem et sine pondere terram
spirantisque crocos et in urna perpetuum ver,

qui praeceptorem sancti voluere parentis
esse loco. metuens virgae iam grandis Achilles
cantabat patriis in montibus et cui non tunc
eliceret risum citharoedi cauda magistri;   (7.207–12)

May the gods make the earth light on our forebears' shadows, and make
fragrant crocus bloom in eternal spring in their urns, for they wanted a
teacher to enjoy the sacred respect of a parent. Achilles was no longer a child
when, singing in his native hills, he still feared the cane, and would never
have laughed at his music teacher's tail.

The centaur had long been a mythical creature somewhat uncomfortably posed between pathos and ridiculousness: on the one hand
he has superhuman powers and occasionally performs noble roles in
high poetry, on the other hand he is an anomaly in his very consti-
tution, a fair match for Horace's laughter-provoking mermaid at the
beginning of *Ars Poetica*. Like that mermaid, he is beautiful at the
front and the head, but ends in the undignified shape of a beast down
under. Significantly, it is the 'material lower stratum', the funny part
of the body comprising belly, genitalia, feet, and tail, that gets the
animal form in both cases. Also, much in line with the rules of the
grotesque, the incongruity comes as a surprise: when the creature's
face first peeked through our door, it looked a well-shaped human
being, and we were not at all prepared for what the lower part of him/
her would look like. Here Juvenal performs a humorist's *praeteritio*—
by pointing out what joke should not be made, he in fact makes that
very joke.[124] Note further that *cauda* is not only the word for tail
(which would draw attention to Chiron's grotesque, inhuman appearance) but also a common euphemism for the penis (which
would presumably be that of a horse in Chiron's case). A technique
which Horace had employed in a passage describing how one could,
yet should not, laugh at a bumpkin-like character with a splendid
soul inside (*S.* 1.3.29–34) consisted of almost-laughing at something,
and then suddenly turning and channelling the humorous energy
piled high within the reader in another direction. The reader could
now be led to mock the mockers with whom he was almost asked to

---

[124] Cf. the classical case of this, the dialogue between Dionysos and his servant at
the beginning of Aristophanes' *Frogs* (1–18), where they go through all the jokes they
will not make in this play because they are too crude.

sympathize a moment earlier.[125] What Juvenal does in the passage
under discussion is similar, only sharper. The Juvenalian persona asks
us not to laugh at the miscreation of the centaur, for he is a good
monster, opposed to the present-day monstrosities that are the real
target of J. 7 in its entirety. Yet the jest he warns against is particularly
grotesque and potentially salacious, showing off the enormity char-
acterizing even heroes in this satirist's universe.

Positive monsters of the Golden Age (J. 6; 13; 14)

Turning now to the last group, that of the best of monsters, I would
first like to explain what specimens I will consider in this section, and
why. My discussion will be limited to some passages which (directly
or indirectly) describe the Golden Age and the inhabitants therein,
i.e. young gods and primitive mortals. For reasons which I shall set
out presently, these passages are at the farthest remove from what
Juvenal most resents, monetary greed and sexual incontinence. Despite this 'goodness', they are still fairly ugly and grotesque—in short,
monstrous—and risible, fully in the style of satire, unlike, for instance, the glimpses of the bucolic detected in J. 3,[126] which are
merely sweet and filled with pathos. The images of the Golden Age
also play out the contrast between past and present times and morals,
a theme essential in satire in general and in Juvenal in particular.
Further, they are compact, rich descriptions, which makes them
suitable for analysis and compensates for the fact that I examine
only a few examples of a whole group of images. Finally, they have a
special significance in that they tell of the Golden Age, a traditionally
positive motif from the higher genres, without distorting it out of
recognition, and, as I shall argue, without wholly subverting it *qua*
Golden Age, i.e. as a better way of living, set in the remote past. It has
been ingeniously suggested that *satire* stands in a kind of inside/
outside relationship to the genre (or mode) of *utopia*.[127] This would
be so because satire usually attacks the morals of its contemporaries,
with the implicit (and in some cases even explicit) claim that

---

[125] See the discussion in Ch. 2 § 'Horace: profitable irony'.
[126] Witke, *Latin Satire*, 128–51.
[127] R. C. Elliott, 'Saturnalia, Satire, and Utopia', *Yale Review* 55/4 (1966), 521–36.

somewhere there exists the ideal society that is the opposite of what is being attacked; whereas utopia, in turn, focuses on the description of an ideal community living Nowhere, from the underlying understanding that life in known places is the opposite of this ideal. Thus utopia would have satire as the dark negative to its golden picture, and satire's derisive caricature would be cast into relief by utopia's mirage. With this illuminating delineation as a background it may be noted that Roman satire, much more than later satires, is prone to spelling out the utopian pole. This can be done in earnest, as in Persius' *Satire* 5; with light irony, as is often the case in Horace (we have seen some of this in the above discussion of his persona-directed humour); or it may, interestingly, be done with harsh humour, as happens in Juvenal's pictures of the Golden Age. This last procedure creates the image of a world which is complete in that it has both poles, the satiric and the utopian, but which is dark all over, even in its brightest spots. It is grotesque but differentiated.

What, then, is the function of Juvenal's brightest monsters, the ones inhabiting his patches of utopia? I would like to suggest that they are there to state satire's claim to the good part of life as well as the bad side that is the genre's obvious speciality. In this way it completes the satirist's claim to describing the whole of life, and so create a full world-view with the same grand ambition as epic. Only this is to be a purely human world, where all is measured by the standard of man. As several scholars have rightly observed, satire usurps the domain of epic—highjacks the metre, snatches the personages—but it does so through lowering, degrading most aspects of the sublime genre, and thus it creates something new.[128] To this I wish to add the observation that humour is an excellent means of translating the sublime and supernatural to the human scale. Juvenal wanders through all the realms and times of the world: heaven, earth, Hades, the Golden Age, even peeks into the future;[129] and where he

---

[128] Anderson, 'Roman Socrates', 12; Braund, *Roman Satire*, 3; Henderson, *Writing down Rome*, esp. 250, 260–1, 267–9.

[129] e.g. Mount Olympus at J. 13.42–9; Hades at 2.149–58 and 3.264–7; Golden Age at 6.1–13 and 13.38–52; future at 1.147–8, 2.135–6. It is interesting to note that Juvenal thus fulfils one of the crucial requirements which Bakhtin sets up when defining his super-genre *Menippea*, namely that the action move over the 'three-planed construction' of heaven–earth–underworld. Bakhtin's view of his *Menippea* is

passes everything is turned into human size with help of humour. Humour shrinks the gods, shines a light into the Underworld, and makes sure the inhabitants of the mythic past are substantial and sturdy. The result is epic inside-out—hilarious and boldly ambitious at the same time.

The three passages that will be treated in some detail here are the two direct descriptions of the Golden Age (6.1–13; 13.38–52) together with one picture of past rural life (14.166–71), which, though not strictly speaking about the Golden Age (since there is already agriculture), nevertheless exhibits several traits typical of this motif. This last passage is chosen for the expressiveness of its details, while a few other places reminiscent of the motif are left in the background,[130] with the hope that the instances quoted will be representative. The three examples will be discussed together, because their common features outweigh their specific functions in their respective satires.

First comes the famous description of the family in the Saturnian age, at the beginning of the sixth satire:

> Credo Pudicitiam Saturno rege moratam
> in terris visamque diu, cum frigida parvas
> praeberet spelunca domos ignemque laremque
> et pecus et dominos communi clauderet umbra,
> silvestrem montana torum cum sterneret uxor
> frondibus et culmo vicinarumque ferarum
> pellibus, haut similis tibi, Cynthia, nec tibi, cuius
> turbavit nitidos extinctus passer ocellos,
> sed potanda ferens infantibus ubera magnis

that it is an enormously broad genre (ranging from Menippus to Dostoyevsky), and that it is not defined by formal characteristics such as prosimetron or limits in time and culture, but by the presence of fourteen elements—mainly thematic—which he presents. In his view, the genre is not a form passed on by influence or knowledge of it on the part of the author, but a deep structure characteristic of human thinking, which, after being forgotten for generations, may spring up in a writer who has not heard about it. The 'three-planed construction' is number six of Bakhtin's elements, and his example of a work that qualifies as *Menippea* in this respect is Seneca's *Apocolocyntosis*; Juvenal would be alone among the Roman verse satirists to fulfil this point (M. M. Bakhtin, *Problems of Dostoevsky's Poetics*. Russian orig. in 1963 (2nd, enlarged and rev. edn.), ed. and trans. C. Emerson (Minneapolis:Universityof Minnesota Press,1984), 116).

[130] e.g. 3.309–14, 14.179–88.

et saepe horridior glandem ructante marito.
quippe aliter tunc orbe novo caeloque recenti
vivebant homines, qui rupto robore nati
compositive luto nullos habuere parentes.   (6.1–13)

I believe that Chastity lived on earth in Saturn's reign, and was long to be
seen when a cold cave offered people their only small house, their hearth and
home, and when the same shade closed in on the cattle and their masters.
Then the mountain wife would spread the woodland bed with leaves and
straw and the furs of animals, their neighbours. She was hardly like you,
Cynthia, nor like you whose bright eyes were dimmed by the death of a
sparrow, but she gave her breast to suck to her big babies, and was often
bristling with more hair than her acorn-belching husband. For then, when
the earth was new and the sky was young, people lived differently; the people
who were themselves born from the bursting wood of the oak, or made of
clay, and who had no parents.

Second, there is the smiling story of the young gods who ruled the
world at a time when immorality was so rare that people gaped at it;
this is told in contrast to the contemporary world, where a good man
is so unheard of that if one were to appear, he would be considered a
prodigy:

quondam hoc indigenae vivebant more, priusquam
sumeret agrestem posito diademate falcem
Saturnus fugiens, tunc cum virguncula Iuno
et privatus adhuc Idaeis Iuppiter antris;
nulla super nubes convivia caelicolarum
nec puer Iliacus formonsa nec Herculis uxor
ad cyathos et iam siccato nectare tergens
bracchia Volcanus Liparaea nigra taberna;
prandebat sibi quisque deus nec turba deorum
talis ut est hodie, contentaque sidera paucis
numinibus miserum urguebat Atlanta minori
pondere; nondum imi sortitus triste profundi
imperium Sicula torvos cum coniuge Pluton,
nec rota nec Furiae nec saxum aut volturis atri
poena, sed infernis hilares sine regibus umbrae.   (13.38–52)

Once the natives lived this way, before Saturn, fleeing, laid down his crown
and took up the country sickle instead; when Juno was still a slip of a girl and
Jove lived as a common man in the caves on Ida. There were no feasts among

the gods above the clouds, no Trojan boy or pretty wife of Hercules to serve the wine, and Vulcan wiped off his arms, black with soot from the Liparaean smithy, only after gulping down his nectar. Every god had lunch on his own. There wasn't such a mob of gods as there is today, so the stars, content with a few deities, weighed less heavily on poor Atlas' shoulders. The gloomy rule over the depths of the underworld had not yet been assigned to grim Pluto and his Sicilian spouse; there was no wheel, no Furies, no stone or punishment inflicted by a black vulture. Instead, the shades were frolicking, without any infernal kings.

Third, there is the idyllic sketch of past times' happy rural life, characterized by modesty and equality:

> saturabat glebula talis
> patrem ipsum turbamque casae, qua feta iacebat
> uxor et infantes ludebant quattuor, unus
> vernula, tres domini; sed magnis fratribus horum
> a scrobe vel sulco redeuntibus altera cena
> amplior et grandes fumabant pultibus ollae.
> nunc modus hic agri nostro non sufficit horto.   (14.166–71)

such a plot of land would feed the father of a family and the crowd in his hut, where his wife lay pregnant and four children played, one a slave-boy, three sons of the master. But their elder brothers would be met by another, larger, supper when they came home from ditch or furrow: great cauldrons of porridge would be steaming. Today this amount of land would not be enough for one of our gardens.

Let us first recapitulate why the inhabitants in these scenes may, in a sense, be counted among Juvenal's monsters. In all cases they are bigger than humans and smaller than gods, they are something in between, the anomalies of an early age when current standards had not yet settled down. The woman in J. 6 is big as a mountain[131] and hairier than a man, her babe is likewise enormous. The whole family is intermingled with animals: they live under the same roof, and the acorn-belching husband obviously has the table-manners of a beast. Of the elder brothers expected home in J. 14 it may be surmised that they are big, since they require a *cena amplior* ('larger supper') and

---

[131] Juvenal seems to be making a pun with 'montana uxor': it may mean either that she is *like* a mountain, or that she is a mountain dweller. I believe we are meant to catch both meanings.

grandes ollae ('great cauldrons'). The gods in J. 13, on their part, indulge in undignified, typically human behaviour such as taking one's after-work drink before washing one's hands, having simple lunch alone (*prandebat sibi quisque deus*), getting tired from the burden on one's shoulders. The ghosts in the underworld take pleasure in their anarchic lifestyle, a far cry from the atmosphere in Hades later, under Jove's rule. The monstrosity of these characters is on the one hand in line with what is usually on scene in literary descriptions of the Golden Age, where the conditions are often a (positive) inversion of normal conditions,[132] on the other hand, here it is specifically slanted in the direction of the grotesque and the gigantic—of course with a comic effect.

At least as regards the Saturnian matron, the prevailing reading today is that she is monstrous and primitive, not that she is virtuous.[133] Since I want to argue that she (like the rest of the Golden Age pictures) is *both* a monstrous *and* a positive image at the same time, I must now focus on the reasons for seeing her positive side, as well as the good traits of the other Golden Age scenes. The reasons that will be discussed here may be arranged around four points: (1) the contrast between surface and essence; (2) the opposition to especially loathsome sins; (3) modest poverty; and (4) endearing features.

1. By the contrast between surface and essence I mean that while these characters are mocked for being ugly, dirty, and ill-dressed, they are worthy on the inside, in their morals. This constellation is the reverse of the hypocrite, a type hated by satire, and treated by Juvenal, as in the form of the stern-looking pathics in J. 2 or the legacy-hunters who offer rich sarcifices for the health of childless Croesuses whose death they are in fact eagerly awaiting (J. 12). Juvenal's favourite among his predecessors, Lucilius, had made it his business

---

[132] The motif had been used by e.g. Hesiod (*Op.* 109–19), Lucretius (an atheistic version of the world's ages and man's civilization, *DRN* 5.772–1457), Virgil (*G.* 1.118–46, and differently in the Golden Eclogue, *E.* 4.18–45), Horace (*Epod.* 16.41–66), Tibullus (1.3.35–50), and Ovid (*Met.* 1.89–150). D. Singleton ('Juvenal VI.1–20, and Some Ancient Attitudes to the Golden Age', *G&R* 19 (1972), 151–65) discusses the Golden Age of J. 6 in the context of the motif's tradition.

[133] Cf. Singleton, 'Attitudes to the Golden Age'; Henderson, 'Satire Writes Woman'; and id., *Writing down Rome*; B. K. Gold, ' "The House I Live In Is Not My Own": Women's Bodies in Juvenal's *Satires*', *Arethusa*, 31, 3 (1998), 369–86.

to 'strip off the skin, in which each went sleekly groomed in public, while inwardly foul',[134] and the other Roman satirists had followed. The opposite type, the person with a dishevelled, ridiculous appearance and an excellent character and/ or a great talent hidden within, had been used by Horace to describe himself, and I have argued above that he based his version of the image on the figure of Socrates.[135] In this way not only the hypocrite, but also his inverse, the outwardly laughable paragon of virtue, had a precedent in Roman satire. More specifically, Juvenal plays off something of this contrast at the level of the individual satires where the Golden Age pictures appear. So the massive woman in J. 6 is expressly compared to two beloved ladies from the altogether different genre of lyric poetry: Catullus' Lesbia and Propertius' Cynthia. Juvenal's primitive housewife is said to be unlike them, *haut similis*, and in the same sentence we hear some of the points of this dissimilarity—that she breast-fed her child and that she was often even more bristling with hair than her mate. Cynthia is simply named, while Lesbia is described with the *literary* fact that she cried over her dead sparrow until her bright eyes (designated with the Catullan form *ocelli*) turned red. There are several significant aspects to these lines: the cavewoman is unlike the beauties in one point of behaviour (breast-feeding, a token of female virtue and a traditional ingredient in descriptions of the Golden Age) and one point of looks (she is very hairy, which Lesbia and Cynthia were certainly not). Furthermore, for his comparison the satirist chooses two emphatically literary creations, paper dolls with the aura of lyric beauty but not the smell of mortals. This makes his woman, by contrast, seem more real, although she is at bottom also a mythic character; in addition, she is *realistic* where the love heroines are *idealized* and idle in their behaviour. The passage is surely also a contrast of genres, where satire, with its page smacking of the human, carries the day. Thus the girls and their genre of lyric poetry exhibit the hypocrite constellation of inside and outside, i.e. they are lovely on the surface but debauched beneath it, while the *montana uxor*, like her genre satire,

---

[134] So in Horace's formulation, 'detrahere et pellem, nitidus qua quisque per ora| cederet, introrsum turpis', *S.* 2.1.64–5.
[135] See Ch. 2, § 'Wearing the satyric mask of Socrates'.

shows the opposite constellation, i.e. ugly and ridiculous in appearance but virtuous in essence. Similarly, in the thirteenth satire the simple but happy life of the young world is contrasted with the contemporary scene, where elegance is cynically combined with perjury and deceit. The poem's addressee Calvinus, who is expecting to have a loan paid back to him, will be laughed out of court as incredibly naïve (13.35), and even the persona ironically calls him a child.[136] In the fourteenth satire, present-day *luxuria* and greed are opposed to the idyllic picture in our quotation, and a few lines further on, where it is recounted how a farmer of olden times would advise his sons, he is made to say that it is 'foreign purple', i.e. royal luxury, that has destroyed Rome, and that the people who are not ashamed of rough clothing and hard work are not even tempted to do forbidden things (14.179–88). Again, an inelegant outer appearance covering a moral soul is contrasted with the opposite combination.

2. Life in Juvenal's Golden Age photographs is opposed to the sins he hates the most. Sexual licence, *impudicitia*, a major theme in his satires, is said to have been absent from the Saturnian age of the cavewoman at the opening of J. 6; it was absent *only* from that age, for even with the Silver Age it came to mankind. The cavewoman herself, though fertile, is completely unerotic (and let us remember that erotic women are always bad women in Juvenal)—this is a picture from before the Fall. In the Golden Age in J. 13, too, the expression 'nec puer Iliacus formonsa nec Herculis uxor | ad cyathos' may suggest that there was as yet no room for adultery (Ganymede) nor erotic pleasure (beautiful boys and girls serving at table). Juno, too, was still a little virgin, *virguncula*. These examples also clearly show that there was no vanity, which both in women and *cinaedi* (the still absent Ganymede again) is one of Juvenal's favourite targets. In J. 14, the woman of the house is, if possible, even less sexually–socially vain than in the other passages, simply lying down and being pregnant. In all three citations the characters are doing some hard, honest work (actually a breach against the tradition, according

---

[136] Cf. also the lines about the stern human laws of the Golden Age, when respect for one's elders was always required, independently of such superficial privileges as being richer in strawberries and acorns (13.53–59, contrasted with vv. 60–70).

to which work was introduced in the Silver Age): the woman in J. 6 is making the bed and caring for the child, in J. 13 Vulcan is toiling in the comically human *taberna* where he has his smithy, and the elder brothers are digging or ploughing in J. 14. This is all opposed to laziness and leisure, and above all it is opposed to the quick, dishonest ways of making money practised everywhere in contemporary Rome: informing, legacy-hunting, prostitution, murder. Foremost among the vices Juvenal satirizes, however, is greed, with the related traits of luxury and of stinginess, sometimes combined into *luxuriae sordes*. The negation of this vice is explicitly present in all the Golden Age texts, where the inhabitants live without affluence but are happy with what they have—and this brings us to the third point.

3. These characters, then, live in relative poverty, and this the satirist directly connects to their moral excellence, not least in the realm of sex. Further down in *Satire* 6, in lines 287–300, he says that in the *poor* old days there was neither time nor need for sins such as debauchery at Rome; it was only with the curse of a long period of peace ('longae pacis mala', 292) that luxury, trailing along vice, invaded the city: 'nullum crimen abest facinusque libidinis ex quo | paupertas Romana perit' ('No crime or deed of lust is lacking here since the fall of Roman poverty'), 294–5.[137] Connecting the two vices he most abhors, greed and sexual incontinence, Juvenal makes the claim that it was *obscena pecunia* ('filthy money') and *divitiae molles* ('pansy riches'), 298, 300, that brought along bad morals to Rome, an imported product like money itself. In the quotations describing the Saturnian age we may observe in what scarcity life was led: the cold, smallish cave in the sixth satire was shared with the animals and—in obedience to the rules of that age—nothing but acorns was on the menu; in the fourteenth satire a large crowd of a family had only a little spot of land, *glebula*, had to share a simple hut, *casa*, and had not improved their food more than to porridge and home-grown vegetables. Even among the gods in J. 13 the conditions were relatively tight, and in a feast of Horatian 'simple-and-right-living'

---

[137] This passage and its context have been discussed in more detail in Ch. 1 § 'A resisting reading of Juvenal's women'.

vocabulary,[138] Juvenal gives them no dinner parties, *nulla convivia*, has Jove live as a mere private citizen in his cave and the stars be satisfied with only a few godheads, 'privatus Iuppiter antris, contenta paucis', and loads Atlas with a smaller load, 'miserum urguebat Atlanta minore pondere'.

4. The Golden-Age monsterlings have several endearing features. Unlike everybody else in Juvenal, they have a functioning social structure, complete with mutually loyal families and communal equality. In J. 6 the wife performs her duties in that she takes care of the house and specifically of the marriage bed (*torum*) and in that she breast-feeds her child, this latter point in contrast to the modern ladies who spare their looks. The people in J. 14 already have a *pater familias* at the head of their family, the pregnant mother is allowed to rest, the elder sons are properly fed upon coming home from honest work, and the four younger children play indiscriminately in the unbiased configuration three free-born—one slave boy. In J. 13 the gods have no servants yet, living as private citizens and eating modestly to themselves, and the spirits in the Underworld have no kings to rule them.

Their clumsiness is not altogether negative. Although one must be careful so as not to overstate this, there are a couple of traits that seem humanly sloppy rather than really ugly, in a manner somewhat reminiscent of Horace's self-portraits: the black hands and arms of Vulcan as he eagerly gulps down his nectar in J. 13, the clumsy boots and the primitive fur coat in the passage with the farmer's speech to his children further on in J. 14 (mentioned above): 'quem non pudet alto | per glaciem perone tegi, qui summovet euros | pellibus inversis' ('who is not ashamed to put on high boots as he walks over the frost, and who keeps the winds off with a fur-lined coat'), 14.185–7.[139]

---

[138] For this vocabulary, see Mette, 'Genus tenue—mensa tenuis'.

[139] Even the great size of the cavewoman in J. 6 is perhaps not as shocking as it would have been if only the *petite* ideal were accepted—further on in the same satire a pygmy girl is piling up her coiffure, trying to look like the famously tall Andromache, while Juvenal mocks her vain attempts (6.502–7). One should, however, tread cautiously here, for the cavewoman is undoubtedly more ugly than not.

Again unlike most characters in Juvenal, and surprising in monsters, they possess moderation: they seem to feel joy (*hilares umbrae* in J. 13), but not ecstasy. In all three texts the monsterlings live in serene peace far from the madding crowd of Rome, where a satirist only needs to stand in a street-corner in order to fill thick notebooks with satirical material.

Most importantly, these passages are dominated by life and fertility *contra* death and sterility, which characterize the contemporary scene in Rome according to Juvenal. As has been noticed, J. 6 may be said to draw a circle from death to death in that close to its beginning, it features an admonition to the addressee that suicide is less painful than getting married (6.30–2), and ends with a description of how women murder their husbands (6.655–61).[140] Between these mentions at beginning and end we are told that contemporary Roman women try not to get pregnant, undergo abortion, and kill their children and stepchildren—in short, they spread death about them everywhere they go. But the Neanderthal woman in our quotation, at the very opening of the poem and so before the first reference to violent death, stands outside this vicious circle, and she is fertile and caring. It should be noted that the line where she gives her breast to the huge child immediately follows the line about Lesbia crying over the *dead* sparrow. If we allow for an allusion to the (ancient) interpretation that the *passer Catulli* stands for his penis,[141] we get a picture of the idle paper beauty crying over impotence and sterility, side by side with the life-giving breast of the Golden Age woman. In *Satire* 14, again, the family is fertile: the woman has had at least five children already (the three younger ones + at least two out in the field) and is now pregnant again. As in J. 6, this family, too, welcomes children and takes care of them. Their patch of land nurtures them and keeps them from getting hungry; the richly associative verb

---

[140] See Ch. 1 § 'A resisting reading of Juvenal's women', p. 134.

[141] Cf. esp. Martial 11.6.16, 'donabo tibi passerem Catulli' ('I'll give you Catullus' sparrow'), as well as Mart. 1.109.1 and 7.14.4; Plin. *NH.* 10.107; *Priap.* 26.5; and not least Fest. 312: 'strutheum ... vocant obscenam partem virilem, <a> salacitate videlicet passeris, qui gr<a>ece στρουθός dicitur' ('the obscene male member is called "strutheus", this because of the salaciousness of the sparrow, which is called στρουθός in Greek').

saturabat is used here. In J. 13, Hades, the kingdom of death, has not yet been properly set up.

Thus Juvenal's grotesque humour helped him describe widely differing poles of human experience, including even such affirmative motifs as those inherent in the Golden Age, which are deeply alien to his world-view, and which he—though not avoiding them entirely—took care to place at the very periphery of his universe.

In summary it may be said that while these pictures of gods and men in the Golden Age present them as monsters on the surface, their insides do not follow, and are sometimes even explicitly contrasted with their imperfect looks. These kind monsters are monsters for show (*monstro*), but hardly for warning (*moneo*). Juvenal uses them to expand the realm of his satire so as to include the Golden Age, Mount Olympus, and Hades. In order to be made satirical, these places have to be colonized with comic creatures, preferably of a human stature. If they cannot become properly human, then their size and strength at least have to be exploited for their comic potential, have to be stripped of their awe-inspiring honour—and what better way to achieve this than to make them into funny monsters, properly playing on the closeness between the awesome and the ridiculous. Thus even the remotest corners of the world—and when it comes to satire these are the (few!) corners of moral goodness—are usurped, with the curious result that the prodigious universe of Juvenal's satire has to include not only a plethora of horrible monsters but also *better* monsters, which are ugly and laughable only on the outside. In this way the apparently unnecessary non-aligned humour helps to complete the ambitious grotesque world of the last Roman satirist.

What in Horace was like the optical grey of the great masters of harmony, in Juvenal becomes the grotesque tableaux of Hieronymus Bosch. But in fact Horace's and Juvenal's techniques have a crucial thing in common: their bold aspiration to present the whole of life in their work. In capturing the extremes of the scale, they hope, and to a great extent succeed, to give an impression of life in its entirety. As Juvenal puts it:

quidquid agunt homines, votum, timor, ira, voluptas,
gaudia, discursus, nostri farrago libelli est.   (1.85–6)

whatever men do, their prayers, fears, angers, pleasure, joys, their running to
and fro—all of this is fodder for my little book.

The very fact that their satires' incongruities are not ironed out, that
their equations do not add up, and that their paradoxes remain just
that, paradoxes, adds a lively openness to the world they depict.
This—very much an effect of their non-aligned humour—is what
allowed the styles of Horace and Juvenal, unlike that of Persius, to be
taken up and elaborated by later writers. And in this, I submit, they
also formed a link in the chain leading from the most ambitious
classical genre, epic, to the most ambitious and most open of our
genres today, the novel.

Epilogue: The Genre Devours Itself

In Juvenal's fifteenth satire satiric humour reaches its limits. The kernel of J. 15 is a narrative about how two feuding Egyptian villages engage in a fierce battle which ends with one tribe catching a man from the other village, and eating him in their fury. Before coming to its end, Juvenalian humour flashes a final burst of grotesque funniness, a rush of what modern jargon would call 'sick humour', in the detailed description of a man torn to pieces and eaten without time-consuming culinary preparation:

> labitur hic quidam nimia formidine cursum
> praecipitans capiturque. ast illum in plurima sectum
> frusta et particulas, ut multis mortuus unus
> sufficeret, totum corrosis ossibus edit
> uictrix turba, nec ardenti decoxit aeno
> aut ueribus, longum usque adeo tardumque putauit
> expectare focos, contenta cadauere crudo.   (15.77–83)

One man tripped as he rushed along in exceeding panic, and was caught. But the victorious mob chopped him up in many bits and pieces so that this single dead body would be enough for many. Then they ate him, gnawing his bones, not bothering to boil him in a brass cauldron, or roast him on spits. They found it such a drag and such a bore to wait for the fire to take, so they made do with a raw corpse.

In this passage the harsh parody of a battle situation, and the incongruous intertwining of ghastly 'realistic' detail with detached cooking terminology combine to create grim and questionable humour: is this still funny?

Several theoretical discussions of humour, including that of Cicero in the second book of *De Oratore*, claim that the laughable borders on the outrageous, but that they are mutually exclusive. Humour may grow sharp and provocative by stepping close to its border with the outrageous (the incongruity is strong, the shock-value jolts the audience), yet if it steps over the border, it is no longer humour. Thus Cicero says that what we find funny consists in the faults of people who do not excite particular feelings of pity, love, or indignation:

itaque ea facillime luduntur quae *neque odio magno* neque misericordia maxima digna sunt. quam ob rem materies omnis ridiculorum est in iis vitiis, quae sunt in vita hominum neque carorum neque calamitosorum *neque eorum qui ob facinus ad supplicium rapiendi* videntur (Cic. De Or. 2.238)

Those things are easiest to joke about which deserve *neither great hatred* nor great pity. Thus the material of the laughable lies in faults in the life of people who are neither dear to us, nor miserable, *nor of such a kind that they seem fully ripe for immediate punishment for the crime they have committed.*

The scene in J. 15 involves people who clearly fit Cicero's category of people whose crime calls out for punishment, thus arousing indignation beyond laughter. In Juvenal's treatment, the cannibalistic motif lies on the border between the funny and the no-longer-funny.

Together with humour, the genre of satire as a whole reaches its limits here. At v. 29, before beginning the actual narrative of the event, Juvenal warned us that this collective crime of a people is more serious than all the tragedies:

> nos volgi scelus et cunctis graviora coturnis;
> nam scelus, a Pyrrha quamquam omnia syrmata volvas,
> nullus apud tragicos populus facit.   (J. 15.29–31)

My story is about the collective crime, and more serious than all the tragedies. For a crime is never committed by a whole people in the tragedians—you won't find an instance of this even if you search through tragedy's wardrobes from Pyrrha on.

Juvenal had made a similar meta-literary comment once before, in J. 6, when describing women who murder their children. There he had said that the subject matter, at this point, seemed to require satire to transgress its generic limits and take up the devices of tragedy, but in fact what he was telling was the truth:

fingimus haec altum satura sumente coturnum
scilicet, et finem egressi legemque priorum
grande Sophocleo carmen bacchamur hiatu,
montibus ignotum Rutulis caeloque Latino?
nos utinam vani.   (6.634–8)

Am I making this up, letting my satire take up the high stage-shoes of tragedy, that is? Have I transgressed the genre limits of my predecessors, raving in ecstasy with my mouth gaping in the manner of Sophocles, shouting a song yet unknown to Rutulian hills and Latin skies?

I wish it were all nonsense!

In J. 15, we may observe that Juvenal makes much the same statement when he says that this story is graver than any tragedy—the story of man-eaters is neither satire, nor even tragedy. The material is *graviora*, i.e. 'more serious', 'heavier', it is planned, at the outset, to go beyond *ridiculum*, the laughable. Yet humour is undeniably present in the picture of the macabre feast on human flesh. The image of the feast, and of food, in Roman satire is intimately connected to the essence of the genre itself. The etymological link between the genre name, *satura*, and food (through *lanx satura*, the full dish of offerings) lived on, being variously exploited throughout the history of Roman satire. As has been convincingly shown by Gowers in her study *The Loaded Table* (1993), food described in the satires may be taken as an image of the genre.

When in J. 15 the food becomes cannibalistic, the projected image is extreme. If food stands for the genre of satire, and the food is human flesh, devoured by humans, then the genre of satire is devoured by its like, i.e. satire devours itself.

Juvenal's last satire, J. 16, whose main topic is the roughness of soldiers, has come down to us in an unfinished state. In this sixteenth satire there are only fragments of satiric humour, reminiscent rather of Juvenal's early satires. The fragments of humour are symbolized by fragments of human bodies: the knocked-out teeth, one eye, and black piece of flesh in the face of a beaten civilian (16.10–12), and the boots, legs, and fists of his aggressors, the soldiers (16.13–4, 24, 30).

After the explosion of grotesque humour in J. 15, satire had nowhere else to go. As with the victim of cannibalism in J. 15, so

with the genre of satire, there briefly existed some bits and pieces—
'frusta et particulas' (15.79)—before these too were devoured.

Yet this is not the end of the story. In Graeco-Roman myth, the god
Kronos (Saturn) devoured his children. His last child, Zeus, was
saved and in time grew up, killed his father, and freed his siblings
from Kronos' belly. Likewise, history in later times freed devoured
satire and returned it to life. And as in the case with Zeus' siblings,
satire sprang forth renewed and refreshed.

Bibliography

BIBLIOGRAPHIES

ANDERSON, W. S., 'Recent Work in Roman Satire (1937–1955)', *CW* 50 (1956–7), 33–40.

—— 'Recent Work in Roman Satire (1955–1962)', *CW* 57 (1963–4), 293–301 & 343–8.

—— 'Recent Work in Roman Satire (1962–1968)', *CW* 63 (1969–70), 181–199.

—— 'Recent Work in Roman Satire (1968–78)', *CW* 75 (1982), 274–99.

CUCCIOLI MELONI, R., 'Otto anni di studi Giovenaliani (1969–1976)', *BStudLat*, 7 (1977), 61–87.

EHLERS, W. in U. KNOCHE (ed.), *Die römische Satire*. (1949; 3rd edn. Göttingen: Vandenhoeck u. Ruprecht, 1971), 126–30, covering 1956–69.

http://www.otus.oakland.edu/english/showcase/satbib.htm

KISSEL, W., 'Horaz 1936–1975: Eine Gesamtbiographie', *ANRW* II.31.3 (1981), 1403–1558.

MARTÍN RODRÍGUEZ, M. T., 'Juvenal (1979–1992)', *Tempus* 5 (1993), 5–38.

NILSEN, D. L. F., *Humor Scholarship. A Research Bibliography.* (Westport, Conn.: Greenwood Press, 1993).

EDITIONS, COMMENTARIES, AND TRANSLATIONS OF THE PRIMARY TEXTS

Lucilius
MARX, F. (ed.), *C. Lucilii Carminum Reliquiae* (Leipzig: Teubner, 1904).

Horace
BROWN, P. M., (introd., text, trans., and comm.) *Horace: Satires I*, (Warminster: Aris & Phillips, 1993. Repr. with corrections 1995).

KIEßLING, A., and HEINZE, R. (eds.), *Q. Horatius Flaccus. Zweiter Teil: Satiren* (6th edn., Berlin: Weidmannsche Verlagsbuchhandlung, 1957).

MUECKE, F., (introd., trans., and comm.) *Horace: Satires II*, (Warminster: Aris & Phillips, 1993).

RUDD, N. (trans., introd., and notes), *Horace: Satires and Epistles. Persius: Satires* (1973; 4th edn., London: Penguin, 1997).

SHACKLETON BAILEY, D. R. (ed.) *Q. Horatius Flaccus: Opera*, (4th edn., Leipzig: Saur, 2001).

Persius

KIßEL, W. (ed., trans., and comm.), *Aules Persius Flaccus: Satiren*. Heidelberg, 1990.

CLAUSEN, W. V. (ed.), *A. Persi Flacci et D. Iuni Iuvenalis Saturae* (1959; 2nd, rev. edn. Oxford: Oxford University Press, 1992).

LEE, G., and BARR, W. (eds.), *The Satires of Persius*. Text with verse trans. by G. Lee; introd. and comm. by W. Barr (Liverpool: Francis Cairns, 1987).

Juvenal

CLAUSEN, W. V. See above.

COURTNEY, E., *A Commentary on the Satires of Juvenal* (London: Athlone Press, 1980).

GREEN, P. (trans., introd., and notes), *Juvenal, The Sixteen Satires* (London: Penguin, 1974).

LUISI, A., *Il Rombo e la Vestale. Giovenale, Satira IV* (Bari: Edipuglia, 1998).

MAYOR, J. E. B., *Thirteen Satires of Juvenal*: i text of all the satires except 2 and 6, and comm. to satires 1–7 (2nd edn. London: Macmillan & Co, 1877); ii. comm. to satires 8–16 (3rd edn. London: Macmillan & Co, 1881).

RUDD, N. (trans.), and BARR, W. (introd. and notes), *Juvenal, The Satires* (1991; 2nd edn. Oxford: Oxford University Press, 1999).

GENERAL

ADAMIETZ, J. (ed.), *Die römische Satire* (Darmstadt: Wissenschaftlige Buchgesellschaft, 1986).

ANDERSON, W. S., 'Juvenal and Quintilian', *YCS* 17 (1961), 1–91. Reprinted in *Essays on Roman Satire* (Princeton: Princeton University Press, 1982).

—— 'The Programs of Juvenal's Later Books', *CP* 57 (1962), 145–60. Reprinted in *Essays on Roman Satire* (Princeton: Princeton University Press, 1982).

—— 'The Roman Socrates: Horace and his Satires', in *Critical Essays on Roman Literature. Satire*. J. P. Sullivan (ed.), (London: Routledge & Kegan Paul, 1963).

—— 'Anger in Juvenal and Seneca', *California Publications in Classical Philology* 19 (1964), 127–96. Reprinted in *Essays on Roman Satire* (Princeton: Princeton University Press, 1982).

344 Bibliography

ANDERSON, W. S., '*Lascivia* vs. *ira*: Martial and Juvenal', *CSCA* 3 (1970), 1–34. Reprinted in *Essays on Roman Satire* (Princeton: Princeton University Press, 1982).

—— 'The Form, Purpose, and Position of Horace's Satire I, 8', *AJP* 93 (1972), 4–13. Reprinted in *Essays on Roman Satire* (Princeton: Princeton University Press, 1982).

—— *Essays on Roman Satire* (Princeton: Princeton University Press, 1982).

—— 'Rustic Urbanity: Roman Satirists in and out of Rome', *Thalia* 5 (1982), 27–34.

—— 'Juvenal Satire 15: Cannibals and Culture', in A. J. Boyle (ed.), *The Imperial Muse. To Juvenal through Ovid* (Berwick, Victoria: Aureal Publications, 1988).

—— *Barbarian Play: Plautus' Roman Comedy* (Toronto: University of Toronto Press, 1993).

ANTONY, H., *Humor in der Augusteischen Dichtung* (Hildesheim: Verlag Dr. H. A. Gerstenberg, 1976).

APTE, M. L., *Humor and Laughter: an Anthropological Approach* (Ithaca, NY: Cornell University Press, 1985).

ATTARDO, S., *Linguistic Theories of Humor* (Berlin: Mouton de Gruyter, 1994).

BABCOCK, B. A., *The Reversible World: Symbolic Inversion in Art and Society* (Ithaca, NY: Cornell University Press, 1978).

BAKHTIN, M. M., *Rabelais and his World.* Russian original in 1965; trans. H. Iswolsky (Cambridge, Mass.: MIT Press, 1968).

—— *Problems of Dostoevsky's Poetics.* Russian original 1963 (2nd, enlarged and rev. edn.); ed. and trans. C. Emerson (Minneapolis: University of Minnesota Press, 1984).

—— *Sobranije Sočinenij* [Collected works], v (Moscow: Russkije Slovari, 1997).

BARBIERI, A., 'Praeco-poeta, sal e urbanitas', *RCCM* 29 (1987), 111–50.

BAUMERT, J., 'Identifikation und Distanz: Eine Erprobung satirischer Kategorien bei Juvenal', *ANRW* II 33.1(1989), 734–69.

BELLANDI, F., 'Naevolus cliens', *Maia* 26 (1974), 279–99.

BENDORIUTE, A. T., 'Humoras Juvenalio satyrose', ['Das Humor in den Satiren von Juvenalis'], *Literatura* (Vilnius) 25/3 (1983), 39–47.

BERGSON, H., *Le rire. Essai sur la signification du comique* (1900; 17th edn. Paris: Alcan, 1919).

BERNARDI PERINI, G., 'Suspendere naso. Storia di una metafora', *Atti e Memorie dell'Accademia Patavina di Scienze, Lettere ed Arti.* Classe di Scienze morali, Lettere ed Arti 79, parte III (1966–7), 233–64.

—— 'Aceto italico e poesia Luciliana: Hor. *Sat.* I.7', in *Scritti in onore di Carlo Diano.* (Bologna, 1975).

BERNSTEIN, M. A., '*O totiens Servus*: Saturnalia and Servitude in Augustan Rome', *Critical Inquiry*, 13 (1987), 450–74.

BLOOMER, M., *Latinity and Literary Society at Rome* (Philadelphia: University of Pennsylvania Press,1997).

BODEL, J., 'Trimalchio's Underworld' in J.Tatum (ed.), *The Search for the Ancient Novel* (Baltimore and London: Johns Hopkins University Press, 1994).

BOLL, F., 'Die Anordnung im zweiten Buch von Horaz' Satiren', *Hermes* 48 (1913), 143–5.

BOOTH, W., *A Rhetoric of Irony* (Chicago and London: University of Chicago Press,1974).

—— *The Rhetoric of Fiction* (1961; 2nd edn. Chicago: Universityof Chicago Press,1983).

BOYLE, A. J. (ed.), *The Imperial Muse. To Juvenal through Ovid* (Berwick, Victoria: Aureal, 1988).

BOYS-STONES, G. R., *Metaphor, Allegory, and the Classical Tradition* (Oxford: Oxford University Press, 2003).

BRAMBLE, J. C., *Persius and the Programmatic Satire. A Study in Form and Imagery* (Cambridge: Cambridge University Press, 1974).

BRANHAM, R. B., *Unruly Eloquence. Lucian and the Comedy of Traditions* (Cambridge, Mass.: Harvard University Press, 1989).

—— and GOULET-CAZÉ, M-O. (eds.), *The Cynics. The Cynic Movement in Antiquity and its Legacy* (Berkeley and Los Angeles: University of California Press, 1996).

BRAUND, S. H., *Beyond Anger. A Study of Juvenal's Third Book of Satires* (Cambridge: Cambridge University Press, 1988).

—— (ed.), *Satire and Society in Ancient Rome* (Exeter: University of Exeter, 1989).

—— ' Juvenal—Misogynist or Misogamist?', *JRS* 82 (1992), 71–86.

—— *Roman Verse Satire*. Greece & Rome: New Surveys in the Classics 23 (Oxford: Oxford University Press, 1992).

—— 'Paradigms of Power: Roman Emperors in Roman Satire', in K. Cameron (ed.), *Humour and History* (Oxford: Intellect, 1993).

—— and RASCHKE, W., 'Satiric Grotesques in Public and Private: Juvenal, Dr. Frankenstein, Raymond Chandler, and *Absolutely Fabulous*', *G&R* 49 (2002), 62–84.

BREMMER, J., and ROODENBURG, J. (eds.), *A Cultural History of Humour* (Cambridge: Polity, 1997).

BRINK, C. O., *On Reading A Horatian Satire: An Interpretation of Sermones 2, 6* (Sidney, 1965: 3–19).

BRUMMACK, J., 'Zu Begriff und Theorie der Satire', *Deutsche Vierteljahrschrift für Literaturwissenschaft und Geistesgeschichte* 45 (1971), 275–377.

BUCHHEIT, V., 'Homerparodie und Literaturkritik in Horazens Satiren I, 7 und I, 9', *Gymnasium* 75 (1968), 519–55.

CALLIMACHUS, *Fragmenta. Hymni et epigrammata*, ed. Rudolfus Pfeiffer (2 vols., Oxford: Oxford University Press, 1949–53).

CAMERON, K. (ed.), *Humour and History* (Oxford: Intellect, 1993).

CASAUBON, I., *De satyrica Graecorum poesi et Romanorum satira* (Paris, 1605).

CÈBE, J.-P., *La caricature et la parodie dans le monde romain antique des origines a Juvénal* (Paris, 1966).

CECCARELLI, F., *Sorriso e riso. Saggio di antropologia biosociale* (Turin: Einaudi, 1988).

CHAPMAN, A. J., and FOOT, H. C., *Humour and Laughter: Theory, Research, and Application* (London: Wiley, 1976).

CHRISTES, J., and FÜLLE, G., 'Causa fuit pater his: Überlegungen zu Horaz, *Sat.* 1, 6', in C. Klodt (ed.), *Satura Lanx. Festschrift für Werner A. Krenkel zum 70. Geburtstag* (Hildesheim: Olms, 1996).

CLASSEN, C. J., 'Eine unsatirische Satire des Horaz? Zu Hor. Sat. I.5', *Gymnasium* 80 (1973), 235–50.

—— 'Horace—a Cook?' *CQ* 28 (1978), 333–48.

—— 'Überlegungen zu den Möglichkeiten und Grenzen der Anwendung des Begriffes Ironie (im Anschluß an die dritte Satire Juvenals)' in U. J. Stache, W. Maaz, and F. Wagner (eds.), *Kontinuität und Wandel. Lateinische Poesie von Naevius bis Baudelaire*. Franco Munari zum 65. Geburtstag (Hildesheim: Weidmann, 1986).

CLAUSEN, W., *A Commentary on Virgil, Eclogues* (Oxford: Oxford University Press, 1994).

CLOUD, J. D., 'The Client–Patron Relationship: Emblem and Reality in Juvenal's First Book' in A. Wallace-Hadrill (ed.), *Patronage in Ancient Society* (London—New York: Routledge, 1989).

COFFEY, M., *Roman Satire* (London and New York: Methuen & Co, 1976).

COFFTA, D. J., *The Influence of Callimachean Aesthetics on the Satires and Odes of Horace* (Lewiston, NY: The Edwin Mellen Press, 2001).

COLAKIS, M., 'The Laughter of the Suitors in *Odyssey* 20', *CW* 79 (1986), 137–41.

CONNOR, P., *Horace's Lyric Poetry: The Force of Humour* (Berwick, Victoria: Aureal, 1987).

—— 'The Satires of Persius: A Stretch of the Imagination', in A. J. Boyle (ed.), *The Imperial Muse. To Juvenal through Ovid* (Berwick, Victoria: Aureal, 1988).

CORBEILL, A., *Controlling Laughter: Political Humor in the Late Roman Republic* (Princeton: Princeton University Press, 1996).

COSTA, C. D. N. (ed.), *Horace* (London and Boston: Routledge & Kegan Paul, 1973).

DECLOS, M.-L. (ed.), *Le rire des Grecs. Anthropologie du rire en Grèce ancienne* (Grenoble: Editions Jérôme Millon, 2000).

DEDECKER, J., *Juvenalis Declamans. Étude sur la rhétorique déclamatoire dans les Satires de Juvénal* (Gent: Librairie scientifique van Goethem & Cⁱᵉ, 1913).

DE SAINT-DENIS, E., 'L'Humour de Juvénal', *Inform.Litt.* 4 (1952), 8–14.

—— 'L'Humour dans les Satires d'Horace', *RPh* 38 (1964), 24–35.

DESSEN, C. S., *Iunctura Callidus Acri: A Study of Persius' Satires* (Urbana: University of Illinois Press,1968).

DEWITT, N. W., 'Epicurean Doctrine in Horace', *CP* 34 (1939), 127–34.

DIELS, H., and KRANZ, W. (eds.), *Die Fragmente der Vorsokratiker*. Griechisch und deutsch von H. Diels. Achte Auflage herausgegeben von W. Kranz (3 vols., 1952; 8th edn. Berlin: Weidmann, 1956).

DOUGLAS, M., *Purity and Danger: An Analysis of Concepts of Pollution and Taboo* (London: Routledge & Kegan Paul, 1966).

—— 'The Social Control of Cognition: Some Factors in Joke Perception', *Man. The Journal of the Royal Anthropological Institute*, 3/3 (1968), 361–76.

DUNN, F. S., 'Juvenal as a Humorist', *CW* 4 (1911), 50–4.

DUROV, V. S., 'La fortuna di Giovenale in Russia', *A&R* 25 (1980), 51–6.

EARL, D., *The Moral and Political Tradition of Rome* (London: Thames & Hudson, 1967).

ECO, U., *Lector in fabula: la cooperazione interpretativa nei testi narrativi* (Milan: Bompiani, 1979).

—— 'Il comico e la regola', in U. Eco, *Sette anni di desiderio [chronache 1977–1983]* (Milan: Bompiani, 1983).

—— 'Intentio lectoris: The State of the Art', in U. Eco, *The Limits of Interpretation* (Bloomington—Indianapolis: Indiana University Press, 1990).

EDWARDS, C., *The Politics of Immorality in Ancient Rome* (Cambridge: Cambridge University Press, 1993).

EICHHOLZ, D., 'The Art of Juvenal and his Tenth Satire', *G&R* NS 3 (1956), 61–9.

ELLIOTT, R. C., *The Power of Satire: Magic, Ritual, Art* (Princeton: Princeton University Press, 1960).

—— 'Saturnalia, Satire, and Utopia', *Yale Review* 55/4 (1966), 521–36.

ELSNER, J., and MASTERS, J. (eds.), *Reflections of Nero* (Chapel Hill: University of North Carolina Press,1994).

EMPSON, W., *Seven Types of Ambiguity* (London: Chatto & Windus, 1930).

EPICURUS, *Epicuri epistulae tres et ratae sententiae a Laertio Diogene servatae*; accedit *Gnomologium Epicureum Vaticanum*, ed. P. von der Mühll (Leipzig: Teubner, 1922).

EVANS, H. B., 'Horace, Satires 2.7: Saturnalia and Satire', *CJ* 73 (1977–8), 307–12.

FABIAN, B. (ed.), *SATURA. Ein Kompendium moderner Studien zur Satire* (Hildesheim: Olms, 1975).

FERM, O., *Abboten, bonden och hölasset: skratt och humor under medeltiden.* [*The Abbot, the Peasant, and the Hay-cart: Laughter and Humour in the Middle Ages*] (Stockholm: Atlantis, 2002).

FERRARO, V., 'Semipaganus—semivillanus—semipoeta', *Maia* 22 (1970), 139–46.

FESTUS, *Sexti Pompei Festi De verborum significatione quae supersunt: cum Pauli epitome*, ed. K. O. Müller (Leipzig: Weidmann, 1839).

FETTERLEY, J., *The Resisting Reader: a Feminist Approach to American Fiction* (Bloomington: Indiana University Press, 1978).

FISHELOV, D., 'The Vanity of the Reader's Wishes: Reading Juvenal's Satire 10', *AJP* 111 (1990), 370–82.

FISKE, G. C., *Lucilius and Horace. A study in the classical theory of imitation* (Madison: University of Wisconsin, 1920).

FRAENKEL, E., *Horace* (Oxford: Oxford University Press, 1957).

FREDERICKS, S. C., 'Irony of Overstatement in the Satires of Juvenal', *ICS* 4 (1979), 178–91.

FREDRICKSMEYER, H. C., 'An Observation on the Programmatic Satires of Juvenal, Horace and Persius', *Latomus* 49 (1990), 792–800.

FREUD, S., *Der Witz und seine Beziehung zum unbewussten.* (Leipzig - Vienna: Deuticke, 1905)

FREUDENBURG, K., 'Horace's Satiric Program and the Language of Contemporary Theory in Satires 2.1', *AJP* 111 (1990), 187–203.

—— *The Walking Muse. Horace on the Theory of Satire* (Princeton: Princeton University Press, 1993).

—— *Satires of Rome. Threatening Poses from Lucilius to Juvenal* (Cambridge: Cambridge University Press, 2001).

FRIEDLÄNDER, P., 'Lachende Götter', *Die Antike* 10 (1934), 210–26.

FRUELUND JENSEN, B., 'Martyred and Beleaguered Virtue: Juvenal's Portrait of Umbricius', *CM* 37 (1986), 185–97.

FRYE, N., *The Anatomy of Criticism* (Princeton: Princeton University Press, 1957).

GARLAND, R., 'The Mockery of the Deformed and Disabled in Graeco-Roman Culture', in S. Jäkel and A. Timonen (eds.), *Laughter down the Centuries* (Turku: Annales Universitatis Turkuensis, 1994).

GENETTE, G., *Palimpsestes: la littérature au second degré* (Paris: Seuil, 1982).

GERHARD, G. A., *Phoinix von Kolophon* (Leipzig: Teubner, 1909).

GIANGRANDE, L., *The Use of Spoudaiogeloion in Greek and Roman Literature* (The Hague: Mouton, 1972).

GLAZEWSKI, J., '*Plenus Vitae Conviva*: a Lucretian Concept in Horace's *Satires*', *CB* 47 (1971), 85–8.

GOLD, B. K., 'Humor in Juvenal's Sixth Satire: Is It Funny?' in S. Jäkel and A. Timonen (eds.), *Laughter down the Centuries*, i (Turku: Annales Universitatis Turkuensis, 1994).

—— ' "The House I Live In Is Not My Own": Women's Bodies in Juvenal's *Satires*', *Arethusa* 31/3 (1998), 369–86.

GOLDSTEIN, J. H., and MCGHEE, P. E. (eds.), *The Psychology of Humor* (New York and London: Academic Press, 1972).

GOWERS, E., 'Horace, *Satires* 1.5: An Inconsequential Journey', *PCPS* 39 (1993), 48–66.

—— *The Loaded Table. Representations of Food in Roman Literature* (Oxford: Oxford University Press, 1993).

—— 'Persius and the Decoction of Nero', in J. Elsner and J. Masters (eds.), *Reflections of Nero* (Chapel Hill: Universityof North Carolina Press,1994).

—— 'Blind Eyes and Cut Throats: Amnesia and Silence in Horace *Satires* 1.7', *CP* 97 (2002), 145–61.

—— 'Fragments of Autobiography in Horace *Satires* 1', *CA* 22 (2003), 55–92.

GRAF, F., 'Cicero, Plautus and Roman Laughter' in *A Cultural History of Humour*. J. Bremmer and J. Roodenburg (eds.), (Cambridge: Polity, 1997).

GRANT, M., *The Ancient Rhetorical Theories of the Laughable*. University of Wisconsin Studies in Language and Literature 21. (Madison: University of Wisconsin, 1924).

GREENBLATT, S., *Learning to Curse. Essays in Early Modern Culture* (New York: Routledge, 1990).

GRIFFITH, J. G., 'The Ending of Juvenal's First Satire and Lucilius, Book XXX', *Hermes* 98 (1970), 56–72.

HABASH, M., 'Priapus: Horace in Disguise?', *CJ* 94, 3 (1999), 285–97.

HABINEK, T., and SHIESARO, A. (eds.), *The Roman Cultural Revolution* (Cambridge: Cambridge University Press, 1997).

HALLIWELL, S., 'The Uses of Laughter in Greek Culture', *CQ* 41 (1991), 279–96.

HÄNDEL, P., and MEID, W. (eds.), *Festschrift für Robert Muth* (Innsbruck: Amœ: Institut für Sprachwissenschaft der Universität Innsbruck, 1983).

HARDIE, A., 'Juvenal and the Condition of Letters: the Seventh Satire', *Papers of the Leeds International Latin Seminar*, 6 (1990), 145–209.

—— 'Juvenal, Domitian, and the Accession of Hadrian (*Satire* 4)', *BICS* 42 (1997–8), 117–44.

—— 'Juvenal, the Phaedrus, and the Truth about Rome', *CQ* 48 (1998), 234–51.

HARRISON, S. J. (ed.), *Homage to Horace. A Bimillenary Celebration* (Oxford: Oxford University Press, 1995).

HELDMANN, K., 'Die Wesensbestimmung der Horazischen Satire durch die Komödie', *AA* 33 (1987) 122–39.

HENDERSON, J., '. . . When Satire Writes "Woman"', in S. Braund (ed.), *Satire and Society in Ancient Rome* (Exeter: University of Exeter, 1989).

—— *Writing down Rome: Satire, Comedy, and Other Offences in Latin Poetry* (Oxford: Oxford University Press, 1999).

HENDRICKSON, G. L., 'Horace, Serm. I.4: a Protest and a Programme', *AJP* 21 (1900), 121–42.

—— 'Satura Tota Nostra Est', *CP* 22 (1927), 46–60.

—— 'The First Satire of Persius', *CP* 23 (1928), 97–112.

HERTER, H., 'Zu ersten Satire des Horaz', *RhM* 94 (1951), 1–42.

HIGHET, G., *Juvenal the Satirist. A Study* (Oxford: Oxford University Press, 1954).

—— *The Anatomy of Satire* (Princeton: Princeton University Press, 1962).

—— 'Masks and Faces in Satire', *Hermes* 102 (1974), 321–37.

HIPPOCRATES, *Pseudoepigraphic Writings*, ed., trans., and introd. by W. D. Smith. Studies in Ancient Medicine, ii (Leiden: Brill, 1990).

HOBBES, T., *Leviathan* (London, 1651).

HODGART, M., *Satire* (London: Weidenfeld & Nicolson, 1969).

HOOLEY, D., *The Knotted Thong. Structures of Mimesis in Persius* (Ann Arbor: University of Michigan Press,1997).

HORSFALL, N., 'The Legionary as his own Historian', *Ancient History* 29/9 (1999), 107–17.

HOUSMAN, A. E., 'Notes on Persius', *CQ* 7 (1913), 12–32.

INNES, D., 'Metaphor, Simile, and Allegory as Ornaments of Style', in G. R. Boys-Stones (ed.), *Metaphor, Allegory, and the Classical Tradition* (Oxford: Oxford University Press, 2003).

JÄKEL, S., 'The Phenomenon of Laughter in the Iliad', in S. Jäkel and A. Timonen. (eds.), *Laughter down the Centuries*, i (Turku: Annales Universitatis Turkuensis, 1994).

—— and TIMONEN, A., (eds.), *Laughter down the Centuries*, i–ii (Turku: Annales Universitatis Turkuensis, 1994–5).

—— —— and RISSANEN, V.-M. (eds.), *Laughter down the Centuries*, iii (Turku: Annales Universitatis Turkuensis, 1997).

JESSEN, J., 'Witz und Humor bei Juvenal', *Philologus* 47 (1889), 321–7.

JOSHEL, S. J., and MURNAGHAN, S. (eds.), *Women and Slaves in Greco-Roman Culture. Differential Equations* (London and New York: Routledge, 1998).

KANT, I., *Kritik der Urtheilskraft* (1790; 4th edn. Leipzig: P. Reclam, 1878).

KEANE, C., 'Satiric Memories: Autobiography and the Construction of Genre', *CJ* 97,3 (2002), 215–31.

KEITH-SPIEGEL, P., 'Early Conceptions of Humor: Varieties and Issues' in J. H. Goldstein and P. E. McGhee (eds.), *The Psychology of Humor.* (New York and London: Academic Press, 1972).

KENNEY, E. J., 'The First Satire of Juvenal', *PCPS* 188 (1962), 29–40.

KERNAN, A., *The Cankered Muse. Satire of the English Renaissance* (New Haven: Yale University Press, 1959).

KLODT, C. (ed.), *Satura Lanx. Festschrift für Werner A. Krenkel zum 70. Geburtstag* (Hildesheim: Olms, 1996).

KNOCHE, U., *Die römische Satire* (1949; 2nd edn. Göttingen: Vandenhoeck u. Ruprecht, 1957).

—— 'Über Horazens satirische Dichtung: Witz und Weisheit', *Gymnasium* 67 (1960), 56–72.

—— 'Juvenals Mass-stäbe der Gesellschaftskritik', in D. Korzeniewski (ed.), *Die römische Satire* (Darmstadt: Wissenschaftliche Buchgesellschaft, 1970).

KOESTLER, A., *The Act of Creation* (London: Hutchinson, 1964).

KORZENIEWSKI, D. (ed.), *Die römische Satire* (Darmstadt: Wissenschaftliche Buchgesellschaft, 1970).

KRAGELUND, P., 'Epicurus, Priapus and the dreams in Petronius', *CQ* 39 (1989), 436–50.

KRAGGERUD, E., 'Die Satire I.1 des Horaz. Zu ihrer Einheit und Thematik', *SO* 53 (1978), 133–64.

—— 'Die Satire I.7 des Horaz', *SO* 54 (1979), 91–109.

KÜSTER, H., *De A. Persii Flacci elocutione quaestiones*, i–iii (Löbau, 1894–7).

LACAN, J., *Écrits* (Paris: Seuil, 1966).

—— 'Les quatres concepts fondamentaux de la psychanalyse', in *Le Séminaire de Jacques Lacan*, xi (Paris: Seuil, 1973).

LAFLEUR, R. A., '*Amicitia* and the Unity of Juvenal's First Book', *ICS* 4 (1979), 158–77.

—— 'Horace and *Onomasti Komodein*: The Law of Satire', *ANRW* II.31.3 (1981), 1790–1826.

LARSSON, L., *En annan historia: om kvinnors läsning och svensk veckopress* [*Another Story: on Women's Reading and the Swedish Weekly Press*] (Stockholm: Symposion, 1989).

LEEMAN, A. D., 'Die Konsultierung des Trebatius: Statuslehre in Horaz, Serm. 2, 1', in P. Händel and W. Meid (eds.), in *Festschrift für Robert Muth* (Innsbruck: Amœ: Institut für Sprachwissenschaft der Universität Innsbruck, 1983).

LELIÉVRE, F. J., 'Parody in Juvenal and T. S. Eliot', *CP* 53 (1958), 22–6.

Lewis, P., *Comic Effects. Interdisciplinary Approaches to Humor in Literature* (Albany, NY: State University of New York Press,1989).

Lichačëv, D. S., *Istoričeskaja poetika russkoj literatury. Smekh kak mirovozz-renie i drugie raboty* [*A Historical Poetics of Russian Literature. Laughter as Worldview and Other Works*] (St. Petersburg: Aletheia, 2001).

Lotman, *Analysis of the Poetic Text*, ed. and trans. by D. Barton Johnson (Ann Arbor, Mich.: Ardis, 1976).

Lutz, C., 'Democritus and Heraclitus', *CJ* 49 (1953–4), 309–14.

McCabe, K., 'Was Juvenal a Structuralist? A Look at Anachronisms in Literary Criticism', *G&R* 33 (1986), 78–84.

McGann, M. J., 'The Three Worlds of Horace's Satires', in C. D. N. Costa (ed.), *Horace* (London and Boston: Routledge & Kegan Paul, 1973).

McKim, R., 'Philosophers and Cannibals: Juvenal's Fifteenth Satire', *Phoenix* 40 (1986), 58–71.

Marache, R, 'Rhétorique et humour chez Juvénal', in M. Renard and R. Schilling (eds.), *Hommages à Jean Bayet.* (Brussels: Latomus, 1964).

Martyn, J. R. C., 'Juvenal's Wit', *GB* 8 (1979), 219–38.

Mason, H. A., 'Is Juvenal a Classic?' in J. P. Sullivan (ed.), *Critical Essays on Roman Literature: Satire.* (London: Routledge & Kegan Paul, 1963).

Merli, E., 'Identität und Ironie: Martial innerhalb der Tradition der römischen Satire' (Forthcoming at Brill).

Mette, H. J., ' "Genus tenue" und "mensa tenuis" bei Horaz', *Mus Helv.*, 18 (1961), 136–9. Reprinted in H. Oppermann (ed.), *Wege zu Horaz* (Darmstadt: Wissenschaftlige Buchgesellschaft, 1972).

Meyer, W. (ed.), *Pomponii Porphyrionis Commentarii in Q. Horatium Flaccum*, rec. Gulielmus Meyer (Leipzig: Teubner, 1874).

Michels, A. K., '*Παρρησία* and the satire of Horace', *CP* 39 (1944), 173–7.

Miller, P. A., 'The Bodily Grotesque in Roman Satire: Images of Sterility', *Arethusa* 31 (1998), 257–83.

Milner, G. B., 'Homo Ridens: Towards a Semiotic Theory of Humour and Laughter', *Semiotica*, 5 (1972), 1–30.

Miralles, C., 'Laughter in the Odyssey', in S. Jäkel and A. Timonen (eds.), *Laughter down the Centuries* i (Turku: Annales Universitatis Turkuensis, 1994).

Moles, J., 'Cynicism in Horace's *Epistles* 1', *PLLS* 5 (1985), 33–60.

Morreall, J. (ed.), *The Philosophy of Laughter and Humor* (Albany, NY: State University of New York Press,1987).

Motto, A. L., and Clark, J. R., '*Per iter tenebricosum*: The Mythos of Juvenal 3', *TAPA* 96 (1965), 267–76.

Muecke, D. C., *The Compass of Irony* (London: Methuen, 1969).

MUECKE, F., 'Law, Rhetoric, and Genre in Horace, *Satires* 2.1', in S. J. Harrison (ed.), *Homage to Horace. A Bimillenary Celebration*. (Oxford: Oxford University Press, 1995).

MÜLLER, R., 'Demokrit—der "lachende Philosoph" ', in S. Jäkel and A. Timonen (eds.), *Laughter down the Centuries*, i (Turku: Annales Universitatis Turkuensis, 1994).

MURLEY, C., 'Lucretius and the History of Satire', *TAPA* 70 (1939), 380–95.

MUSURILLO, H. A., *Symbol and Myth in Ancient Poetry* (New York: Fordham University Press, 1961).

NAUTA, R. R., ' "Lyrisch ik" en *persona* in de bestudering van de Romeinse poëzie', *Lampas*, 35/5 (2002), 363–86.

NILSSON, N.-O., *Metrische Stildifferenzen in den Satiren des Horaz* (Uppsala: Almqvist & Wiksell, 1952).

NISBET, R. G. M., 'Persius', in J. P. Sullivan (ed.), *Critical Essays on Roman Literature. Satire* (London: Routledge & Kegan Paul, 1963).

—— and HUBBARD, M., *A Commentary on Horace: Odes. Book I* (Oxford: Oxford University Press, 1970).

NORDEN, E., *Agnostos Theos: Untersuchungen zur Formengeschichte religiöser Rede* (Leipzig: Teubner, 1913).

O'CONNOR, E. M., *Symbolum Salacitatis. A Study of the God Priapus as a Literary Character* (Frankfurt am Main: Lang, 1989).

OESTERLEN, T., *Komik und Humor bei Horaz. Ein Beitrag zur römischen Litteraturgeschichte*, i–iii [vol. i, 1885, treats the *Sermones*] (Stuttgart: Verlag der J. B. Metzlerschen Buchhandlung, 1885–7).

OLIENSIS, E., 'Canidia, Canicula, and the Decorum of Horace's *Epodes*', *Arethusa* 24 (1991), 107–38.

—— '*Ut Arte Emendaturus Fortunam*: Horace, Nasidienus, and the Art of Satire', in T. Habinek and A. Shiesaro (eds.), *The Roman Cultural Revolution* (Cambridge: Cambridge University Press, 1997).

—— *Horace and the Rhetoric of Authority* (Cambridge: Cambridge University Press, 1998).

ÖNNERFORS, A., *Vaterporträts in der römischen Poesie, unter besonderer Berücksichtigung von Horaz, Statius und Ausonius* (Stockholm: Paul Åströms Förlag, 1974).

OTTO, A., *Die Sprichwörter und sprichwörtlichen Redensarten der Römer* (Leipzig: Teubner, 1890).

PABST, W., 'Zur Satire vom lächerlichen Mahl', *A&A* 32 (1986), 136–58.

PARKER, A. R., 'Comic Theory in the Satires of Horace', Ph.D. thesis (University of North Carolina at Chapel Hill, 1986).

PARKER, H., 'Loyal Slaves and Loyal Wives: the Crisis of the Outsider-within and Roman *Exemplum* Literature', in S. R. Joshel—S. Murnaghan (eds.),

Women and Slaves in Greco-Roman Culture. Differential Equations (London and New York: Routledge, 1998).

PAVLOVSKIS, Z., 'Aristotle, Horace, and the Ironic Man', *CP* 63 (1968), 22–41.

PERLMUTTER, D., 'On Incongruities and Logical Inconsistencies in Humor: The Delicate Balance', *Humor*, 15/2 (2002), 155–68.

PLAZA, M., *Laughter and Derision in Petronius' Satyrica. A Literary Study* (Stockholm: Almqvist & Wiksell, 2000).

POWELL, J., 'The *Farrago* of Juvenal 1.86 Reconsidered', in Michael Whitby, P. Hardie, and Mary Whitby (eds.), *Homo Viator: Classical Essays for John Bramble* (Bristol: Bristol Classical Press, 1987).

PREISENDANZ, W., and WARNING, R. (eds.), *Das Komische*. Poetik und Hermeneutik 7. (Munich: Fink, 1976).

PURDIE, S., *Comedy: the Mastery of Discourse* (Hemel Hempstead: Harvester Wheatsheaf, 1993).

RADCLIFFE-BROWN, A. R., 'On Joking Relationships', *Africa* 13 (1940), 195–210.

RADERMACHER, L., *Weinen und Lachen. Studien über antikes Lebensgefühl* (Vienna: R. M. Rohrer, 1947).

RADWAY, J., *Reading the Romance. Women, Patriarchy, and Popular Literature* (Chapel Hill: University of North Carolina Press, 1984).

RAMAGE, E. S., 'Juvenal and the Establishment. Denigration of Predecessor in the "Satires" ', *ANRW* II.33.1 (1989), 640–707.

—— SIGSBEE, D. L. and FREDERICKS, S. C., *Roman Satirists and their Satire* (Park Ridge, NJ: Noyes Press, 1974).

RECKFORD, K., 'Studies in Persius', *Hermes* 90 (1962), 476–504.

—— 'Horatius: the Man and the Hour', *AJP* 118 (1997), 583–612.

—— 'Reading the Sick Body: Decomposition and Morality in Persius' Third Satire', *Arethusa* 31 (1998), 337–54.

—— 'Only a Wet Dream? Hope and Scepticism in Horace, Satire 1.5', *AJP* 120 (1999), 525–54.

REEKMANS, T., 'Juvenal's Views on Social Change', *AncSoc* 2 (1971), 117–61.

REI, A., 'Villains, Wives, and Slaves in the Comedies of Plautus', in S. R. Joshel and S. Murnaghan (eds.), *Women and Slaves in Greco-Roman Culture. Differential Equations* (London and New York: Routledge, 1998).

REINHARDT, U., and SALLMAN, K. (eds.), *Musa Iocosa: Arbeiten uber Humor und Witz, Komik und Komödie der Antike* (Hildesheim: Olms, 1974).

RELIHAN, J. C., 'Pardoning Persius' laughter', *Mnemosyne* 44 (1991), 433–4.

RICHLIN, A., 'Invective against Women in Roman Satire', *Arethusa* 17 (1984), 67–80.

—— *The Garden of Priapus. Sexuality and Aggression in Roman Humor* (1983; 2nd, rev. edn. Oxford: Oxford University Press, 1992).

—— 'Not Before Homosexuality: The Materiality of the *Cinaedus* and the Roman Law against Love between Men', *Journal of the History of Sexuality* 3 (1993), 523–73.

RIFFATERRE, M., *Semiotics of Poetry* (Bloomington: Indiana University Press, 1978).

ROCHEFORT, G., 'Laughter as a Satirical Device in Juvenal', Ph.D. thesis (Tufts University, 1972).

RODRÍGUEZ ALMEIDA, E., 'Martial—Juvenal: entre *castigatio per risum* et *censura morum*', in M. Trédé and P. Hoffmann (eds.), *Le rire des anciens* (Paris: Presses de l'École Normale Supérieure, 1998).

ROMANO, A. C., *Irony in Juvenal* (Hildesheim: Olms, 1979).

ROTHBART, M. K., 'Incongruity, Problem-solving and Laughter', in A. J. Chapman and H. C. Foot (eds.), *Humour and Laughter.: Theory, Research, and Application* (London: Wiley, 1976).

RUDD, N., 'Libertas and Facetus. With Special Reference to Horace *Serm.* I,4 and I, 10', *Mnemosyne*, 10 (1957), 319–36.

—— *The Satires of Horace* (Cambridge: Cambridge University Press, 1966).

—— 'Association of Ideas in Persius', in *Lines of Enquiry* (Cambridge: Cambridge University Press, 1976).

—— *Themes in Roman Satire* (London: Duckworth, 1986).

RÜTTEN, T., *Demokrit—lachender Philosoph & sanguinischer Melancholiker. Eine pseudohippokratische Geschichte* (Leiden: Brill, 1992).

SACK, V., *Ironie bei Horaz.* Diss. (Würzburg, 1965).

SALLMANN, K., 'Die seltsame Reise nach Brundisium. Aufbau und Deutung der Horazsatire 1, 5', in U. Reinhardt and K. Sallmann (eds.), *Musa Iocosa: Arbeiten uber Humor und Witz, Komik und Komödie der Antike* (Hildesheim: Olms, 1974).

SANTARCANGELI, P., *Homo ridens: estetica, filologia, psicologia, storia del comico* (Firenze: Olschki, 1989).

SCHAEFER, A. (ed.), *Ironie und Dichtung. Sechs Essays* (Munich: Beck, 1970).

SCHINDLER, W., 'Komik-Theorien—komische Theorien? Eine Skizze über die Deutung des Lachens von der Antike bis Heute', *AU* 29 (1986), 4–19.

SCHLEGEL, C., 'Horace and his Fathers: Satires 1.4 and 1.6', *AJP* 121 (2000), 93–119.

SCHMELING, G. (ed.), *The Novel in the Ancient World* (1996; 2nd, rev. edn. Leiden: Brill, 2003).

SCHMIDT, E. A., 'Vom Lachen in der römischen Satire', in S. Jäkel and A. Timonen (eds.), *Laughter down the Centuries*, ii (Turku: Annales Universitatis Turkuensis, 1995).

SCHÖNERT, J., *Roman und Satire im 18. Jahrhundert. Ein Beitrag zur Poetik.* Germanistische Abhandlungen, Bd. 27. Diss. (Stuttgart, 1969).

SCHOPENHAUER, A., *Die Welt als Wille und Vorstellung* (1819; 3rd edn., Leipzig, 1859).

SCHRÖTER, R., 'Horazens Satire 1. 7 und die antike Eposparodie', *Poetica* 1 (1967), 8–23.

SEECK, G. A., 'Die römische Satire und der Begriff der Satirischen' *A&A* 37 (1991), 1–21.

—— 'Über das Satirische in Horaz' Satiren *oder*: Horaz und seine Leser, z.B. Maecenas', *Gymnasium*, 98 (1991), 534–47.

SEGAL, E., *Roman Laughter. The Comedy of Plautus* (Cambridge, Mass.: Harvard University Press, 1968).

SHACKLETON BAILEY, D. R., *Profile of Horace* (Cambridge, Mass.: Harvard University Press, 1982).

SHERO, L. R., 'The Satirist's Apologia', *University of Wisconsin Studies in Language and Literature. Classical series II*, xv (1922), 148–67.

—— 'The Cena in Roman Satire', *CP* 18 (1923), 126–43.

SINGLETON, D., 'Juvenal VI.1–20, and Some Ancient Attitudes to the Golden Age', *G&R* 19 (1972), 151–65.

SKUTSCH, O., 'Messius Cicirrus', in (eds.), *Studies in honour of T. B. L. Webster.* J. H. Betts, J. T. Hooker, and J. R. Green (Bristol: Bristol Classical Press, 1986).

SQUILLANTE SACCONE, M., 'Techniche dell'ironia e del comico nella satira di Persio', *BollStLat* 10 (1980), 3–25.

STACHE, U. J., MAAZ, W., and WAGNER, F. (eds.), *Kontinuität und Wandel. Lateinische Poesie von Naevius bis Baudelaire: Franco Munari zum 65. Geburtstag* (Hildesheim: Weidmann, 1986).

STALLYBRASS, P., and WHITE, A., *The Politics and Poetics of Transgression* (London: Methuen, 1986).

STEWART, Z., 'Laughter in the Greek Philosophers: a Sketch' in S. Jäkel and A. Timonen (eds.), *Laughter down the Centuries*, i (Turku: Annales Universitatis Turkuensis, 1994).

SULLIVAN, J. P. (ed.), *Critical Essays on Roman Literature. Satire* (London: Routledge & Kegan Paul, 1963).

SURLIN, S. H., 'The Evaluation of Dogmatic Television Characters by Dogmatic Viewers: "Is Archie Bunker a Credible Source?" ' (Paper presented at the *International Communication Association*'s Annual Convention, Montreal, 1973).

SÜSS, W., *Lachen, Komik und Witz in der Antike* (Zurich and Stuttgart: Artemis, 1969).

TENNANT, P. M. W., 'Biting Off More Than One Can Chew: A recent trend in the interpretation of Juvenal's 15th Satire', *Akroterion* 40 (1995), 120–34.

TER VRUGT-LENZ, J., 'Horaz' "Sermones": Satire auf der Grenze zweier Welten', *ANRW* II.31.3 (1981), 1827–35.

THORPE, P., 'Thinking in Octagons: Further Reflections on Norms in Satire', *Satire Newsletter* 7 (1969–70), 91–9. Reprinted in B. Fasian (ed.), *SATURA. Ein Kompendium moderner Studien zur Satire.* (Hildesheim: Olms, 1975).

TRÉDÉ, M., and HOFFMANN, P. (eds.), *Le rire des anciens* (Paris: Presses de l'École Normale Supérieure, 1998).

TURPIN, W., 'The Epicurean Parasite: Horace, Satires 1.1–3', *Ramus* 27 (1998), 127–40.

VÄÄNÄNEN, V., *Introduction au latin vulgaire* (1963; 2nd, rev. edn. Paris: Klincksieck, 1967).

VAN ROOY, C. A., *Studies in Classical Satire and Related Literary Theory* (Leiden: Brill, 1965).

VARRO, *Satires ménippées*, ed., trans., and comm. by J.-P. Cébe (13 vols., Rome: École française de Rome, 1972–99).

VOGT-SPIRA, G., 'Das satirische Lachen der Römer und die Witzkultur der Oberschicht', in S. Jäkel, A. Timonen, and V-M. Rissanen (eds.), *Laughter down the Centuries*, iii (Turku: Annales Universitatis Turkuensis, 1997).

WALLACE-HADRILL, A. (ed.), *Patronage in Ancient Society* (London and New York: Routledge, 1989).

WALTERS, J., 'Making a Spectacle: Deviant Men, Invective, and Pleasure', *Arethusa* 31 (1998), 355–67.

WEBER, H., 'Comic Humour and Tragic Spirit: The Augustan Distinction between Horace and Juvenal', *Classical and Modern Literature* 1 (1981), 275–89.

WEISINGER, K., 'Irony and Moderation in Juvenal XI', *CSCA* 5 (1972), 227–40.

WESSNER, P. (ed.), *Scholia in Juvenalem vetustiora* (Leipzig: Teubner, 1931).

WEST, D., 'Of Mice and Men: Horace, Satires 2.6.77–117', in A. J. Woodman and D. A. West (eds.), *Quality and Pleasure in Latin Poetry* (London: Cambridge University Press, 1974).

WHITBY, MICHAEL, HARDIE, P., and WHITBY, MARY (eds.), *Homo Viator: Classical Essays for John Bramble* (Bristol: Bristol Classical press, 1987).

WHITEHEAD, J. K., 'Towards a Definition of Etruscan Humor', *EtrStud* 3 (1996), 9–32.

WIESEN, D. S., 'Juvenal and the Intellectuals', *Hermes* 101 (1973), 464–83.

WILSON, C. P., *Jokes: Form, Content, Use and Function* (London: Academic Press, 1979).

WINKLER, M. M., *The Persona in Three Satires of Juvenal* (Hildesheim: Olms, 1983).

—— 'Satire and the Grotesque in Juvenal, Archimboldo, and Goya', *AA* 37 (1991), 22–42.

WITKE, C., *Latin Satire. The Structure of Persuasion* (Leiden: Brill, 1970).

WOODMAN, A. J., and WEST, D. A. (eds.), *Quality and Pleasure in Latin Poetry* (London: Cambridge University Press, 1974).

WOODMAN, T., and FEENEY, D. (eds.), *Traditions and Contexts in the Poetry of Horace* (Cambridge: Cambridge University Press, 2002).

ZETZEL, J. E. G., 'Horace's Liber Sermonum: the Structure of Ambiguity', *Arethusa* 13 (1980), 59–77.

—— 'Dreaming about Quirinus: Horace's Satires and the development of Augustan poetry', in T. Woodman and D. Feeney (eds.), *Traditions and Contexts in the Poetry of Horace* (Cambridge: Cambridge University Press, 2002).

ZINN, E., 'Elemente des Humors in augusteischer Dichtung', *Gymnasium* 67 (1960), 41–56 and 152–5.

—— 'Ironie und Pathos bei Horaz', in A. Schaefer (ed.), *Ironie und Dichtung. Sechs Essays* (Munich: Beck, 1970).

Index Locorum

General Index

'Humour', 'satire', and the names of the Roman satirists are not included in the index, since these items are treated throughout the study. References to modern scholars in the footnotes are not listed.

Lightning Source UK Ltd.
Milton Keynes UK
UKHW010613130223
416869UK00001B/30